HISTORY OF GERMANY
IN THE NINETEENTH CENTURY

CLASSIC EUROPEAN HISTORIANS

A SERIES EDITED BY LEONARD KRIEGER

Heinrich von Treitschke

HISTORY OF GERMANY IN THE NINETEENTH CENTURY

Selections from the Translation of
Eden and Cedar Paul

Edited and with an Introduction by
Gordon A. Craig

THE UNIVERSITY OF CHICAGO PRESS
CHICAGO & LONDON

GORDON A. CRAIG is J. E. Wallace Sterling Professor of Humanities and chairman of the Department of History at Stanford University. Among his many publications are *The Politics of the Prussian Army, 1640–1945, Königgrätz,* and *War, Politics and Diplomacy.*

The University of Chicago Press, Chicago 60637
The University of Chicago Press, Ltd., London

Library of Congress Cataloging in Publication Data

Treitschke, Heinrich Gotthard von, 1834–1896.
    History of Germany in the nineteenth century.

    (Classic European historians)
    Selections from the translation of the author's work
first published under title: Deutsche Geschichte im
neunzehnten Jahrhundert.
    Bibliography: p.
    Includes index
    1. Germany—History—1789-1900.   2. Germany—intel-
lectual life.   3. German literature—History and criticism.
    I. Craig, Gordon Alexander, 1913-   II. Title.   III. Series.
DD203.T78213 *1975*   943'.07   75-5072
ISBN 0-226-81278-2

60,091

Contents

v

Series Editor's Preface

ALTHOUGH we are accustomed to think of the nineteenth century historiographically as the period which witnessed the emergence of scientific history as a professional discipline, the bulk of the classic European historians produced by that century consisted not of those who adhered strictly to this model—although the future of the field lay in such adherence—but of those who joined the amateur tradition of history as a kind of didactic literature with the new scientific methods of opening up the past. Whether they were actually amateur historians who absorbed the new taste for original research, like Carlyle, Engels, and Gregorovius, or whether they were professional historians who retained the moralizing and literary aims of pre-scientific history, like Guizot, Michelet, and Acton, this group of historians organized massive collections of new knowledge about the past with the cohesive force of the dramatic unities and the principles of civic morality to produce the histories in the grand manner for which we have been nostalgic ever since. They have been charter members of the Classic European Historians almost by definition, since the series has been dedicated to historians who have been notable for the way they thought about history and to works that have been notable for their presentation of important historical subjects, a combination especially appropriate to a group that was articulate in relating history to life in general and that provided a satisfying fullness of substance and respectability of method to the large topics provoked by that relationship.

Heinrich von Treitschke and his *History of Germany in the Nineteenth Century* belong to this illustrious company. For

Treitschke was one of the "political historians" whose own political activity and whose frank dedication of their historical writing to a political purpose obviously carried on the traditional involvement of history with the rest of living; and his *History* remains one of those books whose unrivalled marshalling of material and inimitable expression of untrammelled passion continues to be read for its authority as a commentary as well as for its testimony as a source. The title, to be sure, is a bit misleading since Treitschke's five volumes got only to the eve of the Revolution of 1848 before death cut him off, but the period he did cover was a complete era and the coverage is all the richer for the limited span.

And yet Treitschke has a most distinctive place in the society of nineteenth century historians that he joins. In general, the preconceptions which they brought to their history were liberal, open-ended, cosmopolitan (let us recall that Taine's philosophy of history was radical even if his politics were not; only the Rankeans tended toward generic conservatism, and they belonged to an opposing historiographical grouping). It is easy to see how this kind of assumption could accommodate and even promote the actuality of a European historical process which showed a developing liberalization of conditions since the early Middle Ages. But, as Professor Craig demonstrates convincingly in his incisive introduction, not only was Treitschke's avowed purpose parochially nationalistic, but this purpose did in fact infect his history with narrow partisanship and with bigotry. The peculiarity of Treitschke's place among the great politicizing historians of the nineteenth century, then, is that of a limiting case: because his political and social stance ran counter to the open-mindedness expected in the pioneering scholar and because it ran counter, as well, to the tendency of a good part of the history about which he was writing, the undeniable merits of his book show that it is not only appropriate preconception, but preconception itself, that has been compatible with great history.

The merits of the book lie undoubtedly in the breadth and intensity with which Germany is treated in a period when the diversity and the diffusiveness of the national life pose formidable obstacles to such a history. There would seem to be three reasons for Treitschke's success in granting full measure to the variety of German life in the first half of the nineteenth century while still making it coherent. First, his nationalism, while undoubtedly conservative and exclusive by the time he wrote, was liberal and comprehensive for the time he was writing about. Hence, while it undoubtedly distorted some of the material that was refractory from the national—and especially from Treitschke's pro-Prussian national—point of view, his idea of national unity did serve to give his history both definition and integration. Secondly, Treitschke felt driven to seek knowledge of what he hated almost as much as of what he loved. Professor Craig has shrewdly recalled that Treitschke approached the terrain of scholarship like a field of battle, and he felt keenly, in line with this orientation, the injunction to "know your enemy." Certainly Treitschke's unfavorable judgments of what he abhorred must be discounted even more than his favorable judgments of what he advocated, but the point remains that he often gave as full coverage to the one as to the other. We meet here one of the general inferences that may be drawn from Treitschke: that what matters is not the direction of the bias with which the historian approaches his material but whether the bias opens up or closes down his need to know. The third factor which makes the *History* a book that transcends Treitschke's explicit purpose and perspective is the surprising versatility that the work evinces. It is perhaps because historians have been so callow in examining their own assumptions that others have tended to assess them simplistically, and certainly Treitschke is himself partially responsible for his consistent reputation as a narrow political nationalist not only in his politics but in his history as well. But what this judgment overlooks is Treitschke's cultural—and especially literary—interests and capacities. Professor Craig rightly points out that Treitschke had poetic ambitions, and he retained throughout his life an aesthetic sensibility that paid off historiographically in his appreciation of German intellectual history.

Treitschke's *History of Germany in the Nineteenth Century*, then, confirms for history the lesson that most of us have learned,

whether as students or as scholars, about all cultivation of the
sciences and of the arts—that the products of the mind have a life
of their own and cannot be judged by the qualities of their
producers. But we have also learned that what is opaque and
obscure in these products can often be understood by the
invocation of the qualities of their producers. Treitschke himself
would not endorse this distinction between knowledge and
judgment, but it is one that applies eminently to him and that
lies behind this re-edition of his great work.

LEONARD KRIEGER

Editor's Introduction

IN 1914, when the first volume of the English edition of Treitschke's *Deutsche Geschichte* was published, William Harbutt Dawson wrote an introduction in which he spoke with high praise of its author. It was Treitschke's supreme merit, he wrote, that "he voiced the new life and self-consciousness of modern Germany in a way that no other man—no statesman, no writer of any kind, and certainly no historian—had done before. At last there stood forth a man, like to that earlier patriot-historian of Bonn, Ernst Moritz Arndt . . ., who was able and determined to do justice, not only to the past of the German nation, but to its present and future, to assert its claims and rights, to formulate its aims and ambitions, and to interpret to the world its individuality and outlook." Dawson added that "moderation was not [Treitschke's] special grace" but admitted that, if the personal element in his writings was a weakness, it was "a weakness counterbalanced by so many excellences that it is easier to condone than condemn it."[1]

When the seventh volume appeared in 1919, Dawson's tone had changed decidedly. "Perhaps more than any other man," he wrote, "Treitschke is responsible for the excessive egoism, the self-glorification, boastfulness and inflated estimate of itself which have been the bane of the German nation since 1871." His influence, Dawson continued, had been nothing short of disastrous, for it had "perverted the national mind in the service of a

---

1. Heinrich von Treitschke, *History of Germany in the Nineteenth Century*, trans. Eden and Cedar Paul, 7 vols. (London, 1914–19) I, viii, ix, xii (hereafter cited as *History*).

xi

narrow, false, ungenerous patriotism" and had taught it to pursue "aims and ambitions which were destined to lead it out of the right course and in the end to overwhelm it in disaster."[2]

The First World War had, of course, intervened between the writing of these opinions, which accounts for Dawson's radical change of front. Even so, both of his judgments are largely true, and this explains why the serious student of German history can neglect Treitschke's writings only at the risk of losing an understanding of the psychological factors that contributed to the fateful course of German politics before 1914. Treitschke set out deliberately to make himself the preceptor of the German people, to impart to them the pride and self-assurance that they would need in order to fulfill their historic tasks. Like many another teacher, he became the victim of his pedagogical techniques and, having begun by exaggerating the magnitude of the German achievement in 1871, he was carried on to wilder exaggerations and, in the end, to strident claims of national superiority, partly because of the success of his rhetoric, more perhaps because of his nagging fear that the traditional divisiveness of the Germans might reassert itself. In the end he became a tub-thumper of disastrous resonance, but not, it may be suspected, one who was entirely happy in his role. As Raymond Sontag has written, he became a mirror of "the arrogant pride and the confused doubt of post-Bismarckian Germany."[3]

Aside from the *History*, the most accessible of Treitschke's works for western readers are the lectures on politics that he delivered to large and enthusiastic audiences at the University of Berlin during the last twenty years of his life. In printed form,[4] they suffer from the serious disadvantage that they are not the product of Treitschke's pen but a compilation made from the notes of his students. In general, their substance is accurate, although not invariably so, and there are many inconsistencies. Moreover, only faint echoes of Treitschke's vigorous and poetic

2. Ibid., VII, x, xi.

3. Raymond James Sontag, *Germany and England: The Background of Conflict, 1848–1894* (New York, 1938), p. 339.

4. Heinrich von Treitschke, *Politics*, trans. Blanche Dugdale and Torben de Bille, 2 vols. (New York, 1916).

style have survived the process of collation and transcription. Anyone who wishes to understand why Treitschke was the most popular university lecturer and the most widely read historian of his times should, therefore, avoid the *Politics* and turn to the *History*.

I

As he does so, he should be aware that it was more than a mere book. One of the problems that faced Germans after 1871, when the new Reich was founded, was that of self-recognition and identification with the new creation, and a symptom of this was the difficulty of finding agreement on the question of national symbols. The Germans had been divided for so long that it was hard to find anything of common sentimental value that could be commemorated in symbolic form. A sculptor who was called upon to design a national monument was apt to throw up his hands in despair and decide that the safest solution would be another statue of Bismarck.[5] But what could not be wrought in stone, Treitschke achieved in prose. With the first volume of the *History*, which appeared in 1879, he literally created a national historical tradition for the new empire, by identifying the history of Prussia with that of Germany and bringing "vigorously forward the men and the institutions, the ideas and the changes of destiny, which ... created [the] new nationality."[6]

Like everything that he wrote, the *History* was a labor of passion and of love. Treitschke was what the Germans call a *Kampfnatur*, a man of combative temperament. The mere process of historical research was for him a highly emotional undertaking, as the young Friedrich Meinecke noted, watching the old historian grimace and snort as he strove with the documents in the *Preussisches Staatsarchiv*;[7] and he approached the task of writing, in Wilhelm Dilthey's phrase, like a Hussite

5. Thomas Nipperdey, "Nationalidee und Nationaldenkmal in Deutschland," *Historische Zeitschrift*, 206 (1968), 542 ff. See also Theodor Schieder, *Der deutsche Kaiserreich von 1871 als Nationalstaat* (Cologne, 1961).

6. Dedicatory Preface, *History*, I, xiv. See also Helmut Böhme, *Deutschlands Weg zur Grossmacht: Studien zum Verhältnis von Wirtschaft und Staat während der Reichsgründungszeit 1848 bis 1881* (Cologne, 1966), p. 552.

7. Friedrich Meinecke, *Erlebtes 1862-1919* (Stuttgart, 1941), pp. 130-34.

captain of foot going into the field.[8] On occasion he seemed a bit rueful about this—"I grow too easily excited," he wrote to Heinrich von Sybel in 1864, "but in time I hope to become a historian"[9]—but these moods were not of long duration. He had no admiration for what he criticized as the "bloodless objectivity" of the Ranke school of historians.[10] In his view, the historian's duty was to be both teacher and judge, recording the events of the past as accurately as possible but expressing his moral judgment of the actions he reported. Nor was this all. "You will not blame me," he wrote when he dedicated the first volume of the *History* to Max Duncker, "because now and then, out of the equable peace of historic discourse, there sounds a louder tone. The narrator of German history fulfills but half his task when he indicates the connection of events and expresses his opinion with frankness; he should also himself feel and should know how to awaken in the hearts of his readers—what many of our countrymen have already forgotten in the disputes and vexations of the moment—a delight in the fatherland."[11]

Treitschke's purpose was to arouse "that unanimous sense of joyous gratitude which older nations feel towards their political heroes,"[12] and it was strengthened by the concern he felt over the serious political, economic, and religious conflicts that embroiled the German people in the empire's first decade. But this missionary desire to weld his people together in a firmer union had deeper roots. They extended back to his university days at Bonn and Leipzig, when he had studied with F. C. Dahlmann, an early proponent of German unity under Prussian leadership,[13] and with Wilhelm Roscher, the leader of the school of national economy,[14] and had fallen under the influence of Roscher's teacher, the historian Georg Gottfried Gervinus.

8. R. Hamann and Jost Hermand, *Die Gründerzeit* (Berlin, 1965), p. 162.
9. G. P. Gooch, *History and Historians in the Nineteenth Century*, rev. ed. (London, 1952), p. 153.
10. Walter Bussmann, *Treitschke, sein Welt- und Geschichtsbild* (Göttingen, 1952), p. 200.
11. Dedicatory Preface, *History*, I, xv.
12. Ibid., p. xiii.
13. Treitschke's tribute to Dahlmann appears in Heinrich von Treitschke, *Aufsätze, Reden und Briefe*, 4 vols. (Berlin, 1929), I, 509–82.
14. On Roscher's influence, see Bussmann, *Treitschke*.

The importance of Gervinus in Treitschke's development as a historian has been generally overlooked,[15] perhaps because of their political differences (Gervinus repudiated the Reich of 1871 as a dangerous anachronism in an age of political and material progress) and because of the severe judgment of Gervinus that appears in the last volume of the *History*.[16] Yet Treitschke's basic approach to history, his reliance upon historical analogy to support his generalizations, his skillful use of literary materials, and his unfailing didactic purpose owed much to this eccentric and cantankerous outsider, who spent his scholarly life trying to awaken the German people to some sense of their political immaturity, so that they might correct it. Gervinus's first ambitious attempt to do this took the form of a massive *History of German Poetry*, which he began to write in the late 1830s. Like Treitschke after him, Gervinus scorned "the usual spiritless *Faktensammler* who merely puts things together like a chronicler and then wants to be considered a historian;"[17] and this work, therefore, was no mere compilation. Wilhelm Dilthey later wrote that it first revealed to him the possibility of finding a connection between cultural history and philosophical thought.[18] But Gervinus's purpose was political, and his book was meant to demonstrate that the national spirit, having attained its most magnificent expression in the literature of the classical age, could find no further sustenance in the present age of literary *Epigonentum* and corruption and would be revived only by a redirection of energy and talent from aesthetic contemplation to political action. When this argument had no perceptible effect, and when the Germans once more demonstrated their political incapacity in the abortive unity movement of 1848–49, Gervinus tried again, this time with the *Introduction to the History of the Nineteenth Century*, a bold attempt to reveal the pattern of the

15. Gervinus is not mentioned at all in Andreas Dorpalen, *Heinrich von Treitschke* (New Haven, 1957). See, however, Bussmann, *Treitschke*, pp. 190, 207, 210.

16. *History*, VII, 180–81.

17. "Grundzüge der Historik" (1837), in Georg Gottfried Gervinus, *Schriften zur Literatur*, ed. Gotthard Erler (Berlin, 1962), pp. 56, 99.

18. K. Höfele, *Geist und Geschichte der Bismarckzeit, 1870–1890* (Göttingen, 1967), p. 345.

past five hundred years of European history and to chart the future by revealing the forces of movement and progress that the Germans must make their own if they were to realize themselves as a nation. The immediate result of this effort was that Gervinus was haled before the Badenese High Court on charges of treason and, for the second time in his life, lost his academic position— the first time having been in 1837, when, with Dahlmann, he had been one of seven Göttingen professors who were expelled by the king of Hannover for refusing to repudiate their oath to a constitution granted by his predecessor.

Gervinus's trial for high treason was the *cause célèbre* of 1853,[19] when Treitschke went to Leipzig to study with Roscher, and he sought out the *Introduction* and read it carefully. He refused to accept its political conclusions, which were the reason for the trial—the argument, for example, that the monarchical form of government was bankrupt and that democratic republicanism was the model to which the progressive elements of all nations aspired—but he was deeply impressed by Gervinus's moral earnestness and by the force of his generalizations, particularly by his view that the course of German history was destined to be characterized by three stages: religious independence (the Reformation), independence of the spirit (the classical age of literature), and independence as a state; and that the first two prepared the way for the third but must be left behind in order that all the nation's energies could be concentrated on the effort to attain political independence.[20] As Treitschke summed it up, "a people never makes progress in two areas of its activity at the same time."[21]

It is likely that, in the years that followed, as he completed his formal training and tried to make his mind up about what his career should be, he read Gervinus's earlier works and that they influenced his course. He had for a time thought of devoting

19. The trial records are available in *Der Hochverratsprozess gegen Gervinus*, ed. Walter Boehlich (Frankfurt am Main, 1967).

20. Georg Gottfried Gervinus, *Einleitung in die Geschichte des neunzehnten Jahrhunderts*, ed. Walter Boehlich (Frankfurt am Main, 1967), pp. 176–77.

21. Heinrich von Treitschke, *Briefe*, ed. Max Cornicelius, 3 vols. (Berlin, 1913–20), I, 197.

himself to the world of letters, and he actually published two volumes of verse and began a play about the Teutonic Knights. But as early as 1854, when he wrote his doctoral dissertation for Roscher, the political note was drowning out the aesthetic one, and in the end the career he chose was one that, as in Gervinus's case, combined membership in the academic profession with political activity. His interest in literature did not die; indeed, when, in 1857, he began an association with the *Preussische Jahrbücher* that was to last for more than thirty years, his first essays for this mouthpiece of national liberal opinion were about literary figures. It is worth noting, however, that their essential thrust was political, and that they all read like extensions of thoughts in Gervinus's *German Poetry*, although much improved in style.

These studies of Lessing, Kleist, Uhland, and other German writers, and of Milton and Byron, echo Gervinus's views concerning the degeneration of German literature since the days of Goethe and Schiller and his complaint against the lack of commitment by German intellectuals. Thus the article on Byron —which, in its introduction alone, demonstrates Treitschke's mastery of the essay form—is an attack upon the naiveté of the Germans in comparison with the English, which makes the point that Byron's countrymen are mature enough not to take him very seriously, whereas the Germans are impressed to the point of imitating all his faults. In a passage that would be elaborated at several points in the *History*, Treitschke wrote:

> Most fateful for our literature was Byron through the play of his wit. To understand a joke was never the strong point of the German peoples.... In Germany, largely after Byron's model, the witty feuilleton-style became the modish sickness of the time, and this people, which was only beginning to seek its State and which had hardly any knowledge of serious treatment of political matters in an educated press, accepted wit as sound currency and admired the feuilleton articles of Heine and Börne as political oracles.[22]

22. Treitschke, *Aufsätze, Reden, Briefe*, I, 230.

Similarly, in the essay on Milton, to whom he was perhaps drawn because Milton had suffered from a crippling physical defect, as he did himself, the English poet was held up as a model for German intellectuals, and Treitschke deplored the fact that the "unique combination of artistic genius and civic virtue that we admire in him has not yet found real understanding in Germany."[23] The same note was sounded more forcefully in the study of Ludwig Uhland, whose poetry Treitschke admired for its healthy *Volkstümlichkeit* and whose political instinct he acknowledged, while not forgiving him for having voted against Württemberg's entry into the Prussian Customs Union. Here, like Gervinus, he called upon the poets to leave their arcadian groves and to become involved in politics, and he expressed some hope that they might do so.

Just as we have recently encountered in Italy the notable phenomenon that among the leading thinkers and artists there is hardly one who would not give his heart's blood for a free and united Italy, so now among the Germans a similar transformation is beginning to take place. The nation's heart is turning away from those artists who stand coldly aside during the great political struggle of the present. We now hear less frequently and ever more faintly the saying that was once so current in those circles, namely, that it is not seemly for the artist to trouble himself about the abstractions of political debate "because he has no clear picture of them." The political struggle of the German present is not a struggle over this or that set of political arrangements demanded by this theory or that class interest. It is a matter of saving for the nation the guarantee of any fine success, its proud self-esteem. Whatever is sickly in the life of our people, in art or economics, in faith or knowledge, will not be made fully sound until the Germans have founded their State. But the race of poets to which Kleist, Arndt, and Uhland belong was the first in Germany to understand the unconditional moral significance of questions of state and the first to manifest this in deeds.[24]

23. Ibid., pp. 149–50.
24. Ibid., p. 78.

Like Gervinus, therefore, Treitschke strove from the beginning
of his career as a publicist to combat the traditional *Innerlichkeit*
of the Germans, their tendency to seek refuge from external
reality by withdrawing into themselves, and to arouse his countrymen, with their intellectuals in the van, to fight for their
political independence in the world of states. In defining what
form that independence should take, however, he early parted
company from his old mentor, and by 1863, when the Uhland
essay was written, the two men were moving on sharply divergent paths. When King Frederick William IV had refused the
offer of the imperial crown in 1849, Gervinus had said, "Whatever Prussia's bayonets may achieve, its cause is wholly lost in
Germany," and he had thenceforth worked for the establishment
of a national German republic.[25] Treitschke was too good a
student of Dahlmann to consider such an eventuality. To be sure,
he wanted the Germans to be free—and the sincerity of that
desire was attested to in an eloquent essay, "Die Freiheit,"
written in 1861—but he insisted that true freedom was possible
only when it was guaranteed by a powerful and independent
State.[26] Had not Dahlmann said, "The road of power is the only
one that will satisfy and appease our yearning for freedom....
Germany as such must finally step forward into the ranks of the
great political powers of the world"?[27] And when one spoke of
power, did he not mean Prussia?

Throughout the 1860s, when Treitschke's was the most powerful voice raised in behalf of a united Germany under Prussian
leadership, he remained oddly ambivalent to the northern power
and its leaders. He was never a sycophant or tuft-hunter and had
no special admiration for the Hohenzollerns, and he detested the
narrow provincialism of the Junker class. Although he believed
that Germany needed a leader with the political talent and the
Machiavellian ruthlessness of Cavour, he could not for a long

25. Hans Rosenberg, "Gervinus und die deutsche Republik: Ein Beitrag zur
Geistesgeschichte der deutschen Demokratie," *Die Gesellschaft*, VI (1929),
124 ff., 127–28.

26. Treitschke, *Aufsätze, Reden, Briefe*, II, 41.

27. Speech of 22 May 1849. See Friedrich Meinecke, *Die Idee der Staatsraison*,
3d ed. (Munich, 1963), p. 464.

time overcome an innate suspicion of the greater Cavour who directed affairs in Berlin. He must have been aware of, and troubled by, his friend Gustav Freytag's shrewd appreciation of Bismarck's style. "Between the romantics and the aesthetes of the aristocracy, the Humboldts, Bunsen, and Usedom, on the one hand, and the constitutional present on the other," Freytag had written, "lies a thin cultural layer of undomiciled [*touristischen*] dilettantes. Young Germany and the Junker class in its elegant types—Freiligrath, Lenau, Fürst Pückler, Lichnowsky—insolent, taking pleasure in risks, without firm principles, without a school, chiefly dependent upon French education. The greatest late fruit of this growing period, which in literature stretches from 1830 to 1840, is, or so it seems to me, Bismarck. The salient feature is lack of reverence, a tendency to regard everything capriciously and from a personal point of view, and at the same time . . . a vital energy that is fresh and impudent."[28] Treitschke distrusted Bismarck's aristocratic background, his sublime indifference to principle, and his arrogant violation of constitutional liberties. As late as 1866, when the Prussian Minister President, recognizing the power of his pen, offered him a position in the Prussian propaganda service, an opportunity that would almost certainly have led to a professorship in Berlin after the war was over, Treitschke declined on the grounds that a government that denied parliament its budget rights could not claim his allegiance.

And yet, if unity was to be achieved, was there any alternative to Bismarck? "If you watch our middle class at close range," Treitschke confessed to his fiancée in 1866, "[if you see] how honorable these people are when they write books, wrap up parcels, or add up bills, and how cowardly and short-sighted in politics, you can't help seeing that, as a rule, only aristocrats (of birth or mind) make good statesmen."[29] And, similarly, was there any alternative to the Prussian army, which had as scant a regard for constitutional principle as Bismarck himself? Faced with these questions, Treitschke stifled his doubts, taking comfort in Dahlmann's law that circumstances alter cases and in the Hegelian

28. To Stosch, 24 September 1868, in *Gustav Freytags Briefe an Albrecht von Stosch*, ed. Hans F. Helmolt (Leipzig, 1913).
29. Dorpalen, *Treitschke*, p. 114.

view that reason has its own cunning. In 1861 he was still arguing
that a Prussian military conquest of Germany must be accompanied by a definitive break with the Junkers and by the establishment of "the most democratic state possible" in Prussia.[30] In 1864
it was still his conviction that the solution to the German question
must be a unitary rather than a federal state, so that specific
Prussianism, with all its connotations of feudalism and absolutism,
might be destroyed.[31] But in 1865 he was already weakening and
was writing that "the aggrandizement of Prussia, which is
proceeding step by step, scarcely corresponds to our ideals, but it
seems to me a lesser evil—indeed, a stroke of fortune—compared
with Germany's condition today;"[32] and, after 1866, as Prussia
unified Germany in its own way and with none of the constitutional safeguards that Treitschke had once insisted on, he was a
ready convert to the new dispensation. "Who is so blind," he said
after the victory over France, "as to fail to perceive in the
wonderful events of the last days the divine reason [*Vernunft*]
that compels us Germans to become people?"[33] His task, as he
saw it now, was to help protect what had been gained, and his
weapon was the *History*, which was conceived in the year of
unification.

II

It was the opinion of the severest of the early critics of the
History, the Strassburg historian Hermann Baumgarten, that in
effect Treitschke's effort was self-defeating, since his Prussian bias
was so blatant and his understanding of the rest of Germany so
inadequate that his work was more likely to inflame particularism
than to promote national consolidation.[34] On the basis of the first
volume of the *History*, it would be difficult to deny the merit of

30. Heinrich von Treitschke, *Historische und Politische Aufsätze* (Leipzig, 1897), IV, 91.

31. "Bundesstaat and Einheitsstaat," in Treitschke, *Aufsätze, Reden, Briefe*, III, 104-146.

32. A. Rapp, *Grossdeutsch-Kleindeutsch. Der deutsche Staatsgedanke*, 2d ser., vol. I, (Munich, 1922), pp. 239-40.

33. Bussmann, *Treitschke*, p. 334; Heinrich von Treitschke, *Zehn Jahre Deutsche Kämpfe* (Leipzig, 1874), p. 280.

34. Gooch, *History and Historians*, p. 152.

this criticism, for it was largely devoted to lyrical praise of the work of the early Hohenzollerns (who, in Treitschke's presentation, were always much abler to detect what was to the interest of all Germany at any given moment than any of their fellow rulers), as well as to a series of portraits of the Prussian reformers that were singularly free of warts and a spirited account of the final struggle with Napoleon in which rather too much credit for the victory was given to the Silesian army. But even here the Prussian emphasis was modified to some extent by a noble tribute to the classical period of German literature, and in the volumes that followed, Treitschke could hardly be faulted for lack of knowledge of, or appreciation for, non-Prussian contributions to the national cause. The second volume, which was published in 1882, opened with one of his greatest achievements, a survey of the art, literature, and scholarship of the Restoration period, in which he gave new praise to Uhland, saluted the Austrian Grillparzer as a German poet, and wrote movingly of the old Goethe. If it is true that his description of Prussia's commercial diplomacy in the third volume (1885) is rather excessively detailed (Treitschke was sure that when the new *Zollverein* was achieved in 1834, "the eagle eye of the great king looked down from the clouds, and from a remote distance could already be heard the thunder of the guns of Königgrätz"), it is balanced by a series of splendid descriptions of life and politics in the lesser German states. Perhaps more space would have been devoted to the rest of Germany if Treitschke had not been mining the Prussian archives for the first time. Historians find it difficult to restrain themselves when they are revealing things that have hitherto been unknown. Treitschke was the first historian to appreciate the achievement of the Prussian finance minister Motz, and in his time his chapters on the court of Frederick William IV possessed an exciting originality.

On the other hand, the later volumes of the *History* were marked by increasing conservatism and a prejudice that verged on bigotry; there were passages in which the historian seemed to be hunting for enemies of the state with a fervor equal to that of the chancellor whom he now idolized. Even before the publication of the first volume, Treitschke could have been described accurately as a Bismarckian *sans phrase*. Elected to the Reichstag in 1871 as a National Liberal, he had been proud to participate in creating the institutional infrastructure of the new Reich, and he had enthusiastically supported the *Kulturkampf*, which to him as to other National Liberals was a logical consequence of Prussia's conquest of Germany, which they saw as a victory for Protestantism. When Bismarck decided to break with the party, however, Treitschke had no hesitation about following him. He voted for both of the antisocialist bills that caused such a crisis of conscience in liberal hearts in 1878, for he hated socialism, as he had said in a slashing attack upon it and its liberal supporters in 1874, because "the guiding principle of the whole movement is unmistakeably naked sensuality, the fundamental denial of all that raises man above animal"[35]—and doubtless also because its plebeian following threatened German culture, which he was pleased to identify with the people of property and cultivation (*Besitz und Bildung*). In 1879, during the debate over commercial policy, he left the National Liberal party, which was fighting against protectionism, and, as an independent, supported Bismarck's new tariff legislation, although it was plainly in the interest of the Junker landlords, whom he had once reprobated. In 1881 he was a patron of the new *Verein deutscher Studenten*, the organization that had so much influence in swinging student opinion from liberalism and democracy to conservatism, a shift that began, in the words of a modern historian, "in Treitschke's lectures and was directed against Mommsen and the Progressive party."[36] Throughout the 1880s he was a fervent supporter of Bismarck's foreign and colonial policy and his anti-Polish land-development schemes in Posen. Finally, when the fourth volume of the *History* was published in 1889, only the most obtuse could fail to see that its attacks upon the ideas of 1789 and the natural-rights philosophy

35. *Preussische Jahrbücher*, XXXIV (1874).
36. Fritz Fischer, "Der deutsche Protestantismus und die Politik im neunzehnten Jahrhundert," in *Probleme der Reichsgründungszeit*, ed. Helmut Böhme (Göttingen, 1968), p. 67.

were directed less against the liberal movement of the 1830s, with which the volume dealt, than against the left wing of the liberal movement of his own day, the Progressives, who, he felt, were aiding and abetting enemies of the state.[37]

Treitschke's literary judgments reflected the growing conservatism of his politics. Worried about the rampant materialism of his own day—he was one of the first to warn against the *Amerikanisierung* of Germany[38]—he was quick to find its roots in the literature of the 1830s and 1840s. His concern for the moral fabric of the new Reich increased his tendency toward moral outrage to ludicrous proportions. He had always been a bit prudish in his literary tastes; in an otherwise generous and perceptive essay on Heinrich von Kleist in 1858, he had expressed distaste for some of the poet's stories and had revealed that he was appalled by the conclusion of "Die Marquise von O."[39] Now he did not hesitate to speak of "the cynical impudence of Georg Büchner's drama *Danton's Death*" and to condemn it as a work that "can only arouse our loathing."[40]

Even more noticeable and more offensive to some of his admirers was the increased violence of his attacks on the Jews. His defenders have argued that he was never an antisemite in a racist sense and that he was capable of warm appreciation of Jews like Felix Mendelssohn-Bartholdy whom he considered to be "good Germans." There is something in this. Treitschke's personal attitude toward Jews was marked by the kind of ambivalence felt by his contemporary, the novelist Theodor Fontane, who once wrote in a private letter, "Fine Jews I like, but the ordinary ones are frightful."[41] Nevertheless, one cannot conceive of Fontane writing, let alone publishing, the article that appeared under Treitschke's name in the November 1879 issue of the

37. A useful discussion of Treitschke's politics is to be found in Andreas Dorpalen, "Heinrich von Treitschke," *Journal of Contemporary History*, VII, nos. 3-4 (July-October 1972), 21-35.

38. Erich Marcks, *Heinrich von Treitschke, ein Gedenkblatt* (Heidelberg, 1906), pp. 45 ff.

39. Treitschke, *Aufsätze, Reden, Briefe*, I, 25-26.

40. *History*, V, 530. See this ed., p. 228.

41. *Fontanes Briefe in zwei Bänden*, ed. Gotthard Erler, 2 vols. (Berlin, 1968), II, 139.

Preussische Jahrbücher, announcing to the world that "the Jews are our national misfortune".[42]

The argument of this notorious production was not original; it had been made many times in the speeches of Court Preacher Adolf Stoecker.[43] In brief, it held that Jews were a divisive force in German life because they either persisted in obeying the commands of their own religion or had no religion except that of Mammon, and that they would continue to be the object of legitimate distrust unless they gave up the attempt to be unique and bent their efforts to becoming, in thought and deed, conservative, loyal to the throne, and uncritical of the *status quo*. In sending the piece off to the printer, Treitschke explained to an associate, rather inelegantly, "Somebody has got to tell those guys that it isn't we, but they themselves, who are responsible for the *furia tedesca* that is now breaking loose."[44] He was referring to the increasingly rabid antisemitism that had been promoted by the crash of 1873, which was popularly attributed to stock-rigging by Jewish speculators;[45] but he should have been aware, as others were, that an article of this kind, backed by all of the authority that went with a professorship at the University of Berlin, could only encourage antisemitism by vesting it with respectability. In an open reply to Treitschke, Theodor Mommsen said just that, and he thereupon broke off relations with his colleague. When he heard that Treitschke was being considered for the editorship of the *Historische Zeitschrift* in succession to Heinrich von Sybel, Mommsen vowed that he would never write for that journal again; and in the 1890s he tried, although without success, to block Treitschke's election to the Prussian Academy.[46]

42. Treitschke's article is reprinted, with most of the rejoinders it elicited, in *Der Berliner Antisemitismusstreit*, ed. Walter Boehlich (Frankfurt am Main, 1965).

43. Stoecker's first antisemitic speeches were given in Berlin in September 1879.

44. Boehlich, *Antisemitismusstreit*, p. 239.

45. In June 1875, the *Kreuzzeitung*, the mouthpiece of unreconstructed conservatism, had published an attack upon Jews in high places by a writer named Perrot. See Ivor N. Lambi, *Free Trade and Protection in Germany, 1868–1879* (Wiesbaden, 1963), pp. 84–85. On other causes of the antisemitism of the 1870s, see the statement made by Franz Mehring in 1882, in Paul W. Massing, *Rehearsal for Destruction: A Study of Political Anti-Semitism in Imperial Germany* (New York, 1949), pp. 313–14.

46. Boehlich, *Antisemitismusstreit*, p. 247.

If professional antisemites were encouraged by the article in the *Preussische Jahrbücher*, they had every reason to be delighted by Treitschke's references to Jews in the later volumes of the *History*. In these, even when he seemed to be striving for the objective view, the balance generally tilted against the objects of his discussion. Thus, in his famous chapter on the *Burschenschaft*, while praising the work of Moses Mendelssohn and other Jewish leaders who sought to make German culture their own, and while admitting that the antisemitic outrages in Frankfurt in 1816 were "detestable" and that "the Jews were treated with manifest injustice," he left the impression that popular anti-Jewish feeling was entirely understandable, since the majority of Jews "remained devoted to huckstering and usury, immersed in the gloomy fanaticism of the Talmudical faith, a prey to all the defects of those who have suffered bondage for many generations." Moreover, he added, a great many Jews had dodged military service during the War of Liberation, because of "a profoundly implanted dread of arms," although some of their intellectuals, after the fighting was over, had attributed the victory to the Jewish contribution.[47] In a later passage on the radicalism of the late 1820s and 1830s, he blamed the corrosive influence of cosmopolitanism and Gallomania upon the Jews and wrote that it was "the strange Jewish perversity of self-mockery" that had corrupted the minds of German youth and taught them to regard "impudent abuse of the fatherland as the true index of intellectual ability."[48]

Treitschke was at his most apoplectic when dealing with Jewish influence upon German literature, and his chapter on the Young German movement had an almost fanatical quality. "Cosmopolitanism and hatred of Christianity, bitter mockery and corruption of speech, utter indifference to the greatness of national history—everything in the movement was Jewish." The masterminds of what could almost be described as a conspiracy were, he was sure, Heinrich Heine and Ludwig Börne, Eduard Gans and Rahel Varnhagen, and the Mannheim publisher

47. *History*, III, 44 ff. See this ed. pp. 105–8.
48. Ibid., IV, 556–57. See this ed. pp. 254–55.

Zacharias Loewenthal. "It is true," he added, "that the Hebraic choir-masters were few in number, but the Jew's mysterious faculty for multiplying himself is familiar to all.... This semi-Jewish radicalism had no creative faculty whatever, but it assisted in undermining the foundations of state, church and society, thus contributing to the revolution of 1848."[49]

Whenever he wrote about Heine, Treitschke became so aroused that he lost all restraint, and his opinions acquired an almost zany quality. "Of all our lyric poets," he wrote ponderously, "he was the only one who never wrote a drinking song: to him heaven seemed full of almond cakes, purses of gold, and street wenches, for the oriental was incompetent to carouse after the German manner."[50] Treitschke's general statements were not always accurate,[51] and while Heine may not have written a drinking song, he did write a rather good poem about carousing.[52] In any case, this was a rather curious stick with which to beat a great poet, and it indicates that, when Jewish writers were being considered, Treitschke was interested in things other than literary excellence. His summary judgment of Heine's great satirical epic *Deutschland, ein Wintermärchen* proves this beyond any doubt. "The poem," he wrote, "one of the most brilliant and characteristic products of Heine's pen, is an index for the Germans of what severed them from this Jew. The Aryan nations have their Thersites and their Loki, but such a character as Ham, who uncovers his father's nakedness, is known only to Jewish saga."[53]

In view of what was to happen to the German Jews within fifty years of the writing of these opinions, it is difficult to read them without feeling what the Scots call the cold grues. In his insistence that the Jews must become good Germans, Treitschke

49. Ibid., V, 530. See this ed. pp. 287.
50. Ibid., V, 517. See this ed. pp. 273.
51. Nor, for that matter, his citations. In his Milton essay (1860), he several times misquotes *Paradise Lost* and manages, in a quotation from *Paradise Regained*, to attribute to Jesus words spoken by Satan. See Treitschke, *Aufsätze, Reden, Briefe*, I, 178, 179, 191.
52. Heinrich Heine, *Werke*, ed. Martin Greiner, 2 vols. (Cologne, n. d.), I, 185. ("Im Hafen," *Die Nordsee*, Zweiter Zyklus.)
53. *History*, VII, 134–35.

helped to condition the minds of his fellow countrymen to feel that Jews could *not* become good Germans and, indeed, were secret enemies of everything that good Germans stood for. Before 1914 there were relatively few manifestations of this neurosis, but after the collapse of 1918 and the economic privations that followed it, it became obsessive, which accounts for the fact that so many good Germans tolerated the horrors inflicted upon their Jewish fellow-citizens by the Nazi regime.

Treitschke must, moreover, bear some responsibility for making the debacle of 1918 possible. Through his writings and lectures, he had taught thousands of young men who occupied important positions in state and society in the years before 1914 to place too high a valuation upon the uses of power and to believe that their country was being denied the world position that it deserved by jealous and resentful neighbors. In doing so, he had, as Friedrich Meinecke has said, persuaded all those "who in the world's struggle long for simple lapidary principles" to overlook the basic problems of state life. At a time when the new Reich needed an inner transformation and evolution to cope with new economic and social conditions, he had discouraged change by his insistence upon the complete adequacy of the military-absolutist regime that Bismarck had founded.[54] At moments when this seemed less than completely obvious, he had blamed the discrepancy upon internal and external enemies and the degeneracy of the times and had called for an effort of will to put things right, when an exercise of sustained reflection might have been more profitable.

Yet he was not unaware of the contradictions of his thought or impervious to the claims made on him by the liberalism of his youth. If he believed with Hegel that the essence of the state was power, he had never convinced himself that power was also its purpose and justification. If the state was a necessity in the phenomenal world, it was not a moral value in itself but rather a means to promote and preserve moral values and to create an area of civic freedom in which they could develop. Treitschke never stopped believing this, but his tragedy was that in his hot

54. Meinecke, *Die Idee der Staatsraison*, pp. 467 ff.

love for his people, in his desire to see them strong and respected, in his constant fear that the most dangerous threat to their unity was their lack of confidence in themselves, he had forgotten, and had taught many others to forget, the requirements of freedom, while putting weapons in the hands of its foes. In the end, as he struggled vainly to complete the *History*, there is evidence that he sensed this and was troubled by its possible consequences.[55]

III

The fifth volume of the *History* appeared in October 1894, and Treitschke plunged immediately into the research for its successor, which was to deal with the revolution of 1848. He was not permitted to complete it, for he died in April 1896, a mere eighteen years before a greater revolution would engulf all of Europe and destroy the empire that he had striven to make as firm as a *rocher de bronze*.

Stanford University   GORDON A. CRAIG

---

55. Sontag, *Germany and England*, pp. 337–39.

I
The Founders of the
Prussian State

In his opening chapter, Treitschke describes the constitution of the Holy Roman Empire, the ravages caused in its structure by the Thirty Years' War, and the resultant confusion that "seemed to foreshadow the destruction of the German name." The Electorate of Brandenburg appeared to be as bereft of energy and direction as its neighbors. Content with their own petty concerns, its rulers "looked sleepily over the world out of heavy eyes." But all of that changed in 1640.

THE GREAT ELECTOR, 1640–1688 (I, 33–38)

Then came the Elector Frederick William, a landless prince, the greatest German of his day, thrusting himself with a vigorous impetus into the desert of German life, to inspire the slumbering forces of his state with the might of his will. Never since that time has the strength of the purposive monarchical will of the developing German power known any decline. We can conceive English history without William III, we can conceive French history without Richelieu ; the Prussian state is the work of its princes. There are few other countries in which monarchy has so continually preserved the two virtues upon which its greatness depends : a bold and far-seeing idealism which sacrifices the convenience of to-day to the greatness of to-morrow ; and that strong sense of justice which ever constrains self-interest in the service of the whole. It was only the wide vision of the monarchy that could recognise in these poverty-stricken territorial fragments the foundation-stones of a new great power. It was only in the sense of duty to the crown, in the idea of the monarchical state, that the mutually hostile tribes and estates, parties and churches, which were comprised within this microcosm of German life, could find protection and peace.

Even in the earliest years of the Great Elector the peculiarities of the new German power became plainly manifest. The nephew of Gustavus Adolphus, who led his young army to battle with the ancient Protestant warcry " With God," took over the ecclesiastical policy of his uncle. He was the first to find the saving solution for the quarrels of the Churches, demanding a general and unconditional amnesty for all three confessions. This was the programme of the Peace of Westphalia. But the toleration extended by the Hohenzollerns in the interior of their own dominion went far beyond the prescriptions of this Peace. In accordance with the imperial law Brandenburg was recognised as a Protestant estate, and yet this was the first state in Europe in which complete religious freedom was secured. In the Netherlands the multiplicity of unassociated sects was dependent simply upon anarchy, upon the weakness of the state ; but here freedom of conscience rested upon the laws of a powerful state-organisation which would not allow itself to be deprived of its right to supervise the Churches. In the other territories of Germany there still everywhere existed one dominant Church, whose power was restricted only in so far as it was unable altogether to forbid the other creeds to hold religious services ; in Brandenburg the throne stood free above all the Churches and protected their equality. While Austria was forcibly expelling its best Germans, an unparalleled hospitality threw open the frontiers of Brandenburg to the toleration of every belief. How many thousand times in the Mark was uplifted the hymn of gratitude of the Bohemian exiles :

"Thy people, else in darkness, by error quite surrounded,
Finds here abundant house-room, secure, on freedom grounded!"

When Louis XIV revoked the Edict of Nantes, the Lord of Brandenburg, as spokesman of the Protestant world, set himself in bold opposition, and in his Edict of Potsdam offered protection and shelter to the children of the martyr-Church. Wherever the flames of the ancient religious hatred were still raging among the German people, the work of the Hohenzollerns was one of guardianship and reconciliation. They summoned to the Spree the Jewry of Vienna ; *via facti,* and without asking the leave of the empire, they secured the Protestants of Heidelberg in the possession of their churches ; for the Protestants of Salzburg they provided a new home in East Prussia. Thus into the unpeopled eastern Mark there streamed year after year an abundance of young life ; the German blood which the Hapsburgs rejected fertilised the land of their rival. At the death of Frederick II about one-third of the population of the state was made up of the offspring of immigrants who had found their way into the country since the days of the Great Elector.

It was this Church policy of the Hohenzollerns which closed the epoch of the religious wars, ultimately compelling the best of the temporal princes to follow in Brandenburg's footsteps, and at the same time depriving the spiritual estates of the last justification for existence—for why should there be any more spiritual princes of the empire now that freedom was assured to the Catholic Church beneath the wings of the Prussian eagle ? By the Peace of Westphalia Frederick William acquired the great foundations of Magdeburg, Halberstadt, Minden, and Kammin. No other state in Germany was so greatly enriched by the goods of the Roman Church ; yet the seizure was justified, for therewith were also taken over the great tasks of civilisation which the Church of the Middle Ages had of old performed for the immature state—the duty of providing for the poor and the work of popular education. The same need for self-preservation which compelled the Hohenzollerns to maintain peace between Catholics and Protestants, forced them also to mediate between the antagonisms within the Protestant Church. From the time when John Sigismund first forbade the Lutheran zealots to fulminate against the Calvinists, the idea of Protestant union became characteristic of the Prussian state ; and what had been begun simply from necessity became ultimately a political tradition, became a matter of principle with the princely house.

Just as the Prussian state secured for the Germans peace between the Churches and enabled Germany to take part once more in the activities of the civilised nations, so also did Prussia restore what had been lacking since the opening of the days of religious discord—a coherent will against the foreign world.

Throughout Germany abundant energies were failing to find an outlet in the narrow spheres that were open to them, so that anyone with lofty ambitions hastened to some foreign country ; then came Frederick William to grasp in his resolute hand the scanty resources of the poorest region in Germany, compelling his people to serve their own homeland, and showing Europe once more the might of the German sword. The empire lived upon ancient memories, preserving in the new Europe the political forms of the Middle Ages ; but this North German power was firmly rooted in the modern world; its vigorous state-authority rose above the ruins of the old ecclesiastical dominion and above the ancient rights of the estates ; it lived through the troubles of the present with eyes fixed on schemes for a great future. With a single blow, Frederick William made for his despised little territory a place in the ranks of the European powers, so that, after the battle of Warsaw, Brandenburg could stand side by side with the ancient military states. This strongly-unified and warlike power appeared to rise suddenly, like a new-made volcanic island, out of the raging sea of conflicting sovereignties in Germany, and before the wondering gaze of a people which had long ceased to believe in rapid resolve and high endeavour. So vigorously blew the fresh breeze of purposive political will through the history of the new Prussian state, so tensely and vigorously were all the muscles of its people turned to work, so gross appeared the disproportion between ambition and means, that to friend and foe alike it seemed for a century and a half that Prussia could be no more than an artificial venture. The world regarded as the chance creation of a few favourites of fortune, what was in reality the necessary reconstruction of the ancient national state of the Germans.

In the great struggles for power of the European world, no less than in the contests between the creeds within the German borders, Prussia maintained a difficult intermediate position. So long as Protestant Germany had remained prostrate and lacked the will to arise, Europe consisted of two distinct state-systems which rarely came into contact. The powers of the south and the west were fighting for the dominion of Italy and for the Rhenish Burgundian lands, while the powers of the north and the east disputed for the ruined fragments of the Teutonic Ordensland, and for the command of the Baltic Sea, the legacy of the Hanseatic League.

There was only one desire that was common to the east and to the west, and this was to keep ever open the terrible abyss that yawned in the middle of the Continent. Now uprose the youngest power of Germany, greatly mocked as " the realm of the long borders." Belonging to the European system, its dispersed provinces touched the boundaries of all the great powers of the Continent. As soon as Prussia began to move with an independent will the powers of the west were involved in the affairs of the east, and the interests of the two state-systems became ever more frequently and closely intertwined.

The born opponent of the old order of Europe, established upon Germany's weakness, Prussia stood in a world of enemies, whose jealousies were her only salvation—stood without a single natural ally, for elsewhere in the German nation there was as yet no understanding of the significance of this young force. This, too, was in the time of that hard statecraft in which the state was the mere incorporation of power, regarding the destruction of its neighbours as a natural duty. Just as the House of Savoy won through against the preponderant power of the Hapsburgs and the Bourbons, so also, but in far more difficult circumstances, must Prussia cut a way for herself between Austria and France, between Sweden and Poland, between the sea-powers and the inert mass of the German empire, availing herself of all the means furnished by a reckless egoism, ever ready for a change of front, ever with two strings to her bow.

To its very marrow, electoral Brandenburg came to realise the extent to which foreign elements had eaten their way into Germany. All the unbridled forces of feudal licence which strove against the strict rule of the new monarchy looked for support to foreign aid. Dutch garrisons were established along the Lower Rhine and favoured the struggle of the estates of Cleves against the German suzerain ; the diets of Magdeburg and of the Electoral Mark looked for help to Austria ; the nobles of Königsberg, Polish in their sympathies, appealed to the Polish overlord for help against the despotism of the Mark. In the struggle against foreign dominion, the national unity of these dispersed provinces and the repute of their ruler became established. Frederick William destroyed the barrier of the Netherlands in the German north-west, and drove the Dutch troops out of Cleves and East Frisia ;

he liberated Old Prussia from the Polish feudal suzerainty, and forced the diet of Königsberg to accept his own lordship. Then he made his appeal to the deaf nation in the words, " Remember that you are German!", and endeavoured to expel the Swedes from the realm. Twice the disfavour of France and Austria served to deprive the Brandenburger of the reward of his victories and to cheat him of his dominion in Pomerania ; but none could rob him of the glory of the day of Fehrbellin. At length, after long decades of shame, there came a brilliant triumph of German arms over the first military power of the age, and the world learned that Germany could once more dare to assert her rights. The inheritor of the German ecclesiastical policy of Gustavus Adolphus, destroyed the daring structure of the Scandinavian Baltic Empire which had been established by the sword of the King of Sweden. The two artificial powers of the seventeenth century, Sweden and Holland, began to withdraw within their natural borders, and the new state which arose in their place displayed neither the licentious lust of conquest of the Swedish military power nor the monopoly-seeking mercantile spirit of the Netherlands. It was German ; it was satisfied to protect its own domain ; and to the plans of the Bourbon for world-dominion it opposed the ideas of the European balance of power and of freedom for the nations. When the Republic of the Netherlands seemed likely to succumb before the onslaught of Louis XIV, Brandenburg boldly attacked the conqueror. Frederick William conducted the one serious campaign ventured by the empire for the reconquest of Alsace ; and on his death-bed he concerted with his nephew of Orange the plan for the rescue of Protestant and parliamentary England from the arbitrary rule of the Stuarts, the vassals of Louis. Wherever this young power stood alone its campaigns were victorious, but it was everywhere unfortunate when Prussia was forced to involve itself in the confusions of the imperial army.

Thus in its very inception the new structure of the state showed itself a European necessity. At length Germany had again found one who could extend the empire. With the rise of Prussia there began the long and bloody task of the liberation of Germany from foreign dominion. Despoiled by its neighbours for centuries past, the empire now saw for the first time the foreign powers yielding back a few fragments of German ground. In this single state of Prussia there reawakened, though still but half-conscious and as if drunken from prolonged slumber, the ancient stout-hearted pride in the fatherland. The faithful landsfolk of the County Mark began the little war against the French; the peasants of East Prussia put the Swedes to headlong flight. When the peasant Landwehr of the Altmark, guarding the Elbe-dike against the Swedes, wrote upon their flags, " We are peasants of little wealth, and serve our gracious elector and prince with goods and blood," the disjointed words breathed the same heroic spirit as that which of old, in days of greater freedom, was voiced by the warcry, " With God for King and Fatherland."

Whilst the power of the Hapsburgs was extending beyond the limits of Germany, by the continuous control of destiny the state of the Hohenzollerns pressed ever deeper into the inner current of German life, at times against the will of its chief. Frederick William never ceased to regret his inability to maintain, against the opposition of Austria and Sweden, his hereditary Pomeranian claims in the Peace of Westphalia. As King of the Vandals he hoped to rule the Baltic from the harbour of Stettin, but was forced to content himself with the Saxon-Westphalian Church lands as a substitute for the mouths of the Oder. Yet this diplomatic reverse was in reality advantageous to the state, which was thus preserved from a half-German separate life on the Baltic, so that its central position was strengthened, and it was forced to take part in all the negotiations of internal German policy. Moreover, the whole of North Germany was overlaid with a network of agreements respecting hereditary claims which had been concluded during past centuries by the far-seeing House of Hohenzollern. Any day the fortune of death might bring some new enlargement to the ambitious power.

KING FREDERICK WILLIAM I, 1713-1740 (I, 43-51)

The Great Elector had to struggle throughout his life with the pressure of hostile neighbours. In the great projects of European policy he never lost that strong domestic sense which had characterised most of his ancestors, and which even in the early days of his house had brought to many of its chiefs the cognomen of *œconomus ;* he did all in his power to restore well-being to his country, nurtured the roots of a monarchical officialdom, and began to effect the transformation of the national economy in accordance with the needs of the modern monetary system. But in the storms of this war-filled regime it was impossible to effect a thorough reform of the administration ; the shapeless bundle of territories was with difficulty held together by the personal repute of the ruler and by the unwieldy and antiquated authority of the privy council. It was by the grandson of the Great Elector that the ancient state-system was finally abolished.

The fundamental ideas of the internal order of the Prussian state were so irrevocably fixed by King Frederick William I that even the laws of Stein and Scharnhorst and the reforms of our own days could serve only to develop and not to destroy the work of the founder. He was the creator of the new German administration, of our officialdom and our military caste ; his inconspicuous and laborious activity was not less fruitful for German life than were the deeds at arms of his grandfather, for it was he who introduced into our history a new form of government, the circumscribed national unity of the modern monarchy. He gave meaning and content to the new name of Prussia, united his people in a community for the fulfilment of political duty, and stamped for all time upon the consciousness of this state the notion of duty. Only one who is familiar with the gnarly growth, with the hard edges and angles of the Low German national character, will understand this rigid disciplinarian, will understand his breathless and stormy passage through life—the scorn and the terror of his contemporaries, rough and rude, scolding and quarrelsome, ever at work, forcing his people and himself to labour, a sterling old German, essentially German in his childish frankness, his goodness of heart, his profound sense of duty, and not less so in his terrible fits of hasty anger and in his formless and unconquered solidity. In this royal burgher, the ancient hatred of the North German people for the modish refinements of Gallic manners, as expressed in Lauremberg's Low German satirical poems, became incorporated in flesh and blood ; his severity towards wife and child showed him also the true son of the classic age of German domestic tyranny—an age in which, owing to the enslavement of public life, the energies of the men could find vent only within the narrow limits of the household. Severe, joyless, terribly restricted, did life become under the close-fisted rule of this rigid disciplinarian. The hard one-sidedness of his spirit could value those simple moral and economic forces alone, which served as internal bonds of national union ; with the whole energy of his masterful will he threw himself into the province of administration, displaying here the primitive force of a creative spirit. Firmly and consistently, as of old William the Conqueror in overthrown England, did Frederick William I piece together the structure of a unified state out of the dispersed fragments of his territories. But not to him, as to William the Norman, did the unified state appear as a mere appanage of his own house. Rather, in the mind of the unlettered prince, was there conceived, clearly and vividly, a notion of the state that was accordant with the new doctrine of natural law: the notion that the state exists for the good of all, and that the king is placed at its head to administer with unbiassed justice over all the estates of the realm, to pursue the public weal regardless of all private privileges and preferences. To the development of this idea he devoted his unceasing activities ; and if, when he placed his heavy foot on the loose immorality of the paternal court he also stamped upon the germs of a more abundant culture which had begun to develop under Frederick I, he yet did but what he had to do. The firm and manly discipline of a fighting and industrious people was of greater importance for Prussia's high destiny than were the premature blossoms of art and science.

A gentler hand than his could never have succeeded in bringing the ancient feudal licence under the control of the majesty of the common law ; milder natures than Frederick William and Leopold von Dessau would never have been able to stand against the stormwind which then blew from the Gallic quarter over the German courts. Among all the statesmen of modern history, two only can be compared as organisers of administration with this soldier king : Bonaparte and von Stein. He united to the daring of the innovator, the painfully exact sense of order of the economical householder, who measured the black and white threads with which the official documents were tied and counted the buttons on the gaiters of his grenadiers ; he conceived audacious plans whose realisation has become possible only in the nineteenth century, and yet retained in all his negotiations a secure grasp of the limits of the possible. His prosaic sense, directed towards that which was practically useful and could be immediately grasped, adopted other measures than those characteristic of his heroic grandfather, and yet, in the midst of his care for that which was very small and very near, he always remained conscious of the lofty destiny of his state ; he was well aware that he was collecting and forming the energies of his people for the decisive hours of a great future, and he often said, " I know perfectly well that in Vienna and Dresden they.call me a penny-wise pedant, but my grandchildren will reap the benefit ! "

It was by the army that Prussia was raised to the rank of a European power, and it was by the army that the first breach was made in the old administrative system of the state. For the management of the new taxes which he had introduced to finance his military establishment, the Great Elector had established a number of intermediate boards, the war-commissariats ; thus for some decades the tax-economy of the developing modern state existed side by side with the administration of the crown lands, the last fragments of the natural economy of the Middle Ages. Frederick William I put an end to this dualism. In the general directory he created a supreme authority, and in the war-chambers and domain-chambers intermediate authorities for the whole administration, and also endowed these bodies with judicial authority in questions of public law. The variegated and manifold charac-teristics of the area he controlled forced the king to establish an institution to intermediate between the provincial-system and the real-system ; at the head of the subdivisions of the general directory he placed provincial ministers, who had also to conduct certain branches of the administration on behalf of the state as a whole. Speaking generally, however, a centralised administration was here earlier established than elsewhere on the Continent. Whatever still remained of the ancient feudal authorities, was either abolished or else subjected to the control of the officials of the monarchy ; an unpitying current of reform swept through the profoundly corrupt administration of the towns, did away with the nepotism of the magistrature, forcibly imposed a new and juster system of taxation ; threw the three towns of Königsberg into one, united into a single municipality the two communes of Brandenburg that were separated by the Havel, and placed the entire system of municipal administration under the keen supervision of royal war councillors.

Everywhere the particularism of the estates, of the territorial areas, and of the communes, presented a hostile front to the new and generally applicable order. The nobles murmured against the authority of the bourgeois officials. The proud East Prussians complained of the infringement of ancient charters, now that Pomeranians and Rhinelanders could take office in the Duchy. The law-courts, too, were still living in the circle of ideas of the old feudal state, and, just like the French parliaments, almost invariably took the side of the decaying rights of the parts against the vigorously living right of the whole. It was in the victorious struggle to secure national unity and equality before the law, that Prussia's new ruling class of officials under the crown obtained its schooling. From that homeless race of servants, which during the seventeenth century had flitted from court to court, there was gradually constructed a class of Prussians whose members devoted their lives to the service of the monarch, who found their honour in his, who were vigorous, active, and conscientious like their king. They did not, as had done the feudal lords of the old time, allow their energies to atrophy within the limited fields of territorial interest and nepotism ; they belonged to the nation, they learned to feel no less at home in Cleves than in Königsberg ; and in the class struggles of society maintained against high and against low the law of the land. By an established order of precedence, and by an assured position, the king secured for his officials a respected status in bourgeois life ; he demanded, from every candidate for office, proof of scientific knowledge, and thus founded an aristocracy of culture side by side with the old aristocracy of birth. The result showed how justly he had esteemed the living energies of German society ; the best intelligences of the nobility and of the bourgeoisie streamed to join the new ruling class. Prussian officialdom was for long years the firm support of the German national idea, just as in former days the jurists of Philip the Fair had been the pioneers of French national unity.

The Great Elector had imposed upon his subjects the general liability to taxation ; to this Frederick William I added the obligations of universal military service and compulsory education, thus establishing the threefold group of general civic duties by which the people of Prussia have been trained in an active love for the fatherland. In his mind, powerful for all its limitations, the road was unconsciously prepared for a strong national sentiment akin to the citizen-sense of antiquity. In the eastern march of Germany, ever accustomed to battle, the ancient German idea of military service for all physically fit men had never completely disappeared, even during the epoch of mercenary armies. In East Prussia there lasted on into the eighteenth century the vestiges of the old Polish Landwehr, and Frederick I undertook to constitute a territorial militia for the unified state. In the soldier eye of his son such attempts at an unregulated arming of the people found no favour. King Frederick William understood the superiority of well-disciplined standing armies ; he saw that his state could survive only through the tense employment of all its energies, and yet was unable to effect a permanent provision for the cost of his levies. Since with him every other consideration was subordinated to the demands of political duty, he came to the bold resolve that all Prussians should pass through the school of the standing army. In recent centuries there had been but two political thinkers, Machiavelli and Spinoza, who had ventured to defend the simple and great idea of universal military service ; both these thinkers revived this idea from the history of classical antiquity, and both failed to find understanding among their contemporaries. The needs of domestic economy and an instinctive recognition of the nature of his state now led the rough, practical man who occupied the throne of Prussia to adopt the same view, little as he recked of the moral force of a national army. First among the statesmen of the new Europe did he give expression to the principle : " Every subject is born to bear arms." To construct an army of the children of his country was his life-long ideal. The cantonal regulation of 1733 announced the duty of universal military service.

It was but the establishment of a principle. The notion was still unripe, for it was flatly contradicted by the long term of military service then customary. The poverty of the country and the force of adverse prejudice, compelled the king to make numerous exceptions, so that the burden of compulsory service was imposed, in actual fact, upon the shoulders of the country-folk alone ; and, even thus limited, the duty of bearing arms could not be fully enforced. Unconquerable remained the tacit resistance to the unheard-of novelty, the detestation of the people for the long and severe term of duty. It was seldom possible to make up more than half of the army with homebred cantonists, and the deficiency was made up by voluntary enlistment. Many of the masterless German soldiers of fortune who had hitherto marketed their skins in Venice and the Netherlands, in France and Sweden, now found a home under the flag of the North German power ; the south and the west of the empire were the most fertile recruiting grounds of the Prussian regiments. By such a wonderful and devious route has our nation risen to power and unity. That unarmed third of the German people whose state authorities hardly raised a finger for the defence of the empire paid the blood-tax to the fatherland in the persons of the thousands of its lost sons who fought as mercenaries in the armies of Prussia ; the petty princes of Swabia and the Rhine, who regarded Prussia as their most dreaded opponent, helped to increase the fighting strength of their enemy. As soon as the Prussian army came into existence the empire gradually ceased to be a general recruiting ground ; and, as that army gathered strength, it came to pass that Germany was no longer the battle-field of all other nations.

In the army the king found the means to reconcile the territorial nobility with the monarchical order. The repute of the war-lord had risen greatly since the rude days of the Great Elector, but it was his grandson who succeeded in bringing under his immediate control the nomination of all the officers, and in thus constituting the first truly monarchical corps of modern history. His sense of organisation, always understanding how to adapt political reform to the given social conditions, led him to perceive at once that the hardy sons of the numerous impoverished noble families of the east were the natural leaders of the peasant lads liable for military service. He placed the officers' corps, as a closed aristocracy, at the head of the rank and file ; created in the house of cadets a training school for the officers ; threw open to all who wore epaulettes the way to the highest offices in the army ; kept a strict watch over the honour of the military order ; and endeavoured in every possible way to win the nobles for this knightly caste, whilst preferring to direct the cultured members of the bourgeoisie into the civil service of the administration. How often, with prayers and threats, did he warn the arrogant nobility of East Prussia to provide for their rude sons the discipline of the house of cadets, and, practising his own precept, he made all his own boys serve in the army. Moser refers with admiration to this " hereditary maxim of the Prussian house to accustom the nobles to the military and financial system of the crown." By these means he succeeded in creating out of the semi-savage junkers a brave and loyal monarchical nobility, ready to conquer and to die for the fatherland, and as firmly associated with the life of the state as the parliamentary nobility of England. Everywhere else throughout the high aristocratic world of the Baltic regions feudal anarchy continued to flourish—in Sweden, Swedish Pomerania, Mecklenburg, Polish Prussia, and Livonia ; it was only in Prussia that the nobles were won for the duties of the modern state. The army seemed as if it were a state within the state, with its own courts, churches, and schools ; the burgher regarded with disgust the iron strictness of the inhuman military discipline by which the rough masses of the rank and file were forcibly held together ; he bore unwillingly the blustering arrogance of the lieutenants and their centaurian hatred for the quill-driver's pretensions to learning—a hatred which had been manifest in the officers' circles since the days of the fiery Prince Karl Emil and in the berserker roughness of the Old Dessauer. And yet this army was not merely the best-trained and best-equipped military force of the time, but was also, of all the great armies of the modern nations, the most highly endowed with the civic spirit, the only one which never broke faith with its war-lords and never endeavoured (after the Pretorian model) to set the laws of the land at defiance.

No less uncongenial than the army organisation, appeared, to the Germans, the Prussian system of compulsory education ; the ignorance of the masses was still regarded by the ruling classes as the great safeguard of public order. King Frederick William, however, like his grandfather, admired the Protestant Netherlands as the chosen land of civic welfare ; he had there learned to appreciate the moral and economic blessings of a comprehensive system of school education, and he felt obscurely that the vital energy of Protestant civilisation sprang from the elementary school. Convinced that the oppressed and brutalised masses of the north-east could have their native roughnesses removed only by the compulsion of the state, he decisively anticipated, in this respect also, the legislation of all the other great powers ; and by the educational law of 1717 he directly imposed upon all heads of families the duty of sending their children to school. Very slowly, upon the foundation of this law, the Prussian school system became established. The difficulties attendant upon its development were in part due to the poverty and inertness of the people ; but were in part also the king's own fault, for all popular culture must rest upon the prosperity of independent research and of creative art, and for these ideal activities Frederick William felt a characteristically barbarian contempt.

Thus through the community of arduous civic duties, through the unity of the officialdom and of the military system, the men of Magdeburg and Pomerania, of the Mark and of Westphalia, were welded together into a single Prussian people ; and when Frederick II extended to all his subjects the Prussian nationality he did no more than give a legal sanction to his father's work. However roughly and masterfully the Prussian kingship might manifest its sovereignty against all disloyal opposition, the work of unification yet proceeded far more considerately than did, in the adjoining country, the forcible " levelling of the French soil." The state could not give the lie to its own Teutonic nature ; it was permeated throughout by a powerful element of historical piety. Just as it had endeavoured to reconcile the ecclesiastical differences, so was it compelled in political life to adopt an intermediate position in order to counteract the excess of centrifugal tendencies. Towards the ancient traditions of the territorial areas a tolerant respect was everywhere exhibited ; even to-day the double eagle of Austria may be seen displayed in the market place of almost every Silesian town, and the patron saint of Bohemia still looks out from the citadel of Glatz over the beautiful surrounding country. The arrogant lords who wished to forbid the Great Elector to bury his father with Calvinistic rites were finally, after a severe struggle, reduced to the common position of subjects. The diets lost their ancient rights of government and were deprived of all influence in financial and military affairs ; but were permitted to retain a semblance of life as soon as these necessary changes had been effected.

Until the extinction of the Holy Empire there were only three occasions on which, throughout all the territorial areas which gradually accrued to the crown of Prussia, a local constitution was formally abolished. This occurred in Silesia, in West Prussia, and in Münster, for here the estates became the nucleus of a party hostile to the central government, seriously threatening its predominance. Everywhere else the diets lived on into the new time, remarkable vestiges of that ancient epoch in which the German north still consisted of numerous petty territories. They were the fragments of eggshell that the eaglet still carried on its head : they represented the past of the state ; whereas the crown, officialdom, the army, represented the present. They represented particularism and feudal privilege, as opposed to the national unity and to the common law ; their power still sufficed, at times, to render difficult the great progress of monarchical legislation, but they were no longer able to arrest that progress completely. The diets remained competent to allot certain taxes and to administer the territorial debts ; in this narrow sphere there persisted unchanged the nepotism, the routine, and the empty formalism of the old feudal order ; and the nobleman of the Mark still preferred to speak of his Brandenburg as an independent state under the crown of Prussia. Nor was the feudal office of Landrat abolished, but a place was found for it in the order of monarchical officialdom ; the Landrat, nominated by the crown after being proposed by the estates, was at the same time representative of the knighthood ; and a royal official subordinated to the war-chamber and to the domain-chamber. The king cherished a thoroughly citizen mistrust of the overbearing disposition of his junkers, but he needed the cordial support of the nobility for the establishment of his new military constitution. He therefore sought to appease the disaffected by honours and dignities, leaving to the landed proprietors a portion of their old privileges of taxation and of their other seignorial rights, but always under the supervision of the royal officials.

It was this prudent and tolerant policy which rendered it possible for the king to carry into execution his great economic reforms. He founded that peculiar system of monarchical organisation which for two generations harmonised the traditional organisation of classes with the new tasks of the nation. Every province and every class was made to undertake certain branches of economic and political work on behalf of the crown. In addition to agriculture (which was the principal industry of the entire monarchy), in the electoral Mark and the Westphalian provinces, manufactures, in the coastlands, commerce, and in the Magdeburg districts, mining, must be carried on. The nobles remained the sole great landed proprietors, and had an almost exclusive right to become officers in the army ; the peasantry undertook the work of agriculture and must serve in the ranks ; the burghers engaged in commerce and industry, and must bear the chief burden of taxation.

King Frederick II (the Great), 1740–1786 (I, 56–62, 65–69, 89–90)

The reign of Frederick William came in the poverty-stricken time of the Peace of Utrecht, a period barren of ideas ; the petty arts of Fleury, Alberoni, and Walpole dominated European politics. Perplexed was the simple-minded prince amid the crafty intrigues of diplomacy. He adhered to his emperor with ancient German fidelity ; he wished to put sabre and pistols in his children's cradles that they might help in expelling foreign nations from the imperial soil ; how often with the beer-tankard of the fatherland in his hand did he not raise his resounding shout : " Vivat Germania teutscher Nation ! " Now must the guileless man learn how the court of Vienna, in conjunction with his two ambitious neighbours of Hanover and Saxony, was secretly planning the partition of Prussia, and must witness their helping the Albertiners to the Polish crown, and their surrender of Lorraine to the French ; he must witness their attempts to sow discord in his own household between father and son ; must finally experience their perfidious attempts to deprive him of his sound hereditary right to Berg and East Frisia. Thus throughout his life he was pushed to and fro between open opponents and false friends ; not until the close of his days did he see through Austria's cunning and conjure his son to avenge the tricks played upon the father. At the foreign courts it was currently said, that the King of Prussia always stood on watch with his gun at full cock, but would never pull the trigger ; and when, within the empire, the other Germans were sometimes anxious about the Potsdam military parades, they consoled themselves by saying, " After all, the Prussians are very slow to shoot ! "

The joke missed fire when Prussia found a ruler who combined with the sense of the practicable and with the fortunate sobriety characteristic of the Hohenzollerns, the boldness and the insight of genius. The clear sunshine of youth was diffused over the beginnings of the Frederician epoch, when at length, after so prolonged an arrest, the inert mass of the German world was once more set in motion, and when the powerful opposing forces which Germany contained within its bosom broke into inevitable conflict. Since the days of the Lion of the North, Germany had not again seen a heroic figure upon which the whole nation could gaze with wondering admiration. But the figure which in proud freedom, like that of Gustavus Adolphus of old, strode among the great powers and forced the Germans to believe once again in the wonders of the heroic age, was now that of a German.

The central characteristic of this powerful nature was his pitiless and cruel German realism. Frederick presents himself as he is, and sees things as they are. Just as in the long series of his letters and writings we find not a single line wherein he endeavours to glorify his own actions or to adorn his own image for the benefit of posterity, so also do we find in his statesmanship, even though he did not despise the petty arts and cunning of the age as means to his ends, the stamp of his royal frankness. Whenever he takes the sword in hand he explains with unmistakable definiteness what he demands from the opponent, and does not lay down his weapon until he has attained his end. As soon as he awakens to self-consciousness he is filled with pride and rejoicing to be the son of a free century, which is using the torch of reason to illumine the dusty corners of a world of ancient prejudices and exanimate traditions ; on the ceiling of his bright hall at Rheinsberg was painted a picture of the sun-god, rising victoriously through the clouds of dawn. It is with the self-confident assurance of the disciple of enlightenment that he approaches the phenomena of history, examining them each by each with the judgment of his keen understanding. In the struggles for power among the states he concerns himself only about what is really alive, cares only for the power that can speedily and wisely find expression in effective action. "Negotiations without weapons are like music without instruments," he says frankly. When he is informed of the death of the last Hapsburg he says to his councillors, " I give you a problem to solve ; if one has an advantage in one's hand, should one make use of it or not ? " Never did anyone exhibit a prouder contempt for that boastful powerlessness that pretends to possess power, that immoral privilege which bases itself upon the sacredness of historic right, that dread of action which conceals its helplessness behind an empty respect for forms ; and never did this implacable realism exercise so cleansing, so destructive, so revolutionary an influence as in that great world of fable which was the Holy Empire. Nothing was more remorseless than Frederick's scorn for the sacred majesty of the Emperor Francis, tied to his wife's apron-strings, a worthy king of Jerusalem, occupied in lucrative commissariat-negotiations for the armies of the Queen of Hungary ; nothing could be more cruel than his mockery of the " phantom " of the imperial army, his scorn of the obscure nonentity of the petty courts, of the formal commercial spirit " of these accursed periwig-pates of Hanover," of the vain pride of the landless junkers of Saxony and Mecklenburg, of " this whole race of princes and people of Austria." He that bends the knee before the great ones of this world " is one who does not know them."

With an assured sense of superiority he opposes to the shadow-pictures of the imperial law the healthy reality of his modern state ; a fierce love of mischief speaks out of his letters when he brings home to " the pedants of Ratisbon " the iron necessity of war. Frederick effected in action that which the disputatious publicists of the previous century, Hippolytus and Severinus, had attempted in words alone ; he held up a mirror before the " disagreeable and corpse-like countenance of Germany," proving to all the world the hopeless corruption of the Holy Empire. Well-meaning contemporaries blamed him because he thus exposed to laughter the anciently venerable community, but posterity thanks him, in that he restored truth to a place of honour in German statecraft, as of old had done Martin Luther in the spheres of German thought and belief.

Frederick adopted early in life that strict Protestant view of German history and imperial policy which, since the days of Puffendorf and Thomasius, had dominated the freer spirits of Prussia ;

amid the embittering experiences of his joyless youth he had re-moulded this view with a keen independence. In the Schmalkald rising, in the Thirty Years' War, in all the confused happenings of the last two centuries, he sees nothing but the unceasing struggle of German freedom against the despotism of the House of Austria, that house which " with a rod of iron " ruled the weak princes of the empire like slaves, and allowed only the strong ones to do as they liked. Not without personal satisfaction does he interpret the facts of history in accordance with such a one-sided view, for to direct this one-sidedness towards the light and towards life seems to him the privilege of the creative hero, and he regards it as the task of the Prussian state to lead this ancient struggle to victory. In his earlier years he remained faithful to Protestantism ; he esteemed it the glorious duty of the House of Brandenburg " to work on behalf of the Protestant religion throughout the German empire and Europe," and he contemplated Heidelberg with uneasi-ness, seeing that here in the old leading centre of our Church the monks and the priests of Rome were once more vigorously at work. Even at a later date, when he had become estranged from religious belief, and when from the altitude of his independent philosophical enlightenment he passed a hostile judgment upon the mediocre parson-natures of Luther and Calvin, he remained actively conscious that his state must continue ever rooted in the Protestant world. He knew how all the accomplices of the Holy See were secretly working for the destruction of the new Protestant great power ; he knew that his human ideal of freedom of belief, of the right of all to seek salvation after their own fashion, was attainable only on the soil of Protestantism ; he understood that in new and secular forms he was himself carrying on the struggles of the six-teenth century ; and to his latest work, the plan for the League of German Princes, he attached the significant superscription, " Drawn up after the example of the League of Schmalkald."

The earliest of Frederick's political writings which has come down to us shows the glance of the youth of eighteen already directed towards that region of national life upon which he was to exercise the greatest and most individual forces of his genius—the great questions of statecraft. The crown prince contemplates the position of his nation in the world, finds the situation of its dispersed areas an extremely dangerous one, and draws up, still half in jest, daring plans for the rounding off of the remoter provinces, so that they may no longer remain in isolation. It is not long before these immature youthful proposals reappear as profound and powerful ideas ; three years before his ascent to the throne the great path of his life is perceived with a wonderful prophetic clearness. " It seems," he writes, " that heaven has predestined the king to make all those preparations which a wise foresight undertakes before the beginning of a war. Who can tell whether it may not be reserved for me to make a glorious use of the opportunities thus provided, and to employ these materials of war in the realisation of the designs for which my father's prevision intended them ! " He observes how his state vacillates in an untenable position between the petty territories and the great powers, and is resolved to put an end to this vacillation (*décider cet être*). To enlarge the national area, *corriger la figure de la Prusse*, has become a necessity if Prussia is to stand on her own feet and to do credit to the name of her king.

From generation to generation his ancestors had paid faithful service to the House of Austria, conscientiously refraining from turning to their own advantage the difficulties of their neighbour, but rewarded always with ingratitude, treachery, and contempt. Frederick himself, in the distressing period of his misused youth, had found it hard to endure " the arrogance, the presumption, the overbearing insolence, of the court of Vienna"; his heart was cankered with hatred " for the imperial band " which with its tricks and its lies had alienated his father's heart. His untamable pride was in revolt when at his father's court there was lacking the correct tone of cold refusal for the exacting demands of Austria ; he wrote angrily that a King of Prussia should resemble the noble palm-tree, of which the poet says, " If you wish to fell it, it rears its proud head the higher." With watchful eye he followed the varying fortunes of the European system of states, and came to the conclusion that the old policy of the balance of power was altogether outworn. After the victories of the war of the Spanish succession the time was over for fighting the Bourbon in alliance with Austria and England ; now the moment had come for the new German state " by the terror of its arms " to raise itself to such a height of power as would enable it to maintain its own freedom of will against all its neighbours and against the imperial house.

Thus in the mouth of Frederick, the old and greatly misused

expression "German freedom," acquired a new and nobler meaning.
It was no longer to signify that dishonourable policy of the petty
princes which called in the foreigner to help them against the
emperor, and which betrayed the marches of the realm into foreign
hands ; it was to signify the formation of a great German power
which should defend the fatherland with the strong hand in the
east and in the west ; and which should do this of its own will,
independently of the imperial authority. For hundreds of years
it had been the rule that whoever was not a good Austrian must
be a good Swede (like Hippolytus a Lapide), or a good Frenchman
(like the princes of the Confederation of the Rhine), or a good Englishman (like the scions of the Guelphs). Even the Great Elector,
in the press between neighbours of predominant power, was able
only at intervals to maintain an independent position. It was the
work of Frederick, avoiding on either hand the destructive tendencies
to the acceptance of concealed or manifest foreign dominion, to
institute a third tendency, a policy that was Prussian, and Prussian
only. To this policy belonged Germany's future.

It was not the way of this hater of phrases to talk much of
the fatherland ; and yet his soul was animated by a vigorous
national pride inseparably associated with his keen sense of personal
independence and with his princely sentiment. It seemed to him
to touch his honour that foreign nations should play the masters
upon German soil ; that this should be, was a discredit to his
illustrious blood, for which the philosophic king, with the naive
inconsistency of genius, had a very high respect. When the in-
extricable confusion of German affairs forced him at times to form
an alliance with the foreigner, he never alienated an acre of German
soil, and never allowed his state to be misused for foreign purposes.
All his life through he was exposed to the accusation of faithless
cunning, for no treaty and no alliance could ever make him renounce
the right of free self-determination. All the courts of Europe
spoke angrily of *travailler pour le roi de Prusse ;* accustomed from
of old to dominate German life they found it hardly possible to
grasp the new situation and understand that now at length the
resolute egoism of an independent German state was able to set
itself in successful opposition to their will. Voltaire's royal disciple
began for the German states the same work of liberation that Voltaire's opponent, Lessing, effected for our poetry. Even in his

youthful writings, Frederick strongly condemns the weakness of
the Holy Empire, which had thrown open to the foreigner its Ther-
mopylæ, Alsace ; he rages against the court of Vienna for its
surrender of Lorraine to France ; he can never forgive the Queen
of Hungary for having turned loose upon the German empire the
savage mob of " those Graces of the east," the Jazyges, the Croats,
and the Tolpatsches, and for having for the first time induced
the barbarians of Muscovy to take part in the internal affairs of
Germany. During the Seven Years' War his German pride and
hatred often found vent in grim and scornful words. To the
Russians, who have plundered his peasants of Neumark, he sends
the greeting : " Oh! that with one leap they could sink themselves
in the Black Sea, so that they and all memory of them might
pass away for ever." When the French overran Rhineland he
composed (in French, it is true) an ode which recalls to our minds
the strains of the War of Liberation :

> "To its uttermost sources
> Spumes the ancient Rhine with hate,
> Cursing the shame, that its waters
> Must bear a foreign yoke ! "

" Prudence teaches us how to guard what we already possess ;
but through intrepidity alone do we learn how to increase our
possessions "—such are the words with which Frederick, in his
Rheinsberg days, already betrays how his inmost nature urges him
to rash resolution, to tempestuous daring. It appears to him the
first duty of the statesman to avoid half measures ; and of all
conceivable resolutions the worst of all seems to him to resolve
to do nothing. Yet in this also he displays his German blood,
that from the first he knows how to control his ardent love of action
by cool and sober consideration. One who felt within himself
the heroic force of an Alexander determined to work for permanent
ends within the narrow circle in which destiny had placed him.
In war, sometimes, his fiery spirit leads him beyond the bounds of
prudence ; he demands the impossible from his troops, and fails
through a proud under-estimation of his enemy ; but as a statesman
he always preserves a perfect moderation, a wise limitation, which
leads him to reject at once any too adventurous design. He is

never for a moment befooled by the thought of cutting his own
state loose from the fallen German community; his position in
the empire does not impair his freedom of action in European
policy, while it gives him the right to intervene in the destiny
of the empire itself, and for this reason he wishes to keep his foot
in the stirrup of the German steed. Still less does he dream of
aspiring to the imperial crown. Since the days of the prophecies
of the court astrologers of the Great Elector there had always
persisted in Hohenzollern circles the obscure premonition that the
house was destined to bear the sword and sceptre of the Holy
Empire ; and the Hotspurs, Winterfeldt and Leopold of Dessau,
sometimes ventured to greet their royal hero as the German
Augustus. But Frederick knew that his temporal state could
not carry the Roman crown, that the attempt to assume it would
involve the newcomer among the powers in interminable intrigues,
and said drily, " For us it would be no more than a fetter."

*At the outset of his reign, Frederick invaded the Austrian
province of Silesia and, in the course of a war that dragged on
until 1745, defeated all attempts to dislodge him. This was not,
however, the end of the story, and in the Seven Years' War
Frederick's enhanced stature and the very existence of his state
were challenged by the combined forces of Austria, France, and
Russia. Forced to rely on his own resources because his sole ally,
Great Britain, could supply only limited military assistance,
Frederick held on until the enemy coalition dissolved and peace
was restored in 1763.*

It was solely his
own energy that he had to thank for his victories, and he presented
so brave a front in face of all the old powers, that Horace Walpole
was forced to admit that this King of Prussia now held in his hands
the control of the European balance. Saxony, Bavaria, Hanover,
all the central states, which up till now had remained rivals of the
crown of Prussia, were by the Silesian Wars permanently reduced
to the second rank. High above the innumerable petty oppositions that flourished within the empire there arose the one dominant
question : Prussia or Austria ? The problem of the future of
Germany had been stated. From a free altitude the king now

looked down upon the turmoil of the estates of the German empire, and to all insulting demands could jestingly reply, that those who made them must take him for a Duke of Gotha or for a Prince of the Rhine ! In relation to his smaller neighbours he was now able to assume that role of benevolent patron and protector which, in his *Anti-Machiavel*, he had pointed out as the sublime duty of the stronger ; already in the Reichstag there was forming the nucleus of a Prussian party, and the North German courts were beginning to send their sons to serve in the king's army.

Meanwhile, with astonishing rapidity, the new acquisitions became fused with the monarchy. For the first time upon any considerable area did the state exhibit that strong force of attraction and that formative energy which it has since then everywhere displayed in German and half-German lands. The new energies of the modern world made their way into the neglected province, the victim of feudal and ecclesiastical oppression ; the officialdom of the monarchy overthrew the dominion of the nobles, the strength of law put an end to nepotism, toleration replaced restraint in matters of conscience, and the German school-system superseded the profound spiritual slumber of priestly education. The sluggish and servile peasant learned once again to hope for the morrow, and his king forbade him to abase himself before the officials by kneeling to kiss the hem of their garments.

In that century of struggles for power there was no other state whose working imposed such manifold and widely human tasks. It was the peaceful labour of administration which first gave a moral justification to the conquest of Silesia, and furnished the proof that this widely censured act of daring was a genuinely German deed. By the Prussian rule there was restored to the German nation this magnificent frontier-land which had already been half-overwhelmed by foreign influences. Silesia was the only one of the German-Austrian hereditary dominions in which the policy of religious unity had been unable to effect a complete victory. In the valleys of the Riesengebirge the calm and easy-going German stock had withstood with insuperable tenacity the violent deeds of the Lichtenstein dragoons and the oratorical arts of the Jesuits. The majority of the Germans remained true to the Protestant faith. The Protestant Church, oppressed and despised, despoiled of its goods, continued a poverty-stricken exist-ence ; only the threats of the crown of Sweden secured for this

Church, in addition to the small number of God's houses which still remained to it, the possession of a few sanctuary churches. The Catholic Poles of Upper Silesia and the Czech colonists whom the imperial court had summoned into the land to carry on the struggle against the German heretics, were the props of the imperial dominion. With the entry of the Prussian army the German elements once more gladly raised their heads; joyfully there resounded through the sanctuary churches praise to the Lord, Who after showing severity to His people had now at length displayed a banner for them to follow. Under the protection of Prussian toleration, Protestantism soon regained its consciousness of spiritual superiority, the Polish elements visibly lost ground, and after a few decades the Prussian Silesians, in ideas and customs, resembled their North German neighbours more closely than they resembled the Silesians across the border. The Protestant conqueror, however, left the Roman Church in undisturbed possession of almost all the Church property of the Protestants, and whilst England was constraining its Irish Catholics to pay taxes in support of the Anglican State Church, in Silesia, the Protestant must continue now as formerly to pay taxes on behalf of the Catholic Church. It was only the treasonable practices of the Roman clergy during the Seven Years' War that forced the king to abandon this excess of toleration, which had involved injustice towards the Protestants; and even then the situation of the Catholic Church in Prussian Silesia remained a more favourable one than in any other Protestant state.

The flourishing development of Silesia under Prussian rule sufficed to show that the new province had found its natural master, and that the change in the destiny of the German east was unalterably established. The Viennese court, however, continued to cherish the hope of securing revenge for the past shame, and of reducing the conqueror of Silesia once again to the mediocre situation of the ordinary German prince, just as had been possible in the case of those presumptuous ones who had formerly ventured to raise their hands against the imperial authority. King Frederick knew, moreover, that the final and decisive appeal to arms still lay before him. He attempted on one occasion during the brief years of peace to exclude the son of Maria Theresa from the imperial dignity, so that for the future at least the empire should be separated from the House of Austria, but the scheme was wrecked by the hostility of the Catholic courts. The irreconcilable opposition between the two leading powers of Germany determined for a lengthy period the course of European politics and deprived the Holy Empire of its last vestiges of vital energy. In painful anticipation the nation seemed to foresee the approach of a new Thirty Years' War. That which had been slowly prepared by the quiet labours of toilsome decades appeared to the next generation merely as a wonderful chance, as the fortunate adventure of a talented spirit. Quite isolated in the diplomatic correspondence of the epoch is the far-seeing utterance of the Dane, Bernstorff, who in the year 1759 wrote sadly to Choiseul : " All that you are endeavouring to-day in the hope of preventing the uprise in central Germany of a warlike monarchy whose iron arm will soon crush the petty princes—it is all lost labour ! " The neighbouring powers in the east and in the west vented their anger against the lucky one who, out of the turmoil of the war of the Austrian succession, had alone drawn the prize of victory ; nor was it simply the personal hatred of powerful women that was weaving the web of the great conspiracy which now threatened to enmesh Frederick. It was the general feeling of Europe that the ancient and traditional structure of the comity of states was imperilled as soon as any victorious great power became established in the centre of the Continent. The Roman See was deeply concerned that the detested home of heresy should be once again enabled to give expression to its own independent will ; it was only in consequence of the co-operation of Rome that it became possible for the two ancient enemies, the two great Catholic powers of Austria and of France, to unite against Prussia. The aim was to render the impotence of Germany eternal.

By a daring onslaught the king saved his crown from certain destruction, and when, after seven terrible years, he had defended his German state on the Rhine and on the Pregel, on the Peene and in the Riesengebirge, against foreign and semi-foreign armies. and in concluding peace had maintained the extent of his power over the last village, Prussia seemed to stand once more in the same position as at the outset of the murderous campaign. Not a hand's breadth more German soil had been added to its domain, half the country lay desolate, the abundant work of peace of three generations had been almost completely destroyed, in the unhappy Neumark the work of civilisation had to be begun at the beginning for the fourth time. The king himself could never think without bitterness of these dreadful days, when evil fortune had heaped upon his shoulders all the distresses which a man can bear, and even more ; what he then suffered seemed to him the senseless and evil caprice of a mocking fate, a tragedy without justice and without definite aim. Nevertheless there was a colossal success acquired as the outcome of this struggle, in appearance so fruitless ; the new order of German affairs, which had begun with the foundation of the Prussian power, had proved itself an irrevocable necessity, and this in face of the severest test conceivable. A hundred years earlier Germany had been able to free herself from the Hapsburg dominion only by the struggles of an entire generation, and even to effect this had been forced to pay shameful subsidies to her foreign allies ; now the poorest region of the empire was competent within seven years to repel the attacks of a world in arms, and the victory was gained by German force alone, for the sole foreign power which had come to the help of the king betrayed him in the hour of need. Germany's star was once again in the ascendant ; for the Germans those were true words which were uttered in joyful thanksgiving in all the churches of Prussia : " Many a time have they afflicted me from my youth : Yet they have not prevailed against me."

At the opening of the second campaign it had been the proud hope of Frederick to fight a battle of Pharsalia against the House of Austria, and to dictate terms of peace beneath the walls of Vienna, for this teeming time displayed everywhere the embryonic germs of the great new formations of a distant future, and plans were already on foot for an alliance between Prussia and Piedmont, Austria's other rival. But the battle of Kolin once more plunged the king in despair, and he fought now only for the existence of his state. The attempts he made to summon a counter-Reichstag to oppose a North German union to the imperial league were nullified by the unconquerable jealousy of the smaller courts, and above all by the arrogant opposition of his Guelph allies. The hour was not yet come for the abolition of German dualism, for the reconstitution of the empire ; but by the terrible reality of this war the obsolete ancient formalisms of the German community were morally annihilated, and the ultimate veil was stripped from the colossal lie of the Holy Empire. Never before had any emperor played so brainlessly with the fatherland as did this Loraine-Augustus, who threw open all the gates of Germany to foreign plunderers, surrendered the Netherlands to the Bourbons, and the eastern marches to the Muscovites. And while the emperor thus trampled his oath under foot, and himself deprived his house of all right to the German crown, there was played at Ratisbon the impudent farce of an appeal to the disciplinary powers of the imperial law. The Reichstag summoned the conqueror of Silesia in its antiquated formula, " By these presents must he, the said Elector, be guided " ; the Brandenburg envoy kicked the messenger of the illustrious assembly downstairs ; the eager but miserable imperial army assembled under the banner of the Bourbon enemy of the empire, to be instantly dispersed like chaff before the wind by the cavalry squadrons of Seydlitz. But the German nation loudly acclaimed the victor of Rossbach, the rebel against the emperor and the empire. With this barren satirical comedy the great tragedy of imperial history came in truth to its close ; what still remained of the old German community barely preserved henceforward even the semblance of life.

In domestic politics, Frederick preserved and elaborated on the administrative system established by his father. His most notable personal contribution was in the field of justice.

As a reformer Frederick was active in that province only of the internal life of the state which his predecessor had failed to understand. As regards the administration of justice, almost the only service rendered by Frederick William had been an apt transformation of the mortgage system. His son created the new Prussian judiciary, just as his father had brought into being the modern German executive officialdom. He knew that the administration of justice is a political duty inseparable from the state : throughout all his dominions he secured the complete independence of the imperial courts ; instituted a ministry of justice side by side with the general directory ; placed the entire administration of justice in the hands of a hierarchially ordered state officialdom, which trained its own successors, and which exercised a rigid supervision over the private judicial authorities that still existed in the lowest ranks of the magistracy.   There was a promise of the unconditional independence of the courts vis-à-vis the administration, and such independence was in practice secured except as regards a few instances of judicial power arbitrarily but benevolently exercised by the royal cabinet.   The new judiciary, though not very highly paid, preserved an honourable sense of its duties ; and whilst the courts of the empire displayed venality and partisanship, in Prussia the proud saying was justified (even against the king's will) *il y a des juges à Berlin*   To the youth of the age of enlightenment, who regarded the state as a construction of the human will consciously working towards a definite end, it was a self-evident desire that the state must not be something fixed and traditional in character, but that it must be dominated by a consciously conceived and purposive system of law ; all through his life it was Frederick's idea to effect the first comprehensive codification of the law which had been undertaken since the time of Justinian.   Not till after his death, did the system of civil law come into operation which manifests more plainly than any other work of this epoch the Janus-head of the Frederician conception of the state. On the one hand the legal code is so careful to preserve the traditional social differences that the whole system of the laws was adapted to the ancient feudal division of classes, even preserving for the nobility a feudal marriage law in conflict with the common law ; on the other hand the code pushes the notion of state sovereignty so boldly to its ultimate consequences that many of its utterances anticipate the ideas of the French Revolution, leading Mirabeau to say that in this respect Prussia was a century in advance of the rest of Europe.   The aim of the state is the general welfare ; it is only in pursuit of this aim that the state may impose limitations upon the natural freedom of its citizens ; but in pursuit of this aim it is also empowered to abolish all existing privileges.   The king is no more than the chief of the state, and only as chief of the state does he possess rights and duties. Such were the views of the ruler of Prussia in the days in which Biener and other notable jurists were still maintaining as an incontestable legal principle the rights of the German princes as private owners of country and people.   Consequently the authority of the state, placed above the domain of private rights, exercises an ordering and instructive influence in all private affairs, prescribes moral duties to parents and children, to masters and servants, endeavouring in its promethean legislative wisdom to provide for every possible legal dispute of the future.

This legal code marks the ultimate terms of the ancient absolutism : strict limits were imposed upon authority, and the community was raised to the level of a legal state. At the same time the code, inasmuch as it overthrew the dominion of Roman law, was unwittingly paving the way for a new legal unity of the German people. The mechanical state-idea of the Frederician days was soon superseded by a profounder and more far-seeing philosophy, the incomplete juristic culture of Carmer and Suarez was replaced by the work of historical jurisprudence ; but for many decades the civil code remained the powerful foundation upon which all further reforms of the Prussian state were erected. Among the officials, as among the people, the belief in the dominion of law, a belief which is the pre-condition of all political freedom, became a living force. If the state existed in order to secure the general well-being it followed by an inevitable necessity (although Frederick himself failed to see this) that the privileges of the dominant castes should be abrogated and that the nation should participate in the conduct of public affairs. Sooner or later this conclusion would have to be drawn, for even now, in the enlarged domains of state activity, only a supply of talented human energies could prove adequate for the severe tasks which the kingship was undertaking.

Prussia's fortunes declined sharply after Frederick's death, and the feckless policy followed by the government during the period of the French Revolution led to diplomatic isolation and military defeat. After Napoleon's victories over Prussian arms at Jena and Auerstedt in October 1806 and the punitive Peace of Tilsit in July of the following year, Prussia seemed to have no future except as a French satellite. From this fate she was saved by the exertions of a remarkable group of statesmen who reformed the Frederician state and laid the basis for effective resistance to the French.

THE PRUSSIAN REFORMERS (I, 323-47)

Everything recalled those lamentable days when Wallenstein had occupied the Mark and George William had passed his days in Königsberg as a prince without a country. But what an abundance of love and loyalty had come into existence in the subsequent six generations. Then the diet of Königsberg had bluntly defied the will of its elector. Now, prince and people stood together, like one great family. The poor country house at Memel and the gloomy rooms of the old castle of the Teutonic Knights at Königsberg, did not lack visitors, who wished to give pleasure to their king in his need and to say a kindly word. At the baptism of the new-born princess, the estates of East Prussia appeared as sponsors. In all the shop windows there was hanging the new picture which represented the king standing among his children, dressed in the hideous uniform of the day, and how much more royally did Frederick William know how to endure his hard lot than did the father of the Great Elector. He was filled with profound bitterness of spirit ; more than ever did he need the cordial encouragement of his spouse ; there were hours when it seemed to him as if he could succeed in nothing, as if he had been born only for misfortune. When in the cathedral of Königsberg he read the inscriptions upon the tombs of the Prussian dukes, he chose as a motto for his own hard life, " My days are passed in disquiet, my hope is in God ! " Yet this hope sustained him. He could never accept the conviction that the common souls of the family of Bonaparte who now wore the crowns of Europe were really princes, that in the reasonable world of God, this adventurer of the Napoleonic world-empire, who for all his brilliancy and glory was so inflated and so specious, could permanently continue to exist. He never allowed himself to be persuaded into any personal friendliness towards Napoleon. Even Stein once advised that the mood of the Imperator should be rendered milder by a little timely flattery, and that Napoleon should be invited to act as sponsor at the baptism of the new-born princess. The king rejected the idea unhesitatingly. But to the political proposals of his great minister, he adhered willingly and without reserve. He had a far greater share in Stein's legislation than his contemporaries were aware. Much which now came to perfection was merely the bold execution of those ideas of reform over which the irresolute prince had been brooding for a decade. Thus only do the rapid and striking successes of a single year of Stein's administration become comprehensible.

The new minister found willing helpers also among the officials. It was fortunate for him that it was on East Prussian soil that he had to begin his work of reform. Here, in especial, was keenly felt the untenability of the old division of classes, for the province possessed in its Köllmers a number of free landowners who were commoners. Here had the cultured classes, and especially the officials, long been well-acquainted with the free moral and political views which the two most efficient teachers of the University of Königsberg, Kant and the recently deceased Kraus, had diffused for many years. Most of Stein's laws were prepared in the East Prussian provincial department. At the head of this administration was the minister von Schrötter, an exemplary official of astonishing activity, who had retained even into old age a youthful receptivity for new ideas ; under him were working Friese and Wilckens.[1] Schön was completely filled with the ideas of Kant. In many respects he was a faithful representative of the vigorous, enlightened, and intelligent East Prussian character, but he was a doctrinaire advocate of unrestricted free trade, he was immeasurably vain, was incapable of modestly recognising the services of another, and, moreover, quite in conflict with the characteristics of his fine stock, was untruthful. Beside him worked Staegemann, a highly-cultured and able man of business, endowed with rare industry and rare modesty, who sometimes gave expression to his faithful affection for the Prussian state in profoundly felt, but clumsy, poems. There was also Niebuhr, the man of brilliant learning, too sensitive, too dependent upon the moods of the moment, to find himself readily at home in the equable activity of the office, but invaluable to all by the inexhaustible wealth of his living knowledge, by the width of his outlook, by the nobility of his lofty passion. There was Nicolovius, a profound spirit, strongly affected by the religious tendency of the time. There were Sack, Klewitz, and many others, a brilliant company of exceptional powers. Nearest to the views of Stein among them all, was the Westphalian, Baron von Vincke. He also had formed his views of the state in contact with the nobles and with the peasants of the countryside, but the born Prussian recognised far more frankly than did the imperial knight the services of the salaried officialdom. Vincke could not be reckoned among the poietic intelligences ; his strength lay in kinesis, in the unresting activity of the administrative official.

Hardenberg, who upon Napoleon's orders had for the second

---

[1] Recently shown in the remarkable book by Ernst Meier, *Die Reform der Verwaltungs-Organisation unter Stein und Hardenberg*, Leipzig, 1881.

time been obliged to leave the ministry, sent from Riga a great
memorial on the reorganisation of the Prussian state which he had
there composed in collaboration with Altenstein. In many respects
this corresponded with the ideas of the new minister of state ;
many of its proposals were taken word for word from Stein's own
utterances, such as the idea of an assembly of the estates for the
whole country. Here also, however, there was already manifest
that intimate and profound contrast which always separated the
disciples of the enlightenment from Stein's historical conception
of the state. Hardenberg was first of all a diplomatist. In
administrative affairs he was far from being so well-informed as
Stein, and for this reason in his memorial he inconsiderately incorporated certain general theoretical proposals dear also to Altenstein, the friend of Fichte. His scheme of reform was conceived
" in accordance with the highest idea of the state " ; in commercial
policy the principle of *laisser-faire* was to prevail without restriction. Whereas Stein had from the first regarded the Revolution
with the mistrust of the aristocrat, and desired to transplant to
German soil a few only of its tried results, Hardenberg had been
much more strongly influenced by French ideas. He definitely
indicated as the goal of reform, " the introduction of democratic
principles in a monarchical government " ; in matters of detail,
he wished to follow closely the French example, demanded for the
army conscription with right of purchasing substitutes, and would
gladly have abolished the honorary Landräte (the old-established
administrative chiefs-of-district in Prussia) to replace them by
bureaucratic district officials. He said nothing at all concerning
self-government by the commons. A point common to both these
statesmen was, however, the moral altitude of their sense of the
state. Both of them desired, as Altenstein's proposal expressed
it, " a revolution in a good sense, leading directly towards the
supreme goal of the ennoblement of humanity " ; both of them
knew that France pursued a tendency of secondary importance, directed to the simple manifestation of power ; and they
demanded from the rejuvenated German state that it should
protect religion, art, and science, all the ideal aims of the human
race, for their own sake, and that it should thus secure a victory
over the foreign dominion by means of moral energies.

Stein possessed in a high degree the art indispensable to the statesman of making a good use of the ideas of others. He allowed all the proposals which were brought to him from the circles of the officials to influence his mind, but his ultimate decisions were determined by his own consideration. He laid down the broad line of the leading ideas, but committed the carrying out of these to the councils, and intervened personally only when it was necessary to push the completed work through in opposition to doubt and active resistance. When he came to Memel there was already on foot a proposal for the abolition of hereditary servitude in East and West Prussia. Schön, Staegemann, and Klewitz had worked out the plan upon the king's instructions, appealing especially to the fact that in the neighbouring duchy of Warsaw, the abolition of serfdom was imminent. The new minister at once gave a wider scope to the law, demanding the extension of the reform to the whole area of the state. Since he had begun to think for himself in political matters, he had regarded the lack of freedom of the country people as the curse of north-eastern Germany. The moment seemed to him propitious for the permanent cure of the ancient evil, and with one bold step to attain the end towards which the laws of the Hohenzollerns from the time of Frerderick William I had ever advanced with partial success. The king joyfully agreed; the bold confidence of his minister awakened in him the courage to will effectively that which all his life he had merely hoped for. Thus there was promulgated on October 9, 1807, an edict concerning the facilitated ownership and the free utilisation of landed property, or, as Schön called it, the Prussian habeas corpus act. Thus in unassuming forms there was completed a far-reaching social revolution. About two-thirds of the population of the state now acquired unrestricted personal freedom. On and after Martinmas, 1810, there were to be none in Prussia but freemen. This same law destroyed at a single blow the feudal ordering of the Frederician state. The nobleman received the right to become a peasant and to carry on bourgeois industries, and this right was to be considered a compensation for the privileges previously enjoyed by the nobility in the army. Every kind of landed proprietorship, and every kind of occupation, was henceforward to be open to every Prussian.

But Stein was not inclined to discard the old national principles of the monarchy, and to allow the destruction of petty proprietorship to be effected under the cloak of free competition. It seemed to him that a free and vigorous estate of peasants was the firmest prop of the state, and the nucleus of its powers of military defence. For this reason the right to purchase the lands of the peasants was granted to the larger landed proprietors, but only under restriction; and with the consent of the authorities. Whereas Schön, faithful to the dogmas of the English free-traders, desired to accelerate the destruction of the old generation of settlers on the land, as an unavoidable economic necessity, Stein came to the rescue of the indebted great landed proprietors with a General Indulgence. Thus it became possible to assist the landed gentry through the difficulties of the immediate future, and to retain most of them in the possession of their ancient lands. No less moderate despite its boldness was the new edict which provided free property for the peasants on the domains in East and West Prussia, about forty-seven thousand families ; they were to redeem three-fourths of the services and charges attached to their lands within the space of four-and-twenty years by monetary payments. The remaining fourth was to continue as an irremovable tax. Stein rejected as too radical a disturbance of the accepted relationships of property, the idea of a complete abolition of all the encumbrances upon peasant property. He also determined upon the abolition of thirlage, of the guilds and the selling monopolies of bakers, butchers, and hucksters. His aim was to effect the transformation of all services and payments in kind into money payments, and to abolish the rights to forced labour and other manorial rights, to abolish all servitude and all communal dues ; private property was everywhere to come into its own. In sharp contrast with the Frederician system of the monarchical organisation of labour, the new laws were " to get rid of everything which had hitherto stood in the way of the individual's acquirements of such a degree of well-being as he was competent to acquire in accordance with the measure of his energies." The instructions issued to the executive authorities after Stein's resignation, expressed doubtless in a somewhat more abstract form than Stein had himself used, ran simply : " Industry must be left to take its natural course ; it is not necessary to favour trade, all that we have to do is to see that no difficulties are put in its way."

The remarkable change thus effected in the ancient social system of Prussia, was hardly noticed abroad. This quickly moving epoch had experienced a sufficient number of radical innovations, and how many of them which had been introduced with a great deal of noise had after all come to nothing. The French made fun of the caution with which in Königsberg the footsteps of the Great Revolution were being followed. In Prussia itself, however, the feeling was all the more vivid that the new legislation was profoundly affecting all the relationships of life. The cultured bourgeoisie hailed with gladness the liberation of the country folk; in Breslau the deeds of the royal reformer were commemorated on the stage. But the nobles of the Electoral Mark, led by the valiant Marwitz, raged against the audacious foreigner who, with his school of Franconian and East Prussian officials, was disturbing the good old Brandenburger way. No less unheard-of seemed the Jacobinical phrasing than the revolutionary content of Stein's new laws, which, in accordance with the ancient custom of Prussian absolutism, endeavoured to explain to the people the monarch's intentions in detail, and which in doing this repeatedly referred to the good of the state and to the progress of the spirit of the time. In Priegnitz, the peasants even raised a disturbance against "the new freedom," and the king had to send a force to keep them in order. In the Junkergasse at Königsberg, at the Perponcher Club, worthy gentlemen of the court, of the landed gentry, of the army, were profoundly incensed at the "viper's brood" of the reformer. No one there scolded more fiercely than General York, to whom it seemed that the severe old-time discipline was disappearing from the world, that the time was coming when every cornet would begin to stick up for the rights of man. Even Gneisenau could not follow the minister in all these bold ventures, and it seemed to him that the destruction of great landed proprietorship was imminent, until experience taught him his error. Some of the finest men of the East Prussian stocks of the Dohna, the Auerswald, and the Finkenstein, sent a petition to the king, imploring him to protect the rights of the nobility, and at least to save the noble from military service and from the patrimonial courts. Nor were justified complaints lacking, for although the legislator everywhere expressed his leading ideas with businesslike clearness and definiteness, there were nevertheless in certain matters of detail, owing to the haste with which the work was done, many obscurities and contradictions. But the prestige of the royal command was as firmly established as was the confidence in the justice of Frederick William. Even those who were personally dissatisfied could not imagine that this prince could order an open act of injustice. The reform ran its course. Once again, as so often before, it was by the will of the crown that an act of liberation was effected for the Prussian people.

The second great task which Stein undertook was the completion of the unity of the state. From the proceedings of the Paris National Assembly, he had learned the necessity for a centralised financial system, and from a study of the executive organisation of the First Consul he had come to recognise that the business of the state must be so carried on as to render a unified supervision possible. Even before the war he had recommended the appointment of departmental ministers for the whole state. The extraordinary juxtaposition of provincial ministers and departmental ministers, the intermingling of the real system with the provincial system, was no longer adequate to the needs of an active modern administration. The anxious preservation of territorial peculiarities had been carried so far during recent decades, that the officials of the old school could even speak of the Prussian monarchy as a " federal state." Yet closer examination showed how healthy and full of life was the executive organisation founded by Frederick William I. Now that the undertaking was ventured of carrying his work a stage further, full justice was for the first time done to the remarkable insight of the strict old organiser. Schön esteemed him as the greatest king of Prussia as far as internal affairs were concerned. What was resolved on was not a revolution, but the progressive development and simplification of the ancient institutions. The law of December 16, 1808, concerning the changed constitution of the supreme state authorities decreed that there should be five departmental ministers, for home affairs, finance, foreign affairs, war, and justice, at the head of the entire administration of the state, and the old general treasuries were to be united into a single general state treasury, under the charge of the minister of finance. Stein foresaw how dangerous might become the power of these five men, and he therefore intended to constitute, as the supreme authority of the monarchy, a council of state which should unite in itself all the leading energies of the state service, including the ministers, should advise as to legislative proposals, and should decide the great disputed questions of public law. But his successors failed to carry out this part of his proposals.

Through the appointment of the departmental ministers, the general directory was abolished. There remained, however, the old war chambers, and domain chambers, under the new names of " administrations." The judiciary and the executive were completely separated ; the judicial business of the old chambers was allotted to the "administrations"; they were purged of useless members (for Stein everywhere fought against the practical irre-- movability of the old officialdom, and reserved to the crown the right of dismissing the executive officials at will); the course of business was simplified, and greater independence was secured for the presidents and the heads of departments in the individual branches of the executive. But the advantages of the German *collegial system,* its lack of partisanship, and its careful regard for all the circumstances of the individual case, were too highly esteemed by Stein for him to be willing to exchange that system for the readier mobility of a bureaucratic prefectural administration. The intermediate authorities of the Prussian executive remained colleges and in this form continued to work beneficially for two generations. Instead of the vain display of the general councils which stood beside the Napoleonic prefects giving diffident advice, the German statesmen demanded the active and regular participation of the nation in administrative affairs. Thus there would flow in to the men of the boardroom a wealth of views and feelings derived from the outside world, whilst the people itself would become animated with the sense of fatherland, of independence, and of national honour.

But how was this vigorous activity on the part of the ruled to be incorporated in the firmly ordered hierarchy of the paid officialdom ? It was obviously impossible to transfer to the provincial diets the conduct of individual executive affairs ; nepotism, cumbrousness, the commercial spirit of the old feudal committees, still gave to these bodies an evil repute. For this reason Stein and Hardenberg both conceived the remarkable idea

of proposing that in every government nine of the representatives
sitting in the provincial diets should be co-opted upon the boards
for three years, and that these co-opted members should take full
part in all the work of the boards. This idea shows very clearly
how complete a breach had been made with the old views of bureaucratic self-satisfaction, but it led to nothing. The new institution came into existence in East Prussia alone ; elsewhere the
provincial diets showed little inclination to provide the daily
allowance of money for the notables. The East Prussian representatives soon found themselves to be extremely isolated among their
far more numerous bureaucratic official colleagues ; they felt
themselves to be dilettanti among experts ; those from the country
would not work long in their offices ; the monetary allowances
were not forthcoming; zeal soon cooled, and in the year 1812 the
unlucky experiment was abandoned.[1]   Nor did the new office
of lord-lieutenant at first prove very satisfactory. Whereas
revolutionary France had subdivided its ancient provinces into
powerless departments, Stein, in deliberate contrast, wished to
unite the weakly governmental areas into great and vigorous
provinces. Three lords-lieutenant, for Silesia, for Old Prussia, and
for the territories of Pomerania and the Mark, respectively, were
to supervise the government, not as intermediaries but as permanent
commissaries of the ministry, and as representatives of the common
interests of their provinces. The institution was plainly based
upon the wider relationships of a great state. In the narrow
circumstances of the diminished monarchy, its only effect was to
render more difficult the conduct of business ; not until after the
restoration of Prussia to the position of a great power, did its
utility become manifest.

The social reforms of Stein and the consolidation of the unity
of the state, proceeded from the independent and peculiar working
out of ideas which had been in the air since the outbreak of the
revolution and which were a common possession of all clear intelligences among the Prussian officials.   But a thoroughly creative
action, the free work of Stein's own genius, was the Towns' Ordinance of November 19, 1808.[2]   He regarded the elevation of the

---

[1] Report of Minister von Schuckmann to the king, May 24, 1812.

[2] Stein always definitely described the Towns' Ordinance as his own creation.
It is simply owing to the way in which the work of his office was carried on that
the documents contain so few autograph comments of the minister's (E. Meier,
page 147)

nation out of the dull narrowness of its domestic life, as the last and highest task of his political activity.   He saw that the country was in danger of falling into a condition of sensuality, or of attributing an exaggerated worth to the speculative sciences, and he wished to lead it on towards a vigorous activity which should be of value to the community. By a happy practical insight, he was led to begin his work with the towns. Only after an independent communal life had been awakened among the cultured townsmen, would it be possible for the rude peasants who had but recently been delivered from hereditary servitude, and who still regarded their landlords with great hostility, to be awakened to the rights and duties of self-government. Wilckens played the principal part in the working out of this law. The towns were given the independent control of their finances, of their poor relief, and of their educational activities ; and on the demand of the state, they might also carry on police affairs in the state's name. They were thus to be in a position of almost complete independence *vis-à-vis* the state authority, and were even granted autonomous rights in matters of taxation, no one yet foreseeing how injurious to the community would be the effect of this last privilege. The various ancient gradations of civil right were done away with, and the privileges of the guilds were also abolished. The inhabitants of the towns consisted now of two classes only, citizens and denizens. One who had acquired the freedom of the city, and this was not difficult to obtain, was bound to undertake all communal duties ; for whilst the freedom of property was a leading idea of Stein's law, no less important in that law was the principle that upon the property owner was imposed the duty of service to the community. An elected magistracy, whose members were partly unpaid and partly paid on a very moderate scale, with a representative assembly elected by all the burgesses (who for electoral purposes were listed in separate constituencies), conducted the administration of the town.   Thus the atrophy of German communal life which had endured for two centuries came at length to an end.

This reform seems all the more remarkable in its simple clearness and directness of aim since Stein had no example to follow anywhere in Europe. The careless English municipal constitutions were of as little value to him as examples as was the patrician

domination in his own beloved Westphalian towns. Now for the
first time did there come into existence in Germany modern urban
communities, independent corporations which, nevertheless, were
at the same time trustworthy organs to fulfil the will of the central
authority, and which remained subject to governmental supervision. Hitherto some of the towns had been completely deprived
of independence. Others, like the baronial country-towns, constituted petty states within the state, with their own patrimonial
jurisdiction and their own police, and only too often had the commands of the king to " our vassals, officials, magistrates, and
beloved subjects " been thwarted by the passive resistance of these
ancient municipal dominions. Now at length in the administration of the towns the centralised authority obtained a powerful
prop, and one which corresponded to its own national characteristics.

This reform also had to be imposed upon the nation by the
king's command. The gentry of the Mark, and the officers of the
old school, complained of the republican principles of the Towns'
Ordinance. What horror was felt in these circles when it was learned
that one of the first state officials, the president von Gerlach, had
accepted the election to the position of chief burgomaster of
Berlin ! The exhausted communal sentiment of the bourgeoisie
showed at first very little inclination for the enforced honorary
services ; and it soon became apparent that self-government is
expensive ; whereas Stein and his friends had rather anticipated
a diminution in the cost. The towns, which under the rule of
Frederick William I had been accustomed to strict economy, were
for the most part better disposed towards the new ordinance than
were the old rural communes, which were accustomed to the nepotist
rule of independent magistrates. It was only during the War of
Liberation that a true understanding of the blessings of freedom
awakened among the townsfolk, when the central authority had
almost everywhere to discontinue its work, and when every town
was forced to look after itself. Since then there has become
manifest in our municipal life a second flowering, less brilliant, but
not less honourable than the great epoch of the Hanseatic League.
In educational matters, in the relief of destitution, in foundations
of general utility, the German bourgeoisie once more endeavoured
to compete with the older and richer urban culture of the Romans.

Just as Frederick William I had created the modern German executive officialdom, so did Stein's Towns' Ordinance prove the starting-point for German municipal self-government. Upon this were based the new by-laws, which for two generations, so long as parliamentarism still remained immature, constituted the best and the most secure element of German national freedom. Through Stein's reforms there was reawakened in the German bourgeoisie a lively communal sense and a delight in responsible political activity. It is to these reforms that we owe the fact that the German constitutional state is to-day established upon a firm foundation, that our views as to the nature of political freedom, however erroneous they may at times have been, have never become so vain and formalised as were the doctrines of the French Revolution.

Through the losses of the Treaty of Tilsit, Prussia had once more become a mainly agricultural country. For this reason it was Stein's intention that the Towns' Ordinance should be followed as soon as possible by a Rural Districts' Ordinance. A proposal by von Schrötter and the East Prussian provincial department had already been drafted. Stein demanded free rural communes with village-mayors and village-courts. The last and strongest props of the old feudal order of society, the territorial police and patrimonial courts, must be abolished, for power must be derived only from the highest authority. Stein's plans involved no alteration in the ancient historical character of the office of Landrat ; as formerly, so now, the Landrat was to be a servant of the state, but he was to be at the same time a moderately paid official, a landlord resident in the circles, and the trusted adviser of its inhabitants. But to the experienced eye of the minister, the existing circles seemed too large for the energies of a single man, and he was already considering, in conjunction with his friend Vincke, the appointment of several Landrats in each district ; like the English justices of the peace, they were from time to time to assemble to hold quarter sessions. In addition to the Landrats, there was to be a provincial assembly, constituted of all the principal landowners and of a number of representatives from the towns and villages. The strong representation given to landed property was obviously necessary, for no one yet knew whether the rude peasantry, who had only just become freemen, were competent for representation in the provincial assembly. For this reform also the indefatigable Schrötter had already drawn up a detailed plan which in essential respects proceeded from the same principles as the Circle Ordinance of 1872.

Stein desired that the lord-lieutenant should be assisted by a provincial diet, so that the peculiarities and the separate interests of the great territories should be properly represented within the unified state. He gladly boasted that his scheme for this institution was based upon free property ; he gave the suffrage to all " property holders," and in his mouth this term meant exclusively or chiefly those who held real property in town or country. With a bold hand he had overthrown the legal barriers between the ancient classes. There no longer existed in Prussia any hereditary class differences ; and yet he did not wish in any spirit of levity to overthrow the distinction between the professional classes on the one hand and groups of interests on the other, for this distinction was still a marked one in the popular consciousness. For this reason he demanded a class representation for the provincial diets, in such a way that the country gentry, the towns, and the peasantry, were to name their representatives separately ; and he rejected the proposals of his Silesian friend, Rhediger, who wished to do away completely with the old division of classes. It was enough for Stein if the totality of the burgesses of the town and of the peasants obtained class representation, whereas only a few privileged towns that were immediates of the empire, and among the peasantry only the Köllmers, had taken part in the old feudal diets. Whilst he was still in power the first step was taken towards this end. " In order that the government may be supported by general assent," East Prussia received a new Territorial Ordinance, which secured for the Köllmers equal political rights with the nobles, and gave them the right to representation on the territorial committees.

Finally, over these new provincial estates were to be superposed the Prussian estates of the realm, as a support for the throne, and as an indispensable means for awakening and invigorating the national spirit. In these disordered times, the old absolutism was everywhere feeling its powerlessness. When the stringency of the national finances made it necessary to sell the domains, the king was unwilling to take upon his own shoulders the responsibility for so venturesome a step, and he therefore had the new domestic law concerning the sale of the domains laid before the estates of all the provinces for their acceptance, although he expressly declared that he did this as an act of grace and not as a duty. (In Silesia, which had no estates, the proposal was laid before the representatives of the mortgage institute and of some of the towns.) It was impossible that such a state of insecurity in public law should persist. Stein cherished the idea of a great reform of taxation ; he desired to break with the anxious domestic economy which measured the expenses in accordance with the income, and he wished to introduce for Prussia the bold principle which applies to every national fiscal system which is run on broad lines, that the income must be regulated in accordance with the expenditure. For this reform, and for all the other sacrifices which seemed to him to be required of the reawakening nation, he considered that the approval of an assembly of the estates of the realm was indispensable. For the moment, however, owing to the immaturity of the people, the powers of this body must be deliberative merely.

Such, in essentials, were Stein's proposals for a thorough-going reform, the greatest and the boldest which the political idealism of the Germans had ever conceived. By similar plans Turgot had once hoped to avert the approaching Revolution, but the proposals of the German statesman far transcended the ideas of the Frenchman, in modest greatness, in logical definiteness, and in regard for that which was historically extant. The king was in agreement with all these proposals, but that to which he was least inclined was the summoning of the estates of the realm. It was not that he feared a limitation of his power ; but to his retiring nature, the noise of the debates, the passion of the parliamentary struggle, the necessity for his own public appearance, were repugnant. Brought up in the traditions of a mild absolutism, full of antipathy to the sins of the Revolution, he could not yet completely convince himself that the representative system had become indispensable. It was in fact questionable, in view of the lamentable state of political culture, whether the influence of the estates of the realm would not prove rather a hindrance than a help. From the gentry which, according to Stein's proposals, was to constitute the most powerful element of the united diet, the free assent to a juster system of taxation and to the other innovations proposed by the minister, was hardly to be expected. Even the towns and the peasants showed only too often how little they were able to follow the reforming ideas of the crown.

If, however, Stein's own vigorous personality were to remain in control, if the reform were to proceed as he planned, step by step, if, first of all, by the abolition of the territorial police, the dominant position of the country gentry were to be destroyed, and if then the district assemblies and the provincial diets were to spread through the liberated areas, he might hope to bring the king to understand that the summoning of an assembly of the estates of the realm was necessary on behalf of the unity of the state, as a counterpoise to the centrifugal forces of the provincial diets. In this way, by the free choice of the crown, might be effected the transition from absolute monarchy to a representative system, and the Prussian state might perhaps be spared a whole generation of tentative proceedings. Stein was prepared to build upon the awakening insight in the loyal and good-hearted people. He did not fail to recognise the deep chasm which existed between the over-refined and unworldly culture of the men of learning and the esential roughness of the masses ; but he hoped to bridge this chasm by the reconstitution of the educational system, and it was only his sudden fall which prevented these plans from coming to maturity. Years before, in Münster, he had shown that this branch of internal administration was within the purview of his free and comprehensive spirit, for in Münster he had fought Jesuitism at the University, and had awakened a new life in this ossified institution.

Hand in hand with administrative reform, there proceeded the reorganisation of the army, this also being effected under Stein's personal supervision. The king himself gave the first impetus. In this department, which he regarded as peculiarly his own, he always retained the immediate direction, and never failed to display an apt power of judgment and a penetrating knowledge of affairs. As early as July, 1807, he appointed Scharnhorst to the presidency of a commission for army reorganisation, and submitted to this commission an autograph memorial in which he clearly pointed out all the defects of existing military system, and rightly indicated the means for its improvement. There were associated with

Scharnhorst in this work a number of younger men of talent, who followed with a lively understanding, as did Scharnhorst himself, all the intellectual work of the time, men of statesmanlike intelligence who regarded the army as a popular school, and the art of war as a branch of politics. Their quiet activity served, not merely to sharpen the weapons for the War of Liberation, but also to bring the Prussian army once more into harmony with the new culture, and to endow the German military system for all future time with the characteristics of serious culture and intellectual freshness and alertness.

These officers were united from the outset with the leading statesman by a remarkable and instinctive agreement of moral and political conviction. It sounded like one of Stein's own utterances when Gneisenau, apropos of the French Rights of Man, exclaimed, " First make the human race enthusiasts for duty, and only after that for rights ! " Just as the disciple of Adam Smith was unwilling to apply the principle of the division of labour unconditionally to the national administration, esteeming the skilled business ability of the professional official less highly than that popular maturity which is acquired in self-government, so also did these military experts cherish the belief that it is moral force which ultimately proves decisive in war. However highly they esteemed the essentials of technical training, they regarded as still more important, to use Scharnhorst's own words, " the intimate union of the army with the nation." Scharnhorst wrote soon after the peace : " The sense of independence must be instilled into the nation, which must be given an opportunity of becoming acquainted with itself, of standing on its own feet ; then only will it respect itself, and learn how to gain respect from others. All that we can do is to work towards this end. We must loosen the bonds of prejudice, guide the rebirth of the nation ; care for its growth, and not hinder its free development; more than this it is not in our power to do."

Scharnhorst had long been recognised as the first military writer of his country, as the most brilliant authority among the German officers, but after an extremely varied life he also had at his disposal an exceptional wealth of practical experience. He had seen service in every arm, in the general staff, and in the military colleges. During his training at the military college of Wilhelmstein, he had become acquainted with that exemplary little troop which the talented old warrior Count Wilhelm von Bückeburg had formed out of the young men of his own petty territory ; next as a Hanoverian officer, in the Netherlands theatre of war, he had become closely acquainted with the English Army, which among all the armies of Europe still preserved most faithfully the characteristics of the ancient mercenary system ; he had seen active service against the loosely organised militia of the Republic and also against the well-trained conscripts of Napoleon, and in the war of 1806 he was sufficiently near to the leadership to have learned completely to understand the errors of the Frederician army and the ultimate grounds of its overthrow.   To the simple Saxon, that stiff military conduct which the king demanded from his officers was repugnant.   He went about in an inconspicuous, and almost untidy, dress, with his head hanging down, and his deep-set thinker's eyes turned quite inward.   His hair fell in disorder over his forehead ; his speech was gentle and slow.   In Hanover he was often seen knocking at the doors of the baker's shop, and then sitting quietly with his wife and children at supper under the ¡trees of the Eilenride.   Thus he remained throughout life, straightforward and unadorned in all things.   The simplicity and tenderness of his private correspondence reminds us of the men of antiquity ; in his writings, as in everything else, matter is everything 'and form nothing.   But the superiority of a powerful, continuously productive and thoroughly independent spirit, the nobility of a moral disposition which simply did not know what self-seeking is, gave to this unpretentious man a natural charm which, repellent to men of common mind, slowly and surely attracted magnanimous spirits. His daughter, Countess Julie Dohna, owed everything to her widowed father ; she was spoken of as a royal woman, and was accepted in distinguished circles as if she had indeed been of royal blood.

The equable temperament of the general was more agreeable to the king than was Stein's stimulating and stimulated nature ; none among his counsellors was so near to Frederick William. Scharnhorst returned the confidence of his royal friend without restraint.   It would have seemed to him base to think any longer of past errors ; he admired the moral strength of the unfortunate monarch ; and he never swerved in his loyalty, not even when, in their patriotic impatience, many of his friends became disaffected towards the over-cautious prince. A true Low German, he was of a retiring disposition, quiet, and reserved by nature. Praise sounded to him almost like an insult, and a gentle word as a profanation of friendship. His life led him along a rough road, always among enemies. In Hanover, the plebeian had had to contend with the ill-favour of the nobility ; whilst in Prussia the innovator had to fight against the arrogance of the old generals. When now, by the confidence of the king and by the general acclamation of the army, he was placed at the head of military affairs, for five years he had to carry on the obscure activity of a conspirator, preparing for the War of Liberation under the very eyes of the enemy. He thus learned to control every word and every gesture, and the simple-minded man who despised on his own account every kind of duplicity, became, for the sake of his country, a master in the arts of concealment, unrivalled in the faculty of holding his tongue, cunning and world-wise. With a rapid and searching glance he read the thoughts of those with whom he came in contact ; whereas, when on his side he had to conceal one of the king's secrets, it was necessary for him with ambiguous phrase to lure friend and foe alike upon a false scent. The officers said very truly, that his soul was as full of furrows as his face ; he reminded them of William of Orange, who long before in a similar situation, quiet and self-contained, had prepared for the struggle with the world-empire of Spain. And just like William the Silent, Scharnhorst hid within his bosom the lofty passion, the love of struggle, characteristic of the hero, and during the last war these traits had acquired for him the friendship of the active-minded Blucher. He did not know fear, he would not admit how stultifying can be the anxiety that follows a defeat ; in the courts-martial his sentence was always the most severe against cowardice and breach of faith. In a strange and yet harmonious manner there were combined in this great soul a petty-bourgeois simplicity, and a world-embracing breadth of view ; a yearning for peace, and courage in war ; philanthropic tenderness of heart, and the elemental energy of the national hatred. Perhaps no one suffered so bitterly from the distresses of the time as did this man of silence ; day and night he was never free from the thought of the disgrace of his country. Everyone approached him with reverence, for all felt involuntarily that upon him depended the future of the army.

Among the men who assisted him in the work of army re-

organisation, four proved equally the heirs of his spirit, so that
each one of the four received a portion of the comprehensive talents
of the master. These were Gneisenau and Grolman, the born
commanders ; Boyen, the organiser ; and Clausewitz, the man
of learning. All four of them were, like Scharnhorst himself, poor
and temperate, men of few needs, free from all self-seeking, looking
only to the end which had to be gained, and with all their candour,
men of profound modesty as is natural to the gifted soldier—for
whilst the solitary poietic activity of the artist and of the man of
learning very readily leads to vanity, the soldier works only as a
member of the great whole, and is unable to show what he is worth
unless an inscrutable destiny leads him to the right place at the
right moment. With an excess of modesty, Gneisenau declared
himself to be merely a pigmy beside the giant Scharnhorst. He
lacked the profound erudition of the master, and like so many men
of action, he felt the gaps in his knowledge as if they were a lack
of capacity ; on the other hand, he possessed in a far greater measure
the inspiriting confidence of the hero, that joyful fatalism which
makes the great commander. How proudly and securely did he
now spread his sails when he at length emerged from the erroneous
wanderings of a passionate youth, and when after the long and
dreary calm of a subaltern service, he had attained to the high seas
of life. Every task that destiny offered him he undertook with
a happy facility and readiness ; unhesitatingly the infantry soldier
took over the command of the engineers and the supervision of
the fortresses. Whilst Scharnhorst was cautiously weighing the
dangers of the immediate future, Gneisenau always looked forward
with ardent yearning to the hour of the uprising, and suffered even
fools gladly if they would only take part in the great conspiracy.

A kindred nature was that of Grolman, magnanimous, serene,
and happy, incisive and unsparing in act and speech, created for
the melée, for the bold seizure of the fortune of the moment ; yet
he was to experience to the full the cruelty of the soldier's destiny,
and never in war was he to occupy the first place. In his general
demeanour, Boyen appeared to resemble the general most closely ;
he was a serious and reserved East Prussian who had sat at the
feet of Kant and Kraus, and who, as a poet, was also in close touch
with the new literature. It was only the ardent eyes under his

bushy eyebrows which betrayed the stormy courage that slumbered in the simple and silent man. After his quiet manner he had turned over in his own mind the organising ideas of Scharnhorst, had developed them further, and after the wars he helped to give its permanent form to the new people's army. Finally the youngest of this circle of friends, Carl von Clausewitz, was more than any of the others the trusted pupil of Scharnhorst, deeply initiated into the new scientific theories of war to which Scharnhorst was devoted. Subsequently Clausewitz developed these theories independently, and in a series of works, which in respect of classic form greatly excel those of the master, he secured for the theory of war its place among the number of state-sciences. His was a profound intelligence, and he was a master of historical judgment ; but he was perhaps too critical and too cautious to grasp, as did Gneisenau, the fortune of battle at the propitious moment ; yet he was far from being simply a man of books, for he was a practical and valiant soldier, looking with wide-open eyes upon the tumult of life. He had just returned with Prince Augustus from duress as a prisoner of war. While he was in France, his love for the youthful candour and freshness of the Teutons had risen to the point of enthusiasm. He returned home with the conviction that the French were still in essentials as unmilitary a people as they had been formerly in the days of the wars of the Huguenots when they trembled before the German infantry and cavalry. How can the primitive character of nations alter in ten years ? How could those who had been conquered one hundred times permanently control Germany mighty in arms ?

It was with the aid of such forces as these that the king undertook the work of reconstruction. The whole army was formed anew. Six brigades, two Silesian, two Old Prussian, one from Pomerania, and one from the Mark, were all that still remained of the Frederician army, and constituted the last anchor for German hopes. The troops were given more practical weapons and clothing, the pigtail was done away with, the arts of the parade-ground passed into abeyance, and their place was taken by the strenuous work of field service. All the stores had to be provided anew ; Napoleon's marshals had carried out their work of plunder so thoroughly that the Silesian artillery was unable for many months to undertake any practice for lack of powder. A commission of inquiry made a thorough examination of the conduct during the war of individual officers, and pitilessly cashiered all who were blameworthy or suspect. In the newspaper *Der Volksfreund*, edited by the valiant Bärsch, Gneisenau demanded the abolition of flogging in the army, asking bitterly whether the Prussian soldier was to continue to seek the stimulus of good conduct in the cane instead of in the sense of honour. His views found acceptance, the new articles of war abolished the old and cruel corporal punishments. How changed was the world when Prussian officers could now venture to discuss in the press the defects of the military system !

In another article, Gneisenau sarcastically alluded to the convenient system by which the sons of the Junkers could, while still children, exercise a hereditary right to command the soldiers of the king. In these words he merely gave open expression to what all intelligent officers were thinking. The abolition of the privileged position of the Junkers, and of all the other military privileges of the gentry, was a necessary consequence of the spirit of the new legislation ; and since the Prussians had taken practical note of the efficiency of Napoleon's youthful commanders many Hotspurs demanded that the renowned free promotion of the French should be imitated in Prussia. Scharnhorst, however, went his own way ; he saw the moral evils which had resulted from the adoption of the Napoleonic principle, " young generals, old captains " ; he saw how many rough and unwholesome elements had found their way into the lower strata of the French officers' corps, and how seriously in the French army unbridled ambition had loosened the bonds of true comradeship. The son of the German peasant was well aware why Washington had exclaimed to the Americans, " Take only gentlemen for your officers." He understood why King Frederick William I had allowed his officers to disobey orders when these orders touched their honour. It was not his desire to destroy the ancient aristocratic character of the Prussian officers' corps, but only to substitute the aristocracy of culture for the aristocracy of the privileged nobility.

The regulation of August 6, 1808, concerning the appointment of ensigns, established the principle that in time of peace only knowledge and culture, and in time of war only distinguished bravery and intelligence, could give a claim to officer's rank ; no Junker could now become an ensign simply on the ground of hereditary right, for the position of ensign could not be attained before the age of seventeen years, and only then after a scientific examination ; whilst not until a second examination had been passed, and upon a proposal from the officers' corps, could a young man win his epaulettes. The king impressed it upon the officers that they should never cease to realise their honourable position as educators and teachers of a noteworthy portion of the nation. In the lower grades up to the rank of captain, promotion usually occurred by seniority, but in the selection of the staff-officers and in the filling of the higher posts of command, service was alone determinative. Through these inconspicuous proposals, the officer's position acquired a new character which to us to-day seems a matter of course, since it constitutes a distinctive national feature of the German military system. Now for the first time did the officers' corps gain an inner correspondence with the civil officialdom, now first did it acquire a definite intellectual superiority over the rank and file. The prospect of rapid promotion was open to talent ; and yet the slowness of promotion in the lower grades, the general similarity of culture and of manner of life, resulted in this, that every member of the officers' corps had a definite sense of his position, and that an aristocratic class-consciousness permeated the whole body. The social barrier which in France separated the officer promoted from the ranks from his more cultured fellows, could not here exist.

For no one was the transformation of the military system so momentous, as for the older generation of the landed gentry, whose members still continued to form the majority of the officers' corps. Many years passed away before the actual favouring of the nobility in the army ceased to exist. But the principle was none the less firmly established that even the noble must acquire his commission by the proof of scientific knowledge, and only men of a considerable degree of culture could show themselves adequate for the new and more severe ordering of the service. No longer did the state service offer an asylum for the ignorant, and the reformers already began to speak of the new Prussia as an intelligent state. It was by Scharnhorst that the excessive roughness of the eastern German Junkerdom was first smoothed away, for the house of cadets instituted by Frederick William I had but half succeeded in effecting this change. The old generation, which had despised the quill-drivers, died out, and their youthful successors recognised and revered the power of knowledge.

The fundamental idea of all these reforms was that henceforward the army was to consist of the people in arms, it was to be a national army, to which everyone capable of bearing arms must belong. Recruiting was abolished, the enlisting of foreigners was forbidden ; only a few volunteers of German blood were still admitted. The new articles of war and the ordinance concerning military punishments started with the premise that in future all subjects, even young persons of good education, should serve as common soldiers, and this established the need for a gentler treatment of the rank and file. All thinking officers were at one as to the need for abolishing the old exemptions from military service. The idea of the general liability to service had even before the war been defended by Scharnhorst himself, by Boyen, by Loussau, and by other officers, and it was fully considered by the king. During the unfortunate campaign, this idea had quietly been gaining ground, and it was now clear to every intelligent soldier that the unequal war could only be resumed through the utilisation of the entire energy of the nation. Immediately after the peace, Blucher begged his dear Scharnhorst, " to provide for a national army ; no one must be exempt on any account, it must be a disgrace to anyone not to have served." Prince Augustus, while still a prisoner of war, transmitted a plan for the reconstitution of the army, in which universal military service was the leading idea. Scharnhorst knew, however, what most of his contemporaries had completely forgotten, that this was merely the revival of an ancient Prussian principle. He reminded the king that his ancestor Frederick William I had, first of all the princes of Europe, introduced general conscription ; it was this principle whose application had once made Prussia great, and here Austria and France were merely imitators. It now appeared to be necessary to return to the old Prussian system, and straightway to abolish the misuse of exemptions. Thus only could be constituted a true standing army, an army which would be of equal strength at all times. Almost with the very words of the old soldier-king did Scharnhorst begin his proposal for the formation of a reserve army. The first section opened with the words : " All the inhabitants of the state are by birth defenders of the state."

From the first, the Prussian officers conceived the ideas of universal military service in a freer and juster sense than did the bourgeoisie under the French Directory. The conquered were too proud-spirited to imitate the institutions of the conqueror. It had been bearable that the king's command should except from cantonal duty certain classes of people, either on account of class-privilege or else for economic reasons. But the proposal that a man of means should be able to buy himself exemption from military service, that one subject should sell his skin to another, was utterly un-Prussian, and in conflict with all the traditions of the army. The French system of substitution was indeed recommended by a few civil officials, but not by any single officer of note. Here ideas were more democratic than among the heirs of the revolution ; in plain terms it was demanded that all should be liable to military service, and this demand was made, not simply as a means to the ends of the War of Liberation, but as a permanent institution for the education of the people. Notwithstanding his contempt for military superficialities, Scharnhorst was ever a trained expert ; he was well aware to how small an extent unaided enthusiasm was able to replace the staying power, the skill, and the discipline, of the trained soldier. With his rich historical knowledge he had attained to the conviction that the gentler the manners of the times, the more necessary for the nation was a military education, so that the civilised world might retain the virile virtues of simpler times, so that the vigorous energy of body and soul should not be lost by culture. Gneisenau joyfully acclaimed this manly view of historic life ; it was his desire that military training should begin even at the elementary school, for was the heroic glory of the Spartans no longer attainable to modern humanity ? From his soul, Boyen wrote for all friends of Scharnhorst the verses :

"Valiant men throughout the country wield ye every one the sword ;
Let all classes, as is fitting, fight for hearth and sov'reign lord ! "

Thus there was no dispute about the principle. But how were the enormous difficulties in the way of its execution to be overcome ? To this age, which had so recently emerged from the

barbarism of the ancient military discipline, it seemed an intolerable
severity that the sons of the cultured classes should be enrolled
straightway in the standing army ; moreover, in September, 1808,
Napoleon forced the acceptance of the Treaty of Paris, in accordance with which the ill-used state was forced to pledge itself not
to keep an armed force larger than forty-two thousand men.

Thus the only thing that remained, was to overreach the conqueror by cunning, to find a way round the treaty, and to create,
beside the standing army, a reserve army, a Landwehr, for use in
case of war. And yet even for this end the direct road was closed.
Scharnhorst at once recognised that the simplest plan would be to
provide the Landwehr through the school of the standing army,
to constitute the reserve army out of the trained soldiers who had
served their time. Yet for the moment this was impossible. The
calling up of so great a number of recruits would at once have
aroused the suspicions of Napoleon ; and moreover, a Landwehr
constituted in this way would obviously not attain a notable
strength until many years had passed, whilst month by month a
fresh outbreak of the war was anticipated. For this reason, the
Prussians must content themselves with a militia without any
apparent connection with the standing army, ostensibly intended
only for the maintenance of internal peace, but trained for military
purposes by repeated drills, and with a sufficient supply of arms to
be able to take the field as a reserve army immediately after the
outbreak of war. Four times during the years 1807 and 1810 did
Scharnhorst resume these Landwehr plans, and confer upon
them with the monarch. His first proposal came into effect on
July 31, 1807, quite independently, and long before the Austrian
Landwehr came into existence.

The earlier plans pursued as their main purpose the preparation for military service of the sons of the well-to-do classes, who
would be able to provide their own arms and uniform ; this force
was to be drilled in time of peace under the harmless name of a
" burgher guard " or of the " national watch." In the summer of
1809, the restless military reformer gave a wider scope to these
proposals, in which could already be recognised the elements of
the organisation of 1813. He set a high value upon the heroic
energy of a wrathful people, but he also had a sober vision of the
length of time that would be requisite before he could transform

an armed mob into troops ready and fit for war. His plan was that
the standing army should begin the attack ; meanwhile the reserve
army was to be constituted out of the soldiers that had served their
term, out of the supernumeraries, and also out of all the younger
men liable to cantonal service ; the well-to-do were to join as
volunteer yagers. This Landwehr was to take over service
in the fortresses, and was to effect the investment of places
garrisoned by the enemy ; as soon as it was sufficiently developed,
it was to follow the army, and its place was to be taken by the
militia, or Landsturm, which had meanwhile been assembled and
was to comprise all those still fit to bear arms. Scharnhorst knew
how disagreeable to Napoleon were his memories of the campaign
of La Vendée, and how greatly he dreaded a popular uprising. It
was Scharnhorst's hope to open the War of Liberation with a small
army which should base its actions upon a few fortresses or
entrenched camps, and with such an end in view, he had an
extremely careful study made of the unfavourable ground of the
North German plain. When Gneisenau learned of Wellington's
Portuguese victories, he even hoped to reconstitute a Torres Vedras
upon this plain, out of the little town of Spandau.

All these hopes came to nought. As soon as Napoleon was
informed of the Prussian plans for a new Landwehr, he at once
uttered masterful threats. His detested opponent was not to go
a single step outside the provisions of the Treaty of Paris—while
he reserved to himself the right to trample these provisions under
foot. At length it became clear that the constitution of a Landwehr remained impossible so long as Prussia was not yet in a
position to declare war against France. Until then, all that could
be attained without arousing the suspicion of the Imperator, was
to undertake a more rapid training of the men of the standing army.
The legally established age for the service of those liable to military
duty was twenty years, and this was left unchanged ; but as many
of them were called up as possible, and were sent home again in
a few months when they had received a tolerable training. The
strength of the army allowed by the treaty was not observed with
undue strictness. For years, the bodyguard in Berlin, whenever
the force went out into the field for manœuvres, left a portion of the
men in barracks, so that Napoleon's spies could not ascertain the
strength of the battalions. It was impossible to avoid that many of

those fit for service should evade the more severe levies by flight, whilst on the other hand many conscripts entered Prussia from the territories of the Confederation of the Rhine. On the whole the people showed a self-sacrificing loyalty towards the king. It happened on one occasion that the peasants of the neighbourhood stole a cannon during the night from the ramparts of the Westphalian fortress of Magdeberg, and brought it by boat to Spandau— their tribal lord needed weapons to use against the Frenchmen. Through this system of partial training Scharnhorst gradually succeeded in building up a force of 150,000 soldiers. It was a tragical spectacle, that of this great man endeavouring year after year to elude the notice of his omniscient enemy by a thousand wiles and tricks. His soul longed for the joy of battle ; he was willing to sacrifice the last man and horse in the country so that Germany might once more be free ; yet ever again and again the watchful opponent rendered vain his plans of military preparation. It was not until the hour of open battle struck that in a moment there sprang to life all that had been quietly prepared in five years full of arduous labour, full of nameless anxieties. Scharnhorst and no other was the father of the Landwehr of 1813.

Stein's reforms contributed powerfully to the national awakening of 1813 and the army that had been transformed by Scharnhorst played a distinguished part in the campaigns of the Grand Alliance and in the final defeat of Napoleon, which are described in rich detail in the second half of Treitschke's first volume.

II
The Restoration, 1815-1830

*No account of the post-Napoleonic period in Germany has ever
approached Treitschke's in color, variety, and detail. The Prussian
bias is noticeable, approaching shrillness in the account of
Metternich's success in winning approval for the Carlsbad
Decrees. But it does not prevent Treitschke from feeling pride in
the intellectual achievements of non-Prussians or from acknowledging the merits of other German governments, as is apparent
in his chapter on Bavaria, which is included here, along with his
more caustic descriptions of life in Saxony and Electoral Hesse.*

INTELLECTUAL CURRENTS (II, 235–49, 251–66, 267–70, 278–80)

Throughout the world, the decade following the overthrow
of Napoleon was a blossoming time of the sciences and the arts.
The nations which had just been fighting so fiercely one with
another, now engaged in a fine rivalry in respect of the fruits of
their intellectual life ; never before had Europe approximated
so closely to that ideal of a free world-literature of which Goethe
dreamed. In this peaceful rivalry, Germany took the first place.
What a change from the days of Louis XIV, when our nation
had been forced to go humbly to school to all the other nations
of the west. Now the whole world revered the name of Goethe.
The quaint guest-chambers of the Erbprinzen and of the Adler
in Weimar were always full of distinguished Englishmen who
desired to pay their respects to the prince of the new poetry. In
Paris, Alexander Humboldt enjoyed a repute which exceeded
that of almost any native man of learning ; when a stranger entered
a hackney-coach and gave the address of the great traveller, the
driver respectfully lifted his hat and said : " Ah ! chez M. de

Humboldt ! " When Niebuhr came to Rome as Prussian ambassador, no one in the world-city ventured to contest with him the glory of being the first among all men of learning.

Foreigners spoke little of our state, of its warlike deeds. To all the foreign powers the sudden revival in strength of the centre of Europe was disagreeable, and they all rivalled one another in the endeavour to consign to oblivion Prussia's share in the liberation of Europe. Not one of the foreign military historians who in these years of historical production described the most recent campaigns, did anything like adequate justice to the services of Blucher's headquarters staff. The old prestige of the Prussian army, which in the days of Frederick had been dreaded by all as the greatest army in the world, had by no means been re-established by the victories of Dennewitz and Belle Alliance. Since it is always difficult to gain a comprehensive view of the true course of a coalition war, the public opinion of Europe gladly contented itself with contemplating the simple conclusion that since the Prussians had been beaten when they fought alone at Jena they had been saved only by foreign help. For this reason, too, no one in foreign lands had any interest in the political institutions to which Prussia owed her freedom. Now, as before, Prussia remained the least known and the most completely misunderstood state of Europe. Moreover, the new Reichstag of Ratisbon, which now assembled in Frankfort, aroused the scorn of Europe by its fruitless disputes. Soon after the wonderful uprising of our nation, the old and convenient opinion became generally current that by a wise provision of nature the German nation was foreordained to eternal weakness and dissension. All the more willingly did people recognise the intellectual greatness of this powerless nation ; it was solely to their artists and to their men of learning that the Germans owed the fact that by all the civilised peoples of the west they were once more regarded as one among the great nations. In foreign lands, they were now spoken of as the nation of poets and thinkers ; in the partition of the earth they should be content with the lot of the poet which Schiller ascribed to them, and, intoxicated with the divine light, should be satisfied to lose the light of earth.

For the first time since the days of Martin Luther, the ideas of Germany once more made the round of the world, and now found a more willing acceptance than of old had the ideas of the Reformation. Germany alone had already got completely beyond the view of the world-order characteristic of the eighteenth century. The sensualism of the days of enlightenment had been long replaced by an idealist philosophy ; the dominion of reason by a profound religious sentiment ; cosmopolitanism by a delight in national peculiarity ; natural rights by a recognition of the living growth of the nations ; the rules of correct art by free poesy, bubbling up as by natural energy from the depths of the soul ; the preponderance of the exact sciences by the new historico-æsthetic culture. By the work of three generations, those of the classical and of the romanticist poets, this world of new ideas had slowly attained to maturity, whereas among the neighbour nations it had hitherto secured no more than isolated disciples, and only now at length made its way victoriously through all the lands.

With wonderful elasticity did France resume her intellectual labours after the long and heavy slumber of the imperial age. Madame de Staël's book upon Germany, which the Napoleonic censors had suppressed as an affront to the national pride, was now in everyone's hands, and gained everywhere adherents for German ideas, which were given the comprehensive name of romanticism. The dominion of the sensualist philosophy collapsed before the criticism of the doctrinaires ; a compact circle of men of talent, such men as Mignet, Guizot, and the Thierrys, opened to the French an understanding of the world of history. The age of Louis XIV, which even the revolutionary thinkers of the eighteenth century had still regarded as the epoch of classical beauty of form, began to lose its prestige, and soon there uprose a new school of poets to liberate France from the tyranny of academic rules, so that Victor Hugo could say with considerable truth of his own people that romanticism is in literature that which liberalism is in politics. Yet more vigorous and more direct was the exchange of ideas between Germany and England ; the Germans now repaid to the British what they had once received from Shakespeare and Sterne. Walter Scott, the most fruitful and best-loved poet of the age, went to school to Bürger and Goethe, drawing from the profound spring of sagas and folk-songs which the Germans had unlocked for the world ; by his historical romances the

broad masses of the European reading public was first won over
to romanticist ideals.   Some of the Italians, too, above all Manzoni,
entered the path of the new poetry ; but among this semi-antique
people of Italy, romanticist poetry could just as little attain to an
undisputed dominion as had in former days the northern artistic
form of Gothic architecture.

Everywhere there was an awakening of spirit.   In Germany
itself, the wealth of this fruitful epoch seemed less striking than in
neighbouring countries, for the classical age of our poetry had barely
come to an end, and the great majority of the younger poets
regarded themselves, when compared with the heroes of those
great days, as nothing better than a generation of epigones.   All
the more powerfully and fruitfully did the creative energy of the
German spirit unfold itself in the domain of science.   Almost
simultaneously appeared the epoch-making writings of Savigny,
the brothers Grimm, Boeckh, Lachmann, Bopp, Diez, and Ritter ;
whilst Niebuhr, the Humboldts, Eichhorn, Creuzer, and Gottfried
Hermann, went vigorously forward along the paths they had
already opened.   The current of new ideas flowed everywhere
unceasingly.   There was an overplus of brilliant men, as there
had been in former days when Klopstock led the revival of German poetry.   And just as had previously been the case with the
pioneers of our poetry, so now this new generation of learned
men was permeated with an innocent and youthful enthusiasm,
with a serene ambition which sought nothing more in the world
than the blessedness of knowledge, and the increase of German
glory through the activities of free investigation.

The dry dust which had so long lain upon the works of German
learning was, as it were, wafted away ; the new science felt itself
to be the sister of art.   Its disciples had all drunk from the cup
of beauty, and many of them had even received the determinative
impressions of their lives in the circles of the poets.   Diez continued to cherish after many years the sheet of paper on which
Goethe had once written for him the title of Reynouard's
Provençal researches, and had thus indicated to the young man
the way to his life work.   Boeckh and Creuzer had idled, revelled,
and caroused so many nights with the enthusiasts of Heidelberg
romanticism ; I. Bekker had delved with Uhland among the
treasures of the Paris library ; the impish Bettina Arnim some-

times played her mischievous tricks in the studies of Savigny and of the brothers Grimm. They all looked up with veneration to old Goethe, assembling round this central spirit to form as it were an invisible church, round this man who had received the veil of poesy from the hand of truth herself, and who incorporated the ideal of the age, the living unity of art and science, at once in his life and in his works. All endeavoured to express the results of their researches in a nobler and worthier form ; the chaste simplicity of Savigny's writings, the powerful sentiment and the abundance of unsought, vivid, and intuitive images in the pithy style of Jacob Grimm, put to shame the sugary artificiality of many later poets. In all the works of these investigators, a warm heart and that creative imagination which reshapes historic life had just as great a share as had industrious research and critical acumen.

Just as the poetry of the previous generation had inspired the men of the rising generation, so the speculative work of the previous age made its way into the flesh and blood of the new science. It was only because the German spirit had so long been profoundly immersed in the problem of the unity of being and thinking, that that spirit now became able to diffuse itself throughout the world of history without becoming superficial and without losing itself in a mass of details. It was not in vain that all these young lawyers, philologists, and historians had sat at the feet of the philosophers. They wished to reach out through history into the secret of the human spirit itself ; they endeavoured, as W. Humboldt declared of himself, to gain a view of how man had come to be, and thus to acquire some idea of what man may be and ought to be, to approach more closely to the ultimate questions of existence. Hence was derived the comprehensive outlook, the splendid multiplicity, of this generation of learned men. It was only so recently that the wide field of the world of history had been first occupied ; whoever drove his ploughshare through this virgin soil, subsequently scattered the seed with no niggard hand, so that it was dispersed also upon his neighbour's land. Almost all the notable men of learning were simultaneously at work in several fields, and every one of them, when immersing himself in some particular form of study, never failed to keep his glance fixed upon the great interconnection of the sciences. It was the pride of this fruit-bearing generation to propound brilliant hypotheses, and to illuminate wide prospects which the scientific researches of individual workers in two successive generations have since made accessible to the whole world.

Through the blossoming of science, the universities entered the foreground of the nation's spiritual life. They had ever taken a rich share in the struggles and transformations of German thought ; but now they assumed the leading position in the domain of the spirit, as they had done once before in the epoch of humanism and at the outset of the Reformation. University professors gradually acquired a determinative influence upon the activities and views of our nation, such an influence as they possessed in no other country ; among the leading authors of the ensuing decades, there were but few who had not held an academic position for a shorter or longer period. The university of Berlin soon outsoared all others ; here, during these years, there were at work the most ardent reforming minds in German science ; yet Berlin was never more than first among equals, for this country offered no opportunities for a centralisation of culture. Never have our universities been so truly free, fulfilled with such profound inward happiness, as in these quiet years of peace. The quarrelsome youths brought home from the battle-fields, in addition to their unmannerly Teutonism, to their arrogant political dreams, a fine enthusiasm, and a warm receptivity for ideals ; the deplorable roughness and intemperance of earlier times did not return. Education remained free from corporate coercion and corporate tendencies, for all felt that in science everything was still in a state of youthful growth. No one was astonished when a man of learning, even of mature age, changed from one faculty to another, or when a philologian like Dahlmann, who had never heard a historical lecture, was summoned to the chair of history. When a man displayed the stuff of which a master is made, no one asked whose pupil he had been. Most of the university lecturers did their professorial work with admirable zeal ; but if a fine spring day lured them into the neighbouring hills, even the most industrious among them did not hesitate to write up on the door of his lecture-theatre *hodie non legitur.*

The students of all faculties thronged round notable teachers of philosophy, history, and philology, and many of them continued to pursue such studies for years before thinking of engaging in a professional occupation for themselves. The classical state schools, avoiding mind-destroying polymathy, still knew how to awaken in their pupils a permanent delight in classical activity and an impulse towards free human culture. The disease of the universities of to-day, the dread of examinations, was still almost entirely unknown. The princely schools of Saxony, and the convent schools of Würtemberg, anciently celebrated homes of classical learning, sent their senior students to the university as soon as the teachers considered that the time was ripe, the state leaving them to do as they thought best. Entry into the state service and the ecclesiastical service of the petty states was for the most part secured by young men who had finished their university career, and was secured by patronage, in accordance with the ancient patriarchal manner. It was only in Prussia, after the reorganisation of the administration by Frederick William I, that a system of regular state-examinations had come into existence, and from Prussia this mechanical ordering, which was unquestionably juster, and was demanded by the manifold relationships of a great state, gradually made its way into the petty states. But here also a very moderate standard was exacted, for the state needed many young officials for its new provinces. The idealistic tendency of the time forbade that studies should be anxiously directed with the view to the earning of a living. Youth still enjoyed undisturbed academic freedom ; everyone listened and learned as fancy directed him, if he did not prefer to pass his golden student days in the sole pursuit of uncontrolled enjoyments.

Such was the life of the little learned republics, happy free states of absolute social equality and freedom from restraint, raised, as it were, above the pettiness of everyday life. Men of great talent, who in every other country would have demanded a wide stage for their activities, felt perfectly happy in the poverty and exiguity of these little university towns, with their ancient castles and narrow, winding streets, where every house had memories of some merry wit among the students, or of some distinguished professor. Here science was supreme ; the professor, revered by a grateful audience, regarded himself with frank self-satisfaction. Often enough there occurred fierce intellectual disputes,

after the German manner ; the scientific opponent was apt to
be regarded as a desecrator of the temple, for everyone was
whole-heartedly devoted to his own researches. But these
straightforward and frugal-minded men were little troubled
with vulgar ambition. They made it a point of honour to
despise the display and comfort of material existence ; they still
all firmly believed in the proud saying of Schiller : " In the end
we are idealists, and would be ashamed that it could be said
of us that things formed us, and not that we formed things."

Even after decades had passed, in Tübingen people used to
speak of the wealthy bookseller Cotta, who had first introduced
the unheard-of luxury of a sofa into the unpretentious town of
the Muses. The youthful incompleteness of our civilisation,
which still knew nothing of the many-sided social activities of
the life of great towns, redounded to the advantage of
reflectiveness and the peaceful pursuit of scientific work. Like
the classical poetry of an earlier day, so now the new research
remained perfectly free, almost untouched by the favour of the
court and by official influence ; not even the prosecution of
the demagogues was able to disturb the inner life of science.
Although now almost all the German states, nobly competing
one with another, endeavoured to secure the activities of leading
teachers for their respective universities, in the eyes of the courts
and of the bureaucracy even a professor of European reputation
was merely a professor, without rank at court. The man of
science, on the other hand, looked down with all the pride of
idealism upon the aims of commercial life. Every teacher
appealed to the best intelligences among his pupils to devote
themselves entirely to science ; mediocrities were good enough
for the handicraft work of the soldier and the official, and above
all for the thoroughly despised world of business life. An
incomparably greater preponderance of the spiritual energies of
the nation devoted itself to learned activities, and it remains a
fine testimony to the fertility of this generation that, none the
less, the officialdom now numbered among its ranks an extraordinary abundance of men of talent.

Now, just as sixty years before, while the political life of
the nation was flowing subdivided in innumerable streams and
streamlets, it was only the authors and the men of learning who

spoke directly to the nation as a whole. For this reason they regarded themselves as the chosen representatives of the people and of its highest goods ; it was but very slowly that a few politicians gained general repute beside them. The whole epoch exhibited, for good and for evil, the characteristics of a literary age. Even now, a poem by Goethe, an incisive criticism, or a learned feud, such as that between the symbolists and the critical philologians, aroused far greater interest among the leading spirits of the nation than did any event in the world of politics. Karl Immermann voiced the very spirit of this romantic age when he declared that he could not follow a parliamentary debate with attention, because he could not form any mental picture of such void abstractions. The complete sacrifice of the free personality in the service of the state remained no less antipathetic to this generation than was the life of political parties, with its voluntary limitations and its fundamentally unjust hatreds. To the German, the highest of all aims was still to live out his own life, to develop his own ego, in its free peculiarities, in all possible directions, and, as W. Humboldt expressed it, to pay more attention to the doing than to the deed.

Although the dominant tendency of the age ran absolutely counter to the enlightened cosmopolitanism of the years before the Revolution, this romantic generation had none the less preserved many of the humanly lovable virtues of the philosophic century. The young Teutonisers might arrogantly decry French triviality ; the leaders of science and art continued, after the old and genuine German manner, to exhibit gratitude and receptivity for every fine work of poetry and research, even if it came from much-abused France. Notwithstanding the mystical enthusiasm of the time, the old broad-minded tolerance still persisted. The contrasts of religious life had not yet become accentuated; they did not as yet exercise, as they do to-day, a falsifying and embittering influence in the sphere of politics. No one was surprised if a liberal was at the same time a strict church Christian. To everyone it seemed perfectly in order that Catholic ecclesiastics should attend the consecration of a Protestant church ; even zealous converts like F. Schlegel, Stolberg, and Klinkowström remained on terms of cordial friendship with some of their old Protestant associates. The struggle of the literary parties did not render impossible the recognition of the human value of an opponent, nor exclude a genuine delight in every happy discovery. Uproarious youths prided themselves upon their Germanic strictness of morals ; mature men displayed in their moral judgments a fine and liberal mildness, which was in truth far more German. Exhibiting consideration for human weakness, they placed little value upon that correctness of conduct which to the prudish sense of the present day appears to be the only token of morality, and willingly let a hot-blooded friend go his own way, if he would but co-operate in the work of a free human culture, and if only he did not lose faith in the divine destiny of our race.

It was not without reason that the poets and men of learning looked down with contempt upon the prose of philistinism. They lived in a free and intelligent sociability which knew how to ennoble life by the serene play of art and which approximately realised Schiller's ideal of an æsthetic education. The exchange of ideas in correspondence and conversation, the natural means for the intercommunication of daily impressions, had not yet been rendered obsolete by newspapers. There yet existed the basis of all social charm, the frank and daily intercourse between the two sexes, for women were still able to follow in their entirety the thoughts of men. There was not a town in the realm without its connoisseurs, collectors, and critics, without its circles of lovers of the theatre and of the arts. When the cheerful populace of the smaller towns assembled for their simple meals by the gloomy flickering light of tallow candles, all contributed according to their respective capacities in the way of riddles and witticisms, songs and rhymed toasts—since for many years past every cultured German had known how to provide on his own initiative for the poetic needs of the household. Social life was warmed by cheerful pleasures ; in a game of forfeits a kiss was still permissible in all honour ; the free-spirited girls of the day, who were none the less carefully trained for domestic life, still frankly admitted that Käthchen of Heilbronn was a figure altogether after their taste. In the narrower circles of the initiates how much fine intelligence and wit, how much merry humour and eager enthusiasm, now prevailed—as when Ludwig Devreint and Callot-Hoffmann celebrated their extravagant bacchanals all through the night in the taverns of Lutter and Wegner ; or when Lobeck and the Königsberg philologians joined in a drinking-bout after the Greek manner, their heads crowned with roses, talking in Greek of the heroes of Homer and of the fortunate island of the Phaeacians. The social life of the day, notwithstanding its occasional beastliness and excesses, exhibited none the less an abundance of noble intellectual enjoyments, of which music almost alone has been preserved amid the dulness and the weary ostentation of modern society. The women who had been young during those years, seemed, even in advanced age, to the posterity of a duller generation, to be illumined as by a poetic charm ; they won the hearts of all by their inexhaustible amiability, by their refined understanding of everything that is human.

Doubtless there was also manifest at the same time an indication of the commencement of decay. Literature had for some time run to seed ; writers offered to readers what they thought the readers wanted, whereas the classical poets of earlier days had spontaneously expressed what already lay half-conscious in the soul of the nation. The love of novelty and the sensuality of the reading world were exploited by a mass of trivial light literature ; since a national style had not come into existence in any branch of creative literature, profounder natures readily lapsed into arbitrary and strained experiments, so that Goethe characterised these years as the epoch of forced talents. The fashionable intermingling of poetry and criticism rendered it easy for a barren dilettantism to increase beyond measure. Whoever moved in the circles of romanticism, repeating the catchwords of this school, and sometimes cudgelling his brains over the design for a drama or an epic poem, regarded himself as a poet, and forgot the consciousness of his incapacity in the favourite consolation that the artist was made in the world of thought and aspiration, and that Raphael, even if born without hands would have been the greatest of all painters. The terribly misused word " genius " was a charter for every folly, every extravagance. The straightforward human understanding was apt to be ruined by ingenious toying with new ideas and

with surprising points of view. The belief in the boundless
rights of the sovereign personality, the general desire to be
something different from other men, led some to moral anarchy
and others to vain self-admiration. With nervous sensitiveness, people watched every breath of their own beautiful spirits.
In the letters of Gentz and in the memoirs of Rahel Varnhagen,
the barometer plays the part of the mysterious elemental energy
which bestows upon genius the dark and the bright hours.

The thoughts of the nation were still so completely
dominated by literature, that even the great contrasts of
political and religious life frequently found expression in
learned disputes. Such was the nature of the struggles
between Savigny and Thibaut, between Voss and Stolberg.
When Gottfried Hermann took the field against Creuzer and the
symbolists, he regarded himself as the champion of freedom
against the *tenebriones*, the men of darkness in the state and in
the church. Even the purely political parties, whose weak
beginnings were now at length becoming manifest, emerged
directly out of literary life. The immediate intervention of
political theory in the destiny of states, which so strikingly
distinguishes modern history from the more ingenuous days of
antiquity and of the middle ages, was nowhere more conspicuous
than here in the land of learning. German liberalism sprang,
not from the class interests of the wealthy and self-conscious
bourgeoisie, but from the academic ideas of the professors.
With the indefinite historical yearning for the great days of the
old emperordom, which had first come into existence in literary
circles during the epoch of foreign dominion, there gradually became
intermingled the doctrines of the new philosophy regarding
the natural right of the free personality ; to these were
subsequently added a few phrases from Montesquieu and
Rousseau ; and finally, in addition, a large proportion of the
unconscious prejudices of the learned caste. Thus there came
into existence a system of ideas which were supposed to
correspond with the law of reason, and were to lead our
nation through freedom back to the attainment of its ancient
power. In the writings of Rotteck this doctrine was
produced in a condition of complete elaboration, like a
philosopher's system and, just like such a system, put forward

a claim to perpetuate itself through the world by the might of reason, by its theoretical incontrovertibility. The over-throw of the Napoleonic world-empire had been effected solely by the power of ideas which had been born in the circles of the brain-workers, had from these passed to the nation, had finally overpowered even the hostile crowns, and had led to the holy war—this view was assumed by literary politicians to be indisputable ; thus it seemed that Germany's internal liberation would also be well secured if only all parties would fully accept the sacred truths of the new constitutional doctrine, and would hold firmly to this creed with the faithful conviction of the man of learning or of the martyr of the church. To this generation of well-meaning doctrinaires it still remained altogether unknown that the state has power, and belongs to the realm of the will. It was not until decades had passed, filled with crass confusions and profound disillusionments, that German party life could outgrow the cradle of doctrine and raise itself from a policy of belief to a policy of action.

In the Latin countries, poetry, when it had attained to classical perfection, had everywhere and for a long period given form and direction to the spirit of the nation. So extreme was the stubbornness of the Germans that even during the golden days of Weimar they would never yield to the dominion of a rule. Whilst Schiller and Goethe still stood at the summit of their creative activities, romanticism was already beginning a fierce attack upon the classical ideal. When the War of Liberation had reduced the literary struggle to silence, the anxiety about the fatherland repressed all other thoughts ; the few writings which ventured forth during this wild time seemed to unite in advocating Christian and patriotic enthusiasm. But hardly had peace been concluded when the sharp contrasts which the manifold life of Germany contained, once more and in a moment broke forth into active life. Even half-forgotten thoughts from the first years of the Revolution, ideas which had been sup-posed to have been long outgrown, re-emerged into the light of day ; for it is the lot of every literature which is no longer in its first youth to find that at times the past once more comes to life, and that the shades of the dead take part in the struggles of the living. Rationalism and religious sentiment, criticism

and mysticism, natural rights and historical doctrines of the
state, Nazarene and Hellenic ideals of nationalism and
cosmopolitanism, liberal and feudal tendencies, struggled and
intertwined in perpetual change.

It was not merely the timid Gentz who complained in alarm
that the long-desired time of peace had brought to the Germans
a war of all against all. Even Arndt, who was ever sanguine,
could not conceal his disgust when at the court of the young
crown prince of Prussia he saw Alexander Humboldt, the
advocate of a purely scientific cosmopolitanism, and at the same
time the brothers Gerlach, hotspurs of Christo-Germanic
religious fanaticism. He anxiously asked how, in view of the
immeasurable divergence of sentiments, this nation could ever
attain to internal peace, to firm decision. In the long run,
indeed, the healthy sense of the nation succeeded in grasping
and retaining all that was genuine and viable in this anarchical confusion. Nevertheless, many a fine talent succumbed
hopelessly amid the confusion of opinions ; and whoever found
courage to take part in the struggles of the German spirit had
to be prepared to accept a lot of renunciation. Every notable
intelligence, even if high above the sectarian spirit, was forced,
willingly or unwillingly, into the struggle of the literary parties
and was extolled beyond measure by one faction, while being
abused by the other with all the lack of restraint characteristic
of German fault-finding ; those only who had attained to a great
age might hope, like Savigny and Uhland, to secure belated
recognition even from their opponents.

*   *   *

Even in the serene and youthful days of our classical
literature, unrestrained criticism had frequently hampered the
free natural growth of poetry. Now, when during seventy years
Germany had experimented in almost all conceivable artistic
styles and had made trial of even more manifold æsthetic
theories, artistic creation showed itself to be affected with the
disease of learned over-refinement. No branch of poetic art
suffered more severely in this respect than the drama, which

needs popular favour as flowers need the sun. Goethe had good reason for calling the arrogant spokesmen of romanticism " starvelings yearning for the unattainable " ; notwithstanding their talented flashes of thought and their high intentions, they completely lacked the gift of architectonic, the constructive and convincing energy of the creative genius. Although they had promised themselves to oust the classical ideal by a popular poetising, their works, after all, remained unknown to the people, and were the property of no more than a small circle of admiring connoisseurs. To them, art was, as it were, a magic philtre, one which the philistine was incapable of enjoying, and which was intoxicating to those alone who possessed divine grace ; under its influence these rare spirits forgot reality and smiled upon life as upon a foolish masque. This sovereign disdain which prided itself upon " pursuing sport as earnest and treating earnest as sport " conflicted with the healthy sentiment of the crowd.

Of the older German dramatists, the romanticist art-critic would allow a high rank to Goethe alone, and Goethe had hardly thought of writing his most mature works for presentation on the stage ; the peaceful sensual beauty of his *Iphigenia* and of his *Tasso* were not fully conceivable except to the mind of the reader. Lessing was no longer counted among the poets ; Schiller's tragic passion was mocked as empty rhetoric ; even Heinrich von Kleist, the one dramatist of genius whose outlook was closely akin to that of the romanticists, remained long unnoticed by the critics of this school. The two most efficient dramatists of the period, Iffland and Kotzebue, who continued to dominate the stage even for a decade after their death, were regarded by the arrogance of the romanticists with such unjustified contempt that youthful talent was necessarily frightened away from the drama. All that the romanticists could see in one of these writers was his honourable philistine sensibility, and all that they could see in the other was his insipidity and the commonness of his thought ; in neither could they recognise the exceptional technical talent, nor yet the fortunate gift of ready invention, whereby both put to shame their obscure critics. Of the dramatic endeavours of the romanticists themselves, but few ever appeared before the foot-lights, and all those that did thus appear stood the test badly. The leaders of the school soon turned their backs upon the stage, speaking with scorn of the common prose of theatrical success. Utterly regardless of the vital conditions of the modern theatre, which on five or seven nights a week had to satisfy an audience wearied by the cares of every-day life, dramatic theory constructed its stately cloud-pictures and made excessive demands, for which not even the splendid stage of the Hellenes could have furnished satisfaction.

The heroes of our classical poetry had never had the same intimate relationships with the stage as in earlier days Shakespeare or Molière. Now, however personal intercourse between dramatists and play-actors became ever rarer. Dramatic art forgot that, above all other arts, it is its fine destiny to constitute a bond of unity between the higher and the lower strata of society. There gradually came to exist within our nation a momentous cleavage which down to the present day has remained a grave evil of German civilisation : the reading public separated itself as an aristocracy from the onlooking and listening public. A large proportion of the daily needs of the theatre came to be supplied by literary journeymen ; spectacular plays and bad translations from the French appealed to the sightseeing spirit of the crowd. Whoever esteemed himself one of the select circle of true poets, commonly loaded himself too heavily with the impedimenta of the æsthetic doctrine to be able to act with that boldness, to laugh with that heartiness, which the stage demands from its rulers ; and such writers incorporated their dramatic ideas in bookish dramas. That mongrel type of poetry with which an over-elaborated modern culture cannot completely dispense, exhibited in Germany a more luxuriant growth than elsewhere. Here, upon the patient paper, all the complicated theorems and fantastical ideas of the wayward German intelligence found free play : tragicomedies and plays for *jeunes filles*, in which every conceivable metre recurred in riotous confusion ; hidden allusions comprehensible only to the poet himself and to his intimates ; literary satires which made art the object of art ; and, finally, exotic poems of all kinds, which had to be read as if they were translations.

The art of dramatic presentation also suffered from the decline in dramatic poetry. How many talented monographs upon the theatre as a means of national education had already been published, and yet, among all German statesmen, Stein alone had made this idea his own, and had drawn the conclusion that it is the duty of the state to care for the stage. When, on his retirement, he sketched the plans of Prussian governmental reorganisation, he placed the theatre, as well as the academy of arts, under the control of the department of public instruction ; yet, barely two years later, they were by Hardenberg brought back into the domain of public amusement, and, with the exception of the court theatre, were subjected to police supervision. In the royal capitals, the support of the court theatres was generally held to be a personal duty of the sovereign, and it soon became manifest that such theatres had more to expect from the free-handedness of artistically disposed princes than from the frugal petty-bourgeois sentiments of the new diets. Hardly had the Stuttgart stage, in the year 1816, been elevated to the position of a national theatre and had been nationally financed, when the diet began to complain of extravagance, and cheerfully acquiesced, three years later, when the king declared himself prepared to strike the maintenance of the court theatre out of the civil list. For the most part the monarchs cared with commendable zeal for the external equipment of their theatres, as well as for the employment of notable individual talent ; the old social prejudice against actors soon became mitigated when the stage was seen to be in such close association with the court.

None the less, the histrionic art gained little through the court theatres. After the death of Iffland, Frederick William entrusted Count Brühl with the management of the court theatre of Berlin. Brühl was an amiable and highly-cultured man, but neither dramatic poet nor actor, and he had merely assimilated, with the zeal of a talented connoisseur, the strict classical principles of the theatrical school of Weimar. The dangerous example was quickly followed ; soon at all the courts the office of theatre-intendant was reckoned among the high court dignities, the control of the greatest German theatres was taken out of the hands of skilled experts and placed in those of high-born dilettantes.

Yet the good traditions of earlier days still persisted for a time. The lack of fine new pieces was not yet too plainly perceptible, for the dramas of the classical epoch could still count upon

general acceptance, and the works of Shakespeare now for the
first time became fully established upon the German stage.   The
court theatres of Berlin, Munich, Carlsruhe, and Brunswick,
were distinguished by many excellent performances, and the
same was true of the long celebrated theatre of Hamburg and of
the new municipal theatre of Leipzig.   In Berlin, the realist
tendency, which had here in former days gained dominion
through the work of Fleck, found a talented representative in
Ludwig Devrient.   What sinister and diabolic energy was displayed in his Richard III, what an extravagance of exuberant
humour in his Falstaff !   Almost more astonishing was the
ability with which he played minor parts ; his Knecht Gotts-
chalk, in *Käthchen von Heilbronn*, so admirably presented simple
loyalty and truthfulness that in the souls of the audience there
was awakened in a moment an understanding of the pristine
energy and greatness of old German life.   None the less, the firm
artistic discipline of the stage became gradually more and more
relaxed.   The new romanticist ethics encouraged every man of
talent to press recklessly towards the front, and to emphasise
his own peculiarities ; while the distinguished intendants had
neither the technical knowledge which might have empowered
them by their own example to maintain in the company a unity
of style, nor yet had they sufficient prestige to enable them to
keep the individual members within bounds.   The brilliant new
court theatres were no longer able to display such equably
cultured and harmonious performances as had formerly produced
delight in Hamburg in the days of Ekhof, and in Berlin in the days
of Iffland.   Moreover, dramatic criticism had for some time
established itself like a noxious fungus upon the healthy tree of
dramatic art.   It had already become the rule that every aspiring
senior school-boy or university student should win his literary
spurs by dramatic criticism ; almost every man of culture occasionally exercised his powers in the tragical handicraft of the
critical spoil-sport.   By far the majority of these notices had the
sole aim of winning renown for the writer by arrogant distribution of blame ;   or else of giving rise to party struggles in
theatrical spheres, struggles in which the populace in the small
towns took part with passionate zeal.   The trouble became still
greater when the political prosecutions began.   Thenceforward

theatrical criticism remained the only domain in which the pens
of the newspaper writers could run freely, for Count Bernstorff, the minister of state, said " the snappish dogs must be
left at least one bone to worry ! "

There were but two poets of this epoch who succeeded in
enriching the theatre with works at once suitable for the stage
and possessed of permanent artistic value.   These were the first
two Austrians since the Thirty Years' War to win for themselves
an honourable place in the history of German poesy.   Just as,
long ago in the thirteenth century, the remote lands of the
Danube had fortunately preserved the ancient German national
epic, when the rest of Germany had long turned already to
knightly poetry, so now these same regions had remained almost
untouched by the wealth of thought, but untouched also by
the errors of the doctrinaire over-refinement of our literary
revolution.   When now at length a few fine intelligences in
Austria became aware of the world of new ideas which had been
opened up in Germany, they occupied a position of fortunate
freedom in relation to the catchwords of our literary parties.
From a distance, more unrestrainedly than the Germans in the
German realm, they could discover that which was genuine and
great in the powerful movement.   Their public was one which
loved spectacles and was gratefully receptive, a public whose
naive and vigorous sensuality had not yet been corrupted by
learned criticism.   They had also before their eyes the fine
example of the great musicians of Austria, who all held in honour
the golden soil of handicraft, and who did not think themselves
too good to work straightforwardly for the stage.

It was just at this time that the Burgtheater, under the
skilful management of Schreyvogel, began to outsoar all the
theatres of Germany.   Here the Viennese learned to know the
finest dramas of Germany, presented artistically and yet simply ;
the admirable dramaturge knew so well how to bring even foreign
works near to the German spirit by clever .adaptation, that such
a play as Moreto's *Donna Diana* seemed almost as homelike to
the audience as a native comedy.   Here there was no field for
subtle artificiality.   The result was that even Franz Grillparzer
was infected, on one occasion only, by the theoretical priggishness
of German romanticism.   His first work, *Die Ahnfrau*, was a

fate-tragedy ; the tragical issue arose, not out of the free activity of the hero, but from " intimately concealed and obscure powers." But the beauty of the language and the ardour of the passion, the stormy progress of the action, and the remarkable and precocious security of the technique, make us almost forget the perversity of the fundamental idea.   Soon, too, the sound sense of the poet broke completely loose from the fetters of the artistic theories of Müllner.   In his tragedies *Sappho* and *Das goldene Vliess* there were displayed   purity   of   form,   precision   of   character-drawing, German seriousness, and the fine and truthful sensuality of the old Austrians—a happy fusion of classic and of romantic ideals.   To   him,   henceforward,   Goethe   remained   the   master beloved with childish veneration, and Weimar the consecrated focus of German life.   In the historical dramas of a later period of his activity, Grillparzer created nothing greater than the elemental character of Medea in *Das goldene Vliess* ; notwith-standing his high artistic diligence he was denied continuous development.   Not his one of those mighty spirits which in irresistible progress gradually come to illumine wider and ever wider circles of the world with the light of their ideas ; but his was an amiable and modest artist's nature, he was a true poet, who, even in the days of the decadence, preserved with invaluable loyalty the traditional ancient principles of dramatic idealism, and was the worthy herald of the new German poetry in Austria.

Soon   afterwards   another   Austrian,   Ferdinand   Raimund, conquered a new domain for German dramatic art.   For years, upon the boards of the Leopoldstadt theatre, he had delighted the audience by his masterly acting as a comedian ; and when now in all modesty he devoted himself to providing his little stage with new matter elaborated by himself, he did not produce, as have done the majority of actor-playwrights, pieces carefully designed to draw a full house and possessing grateful roles, but created works of national art.   He was the originator of the new fairy extravaganza, and since the days of Hans Sachs was the first German poet who really understood how to enthral the whole population with the stage, and who delighted the masses by poetic works in which even cultured persons could take cordial pleasure for a time.   In this child of Vienna, the delight in telling stories was inborn ; from the medley of folk-life he drew his

merry figures, having an inexhaustible supply of those genial
jests and foolish conceits which the Austrians and the Upper
Saxons are accustomed to greet with the delighted exclamation,
" Look here, that is really *too* absurd ! " But behind the unrestrained and sportive action, there was the half-hidden humour
of a profound disposition smiling through tears. How firmly,
too, was the ancient German moral idealism still established in
those blameless days of social peace ! Raimund continually
returned to the question of what is the true happiness of life,
which to the oppressed man of the common people remains the
highest of all moral problems ; and ever and again, whether he
was representing the spendthrift, the misanthrope, or the peasant
as millionaire, he allowed the audience to perceive that happiness
is to be found only in peace of the soul. The masses believed
him ; the old German folk-songs extolling cheerful poverty had
not yet been forgotten. Among the numerous imitators of the
unpretentious folk-poet none came near to the master. The folk-
comedy rapidly became brutalised ; pithy bluntness degenerated
into slovenliness, kindly wit became tedious punning, ingenuous
simplicity sank to dulness. It was not until a much later period,
during an epoch of embittered political and social struggles,
that in North Germany a new form of farce came into existence,
which in wit and incisiveness excelled these innocent fairy-tales
just as much as it was inferior to them in humour and poetic
content.

As far as narrative poetry was concerned, the insatiable
passion for writing and reading characteristic of the epoch
became a source of severe temptation. Never before had so
vast a number of busy pens been simultaneously at work in
all branches of literature. The catalogue of the books which the
Leipzig booksellers had on sale at the fair, swelled to become a
volume of inconvenient size. In every town a lending library
provided for the needs of the reading public. The customs
characteristic of an old-established prosperity could not yet
become developed in this impoverished land ; the Germans found
no shame in the fact that they read more and bought fewer books
than any other people. Nevertheless certain works already
secured a sale which was unheard-of according to the ideas of

the old times : for instance, Rotteck's *Allgemeine Weltgeschichte*, Zschokke's *Stunden der Andacht*, and the translations of Walter Scott's novels. In the year 1817, Friedrich König, the inventor of the cylinder-press, returned home, and at Oberzell near Würzburg founded his great printing establishment which rendered it possible for the book-trade to work for the needs of the masses. Since people gradually became accustomed to accept greedily every novelty in the domain of science and art, discontent was soon felt with the simple classical education upon whose fruitful soil the new German civilisation had flourished. No longer did it suffice to give the mind a strictly formal culture, rendering it possible, starting from a narrow circle of well-secured knowledge, to develop gradually, but freely and continuously, and to acquire new knowledge through independent work. Under the high-sounding name of " realistic culture," there was now demanded a variegated abundance of disconnected memoranda, which might enable everyone to converse about everything. People were ashamed of the frank admission of ignorance ; no one wished to remain in the background when conversation flitted rapidly from the fate-tragedy to the Spanish constitution or from phrenology to the new English steam-engine.

The alert F. A. Brockhaus, with the secure insight of the experienced bookseller, noted this powerful impulse of the time, and from the year 1818 onwards engaged in the elaboration of an older and hitherto little noticed compilation, to constitute a great encyclopædia which, in a convenient alphabetic arrangement, placed at the disposal of cultured Germans " all that it was desirable to know." This was the beginning of that gigantic *pons asinorum* literature which distinguished the nineteenth century, by no means to its advantage. The undertaking, which was as un-German as its name (*Konversationslexikon*), none the less found acceptance in wide circles, and there speedily followed numerous imitations ; this generation, burdened with the heritage of so many centuries, could no longer get along without such crutches. Neibuhr watched with unconcealed disgust the transformation which was gradually taking place in national customs ; he foresaw how uneasy, empty-headed, and desultory, how dependent in its modes of thought, the modern world must become, if the empty arrogance of half knowledge and of polymathy, if the desire for continually changing impressions, should get the upper hand. In a world so fond of reading, a refined sense of form speedily became blunted. What was desired above all was material stimulation, and since every epoch has the authors which it demands and deserves, there was to be found an army of ͵busy romance writers satisfied to provide for the needs of the moment, and to have their names current for a few years in the critical periodicals. It remained henceforward a distinctive characteristic of the new century that works of true poetry lay, like isolated nuggets, dispersed throughout a colossal rubbish-heap of worthless light literature, and that they were discovered only after a considerable time amid the masses of inferior matter. In those unpretentious days, however, it was not, as in our own time, the money-making impulse which led so many interlopers to the German Parnassus ; it was as a rule vanity and literary fashion. Just as in the drama, so also in the field of romance and novel-writing, those of a truly poetic nature seldom displayed a talent for composition, whilst the virtuosi of absorbing and fascinating narrative just as rarely exhibited the formative energy of the poet.

In consequence of the stern realism of the war, that lachrymose sentimentality which had before been chiefly nourished by the writings of Jean Paul, had for a brief period been forced into the background. Now, however, it regained its sway ; in many of the houses of North Germany there prevailed a tasteless, sickly-sweet tone. Many vigorous men of the present generation who grew up in this sentimental atmosphere were filled thereby with such loathing that throughout life they earnestly avoided every expression of aroused sensibilities. The insipid scribbler H. Clauren was the writer best suited to the taste of the great reading public. Fashionable ladies delighted in the heavenly steel engravings and the moving novelettes of the pocket-companions which were then in fashion : " Urania," " Aurora," " Alpine Roses," " Forget-me-Not," or " Evergreen," stood upon the title-page of the elegant gilt-edged volumes. Upper Saxony, which in former days had so often intervened decisively in the mental development of the nation through the activities of vigorous reforming spirits, was for some decades the principal seat of this light literature ; it was as if the " Gottshed-Weisse-

Gellert flood " once mocked at by the young Goethe, had
again broken over the beautiful country. In Dresden, Friedrich
Kind and Theodor Hell, with a few other equally meek and
gentle poets, met weekly at a " poets' tea," displaying for mutual
admiration and regarding with invincible mutual politeness their
dull novels, which were worthy of the Chinese beverage—novels
that were then published in the widely-read *Abendzeitung.* Carl
Böttiger, most prolific of critics, then hastened, as Goethe said,
" to hail as masterpieces the pap of these bunglers and scrawlers."

Ludwig Tieck, who had also removed to the charming town
on the Elbe, distinguished himself by holding aloof from this
void activity. It was plain to him that the mysterious " poesy
of poesy," upon which the romanticists prided themselves,
was essentially nothing more than ingenious connoisseurship.
Although his admirers ranked him immediately after Goethe,
he was numbered among those who *are* rather than *do.* Since in
these days he was but rarely seized with the overwhelming
creative impulse of the poet, he threw himself with a fine zeal,
and with his highly-praised " powers of rapid perception," into
the study of the Shakespearian drama. What he effected by
word of mouth, and by his pen, in the elucidation and imitation
of the great Englishman, was in reality more fruitful for German
life than were the shapeless romances and the literary-satirical
dramatised tales of his youth, which failed to appear as the
ingenuous children of fancy, precisely because they themselves
declared with conscious intention that " they were completely
unreasonable." How many youthful poets and dramatists
gained their first inkling of the true nature of art in the old house
in the Altmarkt, when the poet, in his celebrated evening read-
ings, displayed to his hearers, with a truly sympathetic energy,
the whole world of Shakespeare's figures in all their abundant
vitality. Tieck early attained celebrity, and while still in his
prime was regarded as a patriarch of German poetry. The
paralytic man with the clear eyes of the poet received good-
naturedly and with sympathetic understanding the young men
who came to him on pilgrimage, and although his inspired words
now and again conveyed strange impressions, his gaze remained
ever directed towards the altitudes of humanity ; again and
again he referred his young admirers to the sacred four, the

masters of the new art—Dante, Cervantes, Shakespeare, and
Goethe. It was not until after many years that he himself
resumed the writing of poetry. Even more than Tieck had the
brothers Schlegel become estranged from poetic creation.
Friedrich Schlegel was completely immersed in the intrigues of
ultramontane policy. August Wilhelm Schlegel pursued his
historical and philological studies in Bonn, an ornament of the
new Rhenish university ; the small foppish old gentleman was
always venerated by the students as the representative of a
prolific epoch which had given birth to the new science.

It was only in the young poets who had formerly assembled
in Heidelberg that the poetic vein did not run dry. No one had
wandered farther into the labyrinths of the romantic dream-life
than had Clemens Brentano. Half rogue, half enthusiast, to-day
high-spirited to the verge of insanity, to-morrow crushed and
contrite, a riddle to himself and to the world, the restless man
now wandered from one town to another in the Catholic south,
and now turned up in Berlin in order to read to the brothers
Gerlach and to the other Christo-Germanic members of the
Maikäfer-Gesellschaft his essay upon the philistines, the audacious
declaration of war of the romanticists against the world of
reality. He greeted the War of Liberation with loud rejoicing,
but just as little as Zacharias Werner could he accommodate
himself to the North German Protestant tone of the movement ;
how strangely forced and artificial seemed his war poems, mostly
written for the glorification of Austria :

> Through God and thee, Francis, 'tis shown,
> What Austria wills, she can do !

Subsequently his mystical tendency led him into vulgar superstition ; he spent several years by the sick-bed of the stigmatised
nun of Dulmen, and recorded his observations upon the miraculous
woman in ecstatic writings. And yet the serene, heavenly light
of poetry again and again made its way through the mists in
which his sick spirit was enveloped. Hardly had he finished
giving free rein to his distorted fancy in the wild fantasia of
Die Gründung Prags, an unhappy imitation of Kleist's *Penthe-
silea*, when he pulled himself together, and actually succeeded in

doing that which men of learning had hitherto vainly demanded of romanticism—in producing popular matter in a popular form. He created his masterpiece, *Geschichte vom braven Kaspar und dem schönen Annerl*, the prototype of German village stories. With perfect justice Freiligrath subsequently praised him in the following words : " Well did Brentano know the feelings of the lowly. No other writer has described so frankly and faithfully that which gives its simple greatness to the mental life of the common people—the pent-up energy of untutored passion, vainly struggling for expression and then suddenly breaking out into consuming flame." No less unequal remained Brentano's activities in subsequent years. The romanticist epicures admired his story of the barn-door fowls, Gockel, Hinkel, and Gackeleia ; they could not prize enough the way in which here an artificial conceit was hunted to death, the way in which the life of fowls and the life of human beings were confused one with another in childish sportiveness. Meanwhile, in his better hours, he wrote his *Märchen*, valuable stories of Father Rhine ; of the nixies, and of the crystal castle down beneath the green waters, pictures displaying roguish charm, as dreamily lovable as the Rhenish summer night.

The far stronger and clearer spirit of his friend Achim von Arnim found no satisfaction in the world of fable. At an earlier date, in *Gräfin Dolores*, Arnim had manifested high realistic talent ; now, in his romance *Die Kronenwächter*, he ventured on to the high seas of historic life, vigorously incorporating with his energetic and invincible realism the figures of German antiquity, displaying all the racy frankness, the rough sensuality of old Germany, the uncultivated rudeness of its camp morals, and the disputatiously defiant spirit of the burghers of its imperial towns, showing these to his readers sharply and clearly, like the figures of Dürer's wood-cuts. Yet even to this favoured disciple of the romanticist school there was denied that orderly artist-sense which controls the abundance of the matter. In his romances, the simple and the rare pass immediately into one another without transition, as in life ; the narrative is choked by a thick brambly growth of episodes ; sometimes the writer loses all interest, and sweeps the figures from the board like an impatient chess-player. Despite all its greatness of thought and all its depth of feeling, his work lacks the balance and the unity of the highest art.

Far greater approval was secured among the mass of the reading world by Amadeus Hoffmann, the only novel writer who in fertility and resource could compete with the busy little writers of the pocket-companions. In his extraordinary double life was incorporated the contradictory romanticist morality, which wantonly broke down every bridge between the ideal and the real, and disdained on principle the use of art to glorify life. When he had spent the day in cross-examining the arrested demagogues and in the conscientious and thorough study of the criminal records of the Court of Appeal, the time came with the evening for the sun of his dream-world to rise. Not a word then must any longer remind him of the phantasmagoria of life, then he passed his time carousing with merry intimates or extemporising with musical friends. Thus inspired, he wrote fantasies after the manner of Callot, such as *Die Elixiere des Teufels*, and *Die Nachtstücke*, weird stories of demons and spectres, of dreams and wonders, of madness and crime—the most uncanny ever produced by an over-wrought imagination. It was as if the devil-faced gargoyles had descended from the gutters of our ancient cathedrals. The hideous spectre came so threateningly close, was so plainly perceptible to the senses, that the reader, as if paralysed by a nightmare, was spellbound, accepting everything presented by the bold humour and the diabolical charm of the masterly story-teller. Yet ultimately of the crazy sport nothing remained but the dull numbness of physical terror.

Whilst in the fields of drama and romance so much that was impish was pursuing its restless activities, the lyrical poetry of romanticism attained perfection in Ludwig Uhland. When his poems were published in the year 1814, the matter-of-fact man was ignored by the critics of this school. This worthy petty-bourgeois seemed the very antithesis of the romanticist itch for genius. In Paris he passed his days in diligent study of the manuscripts of old French poetry, spending his evenings silently pacing the boulevards in the company of the no less silent Immanuel Bekker, mouth open and eyes closed, quite unaffected by the alluring brilliancy and the temptations by which he was surrounded. Subsequently leading a simple and well ordered life in his native town on the Neckar, he did not think himself too good to participate in word and action in the prosaic constitutional struggles of Würtemberg. Yet it was precisely this healthy naturalness and bourgeois efficiency which enabled the Swabian poet to keep wisely within the limits of artistic form, and to provide for romanticist ideals a lively configuration which was in harmony with the consciousness of the age. A thoughtful artist, he remained completely indifferent to the literary disputes and æsthetic doctrines of the schools, waiting patiently for the coming of the time of poetic ecstasy which brought to him the blessing of song. He then applied inexorably to his own works the critical acumen which other poets dissipated in the literary newspapers; alone among German writers he exhibited an inflexible artist's pride in retaining in his desk all that was half finished or half successful. His poetic energies were first awakened by the heroic figures of our ancient poetry, by Walther von der Vogelweide, and by those in the *Nibelungenlied*. In the poems of antiquity he deplored the absence of the profound background which allures the fancy into the distances, but an inborn and strictly schooled sense of form preserved him from the obscure exuberance of mediæval poetry. This classicist of romanticism presents his figures to our minds in firm and secure lineaments.

Whereas the earlier romanticists were for the most part attracted to the German primæval age by the fantastic stimulus of the strange and of the antique, what Uhland sought in the past was the purely human, that which was ever living, and above all that which was homely—the simple energy and cordiality of the uncultured Teutonic nature. To him the study of the sagas and songs of old Germany seemed " a real migration into the profounder nature of German folk-life." He felt that the poet, when dealing with matter belonging to a remote period, must give expression to such sensations only as will find an echo in the souls of his contemporaries, and he remained ever clearly conscious of the wide separation between the ages. Never did his delight in the multi-coloured beauties of the middle ages estrange him from the Protestant and democratic ideas of the new century. The same poet who sang so movingly of the

heroes of the crusades, sang also with enthusiasm of the Tree
of Wittenberg, which, with giant branches thrusting upward
towards the light, grew through the roof of the monk's cell ; he
gladly associated himself, too, with the martial singers of the
War of Liberation, and bowed himself humbly before the heroic
greatness of the new-risen fatherland :

> " After such heroic sacrifices
> What are these songs worth to thee ? "

With vigorous scorn he turned his back upon the pseudo-
muse of the sugary romanticist masters, of the tricksters with
assonance, and of the sonneteers, holding firmly to the saying
of the earliest writers, " Plain speaking and good feeling make
the true German song." Vivid popular expressions streamed
spontaneously forth from this master of vigorous language. So
easily did his unaffected verses seem to run, so freshly and
serenely did his figures move, that readers failed to notice how
much artist's diligence was concealed behind the purity of these
simple forms, how deeply the poet had had to explore the
wells of knowledge before Roland and Taillefer, Eberhard der
Rauschebart, and Schenk von Limburg could be presented in so
familiar and convincing a manner. He chose by preference for his
narratives the form of the dramatic ballad, so well suited to the
passionate Teuton temperament; on rare occasions, where the
nature of the matter demanded it, he employed the quietly-record-
ing minutely-descriptive southland romance form. It was not
detail which seemed to him important, but its reflection in the
aroused human heart. The most intimate recesses of the
German temperament lay open to him, and with extraordinary
success at times, in a few unpretentious words, he was able to
disclose some intimate secret of our people. More simply than
in the poem of *Der gute Kamarad* there has never been given
an account of the way in which the contentious Teutons have
always been ready for the fray, from the days of the Cimbri to
the days of the French wars—eager for battle and devotedly
pious, so kind hearted and so loyal.

Even in his narrative verses the power of sentiment was so
strongly displayed that many poems which he himself termed

ballads soon became popular as songs. It was on account of his songs in especial that he was beloved of the ˙people, who hailed him joyfully, at first in his Swabian home, and afterwards throughout Germany, so that he ultimately became the most popular of all our great poets. In the straightforward, profoundly felt words describing the joys and the sorrows of love, the happiness of the wanderer and the pain of parting, the pleasures of wine and of arms, everyone, whether gentle or simple, rediscovered memories of his own life. The High Germans, more particularly, were reminded of home when from between the lines of the poems there always seemed to greet them the Swabian land with its vine-clad hills and sunny rivers, with its cheerful and song-loving inhabitants. The simple strains, resembling those of folk-songs, involuntarily challenged the reader to sing them ; before long, composers rivalled one another in setting them to music. All the youth of the land followed suit. Uhland's songs were heard wherever German soldiers were marching, wherever students, singers, and gymnasts, assembled in happy festival ; they became a power of blessing in the freshly blossoming and vigorous folk-life of the new century. The younger generation, steeled in war, pressed forth from the imprisoned chamber air of the good old time, forth into freedom ; the German *wanderlust* demanded its rights ; old and half forgotten popular festivals were once again honoured. The new folk-songs threw a bridge across the deep chasm which separated the cultured from the uncultured, and led the masses, who read nothing, for the first time to an appreciation of the poetry of their own day. Even though that priceless unbroken unity of national civilisation which had once existed in the days of the Hohenstaufen remained ever unattainable to the learned culture of the modern world, there nevertheless ensued a wholesome return to nature, so that by degrees a portion at least of the finest German poems became dear to the whole nation and comprehensible to all. How fast beat the heart of the Swabian poet when he saw the joy of song newly awakening among his people ; full of confidence he issued to his comrades the spirited exhortation :

" Sing who can, your song forth-giving
    In German poets' forest-ground !
Rejoicing all and truly living,
    When songs from every twig resound ! "

The homely man could never have too much of the noisy
thronging of popular festivals, and he secured at times the
highest reward of the poet when upon a journey in the Rhineland he came by chance in the forest upon young people singing
his own songs with their clear voices ; or when a senior
student of Tübingen was taking ceremonial departure across
the Neckar bridge, and the parting song *Es ziehet der Bursch in
die Weite* reverberated as far as the vineyard of the poet's house
on the Oesterberg.

It is true that his poems embraced a comparatively narrow
circle of ideas ; he sang, as had formerly sung the knightly poet
with the golden harp, almost exclusively of "God's love, of the
hero's courage, of the gentleness of love, of the sweet may-
blossom." In his tragedies, too, he preferred to extol the
tenacious loyalty of ancient German friendship ; his plays lack
the compelling force of dramatic passion. His patriotic poems
do not attain to the vigorous political emotion of his favourite
Walther von der Vogelweide ; the fine Promethean impulse to
fathom the highest problem of existence, the whence and whither
of mankind, rarely touched his peaceful imagination. For this
reason, Goethe would hear nothing of the roses and the wall-
flowers, the blond maidens and mournful knights, of the Swabian
singer ; he failed to recognise that in the writing of songs and
ballads no one rivalled him so nearly as did Uhland, and he
expressed the acrimonious view that in all this there was nothing
which went to the fashioning of human destiny. The Germans,
however, had long before tacitly conspired to follow the old
master's own precepts, saying to themselves, if I love you that
is my own affair. The faithful Swabian knew how impossible
it is to convince a master of his error. His own love was
unaffected by the old man's injustice. He was never weary of
sending Goethe his poet's greeting, and of telling the nation
how, long ago, in the golden springtime this king's son had

awakened the sleeping princess of German poesy, and how the
sculptured foliage of Strasburg cathedral once rustled when the
young poet mounted the winding stair of the tower—" the poet
who now for half a century has been singing the world of the
beautiful."

Although after the age of thirty the taciturn man published
few and isolated poems, and was content as a talented investigator and collector to participate in the great work of the
rediscovery of our primæval age, his reputation as a poet nevertheless continued to increase from year to year. The songs of
his youth could never grow old. Highly cultured and yet
inconspicuous ; an enthusiast for the ancient glories of the
empire and of the Austrian imperial race, and yet a democrat,
to whom " the princes' counsellors and court chamberlains
decorated with dull stars upon their cold bosoms " always
remained objects of suspicion ; in the political struggle fearless
and loyal, as the motto on the national coat-of-arms demands,
to the point of defiant obstinacy—he seemed to the Swabians
the typical representative of his country, the best of the tribal
fellowship. They revered him, declaring : " Every word which
Uhland has spoken has been justified by the event."

A crowd of young poets followed in the master's footsteps,
and soon came to speak of itself as the Swabian school of poets.
Here for the first time in the history of modern German poetry
was the attempt ventured at the foundation of a separate territorial culture, taking, however, the form of a perfectly harmless
particularism. Nothing was further from the mind of these
poets than the intention to cut themselves adrift from the
common work of the nation ; they merely felt cordially happy
and proud because they belonged to this cheerful land of wine
and song, to this stock which had once borne the war-standard
of the Holy Empire, and which was more intimately associated
than any other with the great memories of our middle age.
Amiable serenity and natural freshness were characteristic of
the countless ballads and songs of these poets, they remained
German and chaste, and continued to preserve the pure forms
of lyrical poetry even at a later date when the new cosmopolitan
revolutionary spirit, disturbing nobility of artistic form and
innocence of mind, invaded German poetry. Yet the marvellous

poetical mood of the songs of Uhland was as inimitable as was the roguish humour which enabled him to depict so happily the valiant spirit of the German heroic age. Many of the Swabian ballad-singers gradually lapsed into the rhymed prose of the meistersingers ; their dull amiability could offer no ideas to the new century.

Meanwhile the nation first began fully to understand what it possessed in its greatest poet. Ever more powerfully and commandingly did the figure of Goethe rise before their eyes, as the excitement of the war time passed away, and as the three first parts of *Dichtung und Wahrheit,* which were published during the years of 1811 to 1814, gradually made their way through wider circles. Among the autobiographies of notable men, this book occupies as isolated a position as does *Faust* in the realm of poetry. Since St. Augustine's *Confessions,* no auto-biographical work had described so profoundly, so truthfully, and so powerfully the most beautiful secret of human life, the growth of genius. To the severe saint, the forms of the life of this world seemed to disappear completely in face of the crushing thought of the sinfulness of all creatures, and in face of the yearning after the living God ; but through *Dichtung und Wahrheit* there breathes the spirit of a poet who finds joy in this world, who endeavours to contemplate eternal love in the abundant life of creation, and who from the highest flights of thought returns ever to the simple faith of the artist : " What can be the use of all this array of suns and planets and moons, of stars and milky ways, of comets and nebulæ, of worlds that have been and worlds that are yet to be, if in the end a happy man is not instinctively to rejoice in its existence ? " As honestly as had Rousseau, Goethe recognised the faults and errors of his youth ; but his secure sense of style preserved him from Rousseau's forced and artificial outspokenness which led the Genevese author into shamelessness. Goethe did not, like Rousseau, lay bare even those half-unconscious and contradictory surgings of sentiment which are endurable only because they are fugitive, and which when subjected to detailed analysis appear grotesque, but gave merely the important essentials of his life, relating how he had become a poet.

Whilst of Rousseau's *Confessions* there remains in the end

nothing more than the painful recognition of the sinfulness of man, who oscillates unsupported between his archetype and his caricature, between God and beast, the readers of *Dichtung und Wahrheit* attain to the happy feeling that the German writer has in a twofold sense succeeded in doing what Milton once demanded of the poet, namely, in transfiguring his own life to make it a true work of art. Just as he had inherited talent from his mother and character from his father, and now little by little, but with unequalled steadfastness, diffused his energies throughout the entire domain of human contemplation, imagination, and cognition, so at each stage of his development, did his spirit appear healthy, exemplary, accordant with nature, and therewith extraordinarily simple in all its wonderful transformations. The talented Fanny Mendelssohn expressed the feeling of all readers when she prophesied : " God will not summon this man home prematurely ; he must remain on earth until he has attained an advanced age, and must show his people what living means." Reverence for Goethe was a bond of unity between the best men of this distracted nation ; the higher the culture of any German, the more profoundly did he venerate the poet. The tone of the book manifested the feeling which Goethe had once expressed in youth : that he would not have been astonished if people had placed a crown upon his head. Yet he stood far too high to be tainted by those involuntary tendencies to self-conceit which are found in almost all confessions. The mighty self-consciousness which found expression in these memoirs was the serene repose of a spirit perfectly at one with itself, the happy frankness of a poet who all his life had been engaged in writing nothing but confessions, and who had long been accustomed to answer censorious and envious spirits by saying : " I did not make myself."

Whenever he had intervened in German life he had furnished the highest. Now, too, the figures which he conjured out of memory were illuminated by a spiritual warmth which can be paralleled only by that of the finest of his own free imaginary figures. From the parsonage of Sesenheim there shone a ray of love penetrating the youthful dreams of every German heart, and whoever recalled the happy days of his own childhood, instantly pictured the rambling old house in the

Hirschgraben, the fountain in the courtyard, saw and looked into the deep laughing eyes of Goethe's joyous mother. The poet said in the words of his own old man : " We wander among the shades in the form in which we have left earth." To him another destiny was allotted, for so enthralling was the charm of this book that even to-day when Goethe is named almost everyone thinks first of the kingly youth ; his years of manhood, which he did not himself describe for us, are in the shade when contrasted with the sunshine of these early days of his history.

Just as Rousseau intertwined contemporary history with the narrative of his life, so Goethe, with incomparably greater profundity and thoroughness, gave a comprehensive historical picture of the spiritual life of the Frederician age. Flaming up once more in youthful fire, the old man described the springtime of German art, filled with joyful hopes, described how everything was germinating and pressing upward, how the fresh aroma of the soil filled the atmosphere as it arose from the freshly tilled fields, how one tree stood bare beside another which had already burst forth into leaf. How often had Niebuhr and other contemporaries of Goethe refused to admit that the poet possessed the historic sense, taking this view because he was so fond of immersing himself in nature. Now, however, he performed the two highest tasks of the historian, the artistic and the scientific, showing by his work that the two are one. So vividly did he recall the past for his readers that they all felt as if they were themselves living among the events described, and yet at the same time he enabled them to understand what had happened, to recognise the necessary sequence of events. The work was composed in the days of the Napoleonic world-dominion, at a time when the writer seemed to despair of the political re-establishment of the fatherland ; and yet from every sentence there spoke the confident and hopeful mood of the Frederician epoch. Not a word showed that after the recent defeats the poet had abandoned faith in Germany's great future. Even now, when all the world gave up the Prussian state for lost, and when even the Teutonising enthusiasts turned away with indifference from the image of Frederick, Goethe showed for the first time in stirring words how intimately the new art was

associated with the heroic glories of Prussia : in Germany there
had never been a lack of talented men, but a national strength,
a veritable content, was first given to our imaginative life by
the deeds of Frederick.   Thus the poet had never inwardly
become unfaithful to his nation. He said once in those weary days
that there now remained only one sacred duty, to maintain
spiritual mastery, and amid the general ruin to preserve the
palladium of our literature !

It was a terrible misfortune that Goethe had absolutely no
confidence in the awakening political life of the nation.   Painfully enough did he experience the truth of his own saying, that
the poet is by nature unpartisan, and therefore in times of
political passion can hardly escape a tragical fate.   At times,
indeed, he had intimations of a happier future.   When the
grande armée passed through on the way to Russia, and those who
were disheartened expressed the opinion that now the world-
empire had gained completion, he rejoined, " Wait a while, and
see how many of them will return ! "   Yet when there did
indeed return no more than pitiable remnants of the innumerable
host, and when the Prussian nation arose like one man, the
poet   shuddered   at   the   rough   enthusiasms   of   the   " undisciplined volunteers."   He never forgot how little the Germans
had in former days understood the lofty patriotic sentiments of
Hermann und Dorothea, and he did not believe that his fellow-
countrymen possessed the enduring energy of political will.
From   the   first   he   had   exchanged   ideas   with   the   ancient
civilisation of the west, and now contemplated with sinister
forebodings the passage of the peoples of the east across the
peaceful land of Central Germany, the coming of the " Cossacks,
Croats, Cassubians, and Samlanders, brown and other hussars."
He strictly forbade his son to join the army of the allies, and
had then to suffer the experience of seeing the passionate youth,
ashamed and desperate, undergo a sudden change of sentiments
which led him to display in his father's house an idolatrous
veneration for Napoleon.

Goethe unlocked a treasure-house of wisdom which
yielded the apt word for almost every vital problem of the
emotional life and of culture, a treasure-house which only the
present generation has learned to appreciate.   Many of the

poems of his old age recalled the cryptic runes of Teutonic antiquity over which the heroes might reflect and dream throughout life. At times he ventured into the ultimate mysterious profound of existence, up to the very limits of the expressible, where the articulate word becomes dumb and music takes its place—as for instance in that marvellous song which ever resounds softly through the soul when a ray of heavenly happiness falls into our poor life :

> " Until thou too canst pass this test,
>   ' Dying, live again : '
> Art thou but a gloomy guest
>   On this earth of pain."

Thus he lived on in solitary greatness, unceasingly contemplating, collecting, investigating, writing, advancing through the finite in all directions in order to plumb the infinite, rejoicing in every bright day of the springtime and in every gift of the fruitful autumn, and rejoicing no less in every fresh work of art and in every new discovery in the wide domain of human knowledge. Schiller's more delicate frame had been prematurely worn out in the hard service of the Kantian conception of duty ; to the fortunate and thoroughly healthy nature of Goethe, his titanic and many-sided activities seemed merely the natural and easy unfolding of inborn energies. Those who were not in contact with him, hardly suspected how earnestly he had taken to heart his own severe words : " He only can work who always works ; soon comes the night wherein no one can work ! " Still less did they imagine what a firm faith in God sustained the notorious pagan throughout his old age, how carefully he guarded himself against forestalling Providence, and how in every chance occurrence of the day he recognised the immediate intervention of God—for thus only to the artist was the divine governance of the world conceivable. And since he himself continued to grow day by day, as if this life were never to come to an end, youth always remained especially dear to him. Even though the arrogant roughness of the younger generation was at times an offence to him, in the end he could not be angry when he looked into the ardent eyes of the inspired hotheads ; and he expressed the kindly sentiment that it would be foolish to demand of them, " Come, be an old man with me." To young poets he knew how to hand on the counsel which he had himself received from nature ; they should strive in the first place to become men rich alike in heart and in head, and should keep their minds open to every breath of the times. " The content of poetry is the content of one's own life ; we must advance continually with advancing years, and must examine ourselves from time to time to make sure that we are really alive ! "

Certain zealous renegades, such as Friedrich Schlegel, ventured to speak of the overthrown old god, but men of nobler nature knew that to attack this man was to abuse the nation itself. When Baron von Stein complained of Goethe's holding back in the Napoleonic days, he added modestly, " But after all the man is too great to find fault with." Nowhere had the poet warmer admirers than among intelligent circles in Berlin. Here the veneration of Goethe became a cult ; the ever-enthusiastic high-priestess Rahel Varnhagen continually announced in oracular speeches the fame of the divine poet. The old man regarded from a distance, and with equanimity, the clouds of incense which arose before his altar on the Spree, and from time to time, in his formal, privy councillor's style vouchsafed a civil answer. But he would not permit these worshippers to draw nearer to his person ; he felt that they were making a pretentious doctrine of that which nature had granted to him in the cradle. In the bosom of the elvish little Rahel there beat a grateful, pious, and kindly heart ; amid the artificial ecstasy of this dilettantist adept and demi-artist there was still preserved a woman's secure sense of what is great and strong ; at one time, and for many years, Fichte had been her idol as well as Goethe. But side by side with such amiable characteristics she exhibited a half unconscious and for that very reason immeasurable vanity, so that her admiration for the greatest of German poets was in effect no more than a source of egoistic personal gratification ; she consoled herself for her secret sense of barrenness with the sublime thought that the great spirit of Goethe, reaching out towards the infinite, had scorned to confine its energies within the domain of philology ! " Why should I not be natural," she asked naively, " I could gain nothing better or more manifold by affectation ? " Yet how little real content was there in all the cultured conversation of this æsthetic tea-drinking circle. Much which was there spoken of as talent depended in essentials upon nothing more than the misuse of the German speech, upon the preposterous apposition of unsuitable words. When Rahel spoke of a nobly conceived and ardently executed piece of music as " ein gebildeter Sturmwind," the circle of priests of the higher culture shouted with delight, and her husband inscribed the foolish phrase in his diary in his most beautiful script. But the old hero in Weimar knew the great gulf that is fixed between knowing and doing. Where among his admirers he encountered creative faculty, he was not slow to thaw. How fatherly was his attitude towards the wonder-child Felix Mendelssohn-Bartholdy ; he rejoiced with the happy parents over the magnificent combination of refined culture and genuine talent.

THE BURSCHENSCHAFT (III, 37–76)

How could the students remain quiet in this marvellously excited little world ? The great days of the Jena university had come to a close in the year 1803, and for long it had been impossible for Jena to compare with the intellectual forces of Heidelberg or Berlin ; but the glories of past days continued to cleave to the name, and the unrestrained liberty of Jena student life had always been renowned among the German youth. " And in Jenè live we benè " ran the old student's song. There was no other university town in which the dominance of the students was so complete ; as late as the seventeen-nineties they had on one occasion trooped out to remove to Erfurt, and returned in triumph when the alarmed authorities had yielded to all their wishes. Contrasting strongly with courtly Leipzig, life in Jena continued to exhibit a rough, primitive, and youthful tone, in correspondence with the simple customs of the country. Just as the Ziegenhain cudgel, at that time the inseparable companion of the German student, was to be obtained in perfection only from the Saale valley, so also the pithy Jena regulations were highly esteemed in every students' club and duelling-place throughout Germany ; many extremely ancient customs of the Burschen, such as the drinking of blood-brotherhood, were continued in Jena on into the new century. All roughness notwithstanding, an atmosphere of idealism pervaded these noisy activities, a romantic

charm which was altogether lacking to the clumsy coarseness of
the Berlin gymnastic ground. How many a youthful Low
German, making his student's journey to the Fuchsturm and to
Leuchtenburg, had then first become conscious of the poesy
of the German highlands. With what gratitude and joyful
enthusiasm did the Jena students make first-hand acquaintance with Schiller's dramas in the Weimar theatre. Under the
foreign dominion, the university flaunted its German sentiments
undismayed, so that Napoleon was once on the point of burning
" the odious nest of ideologues and chatterers."

It was inevitable that this patriotic enthusiasm should flame
up more fiercely when the young warriors now returned to the
lecture theatre, many of them decorated with the iron cross,
almost all still intoxicated with the heroic fury of the great
struggle, filled with ardent hatred of " the external and internal
oppressors of the fatherland." This was by far the best generation of students that had been known for many years, but these
young men were unfortunately too serious for the harmless fantasies and the exaggerated friendships which endow student life
with its peculiar charm. The urgently necessary reform of disorderly student customs could be effected only by a generation
far more mature than had hitherto been the average of students,
but in two arduous campaigns these chivalrous young men had
had such profound experiences that they were unable to settle
down once more into the modest role of the pupil ; the danger of
arrogance and conceit, which was in any case in the atmosphere
of the day, was for them almost impossible to escape. Similar
tendencies to Christo-Germanic enthusiasm had once before
showed themselves at the universities, in the days of the literary
Sturm und Drang, when the young poets of the Hainbund were
devoted admirers of Klopstock's *Messiah* and of the heroes of
the Teutoburgerwald, and when they burned an effigy of Wieland,
the poet of sedentary life. What had then been the motive
impulse of a narrow circle was now common to thousands.

How contemptible must the corrupt club-life of the
students necessarily appear to the strict-living new generation,
hardened by campaigning. There still existed far too much of
the barbarism of the old bullying times, although the humanism of
the new literary culture had extended its refining influence even

over university customs. Intemperance and debauchery often
displayed themselves with a lack of restraint which to us of
to-day seems incredible ; gambling was practised everywhere,
even in the open street ; and the ineradicable German love of
brawling so far exceeded all reasonable measure that in the
summer of 1815 among the Jena students, three hundred and
fifty in number, there were one hundred and forty-seven duels
in a single week. The homely popular drinking songs and
travellers' songs of the tuneful days of old had almost disappeared,
and the students sang chiefly lewd ribaldry or the lachrymose
effusions of a dull sentimentalism which belonged to a far earlier
literary epoch. With the disappearance of the Rosicrucians and
other secret societies of the old century, there disappeared also
their spiritual kin, the students' orders. The associations of
students from the same province (*Landsmannschaften*), which
had since then been revived, jealously supervised their closed
recruiting grounds, being characterised by a paltry particularist
sentiment which arrogantly rejected everything that lacked the
true parochial flavour, destroying all vigorous self-respect by
the brutal fagging system (*Pennalismus*). The freshman must
not complain if an impoverished senior student should offer him
blood-brotherhood and an exchange of goods ; the freshman must
then give all that he had upon his person, his clothes, watch, and
money, in exchange for the beggarly effects of his patron. One
who graduated in such a school acquired the art of servility
towards those above and arrogance towards those below.

How often had Fichte, at first in Jena and subsequently in
Berlin, uttered vigorous protests against these disorderly practices. Among his faithful followers there was conceived as early
as the year 1811 the design of constituting a Burschenschaft or
association of German students. The philosopher approved the
undertaking ; but, knowing his men, added the thoughtful warning that the Burschen must avoid confusing what was mediæval
with what was German, and must be careful not to value the
means, namely the association, more highly than the end, namely
the revival of German sentiment. The students of Jena now
associated themselves with these proposals of Berlin. They
knew the seriousness of the profession of arms, and desired to
control the rude lust for quarrels by the institution of courts of

honour. During the war they had fought shoulder to shoulder
as the sons of a single nation, and they therefore demanded the
complete equality of all students, with the abolition of Pennalismus and of all the privileges which at many universities were
still allotted to the counts' bench. But their ultimate and highest
idea remained the unity of Germany : the power and the glory
of the fatherland were to be embodied in one vast league of youth,
which was to put an end to the existence of all the particularist
student societies.

Arndt's *Vaterlandslied* remained the true programme of the
Burschenschaft. Although the poet had taken no direct part
in the young people's designs, he was regarded by friend and
foe alike as the leader of the Teutonising youth. After a long
and tempestuous life of many migrations, he had at length settled
down in Bonn, and built for himself and his young wife, Schleiermacher's sister, a cottage amid a garden on the heights close to
the Rhine, expecting " to enjoy to the full the glories of the
Siebengebirge," and in peaceful happiness to store his energies
for his professional work. It is true that he was as cordially
enthusiastic as the youngest of the students in defence of " the
golden academic freedom, the ancient and glorious chivalry of the
Teutons " ; but when one of the Heidelberg students ques-
tioned him regarding the reform of university life, he expressly
warned his young friends, in his writing concerning the German
student-state, against revolutionary excesses, saying, " It is better
to allow that which exists to prevail than to strive after unattainable perfection." He had long adhered in loyal affection to
Prussia and its royal house, and it was only his old hostility
towards the Frederician age which he was unable to overcome.
Since he had long before vigorously advocated the abolition of
serfdom in his Hither Pomeranian home, his reputation among the
reactionary party had been that of a preacher of equality. This
reputation was utterly undeserved. Arndt's wishes never went
beyond the ideas of his patron Stein ; he wished for an effective
subdivision of classes into a respected nobility, a free peasantry,
and a vigorous bourgeoisie ranged in guilds ; and even Hardenberg's agrarian laws were regarded by him with a certain romanticist hostility.

There was no place for political fanaticism in this open and

serene nature, in the affectionate spirit of this man who could
only find adequate expression for the exuberance of his feelings
by the heaping up of superlatives. To extol as brethren " Father
Jahn and Father Arndt " was possible solely to the uncritical
faculties of youth, and nothing but Arndt's touching modesty
induced him to permit the comparison. In reality the two men
belonged to utterly different strata of intellectual and moral
culture. Although Arndt never acquired the strict methodology
of the trained expert, he had at his command an inexhaustible
treasury of well-secured knowledge, and moved freely upon
heights of human culture to which Jahn was hardly able to lift
his eyes. He often spoke of himself as a hardy countryman, and
as a pedestrian could compete with the best of the gymnasts ;
every day in summer he might be seen taking a long swim in the
Rhine, or at work in his garden, wearing a blue overall. But he
was also at home in society, and assured there of his position ;
all glances turned towards the robust little man with the flashing
blue eyes whenever he began to speak, for the charm of his conversation was irresistible, its flow always natural and energetic,
its substance always brilliant and noble. So thoroughly healthy
a mind could find little satisfaction in the coarse methods of the
gymnasts. He exhorted the students that Germans ought not
to draw their examples from among the rough Spartans or Romans.
" Ask yourselves ' were they happy ? did they make others
happy ? ' "

Among the Jena professors, Fries was the students' favourite ;
these young men who were enthusiasts for the ideas of Fichte
sat guilelessly at the feet of a teacher who had always been one
of Fichte's opponents. In Jena the new doctrine of Hegel was
still considered reactionary, and Fries maintained that it had
grown, not in the garden of knowledge, but upon the dunghill
of servility. Like Luden, Fries exercised far more influence as
a teacher than as a writer. To youthful enthusiasts it was agreeable that the good-humoured but muddle-headed · philosopher
should confusedly intermingle concepts with feelings, and should
thus resolve the moral world into a " sentimental broth," as Hegel
expressed it in a justly severe criticism. The students were
strengthened in their subjective arrogance when, in ambiguous
words, their ingenuous professor continually declared that a man

must remain true to his conviction even if all the world were against him. Fries's philosophy of history seemed to the young folk especially appropriate to the time. He understood how to compress all the wealth of history within the limits of a formal and scanty doctrinal scheme, which has since his day been reiterated by countless learned publicists, and among others by Gervinus. According to this formula: in the east, human life was dominated by religion; in classical antiquity, by beauty; in the Christian world, by intuition; but recently, since the Revolution, the development of popular rights had been the central factor of history—a thesis which unquestionably opened the door to all the impertinences of political dilettantism. Although it was the honourable intention of Fries to guard the students against passionate aberrations, he allowed himself to be moved to many incautious utterances, and ultimately had to experience what almost inevitably happens when the intimacy between professors and students becomes too close; he lost touch with his young friends (who, after all, did not confide everything to their teacher), and failed to notice how revolutionary a spirit was gradually gaining the upper hand.

At the outset, the sole political idea of the Jena Burschen was a vague patriotic sentiment. They were zealots on behalf of an abstract Germanism, such as had formerly been extolled in the *Addresses to the German Nation*, but they had absolutely no notion of the vivid Prussian sense of the state which animated Fichte in the evening of his days. All distinction between Prussia, Bavaria, and Saxony was to disappear in the single concept of Germanity; and since, among all the German states, no other possessed so firmly individualised a life as Prussia, these youthful dreamers, who were continually talking about the glories of the War of Liberation, nevertheless imperceptibly began to follow the same false road as the *Nemesis* and the *Isis*, and to overwhelm with accusations the state which almost single-handed had conducted the war.

Among the founders of the Burschenschaft there was but one Prussian, Massmann of Berlin, an upright young enthusiast of exceedingly mediocre mental endowments, the most confused intelligence among all the berserkers of Jahn's immediate circle. All the others were Thuringians, Mecklenburgers, Courlanders,

Hessians, Bavarian-Franconians, and for them, naturally, it was
easy to contemplate the disappearance of their native states in
a general Germany.   At the Prussian universities the Burschenschaft struck root very slowly, making its first appearance
in Berlin.   In Breslau its first adherents were the New Prussians
of Lusatia ; the Silesians were for a long time unwilling to admit
that to a genuine Teutoniser the state of Frederick the Great
could be of no more account than Bückeburg or Darmstadt.   The
men of Jena, on the other hand, and the revolutionists of Giessen,
who were the earliest adherents of the Burschenschaft movement,
did not merely condemn every justified sentiment of Prussian
self-satisfaction as " un-German Prussianism," but further did
not hesitate to erase from the history of the War of Liberation
all that was Prussian, all that gave that history life and colour.
The song-book of the Burschenschaft, A. Follen's *Free Voices of
Fresh Youth*, when reproducing all the beautiful war-songs which
recounted Prussia's fame, mutilated them in such a manner that
the name of Prussia did not appear in the whole collection.   In
Arndt's *Husarenlied*, Blucher no longer swore in the poet's original
words " to teach the Frenchman the Prussian way " ; now he
was to teach " the Old German " or " the most German " way.
Moreover, the leaders of the Burschenschaft had for the most part
served among Lützow's yagers, and had there, as members of a
" purely German volunteer force," become accustomed to regard
with contempt the Prussian army of the line, although this in
actual warfare had been so much more successful than themselves.   The result was that these enthusiasts for Germanism
were from the first almost as hostile as the gymnasts to the most
living force of our national unity.   It is easy to understand that
a childish belief in the infallible wisdom of " the people " and
a sentimental preference for republican forms were far more
prevalent among the students than among men of maturer years.
Like the majority of older liberals, the students desired representative institutions chiefly because they considered that the
mainsprings of particularism were to be found in the cabinets
alone.   It was Carl Sand's opinion that if only there existed a
constitution in every German land, there would no longer exist
Bavarians or Hanoverians, but only Germans !
    Yet during these first years of the movement there was little

trace of morbid over-excitement. Pretentious, indeed, was the aspect of the students in their extraordinary Christo-Germanic rig-out, biretta, sombre coat, and feminine collar ; nor was their appearance rendered more agreeable by the adoption of the new customs of the gymnasts which soon made their way to Jena. But beneath the rough husk was a sound kernel. Greatly astonished were the authorities when the continuous warfare against university discipline, a warfare which had ever been the pride of the Landsmannschaften, now ceased of a sudden ; and how much more refined became the whole tone of academic life when the songs of Arndt and Schenkendorf were heard at the drinking parties, and when a number of youthful poets, and especially Binzer of Holstein, were continually writing new and vigorous students' songs. Almost all the serious songs which German students sing to-day date from this period ; even the students' inaugural song, the *Landesvater*, now first acquired its fine patriotic sense through some happy modifications. Christian piety, though in many instances too ostentatiously displayed, was for the majority a matter of genuine internal conviction ; many of the young dreamers seemed as it were transfigured by their pious delight in all the wonders which God had worked on behalf of this nation.

A notable feature of the new Teutonism was an ineradicable hatred for the Jews. Since the powerful excitement of the War of Liberation brought to light all the secrets of the German character, amid the general ferment the old and profound hostility to everything Judaic once more made itself manifest. Almost all the great thinkers of Germany, from Luther down to Goethe, Herder, Kant, and Fichte, were united in this sentiment ; Lessing stood quite alone in his fondness for the Jews. Immediately after the peace there began a violent paper-warfare about the position of the Jews, which for five years filled the German book-market with pamphlets on this subject, and in which the younger generation, in especial, participated with passionate eagerness. Since the days of Moses Mendelssohn's valuable endeavours, a portion of the German Jewry had laboured with considerable success to bridge the wide chasm separating their tribe from German customs and German culture.

Many of the leading Jewish families in the great towns had by now become thoroughly Germanised. In the Berlin synagogue, from the beginning of the nineteenth century onwards, the sermons were delivered in German, and in this matter Leipzig and other towns soon followed suit. Then Israel Jacobson, the founder of the great schools at Seesen, arranged for a worthier form of religious service, and David Friedländer warned his co-religionists, in his *Addresses of Edification*, that only if they whole-heartedly assimilated German civilisation could they expect their demand for complete emancipation to be gratified. The mass of the German Jews, above all in the Polish frontier provinces, accepted these ideas of reform with extreme slowness; they remained devoted to huckstering and usury, immersed in the gloomy fanaticism of the Talmudical faith, a prey to all the defects of those who have suffered bondage for many genera-tions. When the French entered the country there was evident in many Jewish circles a readily comprehensible sympathy for the nation which had been the first to grant complete equality to the Jews, and Napoleon understood very well how to flatter the Jewish spirit of cosmopolitanism; the most zealous tool of the French police in Berlin was Davidsohn-Lange, the publisher of the well-known *Telegraphen*.

It was only a part of the Jews, moreover, which manifested patriotic zeal in the War of Liberation. The sons of those cultured families in which German sentiments were already thoroughly developed, faithfully performed their military duties; but many others were held aloof from the army by bodily weak-ness and by a profoundly implanted dread of arms, while many were also repelled by the strictly Christian spirit of the great movement. From the Jews of West Prussia, who were but then laboriously emerging from the Polish mire, it would have been quite unreasonable as yet to expect German sentiments; they displayed such alarm at the idea of military service that upon their urgent petition the king granted them (May 29, 1813) the right to purchase immunity, and this privilege was utilised on so extensive a scale that a great part of the expenses of estab-lishing the West Prussian Landwehr was defrayed out of the fees paid by the Jews for exemption. The only available official list of Jewish soldiers, which includes those enrolled in the great majority of the Prussian regiments, shows that in the year 1813 there were only 343 Jews in the army ; while in the year 1815, when the strength of the army attained its highest figure, there were to be found with the colours, at the most liberal estimate, no more than 731 Jews, an extraordinarily low figure considering the proportion of Jews to the population.[1] After the war, their number sank once more to between two and three hundred. What was there, indeed, to attract them to the colours ? By the law of 1812 they were excluded from commissions, and since the king enforced this rule very strictly, during these long years of peace there was but one Jewish officer in the army of the line, M. Burg, for many years teacher at the school of artillery, a thoroughly modest and efficient soldier. Of course the young Teutonisers had no eye for the complicated historical causes which gave all too easy an explanation of the unmilitarist sentiments of the Jews. At this time, too, the money power of certain great Jewish firms in Vienna, Frankfort, and Berlin, began to make itself plainly perceptible, and was often displayed with purse-proud arrogance ; moreover, political ill-feeling was aroused by the Rothschilds' confidential intercourse with Metternich and Gentz. Then came the years of famine ; horrible tales, true and false, of the cruelty of Jewish usurers ran through the land. The ancient racial hatred revived. Sessa's comedy, *Our Traffic*, a bitter satire of Jewish manners and customs, made triumphal progress through well nigh all the theatres of Germany.

In the literary struggle which now took place there were not infrequently displayed on the Jewish side astounding mendacity and presumption, which served to show more clearly than all the discourses of their opponents what serious considerations could still be marshalled against the complete emancipation of the Jews. Saul Ascher of Berlin mocked at the " Germanomania " of the young generation in a number of malicious writings which exhibited fanatical hatred for all that was German, and for Goethe in particular. He boasted of the unbelieving Jews that it was their destiny in world-history to replace all positive faiths by a freer form of thought, and had the effrontery to ascribe to the

---

[1] *Militär Wochenblatt*, 1843, p. 348.   History of the Organisation of the Landwehr in Prussia (Supplement to the before-mentioned newspaper for the year 1858), p. 120.

members of his race the chief credit for the victories of the War of Liberation: "People forget that in the struggle with France, Germany's army had the worst of it until the Jews came to participate, nor do they remember how successfully these armies fought in the years 1813 and 1814 as soon as the Jews from Russia, Poland, Austria, and Prussia were enrolled in their ranks." Another Jewish author who took the field against Rühs and Fries unashamedly declared, only a year after the Belgian campaign, that at Belle Alliance alone fifty-five Jewish officers had fallen, whereas the Prussian army in this battle had lost in all no more than twenty-four officers. A third writer, plainly well-intentioned, published *A Friendly Word to Christians*, suggesting good-naturedly that since the obstinate Jews would certainly not abandon their ancient customs, the best thing would be if the Christians would for the sake of harmony change their Sunday to the Sabbath. In Frankfort, Hess, a Jewish teacher, declared that all his Christian opponents were either visionaries or the instruments of vulgar selfishness.[1]

In face of such arrogance it was inevitable that unjust and offensive expressions should be used in the other camp as well; nevertheless the great majority of the Christian writers maintained a dignified attitude. Lessing's ideas had quietly secured currency, and no German would any longer write so cruelly about the Jews as Fichte had formerly done. Almost all reasonable persons started from the principle that mere residence in the country did not *per se* suffice to justify a claim to the full rights of citizenship; they were willing to admit the Jews to equality in the domain of civil law, but not—or at any rate not yet—to complete equality in all other respects. However harsh this view necessarily appeared to cultured Jews, it was unquestionable that the mass of their race was still in a neglected condition which rendered complete emancipation inadvisable; a Jew was even found to direct to the German princes a pitiful appeal that they should effect an improvement of the Jewish educational system "in order to uplift my nation out of spiritual gloom."[2]

[1] Saul Ascher, Germanomania, Berlin, 1815, p. 67. Observations on the Writings of Professors Rühs and Fries concerning the Jews, Frankfort, 1816, p. 4. A Friendly Word to Christians by a Jew, place of publication not stated, 1816. M Hess, Frank Examination of Rühs's Writing, Frankfort, 1816.

[2] Patriotic Appeal of a Loyal Israelite to the Princes of Germany, Büdingen, 1816.

The Prussian law of 1812, which conceded to the Jews all civil
rights except admission to the state service, was far in advance
of the narrow-minded provisions of most of the other German
legal systems, and expressed, on the whole, what was regarded
as attainable by the liberals of that day. Even Hardenberg,
Koreff's patron, in general extremely favourable to the Jews,
had no desire to overstep this boundary.

Such were the sentiments expressed by the historian Rühs,
who initiated the anti-Jewish literary polemic, and both Fries
and Luden followed in his footsteps. Even the radical *Oppositionsblatt* held the same view as the Christo-Germanic professors ;
so did Paulus, the leader of the rational Protestants, and Klüber,
the secular liberal publicist. Among writers of note, Kotzebue
was especially friendly to the Jews, for the deadly enemy of the
young Teutonisers was attracted to Saul Ascher by an inner
elective affinity ; yet even he was of opinion that Jewish culture
must be radically transformed " by a species of conversion "
before the Jews could acquire equal rights. Immediate emancipation was demanded by no more than a few isolated and little
known Gentile journalists, as for instance by Lips, of Erlangen,
who desired to make the German nation more lively by an
admixture of Jewish blood.

Hatred of the Jews was so powerful and wide-spread that
even in the detestable Jewish dispute of Frankfort, wherein the
Jews were treated with manifest injustice, public opinion was
almost unanimously adverse to their side. How grossly had
the allied powers sinned against our ancient emperor's town in
conferring upon it the empty title of an untenable sovereignty.
During the days of the empire, though Frankfort had borne the
name of an imperial town, it had always been the emperor's
town, immediately subject to the monarch's commands, and it
was gloriously distinguished before all other German cities by
the vigorous communal sentiments of a wealthy, active, and cultured bourgeoisie. Even now, after the wars, the Senckenberg
institute and the Städel museum were opened, and a number of
societies for the promotion of generally useful activities set
vigorously to work. Under the supremacy of a powerful state-
authority, the beautiful place might have become the paragon
of German municipalities. But now the town and the eight and

a half districts of its domain received the complete independence of a sovereign state. Only as far as constitutional disputes were concerned was an arbitral right reserved for the Germanic Federation, the powers of this body being far inferior to the monarchical authority of the emperor in old times. Moreover, with the arrival of the troop of federal envoys a courtly element was introduced, falsifying the straightforward civic spirit, and involving many of the old patrician families and all the financial life of Frankfort in the intrigues of diplomacy.

Morbid arrogance inevitably resulted from relationships so unnatural. The bourgeoisie regarded " the fathertown " as the capital of Germany, misusing their newly acquired sovereignty with all the unrestraint of that social egoism which almost invariably predominates in municipalities not subjected to the even-handed justice of monarchical state-authority. The new constitution of 1816 was careful to protect the established burghers against foreign competition ; no new-comer could acquire civic rights except by the payment of 5,000 guldens or by marriage with a Frankfort woman. The same sentiment of parochial narrowness also led the town to deprive the Jews of the civic rights which they had purchased from Dalberg. With formidable outcry they at once armed in their own defence, and young Ludwig Börne placed his incisive pen at the service of his oppressed co-religionists. The legal question was far from being so simple as Börne, with pettifogging impudence, maintained. From the point of view of strict law the 440,000 guldens which the Jewish community had paid to the grand duke of Frankfort could not be regarded as the purchase price of civic rights, but simply as a sum paid to compound for the old tax of 22,000 guldens imposed annually on the Jews ; and since the federal act merely guaranteed the Jews the rights they already possessed in the states of the Germanic Federation, little legal objection could be raised to the step taken by the Frankfort bourgeoisie. Consequently the claim of the Jewish community was rejected as groundless by the arbitration court of the Berlin faculty.

When the Jews thereupon applied to the Bundestag with a statement of grievances, the political power of the house of Rothschild emerged for the first time from obscurity and an unprecedented thing happened, for the Bundestag actually showed itself more liberal than public opinion. Hardenberg, in accordance with the old traditions of the Prussian spirit of toleration, from the first instructed the Prussian envoy to insist that the Jews of Frankfort were at least entitled to exercise restricted civic rights ; and, to the astonishment of the uninitiated, Austria supported this view, the reason being that the Hofburg could not get along without the Rothschilds' money. When Metternich and Gentz visited Frankfort in the year 1818, they devoted all their influence (as formerly at the congress of Vienna) to the service of their wealthy protégés. The proceedings now went forward with customary slowness, and in the year 1824, through the instrumentality of the Bundestag, the Frankfort Jews reacquired a portion of their rights. They were recognised as " Israelite burghers," but remained excluded from official positions, and acquired equality with Gentile citizens only in matters of civil law. Even in this last point there were certain petty restrictions. For example, the Jews were not allowed to engage in the fruit trade ; they might possess no more than one house each ; their community was not allowed to celebrate more than fifteen marriages annually. With few exceptions, the newspapers tenaciously espoused the cause of the parochially-minded bourgeoisie of Frankfort, for Dalberg's laws were in ill-repute as the work of the foreign dominion, while there was a general dread lest through the exuberant growth of Hebrew activities the federal town might lose its German character. Luden wrote bluntly, " *vox populi, vox Dei*—the voice of the people is unfavourable to the Jews."

In student circles, this mood of the day was further accentuated by the romanticism of Christian enthusiasm. The students regarded themselves as a neo-Christian knighthood, displaying their hatred of the Jews with a crude intolerance which strongly recalled the days of the crusades. From the first, it was definitely resolved to exclude all non-Christians from the new league of youth. Could this be effected, the Jewish students would in reality be robbed of their academic civic rights, for it was the aim of the Burschenschaft to impose its laws upon the totality of the students, and to abolish all other associations.

As early as the summer of 1814 there was constituted in Jena a society of arms to prepare its members by means of

knightly exercises for the military service of the fatherland. In
the following spring, the members of two Landsmannschafts,
weary of the fruitless old activities, joined certain students
hitherto unattached to any organisation, and on June 12,
1815, the new Burschenschaft was inaugurated, in accordance
with the ancient custom of Jena, by a formal procession through
the market place. It was led by two divinity students from
Mecklenburg, Horn and Riemann, and by an enthusiastic pupil
of Fries, Scheidler from Gotha ; these were all fine young fellows
who had fought valiantly during the war. The first speaker,
Carl Horn, who at a later date became widely known as the
teacher of Fritz Reuter, remained until advanced in age faithful
to the enthusiasms of his youth, and died in the pious belief that
in founding the Burschenschaft he had been engaged in " the
Lord's work." The new association immediately broke with all
the evil customs of Pennalismus, and it was governed in accordance with purely democratic principles by a committee and
executive officers appointed in open election ; its court of honour
reduced the practice of duelling within modest limits, and kept
a strict watch upon the morals of its members.

A year after the foundation of the Burschenschaft all the
other students' corps in Jena had been dissolved, and the Burschenschaft now seemed to have attained the goal of its desire,
to have become a union of all the Christian German students.
In these early days there still prevailed the good tone of a cordial
patriotic enthusiasm. What an abyss separated existing custom
from the roughness of earlier days now that the Burschen sang
as their association song Arndt's vigorous verses :

> To whom shall first our thanks resound ?
> To God, Whose greatness wonderful
> From night of long disgrace is seen
> Forth-flaming in a glorious dawn,
> Who humbled hath our haughty foes,
> Who our strength for us renews,
> And ruling sits beyond the stars
> Till time becomes eternity.

For the emblem of their league and of German unity, which this
emblem was intended to symbolise, the Burschen adopted, in

accordance with Jahn's proposal, a black-red-and-gold banner. Probably these were the colours of the uniform of Lützow's volunteers, and this force had also carried a black-and-red flag embroidered in gold. Some members of the Burschenschaft were indeed bold enough to maintain that in this banner were renewed the black-and-yellow colours of the old empire, embellished by the red of liberty, or perhaps of war (for red had once been the war colour of the imperial armies). But the more zealous members would hear nothing of such historical memories, and interpreted their colours as meaning the passage from the black night of slavery, through bloody struggles, to the golden dawn of freedom. Thus it was that from out these students' dreams there came into existence that tricolor, which for half a century remained the banner of the national desire, which was to bring to Germany so many hopes and so many tears, so many noble thoughts and so many sins, until at length, like the black-blue-and-red banner of the Italian carbonari, it became disgraced in the fury of party struggles, and, once more like the carbonari banner, was replaced by the colours of the national state.

The intention of the Burschenschaft to unite all the students in a single association originated in an overstrained idealism, for the greatest charm of such societies of young men lies, in truth, in the intimacies of individual friendship. The invincible personal pride of the Germans would not so readily allow all to be treated on equal terms. To aristocratic natures, the general use of the familiar " thou," which the Burschenschaft enjoined, was uncongenial. Not alone the rude debauchees of the old school, but also many harmless pleasure-loving young men, were bored by the precociously wise and earnest tone of the Burschen, among whom prestige could be acquired solely by emotional eloquence, or perhaps, in addition, by good swordsmanship. Men of free and individual intelligence, such as young Carl Immermann of Halle, cared nothing for the opinion of the leaders of the Burschenschaft, holding that distinguished student chiefs are very rarely men of talent. The only resource against such opponents was dictatorial severity, and the narrowness characteristic of every new tendency (among young men at least) soon increased in the Burschenschaft to the pitch of terrorism. In Jena it

proved possible for the time being to silence all differences of
opinion, and the conceit of the Burschen now became intolerable.
With important mien, the executive and the members of the
committee strode every afternoon up and down the market place,
deliberating in measured conversation the weal of the fatherland
and of the universities ; they regarded themselves as lords of
this small academic realm, all the more because most of the professors exhibited for these youthful tyrants a quite immoderate
veneration, compounded of fear and benevolence ; even now,
the leaders of the Burschenschaft looked forward to the time
when their organisation would rule all Germany.

Patriotic orations displaying passion and enthusiasm became
more and more violent, already concluding at times with the
triumphant assertion : " Our judgment has the weight of history
itself ; it annihilates." How many old members of the Burschenschaft went down to their graves inspired by the happy illusion
that it was in truth their organisation which had founded the new
German empire. Half a century later, Arnold Ruge described
the long struggle for unity and freedom characteristic of modern
German history as a single great *pro patria* dispute between
Burschenschafts and students' corps. Indisputably, many a young
man of ability acquired his first understanding of the splendour
of the fatherland at a students' drinking party, but the political
idealism of those days was too formless to arouse a definitely
drected sentiment. To the first generation of the Burschenschaft there belonged, in addition to isolated liberal party-leaders
like H. von Gagern, a great many men who subsequently displayed ultra-conservative tendencies, as for instance Leo, Stahl,
W. Menzel, Jarke, and Hengstenberg. Voluble enthusiasm, hazy
egoism, and the persistent confusion of appearance and reality,
were unfavourable to the development of political talent. On
the whole it may be said that from the Burschenschaft there
proceeded more professors and authors, whilst from the ranks
of the corps, the subsequent opponents of the Burschenschaft,
were derived more statesmen.

For the present, however, the Burschenschaft was supreme
in Jena. Its fame was disseminated through all the universities,
where it attracted new students, and at Jena the number of
students speedily became doubled. At other universities, too,

Burschenschafts were established ; in Giessen, for instance, and in Tübingen, where as long before as 1813 a Tugendbund had been founded to counteract academic brutality. Quite spontaneously there now awakened the desire to celebrate the new community at a formal meeting of all German Burschen. In dispersed peoples, the impulse to unity finds natural expression in such free social relationships, extending beyond the bounds of the individual state ; in Germany, as in Italy, congresses of men of science, artists, and industrials were, like stormy petrels, the forerunners of the bloody struggles for unity. Among the Germans it was the students who took the first step, and nothing can show more plainly the inertia of political life in those days. Long before grown men had conceived the idea of coming to an understanding about their serious common interests, among our youth the impulse became active to interchange their common dreams and hopes, and through the play of the imaginative life to rejoice in the ideal unity of the fatherland.

The centenary festival of the Reformation awakened everywhere among Protestants a happy sentiment of grateful pride. In these days even Goethe sang : " Ever in art and science shall my voice of protest rise." The students, in especial, were affected by this mood of the time, because their minds were still influenced by the Christian Protestant enthusiasm of the War of Liberation. When the idea of a great fraternal festival of the German Burschen was first mooted in Jahn's circle, the Jena Burschenschaft resolved to postpone the day of assembly to the eighteenth day of " the moon of victory " in the year 1817, in order to combine the centenary festival of the Reformation with the customary annual commemoration of the battle of Leipzig. Arminius, Luther, Scharnhorst, all the great figures of those who led Germanism in the struggle against foreign encroachments, became fused into a single image in the conceptions of these young hotheads. To the more revolutionary spirits, Luther seemed a republican hero, a precursor of the free " conviction." In a commemorative pamphlet by Carl Sand, which was circulated among the students, the Evangelical doctrine of Christian freedom was fantastically intertwined with modern democratic notions. " The leading idea of our festival," wrote Sand, " is that we are consecrated to priesthood through baptism, that we are all free and equal. From of old there have ever been three primal enemies of our German nationality: the Romans, monasticism, and militarism." By this attitude, the universally German character of the festival was from the first impaired. The Catholic universities of the highlands, which in any case had as yet no regular intercourse on the part of their students with those of North Germany, could not receive an invitation ; the Burschen of Freiburg had to light their fires of victory on the eighteenth of October by themselves, on the Wartenberg near Donaueschingen. The Austrian universities did not come into the question at all, for they were quite aloof from the German students' customs, and, with the exception of the Transylvanian Saxons and a few Hungarians, hardly any Austrians studied in Germany. Even in the Prussian universities, the Burschenschaft had as yet secured so few adherents that Berlin was the only one to accept the invitation. The consequence was that at the festival of the national battle the students of the two states which alone had fought at Leipzig in the cause of freedom were almost unrepresented, and all the extraordinary fables with which the liberals of the Rhenish Confederate lands were accustomed to adorn the history of the War of Liberation found free currency.

Long in advance, and with vigorous trumpeting, the press had heralded the great day. A free assembly of Germans from all parts, meeting solely on behalf of the fatherland, was to this generation a phenomenon so astounding as to seem almost more important than the world-shaking experiences of recent years. During October 17th fifteen hundred Burschen arrived at Eisenach, about half of this number being from Jena, thirty from Berlin, and the rest from Giessen, Marburg, Erlangen, Heidelberg, and the other universities of the minor states ; following the custom of the gymnasts, the vigorous men of Kiel had come the whole distance on foot. Four of the Jena professors, Fries, Oken, Schweitzer, and Kieser, were also present. As the men of each new group entered, they were greeted at the gate with loud hurrahs, and were then conducted to the Rautenkranz, there before the severe members of the committee to swear to observe the peace strictly for three days. Early on the following morning, a fine autumn day, "the sacred train" made its way through the forest to the reformer's stronghold. The procession was led by Scheidler, carrying the sword of the Burschen, and followed by four vassals ; next came Count Keller, surrounded by four standard guards, with the new colours of the Burschen which the girls of Jena had shortly before embroidered for their austere young friends ; the Burschen followed two by two, among them a number of heroic German figures, many of them bearded (which to the timid already sufficed to arouse suspicion of treasonable designs). Delight shone from every eye, for all were inspired by the happy self-forgetfulness of youth which is still able to immerse itself in the pleasures of the moment. It seemed to them as if to-day for the first time they had been able truly to appreciate the glories of their fatherland.

In the banqueting-hall of the Wartburg, which the grand duke had hospitably thrown open, *God is to us a tower of strength* was first of all sung amid the rolling of kettle-drums and the blast of trumpets Then Riemann, of Lützow's yagers, delivered an inaugural address describing in emotional and exaggerated phraseology the deeds of Luther and of Blucher, and going on to exhort the Burschen by the spirits of the mighty dead " to strive for the acquiremen† of every human and patriotic virtue." The speech was not free from the current catchwords about the frustrated hopes of the German nation and about the one prince who had kept his word. As a whole, it was a youthful and obscure but thoroughly harmless outpouring of sentimentality, just as vague and unmeaning as the new pass-word *Volunto !* of which the Burschen were so fond. Nor did the subsequent speeches of the professors and of the other students exceed this measure, for even Oken spoke with unusual self-restraint, warning the young people against premature political activities.

After the midday meal, the Burschen returned to the town and went to church, the service being also attended by the Eisenach Landsturm ; and after church the champions of the Berlin and Jena gymnastic grounds displayed their arts to the astonished Landsturmers. At nightfall there was a renewed procession to the Wartenberg, opposite the Warsburg, this time by torchlight, and here were lighted a number of bonfires of victory, greeted with patriotic speeches and songs. Hitherto the festival had been characterised by a pleasing harmony, but now it became manifest that there already existed within the Burschenschaft a small party of extremists, composed of those fanatical primitive Teutons of Jahn's school who passed by the name of " Old Germans." The Turnvater had felt that this valuable opportunity for a senseless demonstration must on no account be lost. He had suggested that the festival in commemoration of Luther should be crowned by an imitation of the boldest of the reformer's actions, and that just as Luther had once burned the papal bull of excommunication, so now the writings of the enemies of the good cause should be cast into the flames. Since the majority of the festival committee, wiser than Jahn, had rejected the proposal, Jahn had given his Berlin companions a list of the books to be burned, and his faithful followers, led by Massmann, now determined to carry out the master's plan on their own initiative, a proceeding which the committee, desiring to keep the peace, was unwilling positively to prohibit. On the Wartenberg, hardly had the last serious song been finished by the Burschen surrounding the fires, and the true festival been brought to a close, when Massmann suddenly came to the front, and in a bombastic speech exhorted the brethren to contemplate how, in accordance with Luther's example, sentence was to be executed in the fires of purgatory upon the evil writings of the fatherland. Now had arrived the sacred hour " in which all the world of Germany can see what we desire ; can know what is to be expected from us in the future."

Thereupon his associates brought forward several parcels of old printed matter, each inscribed with the titles of the condemned books. Tossed in by a pitchfork, the works of the traitors to their fatherland then fell into the infernal flames amid loud hooting. The parcels contained a wonderfully mixed society of about two dozen books in all, some good and some bad, everything which had most recently aroused the anger of the *Isis* and similar journals. There were burned the works of Wadzeck and Scherer, and, to make a clean sweep, those " of all the other cribbling, screaming, and speechless foes of the praiseworthy gymnastic craft " ; copies of the *Alemannia*, too, found their way to the flames, with issues " of all the other newspapers which disgrace and dishonour the fatherland " ; then, of course, came three writings by the detested Schmalz (while the chorus intoned an opprobrious pun upon the author's name), and the *General*

Code of the Gendarmerie by Schmalz's comrade, Kamptz. Beside
the *code Napoléon*, Kotzebue's *German History*, and Ascher's
Germanomania (followed by a shout of " Woe unto the Jews "),
there was burned Haller's *Restoration*, the choice of this victim
being explained on the ground " the fellow does not want the
German fatherland to have a constitution "—although not one
of the Burschen had ever read this ponderous book. But even
Benzenberg and Wangenheim, liberals both, had to suffer at the
hands of these angry young men because their works had proved
incomprehensible to the Jena journalists. Finally, an Uhlan
warrior's pair of stays, a pigtail, and a corporal's cane, were
burned as " fuglemen of military pedantry, the scandal of the
serious and sacred warrior caste " ; and with three groans for
" the rascally Schmalzian crew " the judges of this modern
Fehmic court dispersed.

The farce was indescribably silly, but no worse than
many similar expressions of academic coarseness, and it demanded
serious consideration only on account of the measureless arrogance and Jacobin intolerance shown in the young people's offensive orations. Stein spoke in very strong terms about " the
tomfoolery at the Wartburg " ; while Niebuhr, ever inclined to
the gloomiest view, wrote with much anxiety, " Liberty is quite
impossible if young people lack veneration and modesty." He
was disgusted by this " religious comedy," by the ludicrous contrast between the bold reformer who had risen in revolt against
the highest and most sacred authority of his time, and on the
other hand this safe passing of fiery judgment by a group of
boastful young Burschen upon a number of writings of which they
hardly knew a line ! At the students' assembly, on the following day, the young men made use of calmer language, being at
least more reasonable than their teacher Fries, who had left them
a written discourse of an incredibly tasteless character, turgid
with mystical biblical wisdom and Saxe-Weimar arrogance of
liberty. " Return," admonished Fries, " to your own places saying that you have visited the land where the German people is
free, where German thought is free . . . Here there is no standing army to burden the nation ! A little land shows you the
goal ! But all the German princes made a similar promise " . . .,
and so on. Certainly Stein had good reason for censuring the

Jena professors as " drivelling metapoliticians," and Goethe
reason just as good when he invoked a curse upon all German
political oratory, for what could be expected from the young
when their revered teacher held up the four-and-twenty hussars
of Weimar as a glorious example for the rest of Germany ! The
same repulsive intermingling of religion and politics which was
displayed in Fries's speech, came to light once more in the afternoon, when some of the Burschen hit upon the idea of taking
Holy Communion. Superintendent Nebe actually conceded the
point, and administered the sacrament to a number of excited
and more or less intoxicated young men—a characteristic example
of that deplorable laxity which in time of trouble has ever distinguished both the temporal and the spiritual authorities of the
petty states.

Notwithstanding the follies of individuals, the festival as a
whole was harmless, happy, and innocent. When in the evening
the young men had said their farewells with streaming eyes, for
most of them there remained a life-long memory, scintillating
like a May-day in youth, as Heinrich Leo assures us. They had
had a brotherly meeting with comrades from the south and from
the north ; they considered that the unity of the disintegrated
fatherland was already within their grasp ; and if only
public opinion had been sensible enough to leave these young
hotheads to themselves and to their own dreams, the good resolutions which many an excellent youth formed in those hours of
excitement might have borne valuable fruit.

But amid the profound stillness which brooded over the
German north, the impudent speeches of the Burschen resounded
far too loudly. It seemed as if friend and foe had entered into
a conspiracy to increase to the pitch of mania the sentiment of
morbid self-conceit, that deadly sin of youth which corrupts its
honourable enthusiasms, as if everyone accepted the boastful
assurance of Carové, one of the Wartburg orators, who had
extolled the universities as the natural defenders of national
honour. With ludicrous earnestness the liberal newspapers
delightedly hailed this first awakening of the public life of the
nation, " this silvery sheen in our history, this blossoming of our
epoch " ; while, on the other hand, the old terror of the domes-
ticated townsman for the students who used to beat night watch-

men clothed itself in a political dress. A whole library of writings and counter-writings illuminated the extraordinary drama from all sides, raising this outburst of students' revelry to the level of a European event. It was natural that the heroes of the occasion should participate with justified pride in this paper-warfare. The most faithful picture of the young people's hazy enthusiasm was given by Massmann in a long report of the festival, in which the stilted oracular phraseology unquestionably served to show how much that was un-German was after all concealed in the Jahnese "strong-manhood." "Although the gloomy winter night of serfdom," he begins, " still lowers over the hills and the streams of the German land, nevertheless the peaks are aflame, and the blood-red gold of dawn gathers strength." The poor young man had now to make severe atonement for the Turnvater's folly. Since he dreaded a prosecution and did not wish to cut too painful a figure before the judges, he had to devote the whole winter term to the belated perusal of all the evil books which he had symbolically burned on the Wartenburg. Another work, presumably by Carové, was dedicated to the writer's Rhenish fellow-countrymen with the wish that the spiritual sun of the Wartburg might illumine them also, might bring them strength and consolation in their misfortune. The majority, however, still remained tolerably quiet. A proposal to publish a political programme was rejected with the definite declaration that the Burschenschaft was not to intervene in politics, whilst a short writing on the Wartburg festival by F. I. Frommann, a member of a respected family of Jena booksellers, was thoroughly modest, being characterised merely by a harmless youthful enthusiasm.

Unfortunately several of the professors who had attended the festival proved far more foolish than their pupils. In a typically coarse newspaper report, Fries did not hesitate to express plain approval of the fire-assize which had dealt with the writings " of some of the Schmalzian crew." To " many who discuss Germany wisely and unwisely," Oken, in the *Isis*, held up the Wartburg gathering as a brilliant example, availing himself of all the pictorial wealth of his goose-heads, donkey-heads, priest-heads, and Jew-heads, in order to pour out fresh scorn upon the authors of the burned writings, whereupon the Jena students, in a masked procession through the market place, gave a dramatic representation of the *Isis* caricatures. Finally Kieser, who, despite his magnetic secret doctrines, was respected by other members of the medical faculty as a man of intelligence and learning, published a work, " dedicated to the Wartburg spirit of the German universities," positively luxuriating in crazy vaunts, saying that the Wartburg festival was " an event of which Germany's peoples will still be proud when centuries have elapsed, one of those events which, like all that is truly great, never recur in history, an event which in its hidden womb may bear fruitful germs, influential for centuries to come ! "

For these outbreaks of academic delusion of grandeur, the petty sensibilities of the members of the opposing party were largely responsible. The age was still but little accustomed to the virulence of political struggles, and almost all the authors who had been selected for condemnation felt that they had been seriously affronted by the tomfoolery of the students. Wangenheim alone bore the insult with good humour, saying that hitherto his colleagues at the Bundestag had regarded him with suspicion as a demagogue, but that since his book had been burned upon the Wartburg they had come to greet him in a more friendly spirit. Many of the others uttered loud complaints, and circulated gloomy reports, as that the charter of the Holy Alliance and the federal act had also been burned by the youthful traitors. Especially infuriated was Privy Councillor Kamptz, and he eagerly grasped the welcome chance of suppressing the academic Jacobins once for all. What a piece of luck it was that the ignorant young men had chosen to commit to the flames his gendarmerie code, a collection of police regulations, to which the editor had added hardly anything ! Sovereign ordinances, among them some issued by Charles Augustus himself, had been publicly burned upon the grand-ducal soil of Saxe-Weimar, and according to Quistorp's work upon *Criminal Law* it was indisputable that the " crime of *lèse-majesté* " had been perpetrated. In two minatory letters to the grand duke, and subsequently in a pamphlet *Concerning the Public Burning of Printed Matters*, Kamptz expounded these ideas, and stormily demanded satisfaction, declaring that German soil had been desecrated, that the century had been defiled by the vandalism of demagogic intolerance, and by vulgar displays on the part of the tools of evil professors.

At the court of Vienna the only feeling was one of alarm and anger. The news from Eisenach led Metternich for the first time to devote serious attention to German affairs, which he had hitherto treated with profound indifference, for he recognised with terror that behind the fantastical activities of these young men there lurked the deadly enemy of his system, the national idea. He immediately declared to the Prussian envoy that the time had arrived " to take strong measures [*sévir*] against this spirit of Jacobinism," and he requested the chancellor to join with Austria in common action against the court of Weimar.[1] In the first moment of panic he even desired the immediate recall from Jena of all the Austrian students at that university. In the *Oesterreichische Beobachter* Gentz published a number of savage articles upon the Wartburg festival, an artful compost of perspicuity and folly. Only with trembling, he declared, could a father to-day see his son depart to the university. Such plaints of nervous anxiety were succeeded by a masterly refutation (based upon an extraordinary wealth of knowledge) of the vainglorious students' fables concerning the wonderful deeds of the volunteers.

In Berlin, the king was much more concerned than were his ministers. Frederick William himself had never been a student, and therefore had no personal experience of the rough humours of student life, so that he was disgusted by the noisy and boastful activity of the young men. In the previous spring he had taken action against the Teutonia of Halle when Carl Immermann had begged him for protection against the terrorism of the Burschenschaft, and he now had inquiries made at all the Prussian universities as to who had participated in the Wartburg festival. The Burschen of Königsberg were commended because they had held aloof ; on December 7th strict commands were issued to the minister of education that all students' associations should immediately be suppressed and membership therein prohibited on pain of expulsion, while the practices of the gymnasts were to be closely supervised. " I shall not hesitate for a moment," wrote the king, " to abolish any university in which the spirit of undiscipline proves ineradicable."[2]

[1] Krusemark's Reports, November 12 and 22, 1817.
[2] Cabinet Order to Altenstein, December 7, 1817.

Altenstein fulfilled his orders with benevolent caution. He had not lost confidence in the good sentiments of the students ; he praised the unaffrighted conduct of the grand duke of Weimar ; and held firmly to the hope " that just as the Prussian universities surpass all the others of Germany in their purposive and free-handed equipment, so also may they continue to excel by giving oexmple of an activity which, while vigorous, remains directed ta right ends." [1] Hardenberg, on the other hand, eagerly endorsed the king's views. It was not that he altogether shared the monarch's anxieties, but the young demagogues' speeches threatened to destroy his most cherished plans. The completion of the constitution remained the ultimate goal of his policy, and this work could never be brought to a successful issue if a spirit of suspicion were to become firmly established in the king's mind. Hence he considered that all manifestations of demagogic sentiments must forthwith be stifled once and for all. Schleiermacher's lectures *Concerning the Doctrine of the State*, though purely scientific in character and utterly devoid of party feeling, had recently, through the instrumentality of some scandalmonger, been made an object of suspicion at court, and had led the king to give vent to a few bitter observations ; Hardenberg lacked courage to open the monarch's eyes by a straightforward word ; instructed the minister of education to forbid the continuance of these lectures " which, without being of any real utility, serve merely to sow dissension " ; and cancelled his order only because even Wittgenstein considered it injudicious. [2] In the like arbitrary spirit did the chancellor accept Metternich's proposals. Since he was intending to pay an immediate visit to the Rhenish provinces, he determined to travel by way of Weimar, and there, supported by the Austrian envoy Count Zichy, to have a word with the grand duke, and to hand to him monitory letters from the emperor and the king.

Amid the general excitement, Charles Augustus alone remained serene and equable ; in youth he himself had long luxuriated in the effervescent spirits of the student, and did not esteem the Burschen's boasting more seriously than it deserved. The *Deutsche Burschenzeitung* which had been announced on

[1] Altenstein to Hardenberg, November 30, 1817; August 25, 1818.
[2] Hardenberg to Altenstein and Wittgenstein, December 7th ; Rother to Hardenberg, December 15, 1817.

the Wartburg was prohibited ; a few other newspapers were admonished ; while a criminal prosecution was instituted against Oken, which ended in an acquittal because in the indictment he was foolishly accused of high treason—the article in the *Isis* had afforded ample ground for a prosecution for libel. A prosecution initiated against Fries was discontinued as objectless, and it was considered sufficient to administer a reprimand on account of his tactless speech. For the rest, the Jena students were left unmolested. On November 26th, through his chargé d'affaires in Berlin, Charles Augustus assured the Prussian government : " The present excitement is general, and is a natural consequence of events ; it may be allayed by confidence and courage, but suspicion and forcible measures would throw Germany into con- fusion." [1] He encountered the emissaries of the two great powers with his customary cheerful candour, and promised to co-operate in establishing a federal press-law   At the grand duke's request, Zichy now paid a visit to Jena, accompanied by Edling, in order to examine this nidus of revolt close at hand, and since nothing remarkable occurred the two great powers temporarily abstained from further steps. But suspicion remained alive, and King Frederick William expressed his disapproval in the strongest possible terms when, in the following summer, Massmann was appointed gymnastic teacher at Breslau. The French govern- ment, which had long been rendered uneasy by the intrigues of the prince of Orange and of the refugees in Belgium, also made serious representations to the court of Weimar. Czar Alexander, the protagonist of Christian liberalism, refused to sound the alarm in the ears of the Germanic Federation, as Metternich wished him to do, but was nevertheless unable wholly to master his secret fears, and in an autograph letter he urged the grand duke to take stringent measures against the press. [2] The dread of an approaching revolution grew ever stronger, and since the foreign powers were all conscious of their sins against Germany they regarded this peaceful land, in which, after all, the traces of an uneasy movement were still few and far between, as the natural centre of the European revolutionary party.

[1] Edling's Instruction to Müller, chargé d'affaires, November 26, 1817.

[2] Altenstein to Hardenberg, August 18th and September 15th ; Report of the Badenese envoy General von Stockhorn, Berlin, February 7, 1818.

The fears of the cabinets had an extremely unfavourable influence upon the students' mood, for now that all the great powers of the continent were up in arms against them, the Burschen considered that they had become central figures in history. The democratic ideas which had hitherto slumbered beneath the cloak of the Christo-Germanic fantasies now came impudently into the open, and together with Körner's songs there was often sung the *Marseillaise* as Germanised by old Voss :

> We come, we come ! Quake, hireling-swarm,
> And take to flight or die !

No one asked to what nation this " hireling-swarm " of Rouget de Lisle had belonged ! The revolutionary party of the " Old Germans " became by degrees sharply distinguished from the innocent masses of the Burschen. While these latter, weary of the eternal political discussions, made for themselves a merry beer-kingdom in Lichtenhain, the " quiet republican statesmen " (as Arnold Ruge termed them) held formal session in their republic of Ziegenhain, discussing in emotional orations whether the unity of Germany could be more effectively secured by the assassination or by the peaceful mediatisation of the princes. A new song *Thirty, or Three and Thirty, it matters little !* referred very plainly to the former method, but there still were to be found a few of gentler nature who desired to grant the king of Prussia a retiring allowance of three hundred thalers *per annum*. Folly began to break all bounds, and the blameless Fries had frequent occasion to learn how the forms of intercourse practised by the gymnasts were developing. He associated with his young friends upon terms which permitted them to address him in the second person singular and had therefore no reason to feel surprised when one of his students wrote to him as follows : " I feel that in future I shall not be writing to Councillor Fries, but to thee, my old friend Fries, whilst thou repliest to thy faithful pupil D. Now look here, thou fine old fellow, we are young people, and we are having a better time of it than didst thou in thy youth."

Shortly after the Wartburg festival, an odious literary quarrel came to add fuel to the flames. To the students, Kotzebue had long been a thorn in the side ; they detested the insipid lasciviousness of his plays and dreaded him as a skilled opponent. In the *Literarische Wochenblatt*, which enjoyed the special favour of Metternich, he advocated the views of enlightened absolutism, sang the praises of Russia with servile flattery, and attacked the idealism of the students (as he attacked everything which surpassed the limits of his own sordid understanding) with so much malice and venom that even Goethe wished him joy of the fireassize on the Wartburg, exclaiming :

> Too long, too long, for mean ends fighting,
> And with base scorn of high things writing,
> Of thine own folk a mock hast made,
> At hands of youth art well repaid.

But the old rascal still possessed his impudent wit and his nimble pen. He uttered many an apt word regarding the intolerable presumption of the students ; he had a sharp eye for their illbreeding ; and when, in his amusing *Commendation of the Asses' Heads*, he joined issue with the *Isis*, he was left victor on the field, for the dull and inflated young men were incapable of meeting him with his own weapons. Kotzebue lived in Weimar as secretary to the Russian legation, and his tenure of this diplomatic post aroused offence, for he was a native of Weimar, he owed his literary repute to the Germans alone, and in his *Wochenblatt* wrote freely about the affairs of the fatherland as a German. But who could expect from such a man the fine feelings of national pride ? It was an open secret that throughout Germany there lived secret agents of the St. Petersburg police. When Faber, the Russian councillor of state, visited Rhineland, Count Solms-Laubach considered it advisable to have him shadowed by the trusty Bärsch. The Russian cabinet owed its knowledge of European affairs chiefly to the reports which Russians of quality living in the west were accustomed to send to the court. Kotzebue also sent occasional reports to St. Petersburg, but he could by no means be numbered among the dangerous spies, for his bulletins consisted exclusively of critical surveys dealing with the most recent manifestations in German literature.

One day Kotzebue's secretary, who lived in the same house with Lindner, the editor of the *Oppositionsblatt*, came to the latter and innocently requested his assistance in deciphering certain passages in a report written by Kotzebue in French. Lindner immediately recognised the nature of the document, asked to be allowed to keep it for an hour, copied the most important passages, and did not feel it dishonourable to communicate forthwith to Luden the bulletin thus purloined. It contained nothing more than a few extracts from the *Nemesis* and similar writings (extracts which, though casual and inexact, gave the sense correctly enough), together with some far from flattering criticisms of Luden's authorship, such as might naturally be expected from a political opponent—the men of Jena were certainly accustomed to treat their enemies far more roughly. Luden, who was not lacking in worldly wisdom, eagerly seized the opportunity of exposing a dreaded opponent and at the same time clearing himself from the suspicion of demagogic sentiments. He had the stolen document printed ; endeavoured by paltry and not altogether straightforward quibbling to prove that Kotzebue had falsified the innocent words of the *Nemesis ;* and branded him as a calumniator. All along the line the liberal press now advanced to the attack upon the " Russian spy," who after all had not spied out any secret, but had merely handed on publicly printed writings. Blow succeeded blow ; a furious dispute began, creditable to neither side. The courts intervened, condemning both parties ; Lindner was exiled, and went to Alsace, where, bewitched by the doctrines of the French, he speedily became a liberalising Rhenish Confederate. The students, however, had at length discovered in Kotzebue a target for the aimless but fierce hatred with which their hearts were filled. The sensuous old fellow in Weimar seemed to them a pattern of all the infamies, the evil genius of the fatherland, and the Burschen sang in threatening tones :

> Still bays the friend of Kamptz and Schmalz,
> Beel- and Kotzebue.

Such was the ferment in the minds of the young, while the nation continued with childish curiosity to discuss every act of folly on the part of the students. In the summer of 1818, as the sequel to a dispute with the bourgeoisie quite devoid of political bearing, the students of Göttingen marched out of the town of the muses, declaring the Georgia Augusta university to be taboo, and caroused for a few days in Witzenhausen, taking the opportunity of drinking destruction to the defunct institution. Such an exodus might perhaps in old days sometimes endanger the existence of a university ; but now, when every one of the federal states demanded of its officials and clergy that they should have attended the territorial university, it was merely something to laugh at. None the less, even this child's play called into existence a sheaf of pamphlets. Councillor Dabelow, the distinguished organiser of the *Empire Anhaltin-Cœthien*, who had been among those to experience the tender mercies of the fire-assize of the Wartburg, implored the exalted governments to take serious measures against the young traitors. As it happened, this able jurist shortly afterwards received a call to Dorpat, and now it seemed to the students clearly proved that the czar had surrounded them with spies. Another author devoted a whole book to the description of the affair of the Göttingen exodus, adorning his work with pictures of the students in the council of the taboo —sinister figures which seemed to have come straight out of the Bohemian forest from the band of Robber Moor. Soon afterwards the students of Tübingen fought the battle of Lustnau, a struggle round a village-tavern of which the poets of the Swabian university still sing to-day ; next the Heidelberg Burschen were seized with the spirit of unrest, and stormed the beerhouse of the Great Tun. All these trifles were ceremoniously described throughout the German press. Alike at the courts and among the people, the student acquired an incredible prestige, being here honoured as a born tribune, there regarded with suspicion as a professional conspirator, while Count de Serre, the French minister of state, wrote to his friend Niebuhr, " I am sorry for your statesmen, they wage war with students ! "

The stout-hearted Charles Augustus alone retained undisturbed his high-spirited confidence. In July, 1818, the Jena students, led by Heinrich von Gagern, held a torchlight procession in honour of the birth of the duke's grandson. He gave them a banquet in the court-yard of the palace, appeared on the balcony in a mood of youthful cheerfulness, and long continued to watch the lively proceedings, beaming with delight. Then, in accordance with the patriarchal custom of the Ernestines, inviting to the prince's christening all the corporations of the country, he included in the invitation three representatives of the Burschenschaft ; as the Hofburg learned with intense anger, these dangerous fellows were actually summoned to the festive board, and were manifestly treated with distinction by the inquisitive maids-of-honour.   Charles Augustus had been tried in the balance and found wanting, and in Metternich's circle he was henceforward spoken of only as the " Old Bursche."

Meanwhile the seed scattered on the Wartburg began to spring up.   Burschenschafts after the Jena model were formed at fourteen universities.   Delegates from these met at Jena in October, 1818. and upon the anniversary of the Wartburg festival the *Allgemeine Deutsche Burschenschaft* [Universal German Burschenschaft] was founded, as a free association of all German students, " established upon the relationship of the German youth to the coming unity of the German fatherland."   A general Burschenschaft of delegates from every university was to assemble annually in the " moon of victory."   The organic statutes describing the aims of the association were quite unobjectionable, demanding unity, liberty, and equality of all Burschen, and the Christo-Germanic development of all their energies in the service of the fatherland.   The only alarming feature was the terrorist spirit which desired to enforce membership upon all students, which declared other associations to be " taboo without further consideration," and which was yet unable to achieve the impossible, for at all the universities except Jena some of the Landsmann-schafts continued to exist in addition to the Burschenschaft.   To particularism, and to its leader, the court of Vienna, it was natural that the very existence of this " youths' federal state," as Fries termed it, should seem extremely dangerous, since here for the first time in the forcibly disintegrated nation was constituted a corporation embracing the whole of Germany.   So new was the phenomenon that even Goethe anxiously asked whether a guild could be tolerated extending throughout Germany but not subordinated to the Bundestag.

Whilst the Burschenschaft was thus spreading more and more widely, its internal strength and unity were already being impaired by a confused segregation into factions.   A generation

inspired with enthusiasm for Schiller's sentimental love of liberty
was from the first inclined to be receptive for the ideas of Rousseau,
and it was inevitable that after several years had been passed in
continuous and lively political discussion the demagogic party
should ultimately gain ground.   The university of Giessen was the
centre of the academic revolutionary spirit.   Here in the west
the doctrines of the French Revolution had long before taken
firm root ;   the arbitrariness of the Bonapartist officialdom in
Darmstadt and Nassau had made the young people bitter, and
when the hour of liberation at length struck for these territories
as well, through an unkindly fate it happened that the students
at Giessen, who flocked to the colours, hardly ever came face to
face with the enemy.   In exhausting marches they learned only
the prose of war. and had no experience of its inspiriting joys ;
they had much to suffer from the roughness of their Rhenish
Confederate officers who did not know how to get on with men
of education in the rank and file ;   and they returned home in
low spirits, loathing the " hireling system," and with no inkling
of the loyal monarchical sentiments of the Prussian army, with
which they had never come into contact.   They swore that Germany had waged the war solely on account of the constitution,
and that all the blood had been shed in vain.

Peculiar to the student leagues of Giessen was a secret intercourse with men of riper years, which in Jena was happily
unknown.   At the time of the war several secret societies against
the foreign dominion had been constituted in the region of the
Lahn, but had never effected anything in particular.   In 1814, in
accordance with a plan drawn up by Arndt, a German Association
was formed in Idstein, and the neighbourhood ;   in the following
year the legal councillor C. Hoffmann, of Rödelheim, founded
a league which was in touch with Justus Gruner, and which
favoured Prussian hegemony.   Some of the members of these
associations speedily abandoned their Teutonising ideals in favour
of cosmopolitan revolutionary notions, and carried on secret correspondence with the Burschen of Giessen.   Among the advanced
revolutionaries were the brothers Ludwig, two of the leaders of
the Nassau opposition, Wilhelm Snell, and above all Weidig,
vice-master at Butzbach, an eloquent apostle of equality, in whose

eyes every government was sinful because God's word prescribed the complete equality of all mankind. The influence of these men and the stifling atmosphere of a thoroughly unhealthy state-system soon produced an extraordinarily fanatical tone in the student life of Giessen. An association of " Blacks " came into existence, and endeavoured to enforce its revolutionary new code, the *Ehrenspiegel* [code of honour], upon all the other students ; the Landsmannschafts, on the other hand, played the part of representatives of particularism, sported the Hessian cockade, and by means of a denunciation secured the dissolution of the Blacks' organisation. But the more zealous members of the suppressed league continued their work in secret.

Their leaders were the brothers Follen, Adolf, Carl, and Paul, three handsome young men of great stature, full of life and fire, ardent republicans all, sons of a Giessen official ; they had one sister, who subsequently became the mother of Carl Vogt. Adolf Follen was distinguished by a fine lyrical talent, which he corrupted by the unnatural emotionalism of his declamatory revolutionary phraseology ; it was to him and to his friend Sartorius that the gymnasts owed their most savage and impudent songs. A more notable man was his brother Carl, a fanatical adherent of the principles of harsh reason, essentially a barren intelligence, but possessing rare dialectic penetration, a man of prematurely ripe character, entirely self-satisfied, one who after the manner of revolutionary prophets knew how to assume the appearance of elemental profundity, impressing many of his young associates as if he had been the Old Man of the Mountain. He was already a demonstrator of law, and charmed the students by that pose of absolute certainty which by inexperienced youth is so readily accepted as a mark of genius ; every one of his words was measured, and not one was ever withdrawn ; with remorseless logic he deduced his conclusions from the premise of the unconditional equality of all, shrinking from no possible consequence. The enigmatical mixture of coldness and fanaticism in his nature, together with the meticulous neatness of his aspect and his minatory expression, recalled Robespierre ; but Follen was no hypocrite, and really practised the austere moral code which he preached. Carl Follen had nothing but a smile for the innocent imperial dreams of the Burschen of Tubingen and Jena, who loved to imagine the crown

of the Hohenstaufen on the head of their William or of their
Charles Augustus; moreover, he regarded their Gallophobia and
their Teutonomania as childish, although he carefully refrained
from parading his own cosmopolitan views, since to do this would
have deprived him of all influence. In a word, he was a Jacobin,
and it is probable that as early as the year 1818 (as the Burschen
of Jena suspected), and unquestionable that from 1820 onwards,
he was in confidential correspondence with the revolutionary
secret societies which, spread all over France, were controlled by
Lafayette's *comité directeur*. His leading principle was that no one
owed obedience to any law to whose authority he had not himself
voluntarily submitted, and that therefore, in accordance with the
old Rousseauist fallacy, the rule of the majority was alone
justified. "Every citizen is chief of the state, for the just state
is a perfect sphere in which neither top nor bottom exists because
every point can be and is the summit."

Thus it was that the proposal for a centralised German constitution, drafted by Adolf Follen, emended by his brother Carl,
and laid before the Jena Burschentag in the autumn of 1818,
contained, apart from a few Teutonising phrases, nothing beyond
a free imitation of the fundamental law of the French republic.
All Germans were to possess absolutely equal rights; legislation
was to be effected by the equal suffrage of all, the majority to
decide; the one and indivisible realm was to be administered in
departments containing an equal number of inhabitants, and
named after rivers and mountains; all officials were to be equally
paid, and must swear fealty to the popular representatives; there
was to be one Christo-German church, and no other creed was to
be tolerated. The schools were to be solely in the rural districts,
and especially designed for instruction in agriculture and handicrafts; at the head of all was to be an elected king with a Reichsrat.
It read just as if the whole thing had been penned by Saint-Just.
Far more destructive to the students than were these radical
doctrines was the influence of that base ethical system which Carl
Follen advocated with all the prophet's inspiration, a preposterous
morality which was even more shameful than the teachings of
Mariana and Suarez. The Jesuits, at any rate, had allowed that
the authority of the church was supreme, but Follen, with facile
logic, starting from the cult of personal "conviction" which

flourished among the students, developed a system of crude subjectivism which simply denied any objective rule to human life. It was bluntly declared that for the righteous man no law was of account. What the reason recognises as true must be realised by the moral will, at once, unconditionally, uncompromisingly, even to the point of annihilating all those who hold different opinions ; there cannot be any talk of a conflict of duties, for the realisation of the reason is a moral necessity. This proposition was known simply as " the principle," and it was on its account that Follen's confidants termed themselves the "Unconditionals." To the members of this sect it seemed that anything was permissible for the sake of popular freedom—lying, murder, or any other crime—for no one had the right to withhold freedom from the people.

Thus did the evangel of the overthrow of all moral and political order make its first appearance in Germany, that terrible theory which, under many different cloaks, was ever and again to disturb the century, and which was finally to receive its extremest development in the doctrine of the Russian nihilists. But Follen draped his nihilism in a Christian mantle : Jesus, the martyr of conviction, was the Unconditionals' hero ; their association-song declared " A Christ shalt thou become ! " Just as impudently were misused the names of the Prussian heroes, and especially of Scharnhorst and Gneisenau, by some from naive ignorance, but by Follen from calculation, for the innocent Burschen were to believe that Germany's warriors had fought for democracy. A widely sung lay by Buri, *Scharnhorst's Prayer*, was adorned by the brothers Follen with revolutionary phrases, and was printed under the false title *Kosciuszko's Prayer*. In this the general was made to swear :

I shrink not back, and if need be through fierce and bloody fights
Will men's great cause defend, the city free of equal rights !

Carl Follen himself also hammered out verses, although his harsh nature utterly lacked poetic gifts ; and the incredible bombast, the savage and bloodthirsty rhetoric of his poems, found many admirers among the students. His master-work was *The Great Song ;* it was widely circulated by Weidig and Sand, but its

leading passages were not fully comprehensible except to initiates.
It opened with an appeal, " The Youth of Germany to the Masses
of Germany."

> Human mass, of life's best things still cheated,
> Which in vain the soul's spring yet hath greeted,
> 　Break to pieces, ancient ice-domain !
> Sink them deep in strong and proud sea-eddies,
> Slave.and tyrant, whose unceasing dread is
> 　Free-state which shall glow with life again !
> Babel's realm of foul and venal nations
> Spues forth equal rights and freedoms, fashions
> Godhood out of human labour-pain.

There follows an impudent street-ballad whose refrain " Brothers,
not thus shall it happen !　People, to arms ! " continued for many
years to resound at all mob-assemblies in Central Germany.　Next
came a communion hymn of free brethren, describing " the holy
order of the martyrs of eternal freedom," its members swearing
upon the host as they grasped their unsheathed daggers, " The
equality of all citizens, the will of the people, is alone autocrat
by God's grace."　They apostrophise the nation, saying :

> People, seize Moloch's crew, and strangle all !

Still more definite is the New Year's hymn of free Christians, set
to a quick and lively air, which serves to reinforce the insolent
meaning of the words :

> The dagger of freedom is ready in the hand !
> Hurrah !　Strike it home through the throat !
> Clad in purple vesture,
> Adorned with crowns and garlands,
> The victim stands ready by the altar of vengeance !

In this strain the poem continues, becoming ever more senseless,
ever wilder, until the concluding verse :

Down with forced labour ; down with crowns, thrones, drones, and
　　barons !
　　　Charge !

Among the hundreds of young men who sang these raging verses, few doubtless gave much thought to the words, but the poet himself was thoroughly in earnest. He had already conceived a plan which he repeatedly discussed with the Unconditionals. Since a revolution was for the moment impossible, it was necessary to assassinate a few traitors in order to terrify and at the same time to stimulate the fainthearted populace. He himself would take no part in these preparatory deeds, refraining, not from fear, but because he proposed to act as leader in the general popular uprising. Without respite he pursued an agitation among the people. In the petition that article 13 should be carried into effect, in all the addresses and meetings urging the grand duke of Hesse to fulfil the promise of a constitution, Follen's hand was at work. For him, the red republican, these measures could be nothing more than means for greater ends. Schulz, his right-hand man of Darmstadt, in a *Question and Answer Booklet*, openly preached revolution to the Hessian peasants.

For a long time the Jena students refrained from sharing the demagogic attitude of the men of Giessen ; and they also rejected Follen's plan for a centralised constitution, although this proposal was favoured by a considerable minority. But by degrees the revolutionary doctrines of the Blacks made their way to the banks of the Saale, chiefly through the instrumentality of Robert Wesselhöft, a rough and vigorous Thuringian of autocratic temperament. Quite without the knowledge of the bulk of the Burschen, he formed within the ranks of the Old Germans a secret society of Unconditionals, composed of men who looked down with contempt upon the blameless masses of the Burschenschaft, and who kept up secret communication by trusty messengers with those of their own way of thinking at other universities. To this group belonged Jens Uwe Lornsen, an unruly berserk northlander from the Frisian isles, widely known at a later date as an advocate of the rights of Schleswig-Holstein. Another member of the group was Heinrich Leo from the Schwarzburg region, small and girlishly beautiful, a born romanticist who amid his native forests had acquired a glowing enthusiasm for the rude and natural life of the primitive Teutons, and a profound hatred for the rigid formalism of classical culture ; it was only through the untamable wildness of his hot blood that for a brief period he was impelled to take part in a modern revolutionary movement which was utterly foreign to his temperament.

The tone of these Blacks was indescribably impudent ; they were absolutely convinced that it was their mission to initiate and direct the emanicipation of the enslaved peoples. A Bavarian wit, masquerading as an enthusiastic disciple of Fries, had recently published an open letter in which he classified the entire human race as Burschen, she-Burschen, teachers-of-Burschen, those-destined-to-become-Burschen, and those-who-had-been-Burschen. The satire was so aptly conceived that many of the Burschen themselves took the letter at its face value, and the same mistake has been made by not a few historians of to-day. For a long time now the Blacks had not been satisfied with such manifestations of foolish impertinence as that of Lornsen, who in the presence of the young duke of Meiningen gave vent to three groans for the thirty or three and thirty. With sinister composure, they daily discussed who should first be " corpsed " in the cause of freedom. Since Metternich was out of reach and not one of the German princes was regarded with especial hatred, the wild talk returned ever to Kotzebue as the first victim. In the autumn of 1818, when it was expected that Czar Alexander was about to pass through Jena, the leaders of the Unconditionals held a secret conclave to consider whether the time had now come to strike a blow against the despot ; anyone whose response to this inquiry showed him to be untrustworthy was henceforward tacitly excluded from the counsels of the initiates. The czar meanwhile had passed on his way without visiting the town, and it was subsequently contended that the leaders of the Blacks were aware of the fact. This may be true, but what had happened to our youth when approval of the cowardly practice of political assassination, one so repulsive to the German sense of uprightness, had come to be regarded as the touchstone of sound sentiments ?

The young peoples' excitement was increased by the alarm of the official newspapers, and unfortunately also by many indiscreet utterances on the part of their teachers. In his lectures, as previously in his *Politics*, Luden advanced the incontestable proposition that the power and the liberty of the state are priceless moral goods, and that on occasion, therefore, other moral goods must be sacrificed to these ; but his intellectual force was not great enough to impress clearly upon the students' minds the profound significance of a doctrine which may so readily be misapplied, and many of his greatly moved audience simply acquired the impression, as did Carl Sand, that the end justifies the means. Fries, too, was in a state of hopeless perplexity in face of the awakening of demagogy, and his expressions of opinion were often confused. Conscientiously warning the students against secret societies, he endeavoured to gild the pill by the use of revolutionary phraseology, and inveighed in such rough terms against the police authority which insisted on " binding to hop-poles the oaks and pines of the German forests," that his words proved exciting rather than calmative. In a confession of faith for young people he said : " I regard as sacred the demand for a new German law and for a vigorous republican system that will secure the unity of Germany. I detest the way in which we are ruled by highly well-born French apes, and in which we are instructed by well-born Latin apes. I loathe the oppression of the people by standing armies, by the salaries paid to the stupid and haughty idlers who act as officers. The people is the army, and the people is master." Even the free spirit of Arndt was not uninfluenced by the bitterness of the epoch. The fourth volume of his *Spirit of the Age*, published in the year 1818, was greatly inferior to the earlier volumes ; the fine emotion of the wars of liberation was no longer adequate. The pride of the students was necessarily strengthened when Arndt depicted for them the Seven Years' War as an empty tale, and described the works of our classical poetry as petty and spiritless, as the offspring of a formless age, lacking love and lacking glory. He innocently suggested that secret conspiracies were permissible only " if a foreign nation or a malicious tyrant were endeavouring to brutalise the entire generation to the level of dogs, monkeys, and snakes," and had no idea that his young readers had long before come to consider that they themselves were ruled by such malicious tyrants. The French and the Poles, he exclaimed, have a constitution, " while our rulers wish to have us lying at their mercy as if we had no more life in us than a lot of wooden posts " ; while for the Prussian army he held up as an example the loose militia organisation of the Swedish army, based on what was

known as the *Indelningsverk*, which in the last war had done
nothing at all. Amid such thoughtless words of incitement, the
patriotic warnings which the good man directed against " the
callow and presumptuous folly of the Germans " were completely
forgotten. Among the professors, anger concerning the disillusionments of these first years of peace, gradually increased to an
inflammatory degree. In the summer of 1818, even Schleiermacher
discoursed as if a new 1806 was approaching—and this at a time
when, apart from a few isolated blunders, the Prussian government
had not as yet done anything open to reasonable criticism.

In the autumn of 1818, Carl Follen removed to Jena as demonstrator. He was the grave-digger of the Burschenschaft, the
destroyer of the frank youthful sentiment which had prevailed in
its inception. Vainly did Fries endeavour to hold his own with
the sinister man ; in the oratorical struggles of the Philosophical
Club, the young demonstrator showed himself far in advance of
the professor, and the students withdrew more and more from
the side of the moderate elder. It is true that the number of
Follen's immediate intimates remained very small, for the young
men's healthy feelings made it impossible for them entirely to
overcome their horror of the apostle of assassination ; his principal disciples were his blind and devoted slave Carl Sand, and
Wit von Dörring, a dissolute adventurer, who subsequently became
a traitor. But the corrupting influence of his doctrines extended
far beyond this narrow circle. Louder and louder became the
talk of " cutting off the tyrants' heads." During the winter,
by an odious fraud (since everything was permissible to the
Unconditionals), the Blacks and their faithful followers got control
of the committee of the Burschenschaft ; then a secret society
was formed whose sworn members were, like the carbonari, divided
into lodges, and were in part unknown even to one another. Since
the outspoken Teuton has no talent for the conspirators' secret
arts, such societies could never rise above the level of a foolish
masquerade ; and yet the matter was not devoid of grave significance when so many isolated young men played rudely and
boastfully with the thought of political crime, and were actually
receiving from Follen the definite instruction that whoever wished
to sacrifice himself for the cause must do the liberating deed without confederates. When one of the older Blacks, Wilhelm Snell,

was at this time dismissed his post, his Hessian comrades issued to the Unconditionals an appeal for the support of their friend " so that the brood may learn to tremble before the higher power which will swing the sword of vengeance as strongly as now it swings the shield of defence, as soon as sin awakens the day of wrath."

At a later date, men who had once been members of the Blacks' organisation considered that much mischief might have been avoided if Follen and one or two of his older associates had been expelled from Germany in good time. But the governments had no detailed information regarding these restless activities, and contemplated them with timid concern. The handful of demagogues continued its evil work, until the day was to dawn in which the seed of criminal words which had been so widely scattered was to be harvested, and in which an unhappy wretch, dagger in hand, was to realise the doctrine of political assassination.

Follen's activities had disastrous results. In the summer of 1819, his faithful follower Sand stabbed and killed the dramatist and sometime Russian agent Kotzebue, in the belief that he was striking a blow for liberty. This senseless act gave Metternich a pretext for fastening the Austrian system of thought control on all the states of the German Confederation.

The Carlsbad Decrees (III, 180–85, 206–7, 213–14, 227)

No one who knows the contagious energy of political crime will deny that, after all that had happened, the crowns were justified in undertaking, and were even compelled to undertake, a strict investigation into the ultimate causes of the murder of Kotzebue and the attempt on Ibell's life, and to initiate severe proceedings against certain writers who openly defended political assassination. Since both the criminals belonged to the Unconditionals, the suppression of the Burschenschaft was unavoidable for a time at least. Yet nothing· but courageous, firm, and calm action on the part of the governments could bring unstable public opinion to its senses once more, and at the German courts there was no trace of such statesmanlike certainty of aim.   Gloomy epochs appear from time to time in which even noble nations seem to be smitten by epidemic mental disorder. Thus almost all the German governments fell a prey to a wild delusion of persecution.   The two enigmatic crimes, the excited language of the newspapers (among which the *Isis* and the *Neue Stuttgarter Zeitung* were especially foolish), the stormy proceedings of the two first Landtags—all these things in conjunction made the minor courts extremely uneasy.   There was superadded the obscure feeling that the nation had, in truth, little ground to congratulate itself upon the Vienna treaties.

The South German courts, which were hailed in the press as pillars of the constitutional faith, displayed themselves the most disturbed of all.   King William of Würtemberg sent the court of St. Petersburg so dire a description of the revolutionary sentiments of the German youth that Stourdza exulted loudly, and even the ultra-conservative Blittersdorff found this appeal of a German prince to a foreign court a contemptible act.   Bahnmaier, the pious theologian of Tübingen, was deprived of a minor post, because in an official report he had truthfully declared that Sand's action was not regarded by the students as a crime, but as a patriotic aberration.   The court of Munich immediately applied to Austria and Prussia, urgently demanding that common measures should be taken against the universities ;   certain teachers who had expressed their satisfaction concerning the death of Kotzebue were immediately suspended from office ; and since Sand sent a message to his king from prison, to the effect that the latter had nothing to fear for himself, the timid Max Joseph immediately drew the conclusion that godless designs were manifestly cherished against other German princes.[1]   Finally, the government of Baden, in whose territory the crime had been committed, had quite extraordinary ideas regarding the extent of the " demagogic intrigues," as the new official expression phrased it.   The investigation had   disclosed   a half truth.   The government believed itself to have ascertained that in the Burschenschaft there existed a secret society " whose principal motto is tyrannicide, and which has its centre in the vicinity of Giessen, in the abode of a certain Follenius."   But the Badenese government did not

[1] Krusemark's Report, May 21 ;   Zastrow's Reports, April 14 and August 4 ; Ministerial Despatch to Zastrow, April 23, 1819.

discover how few and powerless were the Unconditionals, cherishing the illusion that the German Landtags desired to combine to establish a German parliament beside the Bundestag, and then to declare the indivisible German republic. It was consequently with ardent gratitude that Berstett received "the gracious communication of the most sapient views of his majesty the emperor," when Metternich wrote that the Austrian court was determined to take serious steps against the professors and the abandoned writers, "who are daily, in every possible way, instilling their revolutionary principles into the mind of youth, to the point of intoxication." Berstett immediately instructed the Badenese federal envoy to follow the Austrian lead, and declared to the cabinet of St. Petersburg, "We desire to press forward to the source of this hellish conspiracy, which aims at nothing less than the overthrow of all divine and human institutions ; we desire to suppress the despotism which the professors are endeavouring to exercise over the political opinions of Germany, under the ægis of an inexperienced and far too impressionable youth."[1]

Far more momentous was the change of sentiments at the court of Berlin. As with all other important resolves on the part of this government, the reactionary tendency of the year 1819 proceeded from the monarch in person. The king became daily more dissatisfied with his chancellor, and with Hardenberg's "curious" entourage. From the foolish articles of the liberal journals, which Wittgenstein sedulously laid before him, Frederick William concluded that a powerful conspiracy existed, and expressed his gratitude to Eylert, the court bishop, when the latter, on the occasion of the Ordensfest, stigmatised the rebellious spirit of the age in a clamorous speech. When the news of Sand's crime now arrived, and when the murder found so many blinded defenders, the conscientious monarch felt wounded in his most sacred sentiments ; he regarded it as his royal duty to intervene with inconsiderate severity, gave the police authorities extraordinary powers (May 4th), and in addition established a ministerial committee to conduct proceedings against the demagogues. The Prussian students at the university of Jena were ordered to

---

[1] Metternich to Berstett, April 17 ; Berstett to Nesselrode, May 9; to Metternich, May 29, 1819.

leave that town, and although the young fellows at first talked
much of heroic resistance to the tyrannical order, in the end, when
the time expired, they all obeyed to the last man.

Yet not even this experience induced the king to ask himself
whether, after all, the spirit of insubordination in the academic
world could be so powerful as he had imagined. He considered
what Metternich had reported to him concerning the intrigues of
political parties working in obscurity had now been completely
justified by the course of events ; he refused to sign the new gymnastic ordinance when it was laid before him, sent urgent advice
for the adoption of severe measures both to Weimar and to Carlsruhe, on the ground that the " unhappy disorders among the
university youth have attained to a truly alarming height " ; and
commanded Count Bernstorff to consult with the Austrian envoy
Zichy (who had just received instructions by courier) concerning
extraordinary resolutions on the part of the Bundestag.[1] The
new director of the department of police, Privy Councillor Kamptz,
with the support of Wittgenstein, ardently threw himself into the
work of investigation. A Mecklenburger by birth, and therefore
accustomed to a deathly stillness in public life, he really seems
to have believed in the great conspiracy, but at the same time
he desired to avenge himself upon his literary opponents. There
at once flocked to his assistance a rabble rout of depraved men,
who were accustomed to thrive in the miasmatic atmosphere of
mistrust and suspicion : the councillors Tzschoppe, Grano, and
Dambach, men animated by vulgar ambition, who undertook
the journeyman's work of the prosecutions with tenacious and
bloodthirsty zeal.

Whilst the German courts were thus mastered by blind terror,
Metternich luxuriated in the sentiment of gratified vanity. Once
again he had foreseen everything, the devilish plans of the repro-
bates who dreamed of German unity had been disclosed ; now
was the opportunity to exploit the anxiety of the German crowns,
" to give matters the best possible turn, to draw from them the
greatest possible advantage." During the spring of this year,
Emperor Francis visited the Italian courts. Metternich, who
with the Prussian envoy Krusemark, travelled in the monarch's

[1] Bernstorff to Varnhagen, April 23 ; Krusemark's Report, April 16 ; Instructions to Krusemark, May 17 and June 15, 1819.

train, sent to his wife from Rome and Naples reports of the journey which produce on the mind of an unprejudiced reader somewhat the impression as if a commercial clerk greedy of knowledge had written them and Baron Münchhausen of happy memory had appended certain historical and statistical observations. He displayed his sentiment for art by playing the patron to certain fashionable French and English painters. On the other hand, the exhibition which the German painters had instituted in the Palazzo Caffarelli in honour of the emperor was hardly deemed worthy of a glance. The Viennese could make nothing of the high-flown idealism of these Nazarenes ; moreover the artists of San Isidoro had long hair and wore Old German coats, and, notwithstanding the artists' Catholic sentiments, these peculiarities rendered them extremely suspect in the emperor's eyes. The political aim of the journey was ostensibly attained. Emperor Francis was hailed everywhere by the polite world as protector of Italy. He visited the Vatican as guest of the pope, who overwhelmed the ruler of the leading Catholic power with tokens of honour, and decorated the archduke Rudolf with the cardinal's purple. This sufficed to determine Metternich's judgment. Why should he concern himself to glean information about Roman affairs from Niebuhr, the Prussian envoy, who, despite his conservative inclinations, despite his respect for the pope's gentleness and for the sagacity of Cardinal Consalvi, had speedily come to the conclusion that the eternal city had been far happier under Napoleonic rule than under the restored priestly dominion ? To the Austrian statesman, conditions in the Pontifical State seemed altogether admirable, whilst the lazzaroni of Naples beneath the blessings of Bourbon rule were " a hundred-fold more civilised than they had been twenty years before." He declared it altogether impossible that the plaintive but spiritless Italians should ever venture upon raising the standard of revolt—making this prophecy barely a year before the revolution simultaneously broke out in Naples and in Piedmont.

He manifested the same certainty of statesmanlike insight in his judgment of German affairs. To him this outwearied people seemed long overripe for revolution. " I vouch for it," he wrote to his wife, " that in the year 1789 the condition of the world was perfectly healthy when compared with the state of affairs to-day!" Even before the Wartburg festival, he had several times discussed with the South German envoys whether there ought not to be instituted in Vienna a common *foyer* for the observation of the German revolution. Now came one appeal for help after another from the minor courts. They all complained of their own heedlessness, and expressed their admiration for the penetrating insight of the great statesman who alone had foreseen the reckless purposes of the Burschen. How was it possible that this vainest of men should now be free from a self-admiration verging upon lunacy? Since the solitary giant of the eighteenth century had passed away (he doubtless referred to Frederick II), Metternich found that the human race had become contemptibly petty. "My spirit," he declared, "cannot endure anything petty; I command a view which is incomparably wider than that which other statesmen see, or desire to see. I cannot refrain from saying to myself twenty times a day how right I am and how wrong they are. And yet it is so easy, so clear, so simple, to find the only right path!" Thus the idealistic pride of the German youth was countered by the cold arrogance of the man of the world, who was never inspired with enthusiasm for any abstract idea, who had never given a thought to the great interests of human civilisation, but who regarded fear, that meanest of human passions, as his natural ally, and who, amid all the follies of police persecution, continued to imagine himself a wise advocate of statesmanlike moderation, saying: "The sacred mean where truth is to be found, is accessible to but few."

Without even asking for proofs, he regarded it as established that the "Jena Fehm" chose its members by lot, in order to despatch them throughout Germany for the work of assassination; the power of the individual German states was inadequate to deal with so terrible a conspiracy. Consequently when King Max Joseph consulted the court of Vienna, as well as that of Berlin, regarding the suspension of the Bavarian constitution, Metternich returned an evasive answer. The press, the universities, and the chambers must be gagged by the common action of all the federal states, under Austria's leadership. "With God's help, I hope to avert the German revolution just as I have overthrown the conqueror of the world!" He was firmly supported by his monarch. Now, as always, Emperor Francis desired repose. Never must the quiet life of his press, of his postulate Landtags, and of those schools which in Old Austria were termed universities, be disturbed by the follies of his German neighbours. He whole-heartedly approved his minister's theory that every federal prince would commit "a felony against the Federation" should he allow freedom to the press, since, owing to the existence of a common language, the virus of this freedom might infect German-speaking Austria. He declared with cynical frankness that it was necessary to play upon the fears of these weak governments, and he empowered his statesmen, in case of need, to threaten that Austria would secede from the Federation.

On July 22nd, Metternich reached Carlsbad, inspired by the proud conviction that "from this place either the salvation or the ultimate destruction of the social order will proceed." Emperor Francis had abandoned a proposed visit to his Lombardo-Venetian kingdom because the repression of the German revolution seemed a more urgent matter. The intimates with whom the Austrian statesman first conversed were, in addition to Gentz, his two friends of the Vienna congress, the Hanoverians, Counts Hardenberg and Münster. In any case, in all matters where no intervention of parliament was to be feared, Metternich could unconditionally rely upon the highly reactionary sentiments of the tory cabinet, and subsequently he wrote gratefully to the prince regent: "One is always certain to find your royal highness on the road of sound principles." But all other assistance was worthless in default of an unconditional understanding with the crown of Prussia. In order to bring this about, Metternich hastened to Teplitz, and there, on July 29th, had a private conversation with King Frederick William, which determined the course of German policy for years to come. The king showed himself to be extremely discomposed on account of the sinister demagogic plans which, as Wittgenstein assured him, had been disclosed by the latest domiciliary searches ; he was annoyed, and with good reason, on account of the chancellor's inefficiency and the dilatoriness of his ministry, which had kept him waiting seven months for an answer to urgent enquiries. He complained, "My own people fail me," and he committed himself confidingly to the advice of this Austrian who in Aix-la-Chapelle had already given him such admirable counsel. Metternich understood how to strike the iron while it was hot. For Prussia, he declared, the day had now arrived for a choice between the principle of conservatism and political death ; the great conspiracy had its origin and its seat in Prussia, and it penetrated even the ranks of the highest officials ; still everything could yet be saved if the crown would make up its mind not to grant any popular representation in the modern democratic sense of the term, and would content itself with estates. At the same time he handed in a memorial in which he repeated the ideas voiced by him at Aix-la-Chapelle. The king's assent to these proposals was a matter of course, for even Hardenberg's constitutional plan had never aimed at more than a representation of the three estates, and had not dreamed of a representation of the people as a whole.

The worst feature of all was that the state which had restored freedom to Germany, the one which had everything to hope from national unity and nothing to dread, now voluntarily put its neck under the yoke of the Austrian dominion, and therefore, to that portion of the nation which could not see beyond the next day, assumed the semblance of a sworn enemy. The star of the Frederician state had become obscured by clouds of suspicion. By the anxious mood of a noble monarch misled by blind counsellors, and through the perplexities of the aging Hardenberg, this state had been diverted from the paths in which it had risen to greatness, and when Austria had gathered in the Teplitz harvest Metternich declared with satisfaction to the Russian envoy, " Prussia has ceded us a place which many Germans had designed for Prussia herself ! "

As soon as the two great powers had come to an unreserved agreement, the victory of Austrian policy was decided. No one in the Carlsbad assembly was prepared to oppose them on principle. Count Schulenburg, the Saxon, now made common cause with the two Hanoverians, for he, like them, was a strict advocate of the feudal state-system. Baron von Plessen, of Mecklenburg, a man of far more liberal and mobile intelligence, was by the traditions of his homeland forced into more or less the same position. Even the representatives of the so-called constitutional states manifested uncritical docility. Count Rechberg, the true originator of the Bavarian plan for a *coup d'état*, did, indeed, in accordance with the custom of Munich, cherish some mistrust for Austria ; but he was far more afraid of the revolution, and this latter fear decided his conduct, although he had been expressly instructed not to approve anything which infringed Bavarian sovereignty or the Bavarian constitution. Baron von Berstett gave such terrible accounts of the disorders of the Carlsruhe representative assembly that in Gentz's opinion to listen to him was at once a horror and a delight. Marschall of Nassau outbid even the reactionary fanaticism of the Badenese statesman ; nor did Count Wintzingerode leave anything to be desired in respect of hostility towards the demagogues, although to him was allotted the thorny task of avoiding anything that might completely undermine the reputation of the most exemplary of constitutional kings.

The members of the Carlsbad assembly fortified one another in their fears of the great conspiracy, and Metternich was able to handle them so adroitly that Bernstorff wrote to the chancellor, " We can settle everything here, but later it will be impossible ! " So completely did they adopt the Austrian view of German affairs that at length they all came to believe that they were doing a great and good work, and honestly rejoiced in the fine patriotic unity of the German crowns. " The issue lies in God's hand," wrote Bernstorff when their work had been completed ; " but at any rate a great thing has already been achieved in that amid the storms of the time the German princes have been able to express their principles and intentions openly, definitely, and unanimously." The sense of satisfaction was all the stronger because the German statesmen were working entirely among themselves, and no foreign power even attempted to exercise any influence over the Carlsbad negotiations. As yet no one dreamed that this fine spectacle of national independence and harmony was nothing else than the subjection of the German nation to the foreign dominion of Austria.

Never since Prussia had existed as a great power, never since the days of Charles V and Wallenstein, had the house of Austria been able to set foot so heavily upon the neck of the German nation. Just as masterfully as in former days Emperor Charles had imposed the Interim of Augsburg upon the contentious Reichstag of the conquered Schmalkaldians, so now did Metternich

M.

call a halt to a new national movement of the Germans ; just as contemptuously as Granvelle had at that time laughed at the *peccata Germaniæ*, so did Gentz now mock at the tribulations of the Old Bursch of Weimar and his liberal train ; and just as submissively as in those days the weakly Joachim II, so now did a Hohenzollern stand before the Austrian ruler. But Austria had soon to learn that the crown which Emperor Francis had once torn from his own head was not to be regained by the trickeries of a false diplomacy. In earlier days Austria's dominion had always been a misfortune to the Germans ; the more brightly the star of the Hapsburgs shone, the more prostrate was the condition of the German nation. That great emperor who, in Augsburg, had once desired to control Protestantism, had at any rate offered the Germans something to replace their lost freedom, a mighty thought, one capable of filling even a Julius Pflugk with enthusiasm, the great conception of the Catholic world-empire. But what could they offer to the nation, these petty spirits who now endeavoured to tread in the footsteps of Emperor Charles ? Nothing but oppression and coercion, nothing but an unscrupulous distortion of the federal law, which must inevitably make their solitary national institution loathsome to the Germans, throwing as makeweight into the scale the lie that Germany was to be rescued from an imaginary danger.

THE LESSER STATES

The Kingdom of Saxony (IV, 305–29)

In 1815 the king of Saxony was Frederick Augustus I, who had been an ally of Napoleon to the bitter end and had, in consequence, been forced by the victorious powers to cede a large part of his territory to Prussia.

When, in June, 1815, the king returned to his diminished realm, he was inspired with the feeling that he had been severely and unjustly afflicted, and his reception could not but serve to strengthen this view. At the time of the battle of Leipzig a large proportion of the cultured classes had severely condemned his ungerman policy. In the subsequent prolonged period of uncertainty, the feeling of attachment to the dynasty was revived, and this feeling became completely predominant when tidings arrived of the partition of the country and of the impending return of the monarch. The few who had openly advocated the cause of Prussia now remained cautiously in the background; the populace termed them " the Prussians " or " the Germans." In the impotence of such particularism, many people changed their views without being aware of it. Mahlmann, the good-humoured Leipzig poet, editor of the favourite newspaper of the fashionable world, had written a fervent ode to the Imperator when Napoleon established the Saxon kingship, saying : " Terror stalks before him, but bounty comes behind." Just as movingly did he sing the glories of Czar Alexander and the national victory of Leipzig; while for the king's return he composed the new Saxon anthem, " Flourish, thou chaplet of rue ! " The enormous majority of the people were unquestionably straightforward in their rejoicings. They had become so thoroughly accustomed to the unchanging government of their old ruler that they felt themselves unable to live without him, and even during his lifetime he was generally spoken of as " the Just." Similar demonstrations were renewed when Frederick Augustus celebrated his jubilee; several of the districts ceded to Prussia sent ardent congratulations, nor did the new sovereign interfere.

A number of stately tomes, profusely illustrated, announced to the world at large the glories of this " feast of joy of the loyal Saxon nation," describing the triumphal arches, the obelisks, and " the temples of immortality "; reproducing the graceful hymn, " The rue again is verdant, the violet blooms once more." Reported, also, were all the rhymed and unrhymed orations in honour of " the good father of the bees," who had so long faithfully watched over his diligent bee subjects, and who, after having been driven out by foreign robber bees, humble bees, and wasps, had at length been able to return to his innocent children. At times the servility of these children increased to become flat blasphemy. The Dresden Society of the Blue Star, which had been formed during the Prusso-Russian foreign dominion to keep loyalty to the dynasty alive, gave a solemn festival, and at this, after a ceremonious pause, there resounded the word of power :

> Where but two or three assemble
> In Frederick August's name,
> His great precursor's also there.
> God bless the king ! Amen.

What a quantity of loathsome slime had during these wild times covered the still waters of the petty state. These were great days for informers and calumniators. Those who, during recent months, had abandoned the land to its fate, remaining sulkily at home, now cast suspicion upon the excellent officers and officials who had carried on the administration under the Russian and Prussian government. All of these, Generals Vieth and Carlowitz, Baron von Miltitz-Siebeneichen, and others, had rendered themselves impossible, and were compelled to leave the country. The king, after his return, founded some new orders, adorned with the freshly chosen green-and-white national colours, and these distinctions were bestowed, not only upon many faithful state servants, but also upon a number of wretched denunciators.

With the ardent veneration which was henceforward paid to these colours without a history, there was unfortunately associated, and inseparably, an equally passionate hatred for Prussia. Among all the Germans, it was the electoral Saxons who found the greatest difficulty in adapting themselves to the confusions of our modern history and in recognising the creative energies with which it was endowed. The facts were obvious: Prussia's ascent had been due to the decline of Electoral Saxony ; during the last century and a half, almost every great day for Germany had been a defeat for Saxon policy. How could this be understood in a country which had experienced no more than fugitive traces of the national enthusiasm of recent years ? Of the two vigorous Saxons who had contributed so much to fan the flames of this patriotic idealism, one, Fichte, was little known in his own land : men of learning esteemed him as a philosopher ; the clergy did not forget that the Dresden consistory had once accused him of atheism ; his *Address to the German Nation* was hardly known. As for "the dramatic poet Theodor Körner," a few days before his death there had appeared in the Dresden papers a citation against him for the non-fulfilment of his military duties; and people in good society were disinclined to mention his name, for, like his father, he had espoused the Prussian cause. Doubtless the writer of *Lyre and Sword* did not stand alone among the Saxon youths. After the battle of Leipzig many who were enthusiasts for Germany's freedom sent in their names to the army, men who had long ere this demanded permission to fight against France under their own banner of the chaplet of rue. In order to attract young men of the upper classes in larger numbers, the Russian provisional government encouraged the formation of a troop of volunteers modelled upon the Lützowers, and this was joined by numerous honourable enthusiasts, among whom was Krug, the Leipzig philosopher. But participation in this movement was far from general, for the impulsive ardour of the Prussian volunteers was lacking. The new force had poor fortune, and its only sight of the enemy was behind the walls of the Mainz fortress. The patriotic undertaking was no less sterile than was the *Encyclopædic Synopsis of the Military Sciences* which, on the strength of his bloodless warlike experiences, Krug, the ready writer, published immediately after the war. Whilst the entire population of Prussia was fighting for Germany, many excellent young Saxons were still entirely dominated by the philistine views of traditional class pride, and were utterly unable to understand that a man of culture could shoulder a musket. Möbius, the learned young astronomer, voiced the cordial opinion of his Leipzig colleagues when he wrote in the summer of 1814: "I consider it utterly impossible that anyone should think of making me a recruit, me, a fully accredited magister of Leipzig university. This is the most horrible idea I have ever heard of; and anyone who shall dare, venture, hazard, make bold, and have the audacity to propose it, will not be safe from a dagger. I do not belong to the Prussians; I am in Saxon service."

When the partition came, with its rude disturbance of numerous neighbourly relationships, memories of the War of

Liberation and of the misdeeds of the French were speedily forgotten. No longer did anyone ask what Prussia had contributed to the liberation of Saxony in addition to that of the rest of Germany; no one reflected that Talleyrand and Metternich were responsible for the partition, and that Prussia had accepted it only with reluctance. Naturally enough, boundless hatred was felt for the northern neighbour, and this hatred was raised to the pitch of fury when the horrible intelligence was received of the mutiny at Liège. No longer was Saxon particularism proud, as it had been in the days of the electors Maurice and Augustus; it was sullen, spiteful, and venomous, after a fashion utterly opposed to the inborn characteristics of this kindly race. Whoever was a good Saxon must from time to time prove by a volley of abuse directed against Prussia that the Meissen dialect is as expressive and well equipped for rudeness as for politeness. For many years it was a peculiarity of Saxony that at every turn it was possible to encounter men of conspicuous ability and inspired with excellent German sentiments who could speak reasonably upon every topic in the world except Prussia.

During the first days after the partition, this mood found expression solely in a few detestable lampoons. Thus, for example, there appeared a manifestly false despatch from the Saxon grenadiers, describing for the " brothers-in-arms of all the German nations " the abominable crimes of the Prussian " dealers in souls " at Liège. Another pamphlet with an equally fictitious title, *Apologia of Councillor N. for his transfer from the Saxon to the Prussian Service*, developed the fine plan that the Old Saxon officials in the Prussian province of Saxony should secretly endeavour to hinder " the decline of Saxon national feeling and the amalgamation with Prussia " in order to prepare the inhabitants for " the dawn of better days." Further we read : " It is not without the profoundest grief, we may rest assured, that the imperial house of Austria has now yielded to the pressure of circumstances, and consented to the humiliation of a family so closely allied ; of necessity, Austria must dread the rapacious northern eagle, and must as speedily as possible set a term to its advances. France, Bavaria, the pope, the clergy who are so powerful in Austria, all the lesser German princes who see in Saxony an example of the manner in which their own existence is threatened, will speak on our behalf, and will before long fan the flames of discord between the two rivals for supremacy in Germany!" The populace continued to hope for the reunion of the Albertine territories just as obstinately as of old the Ernestines had hoped for the restoration of the forfeited electoral hat. The children in the schools sang the defiant song: "Prussia has stolen our land, but we shall get it back again. Wait, wait, wait!"

Although the king, with his strict sense of justice, faithfully observed the treaty of peace, it was the inevitable result of what had happened that he should now regard a closer union with Prussia as impracticable. Henceforward it seemed to him that his natural ally must be Austria, although whenever there was famine in the Erzgebirge the imperial state made a point of closing the frontier, and in other respects displayed herself a bad neighbour. The tacit animosity against Prussia failed to find plainer expression only because the two German great powers were now allied, and because Frederick Augustus again devoted himself exclusively to the tasks of internal administration. High politics were beyond his circle of vision, but he never failed to feel flattered when the envoys of the great powers gave him information concerning the troubles of the outer world.[1] At the Bundestag, the Saxon envoy obediently followed Austria's lead; and, for the rest, his activities were so inconspicuous that Metternich would occasionally suggest in a friendly way that it might be well for the court of Dresden to display its excellent sentiments in a somewhat more vigorous fashion. Thus it was that the partition long exercised a disastrous influence upon Saxon policy. Among the common people, it fostered a petty particularist spite which completely overshadowed German national pride; alike at court and among the general population, it rendered difficult the appropriate recognition of the great economic interests which bound Saxony to Prussia.

[1] Jordan's Report, November 2, 1826.

Beyond question the country had suffered irremediable losses. In addition to the beautiful Thuringian chapter lands and the greater part of Lusatia, Kurkreis had been sacrificed—Kurkreis, the pride of Upper Saxony—for a just destiny had restored to the home of the Reformation the blessings of a faithful Protestant governance. What precious intellectual energies, too, passed from the state with the loss of the two classical schools of Pforta and Rossleben. In Aster, the army was deprived of its most gifted officer. In Streckfuss, Schönberg, Ferber, and Theodor Körner's father, the Saxon officialdom had to dispense with the candid men who had long recognised and censured the errors of the nobles' regime. Nevertheless the dynasty still retained the more beautiful and richer moiety of Saxony, that which had of old endowed the Albertine state with its peculiar attributes. The area of the country was now, indeed, ludicrously small in comparison with the pretentions of the new kingly crown, but it was sufficient to enable the king-dom of Saxony to secure in the Germanic Federation the next place to that held by Bavaria. How astonishingly multi-farious were the culture and the intercourse of this narrow region. The industrious land took a share in almost every-thing which went to make up German life. The capital, half a royal seat and half a house-of-call for foreigners, continued to preserve almost unchanged the harmonious beauty of the baroque splendours which had once been celebrated by the brush of Canaletto. The gay life of those Polish days had long passed away, and but rarely were the ladies of the nobility borne to the palace in Old Franconian sedan chairs to attend some court festival; it was only the stores of art treasures and the charms of natural scenery which lured crowds of strangers to the Elbe. In this slumberous air, an independent bourgeoisie had never been able to come into existence. Here thrived those devout philistines among whom young Ludwig Richter found his most amusing figures: the controllers and court secretaries, who in the afternoons, after their moderate labours were finished, would wander with their families among the trees; the lesser nobility and the higher officials who spent the summer in their chalets at Loschwitz; and, last not least, the councillors, the artistically minded men of learning from the theatre and from the art-galleries, who in Old Dresden were no less respected than were the privy councillors in Old Berlin. Taking them all in all, they were cheerful and contented folk, ever out of doors, and characterised by immaculate political innocence and docility.

With feelings similar to those felt by Frankfort for the Golden Mainz, the rich town of Leipzig, the opposite pole of the multiform Saxon life, looked down upon her neighbour, the court city of Dresden. Leipzig was a bourgeois town, utterly devoid of beauty, but powerful from of old through a vigorous combination of mercantile and learned activities. After the close of the seventeenth century the German booktrade, scared away from Frankfort by the strict imperial censorship, had become centred on the Pleisse, assisted in this choice by the presence of the university and by the zeal of the electoral Saxons for authorship. Towards 1820, nearly one-third of all German books were printed in Leipzig; every German publisher of note had an agent there, and attended the Easter fair. The smaller publishers of the Catholic highlands, who had hitherto disposed of their school books and devotional works among the peasant farms of the mountain districts through the instrumentality of travellers, were irresistibly drawn into the more orderly activities of the " Protestant booktrade "; and just as literature had been the first bond of our national unity, so did it now create the first recognised universal German corporation, and did this, not as Metternich had once designed through the assistance of the federal police, but by its own spontaneous energy. In the year 1824, chiefly through the initiative of Perthes in Gotha and Fleischer in Leipzig, there came into existence the Union of German Booksellers, and therewith was effected a beneficial centralisation of the trade in literature, such as no other country could boast—a striking testimony, at once to the business efficiency of the German bourgeoisie and to the hidden power of the national idea.

Although Leipzig lacked the advantage of being situated upon a navigable river, from the beginning of the eighteenth century onwards it had taken the lead of all other German towns as a fair-town. It owed this development chiefly to the superiority of the Erzgebirge industries and to the lively spirit of enterprise of its merchants, who were little troubled by the easygoing Electoral Saxon administration, whereas the well-intentioned guardianship of Frederician commercial policy succeeded in ruining the fair-traffic of Frankfort - on - the - Oder. As the German industrial land situated furthest to the east, Saxony was the natural mart for the peoples of eastern Europe, who were still but half civilised, and had not yet completely outgrown the customs of the caravan trade ; and so long as German intercourse was still restricted by internal tolls, by the anarchical systems of coinage and weights and measures, and by the corporative rights and prohibitive rights of the towns, very definite advantages were offered by the intermittently recurrent free trade of the fairs. The attempts now made by the Prussian government to improve the trade of its own fair-towns, Naumburg and Frankfort-on-the-Oder, were labour lost, and served merely to arouse neighbourly resentment. Whenever the Naumburg fair was opened an interim fair was held at Leipzig, with the tacit connivance of the authorities ; as a measure of retaliation, the Prussian traders would during the Leipzig fair hold an accessory leather fair in Lützen. But Leipzig's superiority was decisive ; and with the great increase in urban traffic which occurred here thrice every year, the horizon of the bourgeoisie gradually became widened. The second commercial town of Germany faced the court and the officialdom like a free imperial town, not rebelliously, but in an independent spirit, and inspired with a consciousness that it did not belong to the petty kingdom alone.

The small town of Freiberg was even more important for German mining than was Leipzig for German commerce. Here flourished the first of all mining academies, sending its pupils as far away as Mexico and Peru, and recently acquiring a wide reputation through the work of Werner, for the poorer the natural yield of the precious metals furnished by the Erzgebirge ores, the more intricate had become the artifices for their extraction. Here Humboldt and Buch had passed some of the rich years of youth; here had Heinitz, Stein's tutor, worked; and here had Novalis written the lofty *Song of the Miner*, " That man is lord of all the earth, who gauges earth's profound." Close at hand in Tharandt, Heinrich Cotta, the Thuringian, directed a great institute for the teaching of forestry, which before long became the model for all Germany. Throughout the Erzgebirge, above ground and beneath, there were carried on grandly conceived economic activities, such as elsewhere in Germany were known only on the Lower Rhine. The watercourses of the mountains were interconnected by a system of canals for rafts; the great coal mines of the Plauen and Zwickau basins were already being worked; since the days of the continental system the textile industries had undergone great development; in Chemnitz, C. G. Becker was by now employing more than 3,000 hands in his calico printing works and his cotton mills. Almost all the little mountain towns presented the same picture. At the entrance stood the tall mile-stone, bearing the sign manual of Augustus the Strong; upon the summit of a rock with the river circling round it was an old castle dating from electoral days; on the sides of the hills nestled the trim houses and workshops of the weavers, the clock-makers and the stone-workers, everywhere buzzing with hard-working men, who would live from week end to week end upon potatoes, washed down with draughts of an infusion of chicory, supplied in yellow paper bags by Jordan and Timäus. Yet, notwithstanding the grinding poverty, everything was clean, and the workpeople always consoled themselves with the old phrase, " A pleasant life is ours in the Erzgebirge." There were excellent elementary schools, although the teachers were half starved; and there was manifold technical instruction, centred above all in the Dresden institute for technical education, founded in the year 1828. In this proud old Electoral Saxony there was to be found a magnificent share of German efficiency; and even in Rhineland General Aster would recall with complacency the varied life of his native country, well as he must have known that its restricted relationships could have afforded no scope for his talents.

But this abundance of social energies was impaired and

repressed by a constitution which seemed like a fragment
of topsy-turveydom. Everything which gave the country
importance, science, commerce, and industry, was bourgeois.
It is true that here, as in all the Germanised Slavonic lands,
there existed an incredible number of manorial estates, but
with few exceptions the landed gentry were impoverished,
those of Lusatia alone being tolerably well-to-do, and the
majority of the noble families finding it necessary to seek
a supplementary means of livelihood in court or state service.
With its dense population, and the predominantly urban
character of its civilisation, Saxony resembled the German
west far more closely than the aristocratic agricultural regions
of the Baltic shores ; and yet amid these thoroughly modern
economic conditions, there persisted immutably, like a well-
preserved political fossil, a nobles' regime whose inertia
was hardly exceeded even by that of Mecklenburg. It was
here as plainly necessary to effect a thorough transformation
by a partition of the lands, as it had formerly been necessary
in the Rhenish Confederate territories of South Germany
to effect such a transformation by the enlargement of the
state domain ; the wide mantle of the old constitution hung
in flapping folds around the limbs of the diminished kingdom.
But who could expect the cautious Frederick Augustus, now
advanced in years, to conceive such bold designs ? Who
would have ventured even to breathe these possibilities amid
the exaggerated homage of the days of his return ? The
king imagined that he was fulfilling all the wishes of his
grateful people when with his customary industry and knowledge of affairs he faithfully reinstated the old order, when
he wound up the rusty clock once more. The pendulum
moved again solemnly to and fro, so continuously, so
monotonously, that the Prussian envoy was never able to
report anything beyond "the persistent lack of events of
interest."[1] Of all the reports sent in by Prussian diplomats,
those from Dresden were the most void of matter.

Immediately after his return, the king reestablished the
former rigid court etiquette which when Frederick Augustus
was a prisoner of war in Berlin had given the inhabitants

---

[1] Jordan's Reports, July 12, 1819, and subsequent dates.

of that city so much opportunity for the exercise of their wit. Just as, a man of habit through and through, he continued to display his fine musical talent upon Silbermann's old clavicymbal although the pianoforte had long ere this been invented, so did he desire that his court should retain all the characteristics of 1780, and it was with reluctance that he constrained himself to the tacit recognition of some of the bold innovations which Prince Repnin, the Russian governor, had had the presumption to introduce. Repnin had disbanded the expensive yellow-and-blue Swiss guard, had thrown the Grosse Garten open to the public, and had connected the palace square with the Brühl Terrace by a flight of steps. These audacities of the foreign regime could not now be done away with. Subsequently some of the Dresden art collections were actually opened to the public. Hitherto these had been preserved as a court mystery, and, almost unknown to natives, had been visited solely by a few artists and foreigners, who gained entry, in accordance with the traditional Old Saxon manner, by the payment of a douceur. In other respects the court remained as unapproachable as ever. Day after day two chamberlains stood behind the king when he sat down to meat, solemnly lifting the tails of his coat, first the left and then the right, before pushing his chair beneath him ; every evening he appeared with all his court in the theatre, where Morlachi conducted the Italian opera. On Sunday in winter, after mass, the well- behaved boys of the upper classes waited in the corridors of the palace to admire the dignified train of the returning " Herrschaften " : first of all a great number of runners, equerries, chamberlains, and adjutants ; then the king in his old fashioned dress, powdered and pigtailed, his hands buried in a huge muff ; then followed the princes, Antony and Max, likewise with muffs, carrying their chapeau bras—a marvellous spectacle, which nowhere but in Dresden could have been contemplated with a straight face. The king never appeared on foot in the streets; he never saw the fine monument to his ancestor Maurice, recently restored, for it was in the pleasure grounds a hundred paces from the carriage road. If he wished to see a travelling menagerie, the elephants and the snakes must pay their respects to him in the palace yard. How astonished were the Dresdeners when Max Joseph, paying a visit to the Saxon court, in accordance with his Munich custom cheerfully perambulated the town, and even exchanged words with bourgeois, for the king of Saxony never conversed with anyone who was not of the highest rank.

No one had occasion to sigh more deeply over the oppression of all this court ceremony than the gifted children of Prince Max. Prince Frederick Augustus, the hope of the country, was an amiable young man fond of brilliant conversation, and even showing some understanding ot liberal ideas ; he associated freely with Wangenheim, who lived in Dresden after his dismissal, and the ever-sanguine trias politician confidently anticipated that he would one day be appointed chief of the Saxon ministry.[1] Prince John, the younger son, was a Dante enthusiast, and would at times describe Italy's misfortunes in verses which sounded almost sacrilegious in the mouth of this near relative of the archducal house :

> A tyrant's minions practice arts of hell
> In the proud city once the ocean's queen ;
> Cowards now flee where once the Fabii fell ;
> Where Dante sang, base flatterers now are seen.[2]

Their sister, Princess Amelia, wrote minor dramas. She displayed no striking talent, but her work was characterised by cordial natural sensibility, and by remarkable knowledge of petty bourgeois life.

In the presence of the king, before whom everything was hushed in timid veneration, it was impossible for the comparatively free tone of this youthful court to find expression. Heavy was the hand of the president of the privy cabinet, the prime minister Count Einsiedel, a spare, stiff man, chary of words, his master's most humble servant, and, though still young, absolutely petrified in the usages of the Saxon court and nobility. He was at first regarded with suspicion by the fanatics of particularism, for he had estates in

[1] Wangenheim to Hartmann, February 20, 1824; September 23, 1827.
[2] Wangenheim to Hartmann, January 4, 1824.

Prussian Lusatia, and was therefore one of the enemy's
"vassals."[1] In reality, however, his political horizon ended
at the green-and-white boundary posts; he neither knew nor
cared to know anything of the outer world, his Prussian
ironworks at Lauchhammer alone excepted. Shortly before
the king's return, Count Marcolini, the favourite of many
years' standing, had died. The "Contino," as he was called,
an Italian of the frivolous Old Bourbon school, had been
generally detested in the country; but he had had one merit
at least, namely, that he had exercised a cheering influence
upon his royal friend, and had to some extent counterbalanced the influence of the father confessors. But all
this was altered now, for Count Einsiedel, a rigidly orthodox
Lutheran, was extremely friendly towards the claims of the
Catholic clergy. The minister's predilection for Stephan, the
preacher, who had become the centre of a fanatical sect
at the Bohemian church in Dresden, and who was subsequently shown to be a common hypocrite, aroused well-
grounded discontent. So inflamed was public opinion that
Stephan's participation in the work of the Bible society,
the missionary union, and other perfectly innocent Christian
undertakings, was regarded by the populace as suspicious.
For at this time among the Upper Saxons the Lutheran
rationalism of the old century was still in full force; no one
would hear a word of Evangelical union but every manifestation of a strongly religious sentiment was resisted with
the utmost intolerance as cant and sanctimoniousness.
Under Ammon's rationalistic rule, the circulation of orthodox tracts was absolutely prohibited. The conventicles
of Count Dohna, grandson of Zinzendorf, and the pupils of
Schubert, the poor and pious weavers in the Erzgebirge, had
to keep just as quiet as the Moravian brethren who had
founded Pella-Herrnhut in a charming corner of Lusatia.

The cabinet was assisted by the privy council, whose
powers were purely deliberative, and by the central boards
of justice and police. In financial matters, the dualism of
the feudalist state persisted unchanged. The royal privy
financial council administered the domains, whilst the supreme

[1] Report of Councillor Heun, July 23, 1817.

college of taxation (partly controlled by the diet) had charge of most of the taxes, and the disputes between the financial and the fiscal authorities were unceasing. In the bailiwicks, affairs were in the hands of the bailiffs, state officials drawn from the ranks of the resident gentry, with authority resembling that wielded by the Prussian Land-rats. But the lords of the manor recked little of these administrators, exercising almost unrestricted powers within their own estates, administering justice through patrimonial courts (which the lord justicer could dismiss at will), and controlling their copyholders by the corvée, by heavy taxation, and by tithes. In Lusatia, hereditary servitude still obtained. Finally, in the treaty-dominions of the house of Schönburg the crown possessed little more than the name of sovereignty, but on into the eighteen-twenties it continued to levy import and export duties at the frontiers of this petty vassal state. Hardly less autocratic was the rule of Count Solms-Wildenfels in his tiny mediatised territory; and when the officers of the neighbouring Zwickau garrison came to visit him, he would say to them, " Well, what's the latest news with you in Saxony ? "

The towns, too, looked upon themselves as states within the state; their councils perpetuated themselves by cooptation, as had been the case in Prussia before the reforms of Frederick William I; and in the larger towns they were composed exclusively of lawyers. In Leipzig and Dresden the councils, in virtue of the charters granted by the Polish Augustuses, did not need to give any account of their administration, and the saying was current, " Who can withstand God or the Leipzig council ? " Even when need was pressing, the government rarely ventured to curb the pride of these despotic town councillors; for many years the inhabitants of the Mulde flats had to get along without an indispensable bridge, because the town council of Warzen would not relinquish the profits of a lucrative ferry. Not until 1821 was the administration of Upper Lusatia, hereto-fore in the hands of the estates, entrusted to the government of the regal authorities. Nor was this effected without strong opposition. The little region, although two-thirds of its former domain were now Prussian, greatly desired to remain an independent margravate, distinct from the "hereditary dominions"; nor would it abandon the right of receiving the king-margrave in state, after his accession to the throne. The reception took place at the Upper Lusatian frontier, four hours' walk from Dresden, beneath the fluttering blue-yellow-and-red territorial banners. After all, four of the proud Six Towns of Lusatia had remained Saxon, and among these was Bautzen, the capital of the dynastically minded Wends.

Some of the posts in the judiciary and the administration were reserved by law for the nobles, for in accordance with feudal tradition these authorities were still subdivided into two benches, the noble and the learned. As a rule the higher dignities of state were allotted in rotation among the members of a small circle of titled and influential families, whose numbers had been yet more restricted since the partition, and whose identity was well known to all. It was solely as volunteers that young men of bourgeois birth could enter the nobles' cadet corps, and the only military school they could attend was the artillery school. Not until 1825 was the old method of military recruiting replaced by a conscription system based upon French and Rhenish Confederate models. Even longer, down to as late as 1829, did the old traditions continue in force at the university, whose students were still classed in four nationalities, as Meisseners, Saxons, Franconians, and Poles. The rector had princely rank. Without any state supervision, the university officials carried on in antediluvian fashion the costly and tedious administration of the extensive university estates. Their authority, indeed, no longer extended to all students residing in Leipzig, for this power had been abrogated by an edict of Napoleon; but they still exercised unrestricted sway over every member of the corpus academicum.

In this world of special privileges, it was natural that the clergy should not be subjected without reserve to the authority of the secular state. In 1814, when Pastor Tinius was charged with robbery and murder, the Leipzig law court had first to come to a provisional decision that it was necessary to take proceedings against the accused ; then, in the Nikolaikirche, the poor sinner was publicly unfrocked ; and only after this could he, now a layman, be handed over to the lay assize. But the old privileges of the Lutherans had not weathered the storms of the times. When, in the peace of Posen, Napoleon had bestowed civic equality upon the Catholics, it was not long before the members of the Reformed church (after paying the customary douceurs) secured like privileges. Subsequently Governor Repnin granted equality before the law to the Greek Catholics as well ; while the Jews of Leipzig, who had hitherto been forced to carry their dead to Dessau for burial, were now at least permitted to found a local cemetery. It was characteristic enough that the Russian general should be universally regarded as a pioneer of reform. None the less, Jews were allowed to reside nowhere else in Saxony than in Leipzig and Dresden.

The nobles and the bourgeois rivalled one another in zeal for the preservation of the rigid forms of the ancient guild system. While the towns continued obstinately to complain of the competition of the rural traders, and endeavoured to prevent the marriage of journeymen, the gentry insisted that no peasant's son should be apprenticed to any handicraft until he had spent four years in agricultural occupations, two years of this time being devoted to the service of the lord of the manor. Illegitimate children, unless specially legitimised by the king (on the payment of high fees), remained " of ill repute," and as such were excluded from the guilds and from all respectable occupations.

Since the days of the first elector Augustus there had been no further attempt to carry out a deliberate commercial policy. The mercantile system never found its way into Saxony, and its absence caused no loss, for domestic industry was sufficiently vigorous to be independent of protection. The Polish Augustuses scattered money cheerfully with both hands, cherishing the agreeable delusion that extravagance on the part of the sovereign brings plenty of money into the hands of the people, and even when order had at length been restored to the finances, this powerful manufacturing country remained without proper supervision on the frontiers. The only aims of its economic policy were to secure abundant customers at the Leipzig fairs and to provide cheap commodities for the gentle class among the consumers. Consequently imports were favoured by an extremely low tariff, while internal commerce was hindered by excises and transit dues, and in addition was hampered in Leipzig by the staple right and by a heavy octroi which was enforced until 1823. The taxes on articles of consumption differed in the urban and the rural districts, and the landed gentry and the clergy enjoyed numerous privileges. This ill-considered fiscal system, which paid absolutely no attention to the vital needs of domestic industry, was extolled as the wise "Saxon freedom of trade." When Prussia now established her custom houses in close proximity to the precincts of Leipzig, thus restricting export to the north, and when in many branches of industry the effects of Prussian competition became noticeable, considerable uneasiness was felt. But anger turned against Prussia alone, and was not directed against the paternal government, people even viewing with indulgence the obstinate way in which the cumbrous old convention-coins were retained, although the lighter Prussian thalers had long ere this invaded the entire country. Before long the manufacturers of the Erzgebirge were mainly, and those of Lusatia almost exclusively, dependent for a market upon the smuggling traffic to Austria, and business people of the old school considered this furtive trade a blessing. But anyone who noted the increasing savagery of the frontier districts could not fail to experience much concern, and to ask whether Saxony could continue to exist in this way, cut off from the sea and the northern market.

Like all the other Saxon institutions, the diet, as it proudly boasted, had "arisen from the very spirit of the golden days of eld." It is true that the "exalted loyal estates, prelates, counts, and lords, those of the Ritterschaft and those of the towns," as the official title ran, had been terribly jumbled together. The first estate had since the partition numbered no more than three heads. The Ritterschaft consisted of all lords of the manor who could show eight

ancestors; the German ancestor test was excused only to
the Catholic noble families which had come to Saxony from
Poland, Italy, and Ireland, after the conversion of the dynasty
to Rome. But owing to the enforcement of the test, fully
three-fourths of the lords of the manor were now excluded
from the diet; in the Leipzig circle, where many of
the merchants of the fair-town had bought estates, among
217 lords of the manor, 14 only were eligible. The representatives of the towns were appointed solely by the town council,
and the peasantry was entirely unrepresented. In matters
of legislation the diet possessed deliberative powers merely,
but enjoyed a well-established right of voting supply,
and was thereby enabled to frustrate any serious attempt
at reform. Even Augustus the Strong had rarely ventured
to impose an unapproved tax, preferring to defray the
expenses of his court by selling land and people to
neighbouring princes. None but isolated experts could find
their way through the labyrinth of Saxon fiscal administration.
The land taxes, from which the estates of the gentry were
naturally exempt, were levied in Schockgroschen (60 groschen
pieces), in accordance with a cadaster of the seventeenth
century; but since in the interim the Swedish, the Silesian,
and the Napoleonic wars had ravaged the Upper Saxon
plateau, many changes had taken place since the completion
of the cadaster. Moreover, there were in circulation, besides
the " good," large numbers of " poor, debased, defaced, and
defective " Schockgroschen.

The entire position was so intolerable that in two
instances even the crown could not avoid initiating a trifling
change. For decades past, vain attempts had been made to
unite the hereditary dominions with the lesser accessory
territories; this union had now become unavoidable, for since
the partition no more than a part of Upper Lusatia and a
few fragments of the chapter lands of Naumburg and Merse-
burg had remained to the kingdom. These vestiges were at
length (1817) incorporated in the diet of the hereditary
dominions; nevertheless Lusatia still retained its special
margravial diet, composed of the lords of the manor of
noble birth and of the four remaining Six Towns. Three

years later, after an animated struggle between the Ritter-schaft and the towns, it was decided that the lords of the manor who could not pass the ancestor test might send forty elected representatives to the diet. The prelates, counts, and lords could not, however, be induced to unite with the Ritterschaft to form a single estate, and they considered that they were making a great concession when they agreed to accept the university of Leipzig into their order. When the estates expressed a desire to be furnished with a summary statement of income and expenditure, the king could not make up his mind to accede to the suggestion. Nor was it really necessary to grant the petition, for no one seriously wished to put an end to the hopeless dualism of the financial system, and, for the rest, everything was managed quite honestly.

The king likewise rejected a proposal for the publication of part of the proceedings of the diet, for the inviolability of official secrecy was held to be a pillar of the Old Saxon state ; moreover, alike in Vienna and in Frankfort, publicity of the diet was now looked upon with suspicion as demagogic. When a Leipzig professor published in the Nüremberg *Korrespondent* some details of the proceedings of the estates, he was favoured with an extremely definite expression of " exalted disfavour." To avoid the reproach of doing nothing at all, the king had a brief diet report published in the record of laws, but this was so richly adorned with the flourishes and periphrases of Saxon legal style that no one was able to read it. As a matter of fact, no reader would have found it easy to endure an unabbre-viated account of the proceedings of the diet. For example, in the year 1820, the loyal estates sent in the following address : " Thankfully did the estates praise heaven for that momentous day on which the most exemplary of rulers and the model of all the domestic virtues celebrated the glories of a completed half century. With no less loyal and devoted participation did they receive tidings of the happy events which have recently occurred in the most exalted royal house, and in especial the gratifying bonds by which renewed associations have been formed with the most

illustrious imperial house. This very morning they solemnly
returned thanks to the Almighty for that he has preserved
your majesty in such gratifying health to be a blessing and
a joy to the entire country, that he has given your majesty
energy to endure all the labours and the cares of government
and to continue the customary unexampled application and
activity. In profoundest veneration . . . . " and so on
for several folio pages.[1] With how much effort, too, were
these priceless documents composed! Every proposal was
first discussed seven times, and on occasion nine times, by
the various committees and directories of the diet before
a vote could be taken, so that it was a joke among the
people that the diet spent its time playing puss-in-the-
corner.

When King Frederick Augustus died in the year 1827, alike
at court and among the general population it was widely
expected that his two elderly brothers would have the good
sense to renounce the throne in favour of the young and
vigorous Prince Frederick Augustus. King Antony, however,
was unwilling to forego his rights; and Count Einsiedel
remained in office, under the express condition, to which the
minister willingly agreed, that no changes whatever were to
take place.[2] The new king was a thoroughly good-hearted
man, less formal than his elder brother, but ill fitted for
affairs (having been trained in youth for the clerical profession), and a man of so little account that the veneration
even of the Dresdeners could find for him no other nickname than " the good-natured." Thus it was that the regime
of old men pursued its dull and sleepy course, but among
the common people there was taking place a gradual change
of mood. Here, as in Prussia, during the first years of peace
economic distresses monopolised popular attention, for the
country had suffered terribly. The losses of the villages
on the Leipzig battlefield were officially reckoned at more than
3,500,000 thalers, and this was certainly an under-estimate.
In Dresden, after the peace, a number of the garden plots
on which the cheerful villas of the Antonsstadt have to-day

[1] Address from the diet of 1820.
[2] Jordan's Report, May 17, 1827.

been erected, changed hands at the price of five or ten thalers. Many householders had been ruined simply by the extensive billeting ; the Körners, whose house was assessed at a rental value of 1,085 thalers, had in the summer of 1813, during a period of six and a half months, to billet on the average nearly forty men per diem.[1] The entire war costs of the year 1813 amounted to at least a hundred million thalers. These wounds had at length healed, and now that the evil days had passed the question arose whether the state and the people were maintaining in Germany the position to which history entitled them. It was impossible to rest content in perpetuity with the favourite self-congratulatory phrase, that Germany was the heart of Europe, Saxony the heart of Germany, and Dresden the heart of Saxony.

Devotion to the dynasty was, indeed, still unshaken. The whole country was racked with anxiety concerning the future of the royal house, which for a time seemed extremely insecure, for the marriages of the two young princes remained childless. Urged to the step by the pope and the court chaplain, Prince Max, notwithstanding his advanced age, contracted a second marriage with a young princess of Lucca, but this union also was denied the blessing of offspring. All the greater were the rejoicings when a son was at length born to young Prince John, and in honour of the event enthusiastic Dresdeners were to be seen standing on the bridge holding bottles of champagne and compelling every passer-by to clink glasses with them in honour of the heir to the throne.[2] Yet despite all this servility it was no longer possible to ignore that the unnaturalness of the outworn political forms was beginning to paralyse national life. The industry of the Erzgebirge could not recover a healthy tone ; and while the glories of the Leipzig fairs still persisted, during the rest of the year things seemed by contrast all the duller on the Pleisse. Country customers were already inclining to obtain their requirements of colonial produce by way of Magdeburg, where no excise was charged.

Nations, like individuals, have to endure periods of

[1] C. G. Körner's own calculation.
[2] Reports from Jordan, August 1 ; from Meyern, October 15 ; Witzleben's Diary, July 1825 ; Wangenheim to Hartmann, April 30, 1828.

sterility, during which everything goes wrong. Such an epoch had now arrived for Upper Saxony, so that it became hardly possible to recognise this country, which had formerly abounded in men of first-class intelligence. The reputation of the university, once world-wide, was now limited to Saxony. It possessed at this time a number of respectable experts, but no more than two whose excellence was widely recognised abroad, Gottfried Hermann, and Tzschirner, the eminent theologian, to whose names may perhaps be added that of the voluminous but vapid writer, Pölitz, and that of the indefatigable Krug, who at least possessed the courage to shake up the sleepy Saxon world by his frankly worded censures of public abuses. After the war, Count Heinrich Vitzthum, patron of Carl Maria von Weber, had cherished the hope that Saxony would find due compensation for the loss of political power, and that (like Bavaria, subsequently, under King Louis) she would become a centre of German artistic life. What had been the issue of these proud dreams? The writer of *Lyre and Sword* did not enjoy the favour of the court, for he was suspect on account of his Germano-Prussian patriotism. Saxony had hardly any share in the successes of the new plastic art, for the youthful men of talent, Schnorr, Rietschel, and Richter, were still in the years of development. Tiedge, the meditative author of *Urania*, who, though not Saxon born, was nevertheless honoured in Dresden as a native product, the poetical harpist Therese aus dem Winckell, Tromlitz, Nordstern, and the other stars of the " Dresden Tea and Poetry Society "—these worthies could but radiate a very gentle refulgence over the land.

Mediocrity and petrifaction prevailed everywhere, and now, by the irony of fate, it was the spectacle of Prussian conditions which awakened political discontent among the inhabitants of town and country alike. However much people might abuse the Prussians, it was impossible for them to overlook the obvious fact that the province of Saxony was in all respects better off than the kingdom, and that no one in the province seriously desired to return to the sway of the chaplet of rue. The province possessed everything which was lacking in the kingdom : a sagacious and vigorous administration, friendly to the bourgeoisie ; and a liberal system of municipal government, which contrasted strangely with the nepotism of the Electoral Saxon town councils, and, for this very reason, found its most ardent advocate in the Saxon, Streckfuss. Whilst in the province the relief of burdens on the peasant lands made continuous progress, in the kingdom the existing burdens were actually increasing. As late as 1828, a new order was issued concerning the right of common. Those upon whose land the right of common might be exercised by others could claim the privilege of herding their own beasts upon their own pastures only if they had exercised this privilege from time immemorial !

Thus it was that in Saxony people began to envy the towns' ordinance and the agrarian laws of Prussia, and to this well-grounded discontent there was superadded an utterly baseless suspicion that the royal house was animated by ultra-montane sentiments. It was natural enough that in this Lutheran land—where the idea had once been seriously entertained of introducing a new chronology, the Lutheran (starting from the year 1517), to supplant the Christian—sinister rumours should be continually circulated concerning the Catholic court. These suspicions became all the more irritable in proportion to the degree of servility with which in other respects the king's commands were obeyed, and for long years hardly any other political passion was known to the Electoral Saxon people. King Antony was even more of a bigot than had been his deceased brother, whose custom it was, speaking of Catholics, to say in confidence, " Il est de notre religion." From time to time some ambitious lieutenant or official would go over to Rome upon ques-tionable grounds, but such cases were extremely rare, demonstrably rarer than conversions from Catholicism to Protestantism. Even if at court there had long existed a secret fund for the support of converts,[1] even if a former court lady was deprived of her pension because she brought up her children as Lutherans,[2] these were purely private

[1] Baron von Oelssen's Report, December 28, 1818.
[2] Jordan's Report, November 4, 1828.

affairs of the royal house and did not concern the state. Despite their strictly Catholic sentiments, the Albertines have during the nineteenth century always honourably avoided the deliberate favouring of proselytism. There was no possibility in Dresden of such a Jesuistic propaganda as prevailed at the newly converted court of Coethen, for none of the higher officials would have been a party to anything of the kind.

Nevertheless suspicion was rife, and found fresh nourishment in certain incidents harmless in themselves. In 1824, when the ecclesiastical jubilee was notified for the following year, and when a placard was posted in the Catholic Hofkirche inviting the faithful to offer up the customary prayers for the diffusion of Catholicism and the overthrow of heresy, a storm broke throughout the country. No one marked that in all the churches of Catholic Christendom the same traditional invitation was to be read; no one reflected that the Protestants were also accustomed to pray their God for the diffusion of the pure Protestant faith. An address from the Dresden burghers indignantly asked how this could possibly happen "in a German province from which the light of the Reformation first radiated."[1] Such a clamour issued from the pulpits that the king at length found it necessary to enjoin both parties to hold their peace. Fresh uproar was raised by the Lutherans in 1827 when the crown, against the advice of the estates, promulgated a mandate containing entirely unobjectionable prescriptions about Catholic parishes and the cure of souls. Another mandate left the matter of the religious education of the children of mixed marriages entirely to the free decision of the parents, and this law, manifestly well-intentioned, stimulated Lutheran intolerance to deliver violent attacks. It was universally believed that the Marcolini palace was to become a Jesuit college. A number of similar fables were current, and yet there was but one definite fact underlying them all, namely, that the king and Count Einsiedel favoured Bishop Mauermann with their especial confidence.

Beneath the surface, dissatisfaction became so intense

---

[1] Petition from the burghers of Dresden to the town council, December, 1824.

as to render possible the foundation of an opposition newspaper, an unprecedented event in Saxony. The *Biene* [Bee], edited by Richter, the Zwickau theologian, was not properly speaking a political journal, but a forum for the discussion of public affairs—for by royal privilege politics were reserved for the subsidised *Leipziger Zeitung*. Here it became possible for thoughtful philistines to pour out their troubles to the " dear little bee " and the " worthy bee-father," to express their concern about Pennalismus in the princely schools, about vermin in the university lock-up, about the dangerous condition of the Leipzig shooting-range, about the pug-dogs of the Dresden ladies. But side by side with such puerile grievances, there were serious complaints on behalf of the burdened countryfolk, especially from Schönburg, where the peasants had to hand over to the count a tithe of the grain harvest, and every seventh head of the new born stock ; and there were strongly worded complaints of the abuses committed by the municipal administration, dealing not only with the beer monopoly and the scandalous thinness of the beer from the council cellar, but also with the irresponsible system of town government. The tone of the articles was at times definitely impassioned, and it could be felt that the new king could no longer count upon unconditional devotion. Men of the good old times contemplated with anxiety this contentious insect " which went buzzing about, disturbing everyone." In November, 1829, the *Biene* ventured to publish an " Address from the Saxon People " to the king, the work of Albert von Carlowitz, the most capable member of the Ritterschaft. In this address the writer referred to the example of Weimar, Bavaria, and Würtemberg ; demanded the introduction of a genuine system of popular representation ; recommended a more equitable distribution of the public burdens ; the Ritterschaft would do well to release the king from the charters which guaranteed its members in the exercise of their popular rights !

Still plainer was the language employed shortly afterwards by another respected landowner, Otto von Watzdorf, an outspoken man, who at a much later date, irritated by the ill feeling displayed towards him by the members of his order, was forced into a radical attitude. At this time his position was still that of South German constitutional liberalism. In a *Memorial concerning the Saxon Constitution* he developed the programme of the party, demanding partition of authority, a bicameral system, and ministerial responsibility. The government refused its imprimatur to this essay in contemptuous terms, but it was printed none the less, and widely read. For a long time, now, these two aristocratic liberals had not stood alone. This was plainly manifest when the diet of 1830 again demanded that a summary statement of expenditure should be issued, and, when approving the taxes, it openly declared : " By far the smallest proportion of that which we approve is our own. The spirit of these days demands far more than the people demanded from its representatives in decades past." Once again the crown rejected all innovations, but its language was less confident than of yore. Everyone felt that the old system was tottering. After fifteen years had been wasted in dreamy inactivity, a peaceful transformation of the mouldy structure seemed extremely improbable.

Electoral Hesse (IV, 332–51)

It was not until after the Seven Years' War that, by a disastrous anachronism, all the evils of princely caprice broke over Hesse, at the very time when the clock of the old French absolutism had run down, when public opinion was already noting the activities of the great with a more critical eye, and when well-nigh all the notable princely houses of Germany were earnestly collecting their energies in the endeavour to follow King Frederick's lead. With Landgrave Frederick II, there began in the house of Philip the Magnanimous, and progressively increased, an enigmatic degeneration ; in four generations the glories acquired in five rich centuries were shamefully lost ; and at length this venerable race of princes became detested by the loyal people, and passed to its. destruction unlamented. The Hessians were familiar with their princes' hereditary sin, ungovernable anger ; ill-controlled eroticism had of old brought much misery over the land, when Philip the Magnanimous concluded his double marriage ; but entirely new was the heartless avarice, which was now with sinister regularity superadded to these two weaknesses, and owing to which the rulers necessarily appeared to be the enemies of the ruled.

As long as armies were still composed of soldiers obtained by voluntary recruiting, and serving for pay, no disgrace attached to war service under a foreign flag. It was not until the days of King Frederick that the Germans began to recognise that armed power belongs to the state. Even though, in the Seven Years' War, the Hessians fought as English mercenaries, they were fighting for hearth and home, for their own country's cause. Meanwhile the Prussian cantonal system had been introduced into Hesse (1762) ; and when the traffic in men was now carried on with the persons of these compulsory soldiers, and more vigorously than ever, to the changed sentiments of the time the traditional practice seemed extremely repulsive. Mirabeau, Burke, even Frederick the Great, expressed their reprobation in the severest terms when Landgrave Frederick and his son William, hereditary prince of Hanau, sold by degrees to England 19,400 of their 300,000 subjects, well nigh a third of all the men fit for military service. These men were employed in the civil war against the Americans, regarded by their contemporaries as champions of liberty. " The misdeeds of this German princeling " were pitilessly exposed in the English parliament. The old landgrave had at least been ever careful to preserve the forms of decency, and had concluded with Great Britain a treaty by which the two powers mutually guaranteed the integrity of each other's dominions ; but the hereditary prince composed adulatory epistles to his " magnanimous protector and noble-minded benefactor " George III, placing himself and his army at the king's disposal. Father and son now outvied one another in fiscal arts calculated to overreach the English paymasters. William insisted on special compensation for every killed or wounded Hessian soldier ; Frederick found it more lucrative to receive the soldiers' pay with his own hands and to keep the names of the slain on the active

list for a time. Of the unhappy mercenaries, more than a
third never saw their homes again ; and their name became
a byword, for the Americans applied to everything base and
slavish the contemptuous epithet of " Hessian."

Measureless was the distress of the depopulated land.
Day and night, mounted patrols guarded the frontier to
prevent the escape of men liable to military service. As a
consolation for his people, and since he had no longer to
pay for the army himself, the old landgrave remitted a modest
proportion of the taxes for the duration of the American war.
But to the hereditary prince, even this sacrifice seemed excessive. He was content with remitting taxation in the cases
of the parents and wives of those who had gone to the war,
and announced to his faithful subjects that it was " a real
pleasure " to him " to be able to give such a mark of royal
favour." By the son, the blood-money was thriftily stored
away in his treasury. By the father, on the other hand,
some of it was devoted to the construction of new buildings
in Cassel, while much of the remainder was squandered
upon unsavoury entertainments for the benefit of the French
prostitutes and adventurers who dominated the court and
corrupted the morals of the capital for many years to come.
Despite this extravagance, Frederick II handed down to his
son a princely private estate which had no parallel in
Germany. Nevertheless, the former services of the landgrave
and his house were still so greatly valued that during his
lifetime the loyal estates erected in the Friedrichsplatz a
monument to this " father of the fatherland."

When William IX succeeded to the landgravate, he
remained true to the principles of government previously tried
in Hanau. He put an end to ostentatious display, and extreme
parsimony prevailed in court and state ; but the old debauchery
persisted unchanged. No one was able to reckon the
precise number of the royal bastards. Everyone, however,
knew the counts von Hessenstein and the brothers Haynau ;
and the saying was current that whenever the landgrave could
feel assured once again that he was about to experience the
joys of extra-conjugal fatherhood, it was his custom to raise
the price of the salt in the state magazines another

farthing per bushel. In the Rhenish campaigns, the army (again in English pay) fought once more in a manner worthy of its ancient reputation, and this time for the German realm and for a cause which the prince himself held sacred, for he had the temperament of an autocrat, and detested the revolution. Where his avarice was not involved, his rule was during these years tolerable enough ; and when he was ingloriously dethroned (a victim of his own wiles, and of his failure to forecast the winning side) his loyal subjects instantly forgot all the injustice they had suffered at his hands. On three occasions during the years 1806 and 1809 the Hessians attempted a rising against the foreign dominion. But the wealthy electoral prince was content to levy in Bohemia a small and badly paid volunteer corps ; he had no alms for those upon whom misfortune fell for his sake ; and he wished to pay off the valiant Colonel Dörnberg, the instigator of the second rising, with a paltry two hundred thalers. These sins were likewise forgotten. Upon his return, the entire land of Old Hesse luxuriated in patriotic enthusiasm. Even County Schaumburg, the remote and beautiful dependence on the Weser, was delighted at the restoration of the old regime. But here the well-to-do peasants, established in their farms shaded by oak trees and still accustomed to display the Saxon horse on the buttons of their linen jerkins, had nothing in common with the Old Hessians in respect either of tribal origin or of political constitution. Once a week only did they receive news from distant Cassel, brought by a diligence which invariably broke down at Höxter. Less powerful was the affection for the dynasty in busy Hanau, for this, associated by position and by trade relationships rather with Frankfort and the Rhenish territories, had never felt really at home in its connection with the comparatively poor agricultural region of Hesse ; and the Hanauers, whose blood contained a considerable French admixture, had ever been regarded as turbulent and revolutionary.

Utterly foreign in the reestablished electoral state was a vestige of the ancient bishopric of Fulda, acquired in the peace by the elector through an exchange, and incorporated by him " with my other states " under the pretentious title

of " Grand Duchy of Fulda." Here the church was all
in all. The poverty-stricken inhabitants would still sadly
recount what glorious times there had been of old in the
magnificent rococo palace close to the tomb of St. Boniface ;
how at the banquets of the bishop and his canons the noble
Johannisberger would flow in streams ; how on Palm Sunday
the school children would get their Easter eggs from the
belly of the consecrated donkey ; and how the oppressed
man of the common people, looking on at the splendid
processions or enjoying the free soup provided by the
monastery, could forget his troubles for a time. Even
after the secularisation, a distinctively Catholic life tenaciously
persisted in this rude region of the Rhöngebirge—by no means
intolerant, but in habits and mode of thought differing very
markedly from that of the neighbouring Protestant districts.
In Fulda, the Christmas tree was still unknown, though it
had long before made its way from the Lutheran lands
into other parts of Catholic Germany. This focus of Catholicism accepted with reluctance the rule of the Protestant
elector. When he took possession there was circulated an
extremely disrespectful song : " Fuldans rejoice, Heaven's
kingdom's now at hand. The hero mates with heroes of
like pattern ; stout Hessians now are we, and valiant Catten,"
and so on.[1] But serious resistance was out of the question.
Nothing of the kind could be expected from the inhabitants
of a region which had within ten years enjoyed the successive blessings of episcopal, Orange, French, Berg, Frankfort,
Austrian, and Prussian rule.

With a reasonable amount of justice and benevolence,
no land in Germany would have been easier to rule than
Electoral Hesse. How delighted were the inhabitants to be
freed at length from the accursed dominion of Westphalia ;
everything could be accepted with gratitude from the Nestor
of the German princes. But even Hessian loyalty was
shaken when William, as if he had been asleep all the
time, attempted, with a stroke of the pen, to annihilate the

---

[1] A Brief but Loyal Song of Rejoicing. Fulda, May 22, 1816. The poem is
witty, but unprintable. Its author was presumably Baron von Meusebach.

history of the last seven years. Everything was to return to
the status quo ante November 1, 1806. The regiments then
dismissed on furlough were to reassemble forthwith in their
old garrisons ; the state servants were to resume their former
posts. The major became a lieutenant once more, and the
councillor an assessor—unless the elector preferred to confirm
them in their new dignities on the payment of fresh fees.
The *code Napoléon* and all the Westphalian legislation were
immediately swept away : thousands of persons now regarded
as of full legal age were to become minors once again, because
majority was henceforward, as in old days, to begin at twenty-
five instead of twenty-one. At New Year, 1816, when the
troops returned from the siege operations in France, they had
immediately to resume the wearing of fifteen-inch queues :
one inch before the plait begins, thirteen inches plaited, one
inch curled at the end—thus ran the regulations.

Things would not have been so bad if the follies of
this restoration had at least been dictated by an honourable fanaticism. But the prince's legitimist zeal was aptly
combined with mercantile calculation. Just as he robbed
the purchasers of the domains but held fast to the new
acquisitions of King Jerome, so did he reintroduce the taxes
of Old Hesse while leaving in force the heaviest of the
Westphalian exactions. The Westphalian national debt was
repudiated, but of the Old Hessian debt William would recognise no more than a third because his administrator Jerome
had arbitrarily written it down to that amount. What a
contrast was this to the scupulous honesty of the king of
Prussia. The guild system, the corvée, and the burdens on
the peasants were revived ; but the patrimonial courts were
not restored, for the elector mistrusted the gentry. The
sons of those not of the highest rank were allowed entry
to the university only upon receipt of a special permit from
the sovereign prince.

The state servants, who under the foreign dominion had
at least been able to count with some certainty upon the
receipt of their pay, were once more exposed without defence
to the prince's avarice. In the army it soon became the

rule that on promotion officers should retain their old salary ; there were generals with the pay of a cavalry captain, and not one of them received his due. When four years had elapsed, the father of the country was fleecing his servants so unmercifully that month by month he was able to save thirty-six thousand thalers on his pay-roll and to hide the sum away in his unfathomable treasure chests.[1] Those even who had served their time were for the most part allowed to hunger. When there was a possibility of defrauding a deserving old general of his pension, his record in the service was besmirched with all kinds of trumped-up suspicions. Should any retired officer complain that he could afford nothing to eat but potatoes, the elector's blunt answer was, " For my part, I am very fond of potatoes." Now that England no longer paid any subsidies, the number of men on active service was soon reduced to 1,500 (eighty men in each battalion) ; but taxes had still to be paid for an army of 20,000. In order to effect further savings, the elector, who was building a palace, used the horses of the artillery to do the carting.[2] Not even endowments were safe from the old man's thievish hands. The university of Rinteln having been abolished, part of its property was assigned to the Rinteln gymnasium, and another part to Marburg university, while the balance, a sum by no means to be despised, passed to the insatiable princely treasure chest. The Jews came off best at this time. They had no difficulty in understanding the character of the man with whom they had to deal. Promptly paying over a good round sum in cash, they secured a confirmation of the rights assigned them by the *code Napoléon*.

In this way all the beneficial reforms of the Westphalian regime were abolished. The severities of that regime alone persisted, reinforcing the revived abuses of the good old time. The arbitrariness of the restored prince was so outrageous that even Goethe, who was as a rule disinclined to lend an ear to the complaints of the liberal world, penned the bitter verses :

[1] Hänlein's Reports, January 22, 1816, November 6, 1817.
[2] Hänlein's Reports, May 25 and June 1, 1818.

From the spirit of our age
Far is the rich old prince,
Far, far indeed.
Yet whoever money understands
Understands the time
Aptly indeed !

At court, moreover, there were perpetual disputes between the elector, his son, and his mistress-in-chief ; there were detestable usurious practices on the part of the favourite Buderus von Carlshausen ; and there were continual affronts to the diplomatic corps, whose members could enforce decent treatment by threats alone. How gladly would the excellent Hänlein, the Prussian envoy, have related smooth things of this court which was so closely connected with the royal house of Prussia ; but being a truthful man he had nothing to fill his reports with but stories of sultan's caprices and similar unsavoury matters. The ruler's cynical contempt for mankind was so ingrained that he never even noted the despair by which he was surrounded. At a patriotic festival the inhabitants of Cassel were privileged to read the inscription, appearing in letters of flame over the gateway of the palace : " The father to his children ! "

Upon his entry into the grand alliance, the elector had been compelled to promise the great powers to reestablish his old diet, which in recent decades had been nothing more than a " Geldtag " (money diet), and had not met at all since 1798. After a year's interval, he fulfilled his pledge, and in March, 1815, summoned a "restricted diet" for Old Hesse, consisting of eight prelates and gentlemen, eight urban representatives, and a third curia of five members for the hitherto unrepresented peasantry. The Ritterschaft of the five Hessian *Ströme* (departments) of the Diemel, the Lahn, the Fulda, the Schwalm, and the Werra, had hitherto elected one representative for each *Strom*. The peasantry was to do the like in the future. This introduction of peasant representation was the solitary reform instituted by William I, and it was not inspired on his part by any desire to do justice to the countryfolk ; his sole motive was to provide a counterpoise to the Ritterschaft, for he regarded that order with suspicion. The elector opened the assembly of the estates with words of paternal affection, and then introduced, as the only proposition for them to discuss, a demand for more than four million thalers. He claimed that he had expended this amount on behalf of the country, two million thalers before the year 1806 ; and with the same magnanimity as that with which he had in earlier days remitted taxation for the wives of the mercenaries, he now gave the estates to understand that, as an act of special grace, he was prepared to forego compensation for the burning of the palace in the year 1811.

In face of these claims, the diet maintained the firm and calm commonsense which has since then, amid severe trials, come to be considered the predominant trait of the Hessian character, securing for the inhabitants of this little country the respect of the world. Although the Ritterschaft at times endeavoured to go its own way, the estates held firmly together in all matters of importance, the peasant representatives behaving extremely well. The Prussian envoy admired the courage and thoughtfulness of this diet, and even the Austrian envoy was impressed. Under such a prince, politics was nothing but a matter of business, and after prolonged chaffering the ruler's demand was ultimately abated to four hundred thousand thalers, and the elector was induced to recognise the Old Hessian debt at its full nominal value. But the estates were unable to secure any statement as to the condition of the national finances. Not only were they refused information about the cabinet treasury and the private treasury, which by ancient constitutional usage were the concern of the sovereign prince alone, but they could learn nothing about the state of the war chest, though this contained a part of the English subsidies estimated by the diet at 22,000,000 thalers, and claimed by that body on behalf of the state. The most odious sin of political life in the German petty states, disputes about money, were never so venomous as in Hesse, where the treasures of the princely house had unquestionably been obtained by the blood of the people.

Meanwhile the country began to show signs of ferment. The hereditary chamberlain Baron von Berlepsch, an honest but somewhat eccentric radical, issued a work in which he advanced proof that now in time of peace many of the peasants were paying twice as much in taxes as they had paid under the foreign dominion in time of war, and the countryfolk knew that the writer was speaking the truth. The peasants of the Diemel Strom (131 communes) sent a statement of grievances to the diet concerning the oppressive burden of taxation : " The days of French rule were bad, but if all that has to be paid out be added together, the present days are even worse, and if it were not that we are paying to our beloved elector, who is as good a Hessian as we are ourselves, the country would not have kept quiet so long." They went on to ask, in an artless manner, that the diet should enquire how much of the money that Hesse owed was really owed by the state, and what became of all the money which they were compelled to pay.[1] Before long similar petitions were circulated for signature in the other *Ströme*. Two officers, moreover, applied to the estates in the name of their comrades, asking that a report should be drawn up regarding the illegal withholding of pay ; and even Hänlein found this procedure excusable, however improper from the military point of view, for the unhappy men were hardly able to keep body and soul together.[2]

When the estates reassembled in February, 1816, after a lengthy prorogation, the elector submitted to them a constitution for the new composite state of Electoral Hesse and Fulda. " I do not need a constitution," said the elector to the Prussian envoy, " but I shall give one for the sake of example and of effect." [3] The draft for a constitution, the work of the sympathetic minister von Schmerfeld, contained many excellent prescriptions, but lacked the one essential, the separation of the ruler's private property from the property of the state. In the lively discussions which followed, there were already to be heard from time to time

---

[1] Wishes of the peasants of the Diemel Strom, March, 1816.
[2] Hänlein's Report, June 22, 1816.
[3] Hänlein's Report, January 11, 1816.

the ambiguous battle cries of the dominant constitutionalist doctrine. It was proposed that " the ideal of a happy form of government, the English," should be taken as an example ; to the intense indignation of the elector, the name of *Landesherr* (lord of the land) was replaced by the name *Regent* (ruler) used by the apostles of the law of reason ; and the demand was voiced that the *Regent* should take an oath of fidelity to the constitution as a preliminary to its formal imauguration. Robert, the eloquent urban representative, spoke much of a " general state right " which took precedence of " territorial right." But most of the amendments suggested by the diet were thoroughly reasonable ; and if it was finally proposed that " the united constitution " should be placed under the guarantee of two German powers,[1] this demand was by no means superfluous in relation to such a princely house, nor was it unprecedented in Hessian history. When the elector's father had become a Roman Catholic, Prussia, the naval powers, and the Scandinavian crowns, had guaranteed the Hessian act of assecuration, and had thus obtained for the country the maintenance of the religious status quo.

The elector was in a fury when he saw the unrestricted exercise of his sovereignty thus threatened. He had expected the estates to accept his gracious gift unexamined ; he now announced to them his peculiar displeasure because they had not refrained from displaying " an inadmissible tendency towards the subversion of the old constitution. . . . Every independent state," he continued, " however small it may be, makes it a point of national honour not to permit foreign powers to interfere in its internal affairs, and it is a painful experience to his majesty that the estates should desire conditions to arise in Electoral Hesse by which the country's independence would be endangered."[2] To some of the representatives who had spoken of mediation on the part of the king of Prussia, he uttered personal threats, saying he would treat anyone as a rebel who should look abroad for help.

[1] Observations of the estates upon the proposal for a constitution, with Memorandum of March 29 and Address of April 1, 1816.

[2] Despatch from the sovereign committee to the estates, under date April 6, 1816.

In respect of all these matters a compromise might still have been effected, but no understanding was possible as regards the distinction between the sovereign's private property and the property of the nation, although the demands of the diet were extremely moderate. Bluntly and scornfully, and with manifest intention to force a rupture, the sovereign commissary Johann Hassenpflug declared that what the ruling house had acquired by inheritance and subsidies belonged to the sovereign alone. A curse lay upon the English blood-money, for this was the rock upon which was shipwrecked the first attempt to establish a constitution. In May the elector dismissed his estates with nothing effected, not even permitting them to reassemble after a recess, an unprecedented incident in Hesse. The assembly broke up amid solemn protests of its right to vote supply, reiterating the assertion that the national property belonged to the country and not to the sovereign. Soon afterwards the two officers who had addressed the estates were, without a trial and in defiance of law, sent to Spangenberg, a small mountain fortress which in the history of the minor German states had long played a role similar to that played by Königstein or Hohenasperg; the deepest dungeon in Spangenberg, known as the Karthause, was one which no prisoner had ever left alive. The officers' corps was much enraged, and its members were on the point of throwing up their commissions in a body. When this became known to the elector, he thought it expedient to set the prisoners at liberty.[1]

To the day of his death he continued to rule as an absolute sovereign, and could enjoy the pleasure of reducing salaries all round in the grand duchy of Fulda, and of thus adding several thousands a month to the fund in his cabinet treasury.[2] The debt committee of the estates, which continued to exist as an isolated vestige of the old constitution, was utterly impotent, being unable even to prevent an occasional arbitrary increase of taxation. No one could influence the elector, except that in monetary matters Amschel Rothschild's well-tried advice was gladly followed; even Hassenpflug's power went no further than to enable him to

---

[1] Hänlein's Report, June 24, 1816, and subsequent dates.
[2] Hänlein's Report, June 8, 1818.

procure for his aspiring son, Hans Daniel, the opening of a varied
career in official service.   The weal and the woe of every
Hessian were absolutely dependent upon the incalculable
caprices of the aged ruler, who, as his health broke up,
became ever more cranky and irritable.   When promulgating
the Carlsbad decrees, he fiercely appended the threat : " Here-
with I declare to those of my subjects who shall be proved
guilty of participating in the aforesaid subversive associations,
that they are unworthy of the name of Hessian, and that
they will consequently be expelled in perpetuity from among
my trusty people, and will be deprived of all civil rights." [1]

The quiet interment of the ancient constitution was
received by the nation with unexpected tranquillity, although
the estates issued a printed report of their private proceedings.
The town of Cassel expressed its gratitude to the departing
diet ; and when in the year 1817 the elector issued a
legislative mandate upon his own initiative, it was suggested
that a protest should be lodged with the German great
powers. [2]   But the design was never carried out.   People
had abandoned hope, and what time was there for political
thought amid the economic distresses of this miserable and
neglected land ?   When the traveller gained his first sight of
the red rocks of the Werra or the Fulda valley, richly wooded,
with the river sparkling at their base, or glimpsed the
picturesque basalt domes beside the Eder or the Schwalm, he
imagined that he would find here the cheerful repose which
constitutes the charm of the Central German hill-country.
But in the poverty-stricken villages he was soon astonished
to note the extraordinary gloom of the inhabitants.   Above
all, in the careworn faces of the old peasant women ; in the
sadness of the great eyes gleaming beneath the black head-dress
was often to be seen the tragical record of a long life of
sorrows.

The Hessian stock was never noted for the production of
heroes of art and science ; its strength had always lain in
its valiancy and in its unyielding sense of justice—although
should the power of genius show itself among them, as in
the brothers Grimm, there was then displayed the funda-

[1] Proclamation to the Hessians from the elector, September 30, 1819.
[2] Hänlein's Report, March 17, 1817.

mental greatness of the Germanic character. But hardly ever before had the intellectual life of the country been so sterile. When the university of Marburg, within a brief period, lost Savigny, Creuzer, and Tiedemann, people said that, while able to win for itself young men of talent, it lacked the power to keep them for its own ; and this reputation lasted down to the close of the electoral epoch. Even more distressing was the decline in civic prosperity. No other region of Germany showed so plainly the traces of the Thirty Years' War, no other had so completely lost the prosperity of the sixteenth century. The visitor to Fritzlar who contemplated the beautiful renaissance edifice of the Rymphäum could hardly believe that the inhabitants of the impoverished little country town could ever have built this nuptial house. In every farm, the women worked at distaff and loom to supply the needs of the household, and perhaps to provide a little linen for the market ; but, with the solitary exception of Hanau, this " land of big pots and sour wine," as the Rhenish Franconians termed it, had never developed any vigorous industry. The first weakly stirrings of the spirit of economic enterprise were hampered by an antiquated customs system, by the internal tolls of the electorate, and by innumerable and absurd vexations. Years went by before the final removal of the narrow town-gate at Gelnhausen, which obstructed the great commercial route between Leipzig and Frankfort, making it necessary every year for hundreds of wagons to unload before they could pass through. Nearly half of the land was under forest. The countryfolk lived with the extremest simplicity. In the Schwalm Strom, the region which contained the largest farms of Hesse, coffee was still entirely unknown, and *Covent*, a celebrated small beer of local manufacture, was the only beverage.

Dilapidation and poverty were manifest on all hands, and the Jewish usurers, the vultures that prey upon the miseries of the German peasantry, had long ere this flocked into the country. At the castle of Marburg, rich in memories, the birthplace of Philip the Magnanimous was used as a state prison ; the beautiful church of St. Elisabeth beneath, the earliest example of German Gothic, was in a dirty and half-ruinous condition ; while of the Hohenstaufen imperial palace on an island in the Kinzig at Gelnhausen, the best preserved portions were sold to the housebreakers. Even in Cassel nothing was done to keep the palace in repair, although this was a matter which even in the badly governed lesser states of Germany was apt to receive special attention from the ruling prince. In youth the elector had adorned a few health resorts with pleasure grounds, and had beautified the Wilhelmshöhe park with the ridiculous sham castle of Löwenburg; but now he considered that he did enough when he removed the statue of Napoleon from the Königsplatz and restored to the Friedrichsplatz that of the old *pater patriae*, the trafficker in human flesh. During the fifty years prior to the entry of the Prussians, Cassel remained completely unchanged, the art collections closed, and everything so dead and desolate that when the Göttingen students paid a visit to the town they were able even at midday to awaken the sixfold echo in the round Königsplatz. It was only in honour of his greatly desired but never secured dignity as king of the Catti that the elector began to build the Cattenburg at enormous expense, amounting at times to as much as ten thousand thalers a week. This was a gigantic palace, constructed on lines to fit it for the habitation of an imperial race, but was regarded in the country as a repulsive memorial of petty princely conceit.

A few days before the elector's death, a Prussian official, Hessian by birth, with an unsparing candour which seemed inconceivable to the minor courts, read him a lecture upon his folly. The reproof came from Motz, then president in Erfurt. He had intervened on behalf of his uncle, an elderly general arbitrarily deprived of pension, and when the customary answer was returned that no recognition was accorded to the seven years of Westphalian regime, he did not hesitate to fling in the old prince's face the name of " Sevensleeper " which was universally current in the country. The subjects and servants of the elector, he wrote, would have been happy had they been able to say the same of themselves, " had they, with their wives and children, also fallen asleep for seven years, and, then refreshed for new services to your majesty, reawakened under the changed conditions." He

continued : " Your majesty is rich, but your servant and
subjects are poor " ; and he adjured the old sinner, now in
the evening of his days, to make a worthier use of his
abundant wealth, and do his utmost to relieve the distresses
of the loyal Hessian people, before he was compelled to appear
" before Him who is lord over us all, and who puts down
the mighty from their seats." [1]   Such was the judgment
passed upon the elector's doings by the leading political
intelligence of contemporary Hesse.   When William I died
in February, 1821, there was found among his papers a
political testament, impressing upon the heir the need for
continuing to reign as a true autocrat.

The exhortation was hardly necessary.   In the new reign
the destiny of the country was associated more closely than
ever with the personal circumstances of the princely house.
By nature Elector William II was neither stupid nor malicious ;
but he had been badly brought up, had no taste for intellectual life, was unable to discipline his passions, and was a
commonplace voluptuary and martinet.   To his misfortune,
while his father was yet alive, he fell under the sway of a
mean-spirited woman from Berlin, Emilie Ortlöpp by name,
and for her sake put coarse affronts upon his high-minded
consort Augusta, sister of the king of Prussia.   With
William's ascent to the throne the power of this mistress
attained a level unexampled in nineteenth century history.
Hardly had a brilliant funeral train, led by the black
knight of the house of Hesse, escorted the old ruler's coffin
to Löwenburg, than there ensued the first liberating deed of
the new government, the cutting of the queues.   Loud were
the rejoicings ;   by hundreds these symbols of the bad old
days were to be seen lying on the pavements ˊand in the
gutters of the capital, for the street arabs to play with.
No less cheerful was the intelligence that the construction of
the Cattenburg was to be discontinued ;   and henceforward,
so long as the electorate of Hesse still existed, the pretentious
structure remained as an ill-omened ruin, where beggars
and vagabonds sought shelter by night beneath the lofty

<hr>

[1] Motz to Elector William, January 22, 1821.

arches. In the same year, a proposal for administrative
organisation, drafted by the ministerial councillor Krafft,
was brought forward. By this scheme, after the boastful
manner of the German petty states, the little territory was
subdivided into four provinces, with four local governments
and four financial directories, and with, in addition, a special
board of government for Schaumburg—all this for a population of 600,000 souls. Despite its costliness, the new organisation, modelled upon that of Prussia, was unquestionably better
than the old, an especially valuable point being the clear
distinction between the executive and the judiciary.

These reforms, however, comprised the total of the
praiseworthy deeds of William II. While the coronation was
in progress, the Ortlöpp with her children was installed in
her lover's palace,[1] and, known henceforward as Countess
Reichenbach, enjoyed all the rights of an electoral consort.
The diet was not summoned, although the Ritterschaft remon-
strated on several occasions on account of the omission.
Enjoying uncontrolled power, and associating with the corrupt
riff-raff that followed in the countess Reichenbach's wake,
the elector soon became an utter savage. His rages were
brute-like ; no one was safe from his ill usage—no one at
least who could not summon up courage to respond to the
ferocious despot with blow for blow. Things soon reached
such a pitch that it was matter for congratulation when upon
his journeys through the country nothing worse happened
than " the whipping of one or two postmasters with his
majesty's own hands." [2] Even the Reichenbach had to
beware, but she knew how to take care of herself. If he
attacked her she began throwing expensive vases and cups
about the room, and continued to do so until the infuriated
man realised the costliness of these missiles, so that his anger
was tamed by avarice. As soon as such a scene was over,
she could secure from her lover anything she pleased. Her
brother shone in the sunshine of her favour. This was an
absolute ne'er-do-weel to whom the elector, greatly to the
disgust of the Ritterschaft, assigned the name of an extinct

[1] Hänlein's Report, March 1, 1821.
[2] Thus Hänlein, August 21, 1824.

family, that of the barons Heyer von Rosenfeld. The Rothschilds, the old friends of the family, could now reap their harvest, for though the son had inherited his father's avarice, he was no miser, and, rich as he was, was often in need of kindly financial aid, which his business administrator, Councillor Deines well knew how to secure from the Frankfort house.

Young Hänlein, who had now succeeded his deceased father as envoy, reported to his government that the elector had often declared himself to be firmly attached to Prussia —and there can be no doubt that these assurances were honest. But since King Frederick William was forced to intervene in favour of his ill-treated sister and her little son, the disputes between the two courts were unceasing. On one occasion there was an actual rupture when, under cover of darkness, the elector had had his sister, the duchess of Bernburg, removed from Bonn to Hanau. William's contention was that the poor lady was insane, but all that is proved is that the malady became unmistakable after her removal. Hänlein was recalled, on account of the violation of Prussian territory, and did not return to Cassel for some months, when the elector had apologised.[1] In the better ruled among the German territories the small scale upon which life was conducted rendered it easy to pay benevolent attention to personal and local interests, and herein was to be found the solitary advantage of the system of petty states. In Hesse, however, the outcome of this system was individual persecution. The Reichenbach knew everyone, and everyone's fate depended upon his position in the woman's favour. Upon a summer evening in the year 1823 the elector made a sudden descent upon Cassel from the Wilhelmshöhe, had the alarm sounded and the garrison mustered in the Friedrichsplatz ; then Captain Radowitz of the general staff and three other officers were transferred to small garrison towns, with orders to depart on the instant to their new posts.[2] The men thus banished from Cassel were all friends of the electoral prince, and had made no secret of their opinion of Countess Reichen-

---

[1] Hänlein's **Reports**, February 28, 1822, and subsequent dates.
[2] Hänlein's **Report**, June **14,** 1823.

bach. At a later date, through the favour of Prince Augustus, Radowitz was enabled to enter a new and richer field of activity in Prussia. When Heyer von Rosenfeld was challenged by an officer on account of an unsavoury love affair, the elector, for the protection of this beloved life, immediately promulgated a law by which the duel was proclaimed a capital offence, while the sending of a challenge made the challenger liable to degrading punishment. Especially dreaded were the Reichenbach's accouchements, which recurred with great regularity every year ; at these times the elector, having nothing else to do, would pay evening visits to the government offices, note the names of absentees, and vent his spleen upon all who fell into his hands.

But all these things were trifles in comparison with the tragedy in the princely household. The electress Augusta had long been absent from Hesse, and at length came to an agreement with her husband by which her independent maintenance was secured. The electoral prince steadfastly espoused his mother's cause. He had taken a formal vow that he would never attend Countess Reichenbach's entertainments, and he kept his word, although the theologians at his father's court endeavoured to convince him that the oath was not binding. In 1822 he attended a public masked ball, accompanied by a confidential servant. The two men were of the same stature and wore similar dominoes. An unknown mask offered the servant a glass of grog. The man drank it, and died almost immediately, manifestly poisoned. The elector, who, after his manner, was greatly attached to his son, immediately commanded a strict investigation, and his police were equal to the occasion. They simply ordered that everyone who had attended the ball was to report within forty-eight hours, and that any who should neglect to do so would be arrested on suspicion.[1] Nevertheless this sinister affair was never cleared up. The general belief was that the blow had been launched from the circle of Countess Reichenbach. What a prospect was it for the country when this unhappy prince should some day come to the throne,

---

[1] Notice issued by the supreme direction of the electoral police, Cassel, February 5, 1822.

foolishly brought up, suspicious and unsociable, exposed from early youth to roughness of every kind, with adultery and assassination continually under his eyes! The elector was ever filled with apprehensions, as is customary with despots. On one occasion, when he believed that his life had been attempted by poison, he made his cook, after a formal investigation, take twenty-three solemn adjurations. From 1823 onwards he received a series of mysterious letters, threatening him with death unless he abandoned the Reichenbach. The whole country was disquieted by this affair; numerous arrests were made; "an electoral committee for the discovery of the threats levelled against his highness" promised a high reward to anyone who would throw light upon the origin of the letters. In the end suspicion actually fell upon Manger, the principal superintendent of police, a man generally detested. Confined in Spangenberg, all that he would admit was that he had failed to pursue the investigations to a close because the clues in his possession led to issues which he had not dared to follow up. Manger was sentenced to five years' imprisonment in a fortress, and the elector increased the sentence to one of imprisonment for life, but no further light was thrown on the matter.

The faithful country felt itself betrayed and sold. At first liberal ideas secured in Hesse no more than isolated supporters. A work by Martin, the advocate, demanding the summoning of the diet, aroused no interest. The national conscience, however, demanded its rights. Whenever the beloved electress showed herself she was received with a veneration which reflected unfavourably upon the Reichenbach. In Marburg an obelisk was erected upon the Augustenruh, above the Lahn, in honour of "the princess who loves nature." At times the repressed fury broke forth. After the death of Manger's brother it transpired that he had been a cheat and had killed himself. Thereupon the burghers of Cassel applied to the courts, and secured authority for the destruction of the desecrated town hearse, for the exhumation of the body, and for its reinterment outside the walls of the town.[1] The two excellent ministers, Witzleben

[1] Hänlein's Report, October 3, 1824.

and Krafft, at length resigned in disgust. There remained only Minister Schminke, a man too fond of good living; and Councillor Rivalier, now raised to the rank of Baron von Meysenbug, who would at times place obstacles in the way of the exercise of arbitrary power, but who was on the whole a mere pliable courtier. New and illegal taxes and fines were imposed to fill the empty national treasury. The elector went so far as to have the wax figures of his ancestors removed from the Cassel museum and melted down in order to sell the wax. His private wealth was invested, partly in foreign securities, and partly in the purchase of landed estates in Bohemia for the children of Countess Reichenbach.

In the case of the oppressed and neglected common people, the insane tariff war with Prussia served also to prevent neighbourly intercourse; discontent was rife; smuggling and poaching were on the increase. The last bulwark against despotism was found in the law-courts, which maintained their excellent reputation throughout this trying time. Just as in the days of the old elector Councillor Pfeiffer had intervened on behalf of the purchasers of the domains, so now President Wiederhold and the Cassel supreme court of appeal proved the falsity of the liberal prejudice that the free administration of justice is rendered impossible by the atmosphere of a court. Wherever they could, they championed the rights of the officials, of the creditors of the state, and of the taxpayers; but their power was circumscribed. The electoral state of Hesse shared the aimless futility common to the political life of all the petty German states. The only thing peculiar to Hesse was its unscrupulous tyranny, wherein it contrasted strongly with the well-intentioned stupidity of most of the other German courts, and went far to resemble Naples or Modena. Even more irresistibly than Saxony did Hesse move towards a violent explosion.

The Kingdom of Bavaria (IV, 441-64)

While the petty states of the north were fast bound in profound quietude, a new and hopeful life broke noisily forth in Bavaria.

King Louis was in his fortieth year when he ascended the throne, and in the view of his physicians he was not destined for a long life. It was necessary, therefore, to set speedily to work. He had long been the hope of the patriotic youth of the south, but during recent years had for the most part held discontentedly aloof from the paternal court, for in social graces he could compete neither with his brother-in-law, Eugene Beauharnais, nor with his younger brother Charles, his parent's admitted favourite ; moreover, his pride was hurt by the indecisive political attitude of the cabinet, by the secret appeals for aid which were issued from Munich to the great powers. At length he was master, and could show the nation what it was to have a king who was at once " German, religious, and a defender of popular rights." Frederick the Great was his ideal ruler, although he had little in common with his exemplar beyond an inexhaustible love of work. There was nothing of the brilliant sobriety of the historic hero in this fantastically excitable nature, endowed with insatiable receptivity for all the new political, religious, and artistic ideals evolving in a time of ferment.

A true child of the romanticist movement, King Louis strongly resembled his brother-in-law, the crown prince of Prussia. More fortunate, however, than Frederick William, he was saved from the curse of sterile dilettantism, for among the gifts of his many-sided and sensitive nature, there was one which dominated all the rest, and which gave stability and definite direction to his life—the artistic sense.

> " Ever does the busy worker's mind
> Fashion joys that spring anew to life.
> Never he to time shall fall a prey,
> Living always in a bright to-day,
> And his spirit aye with love is rife."

It is in these terms that he describes immortality in one of his works. It was his ambition to awaken the slumbering sense of colour and form, to reintroduce the world of the beautiful among the life habits of a nation which, despite the masterpieces of its poets and composers, continued to lead a poor, tasteless, and philistine existence ; and he devoted himself to this grand aim with a delight in self-sacrifice which could have been the outcome of nothing else than genuine inspiration. In marked contrast with Frederick William of Prussia, he possessed what enthusiasts commonly lack, an iron force of will, a stubbornness recalling that

which characterised his ancestor, Charles XII of Sweden. Of the
innumerable artistic plans with which his mind was filled, many
never ripened, and many miscarried ; but not one of those which
he seriously undertook to bring to fruition was left in a state of
half completion. Thus it was that next to Charles Augustus he
became the greatest Mæcenas in German history, and he is more
highly esteemed by his successors than he was esteemed by his
contemporaries outside Bavaria. Forgotten are his foolish crotchets,
which to those of his own day seemed now ludicrous, now repulsive ;
healed are the wounds which his capricious and inconstant policy
inflicted upon Bavaria : but there remains as an enduring possession
of the nation an abundance of magnificent works which would
never have come into existence but for the open hand and the
restlessly scheming intelligence of King Louis, works which have
awakened new creative energies in every domain of art and craftsmanship. He made his capital one of those great foci of culture
which have become essential to German life, and royally fulfilled
his promise to bring it to pass that no one could know Germany
without having seen Munich.

Rarely has a single human intelligence fostered such extraordinary contradictions in close and disturbing juxtaposition.
Hellenic sense of beauty, and bigoted Catholic credulity ; honest
love for his people, and an over-esteem for the royal dignity which
approximated to self-idolisation ; enthusiastic Teutonism, and
Wittelsbach dynastic pride—all these qualities were displayed
conspicuously and crudely, for nature, when endowing the king,
had been chary with the plain gifts of common sense, tact, and
moderation. The harmony which he was so well able to appreciate
in works of art was lacking in his own personality. The impatient
movements of the tall figure, the oblique glances of the fiery eyes,
and the hasty, stuttering speech, betrayed a strange inward unrest.
The same man who could engage hour after hour in light, good-
humoured, and innocent converse with his artists at work would,
when infuriated, in some access of masterful caprice, outrage his
friends' most delicate sensibilities, or, crying out " The king, the
king ! " would in the street strike the hat from the head of a passer-
by. A connoisseur of the beautiful, he nevertheless mishandled the
German tongue, using grossly involved sentences and participial
constructions of unparalleled complexity, and he would fashion
seven-footed hexameters with utter disregard of all the laws of

prosody. He worked incessantly from early dawn, and renounced the ordinary comforts of life in order to save money for the purchase of works of art ; but when seized with a passion for a pretty woman, he forgot self-control and consideration for his wife Theresa (whom he nevertheless continued to love), and displayed his desires with a Hellenic unrestraint which could not fail to arouse scandal in the sober-minded modern world.

The Bavarians were partly responsible for the king's extravagances, for when he ascended the throne he was hailed with an exaggerated veneration which might well have turned a cooler head. Thiersch actually declared : " Here is one greater than Frederick ! " Platen announced the artistic and political hopes of the younger generation in a spirited ode :

> " You discern in the marble, not marble merely,
> But the countenance of a future Jove.
> In the coat of arms of ancient tradition
> Your mind figures the roses of modern freedom ! "

Of greater political significance was an emotional address to the new king from Elector Maximilian I which Görres published in the *Katholik*. Herein, the founder of the Catholic league, the man who exercised so strict a control over the feudal licence of Old Bavaria, exhorted his descendant to be loyal to the constitution, to maintain the peace of the creeds, to fight against the zealots in both camps who believed faith and freedom of thought to be incompatible. The leading idea of the writing was not, however, to be found in these flashy liberal catchwords, but in the unambiguous proposition that King Louis was to be protector of the Catholic faith, " so that Bavaria may again become that which it was before the converse was falsely imputed, the shield and corner stone of the German church." The clericalist demagogue believed that in the crowned romanticist he had found the man who would no longer restrict by " so-called organic edicts " the carrying of the concordat into full effect, and the man who would expel from orthodox Bavaria " the evil sect of the fanatics of reason." Görres did not spare turgid expressions of praise.

The lesser Bavarian journalists outvied one another in flatteries whose grossness aroused disgust even in the diplomatic corps.[1] " Bavaria's Louis " was the most German of all the German princes,

[1] Küster's Report, October 11, 1826.

the star for all men of German sentiments, wisdom enthroned ;
upon his wife's feast day, the moon appeared in the heavens to
express humble wishes for the happiness of the royal pair.   Praise
was even bestowed upon the king's military genius, which
unquestionably occupied the last place among his manifold gifts.
He was termed " the laurel-crowned victor of Pultusk," although
every veteran knew how little share the crown prince, then twenty-
one years of age, had had in the glories of that bloody affray.   This
Byzantine tone persisted.   Year after year, when the feast of St.
Louis recurred, Schelling, as president of the university, extolled
the king's glories with a servility which was in odious contrast with
the dignified candour of the ceremonial orations delivered by
Boeckh in Berlin ; nor did the grateful artists spare incense.   A
lithographic print which was widely circulated among the village
inns of the mountain district represented the king amid the magnificent new edifices of his capital, with the inscription : Posterity will
one day speak of him as the Great.   Everything he did was considered a mark of genius.   Even his poems were admired, and this
not at court merely, for so honest a liberal as Andreas Schmeller
exclaimed in delight, " Would it be possible for such growths to
thrive upon ice-bound summits ? "   Beyond the blue-and-white
frontier posts, the unexpected appearance of this unfortunate
collection of verses awakened, indeed, different sentiments.   Conservatives demanded in astonishment whether the Bavarian monarch
had not a single candid friend to give him a kindly hint.   As far
as the members of the opposition were concerned, the barbarous
shapelessness of the Wittelsbach metrical atrocities afforded them
inexhaustible material for malicious jests.   For many years to
come, to the despair of the censors, quotations from King Louis'
poems remained welcome tit-bits for the readers of liberal newspapers, and people became accustomed to make light of the king's
genuine services.   Chamisso alone could find a word of sympathy
for the tragic isolation of the crowned singer of liberty.

The blind admiration of the Bavarians for their new ruler,
following hard upon years spent in the background, could not
fail to strengthen his despotic inclinations.   In the establishment
of the fundamental law, and subsequently in the struggle against
the Carlsbad decrees, he had unceasingly and valiantly displayed
his loyalty to the constitution.   He boasted of belonging to the

leading constitutional princely house of Germany, and in his poem,
A King's Sentiments, he wrote :

> " Glorious to rule by free assent of all,
> And not as despot sways the will-less thrall ! "

With good reason he refused to admit for his Bavaria the validity
of the neo-French doctrine that the king reigns but does not govern,
and with his restless desire to participate in everything that went
on, he made so comprehensive a use of his monarchical authority
that, in reality, without any deliberate infringement of the constitution, his will was universally decisive. Alike the greatest and
smallest in the land were subject to the strange caprices of his
uneasy intelligence. For example, since it pleased him to spell
the name of his country " Bayern," this antique orthography was
insisted on, and no Bavarian printer dared any longer to use the
form " Baiern." The finances, which under the good-natured Max
Joseph had never been in a state of complete equilibrium, were his
first care. In pensions alone, leaving the army out of account,
nearly 5,000,000 gulden were expended every year. " Right is
sacred to me," wrote King Louis to Stein, " and this makes it all
the more difficult to balance income and expenditure, but with
God's help I shall succeed." And succeed he did, though not
without much harshness. The heirlooms received from his father,
even the sword and the articles of daily use, were at once sold by
auction, and he exhibited little consideration for his step-mother,
Queen Caroline. The expenditure of the court was restricted to
the utmost, and two economy committees, under his personal
presidency, were instituted to supervise the national expenditure.

To the general surprise, the king dismissed, not only his old
opponent Rechberg, whose fall everyone had anticipated, but also
Lerchenfeld, minister for finance, a confidant of many years standing,
for the king considered that his methods of retrenchment lacked
thoroughness. Louis at length secured a finance minister after his
own heart in Count Armansperg, a man of the world, young, brilliant,
of mobile intelligence, and with the reputation of a liberal. The
count set to work with bureaucratic stringency, and speedily
acquired in the popular mouth the nickname of " Sparmansperg."
By the remorseless deletion of items of expenditure, he was enabled

as early as the year 1827 to lay before the chambers, for the first time, a budget without a deficit. But the thriftiness of the new regime, beneficial at first, soon became a torment. Hardly had equilibrium been restored to the national finances, when the king demanded of his authorities that out of the prescribed disbursements they should furnish " economies," and these economies he unhesitatingly regarded as a free gain, with which the crown might deal as it pleased. Even during the first months of his constitutionalist zeal, he dolorously admitted to the duke of Nassau that a rigidly limited civil list was " extremely inconvenient " ;[1] not even the wealth of the Wittelsbachs sufficed for his grandiose artistic plans. It was here that the economies were to help him out.

The zealous officials endeavoured by such economies to secure the monarch's favour. Road construction, abolition of the burdens on the soil, care of the elementary schools, and many other important but inconspicuous duties of administration, were grossly neglected. The army suffered most severely of all under this remarkable system of thrift practised by the royal patron of the arts. Amid the joyous acclamations of the liberal world, he immediately reduced army expenditure by 1,000,000 gulden, and subsequently lowered it still further to 5,500,000, whereas Frederick William III, himself economical to excess, spent over 21,000,000 thalers upon the Prussian army, more than double proportionally to population ; it had become the custom in the middle-sized states to leave the defence of the fatherland with an easy mind to the care of Prussia. The nominal strength of the regiments was left undiminished, for the king required a powerful army to support his policy of making Bavaria a great power ; but 16,000 men were sent on furlough every year, whilst the old officers were hardly ever allowed to retire, even if they were no longer able to ride. Field-Marshal Wrede, whose opinion had once counted for so much with the crown prince, now lost all influence, for the veteran soldier recognised the defects in the military system, and the unwarlike monarch could not tolerate contradiction. As early as the days of the July revolution, the army was in such a plight that Bavaria's war-experienced neighbour, King William of Würtemberg, expressed himself as being greatly concerned about the matter ;[2] but it was not until the Main campaign of 1866 that

[1] Blittersdorff's Report, September 9, 1829.
[2] Küster's Report, October 2, 1830.

the evil consequences of this system of false economy, slowly working out to their natural issue, became plainly manifest.

The king opened his first diet with an address from the throne in the monumental style. " It is presumably superfluous for me to offer assurance of my sentiments in favour of lawful freedom, the rights of the throne, and the constitution which extends its protection over all ; nor can it be necessary for me to say that I regard religion as the most important element in life, and that I shall know how to uphold all that thereto appertains." The tedious session led to some noteworthy result : the local council which had long existed in the Rhenish Palatinate was with certain changes introduced into the other circles of Bavaria, and thus a firm foundation was for the first time given to the constitution. It is true that these local councils, constituted after the model of the French *conseils généraux*, possessed extremely restricted powers ; they did not conduct any administrative affairs, but had merely to approve tax assessments and the extraordinary expenditure of the circles. Nevertheless they made it possible for subjects to affect the course of administration by means of petitions, statements of grievances, and expressions of opinion, and thus exercised certain restrictions upon the power of the officials. For the rest, the crown was just as unyielding towards the chambers as in the previous reign. As of old, Zentner, still the ablest man of affairs in the ministry, declared, upon extremely dubious grounds, that the government was entitled to refuse leave to attend the diet even in the case of municipal officials ; consequently Burgomaster Behr was absolutely unable to secure admission to the chamber, although he defended his legal right in a vigorous polemic writing, and had recently in Würzburg been in friendly association with the crown prince. Many of the king's romanticist proposals had to be shelved. Like his brother-in-law in Berlin, he was much concerned about the future of the German nobility, and he, too, believed that it would be advantageous to follow a foreign model, and to introduce the English right of primo-geniture ; but the dissatisfaction of the members of the upper chamber showed him that ancient customs cannot be abolished by the simple fiat of a ruler ; the proposed nobles' law was with-drawn, and even the newly established Rhenish Confederate personal nobility, whose creation was obviously intended to reduce the prestige of the hereditary nobility, remained a Bavarian peculiarity.

The consequences of the presence of a new personality upon the throne were manifested far more plainly in the spiritual life of the country than in the proceedings of the representative assemblies. It was in the world of ideas and of dreams that the new king felt most at home, the man who said of himself :

> " Let me yearn, dream, be an enthusiast ;
> Imagination alone gives satisfaction and delight."

He rescinded the press ordinance which had been enforced after the promulgation of the Carlsbad decrees ; and although the censorship of political newspapers was continued, during these first years of confidence it was by no means severe, the principle being that everyone was to be allowed to express candid opinions regarding the conduct of the Bavarian authorities. Henceforward, too, the church was to enjoy greater freedom than it had possessed under the " enlightened " bureaucratic rule of the late king. Louis, as a faithful Catholic, re-established the ancient family customs of the Wittelsbachs, washed the feet of the poor on Maundy Thursday, and walked devoutly in the Corpus Christi procession ; he restored to the capital its ancient coat-of-arms, of which Montgelas had formerly deprived it because the little boy of Munich had unfortunately been an unenlightened little monk ; he permitted the peasants of Oberammergau to resume the representation of their fine old Passion Play, and hastened to fulfil the pledges of the concordat which had not yet been carried into effect. Eight monasteries and four nunneries were immediately reinstated, beginning with Charlemagne's venerable foundation, the Benedictine abbey of Metten on the Danube. The number of convents gradually increased. With astonishment did the inhabitants of Munich once more see the Benedictines, Capuchins and Franciscans, the memory of whom had long passed away, walking through the streets. The minds of the peasants were now more at ease, when they were again able to buy from the hands of consecrated men of God the water of St. Ignatius, Quirinus oil and Walpurgis oil, the tablets of St. Luke, and the other charms of customary local use. The king soon exceeded the prescriptions of the concordat, inasmuch as he founded two Catholic

schools for boys in addition to the promised seminary for the priesthood. He desired pious priests who should cleanse the orthodox
land of Bavaria from the last dregs of the enlightenment, and failed
to understand how much estranged from the fatherland the clergy
of the coming generation would necessarily become if from earliest
youth they were to be cut off from lay society.

Roth, the Swabian, was appointed chief of the Protestant
consistory, a man of rigidly orthodox views, who regarded the ultramontanes as welcome allies against rationalistic unbelief. Since
the queen-mother had had to remove to Würzburg, her chaplain, the
conciliatory Schmitt, lost his influence, and the strict Lutheranism,
hostile to the Evangelical union, which flourished at Erlangen
under the younger theologians, was everywhere favoured. But the
king was by no means disposed to restrict the freedom of Protestants or to subject the state to the Roman church. He would not
hear a word of the recall of the Jesuits, saying, " They have never
been German " ; and among the other orders he gave the preference
to the gentle and learned Benedictines. His favourite among the
priests was the venerable Sailer, who, now restored to the pope's
favour, had become bishop of Ratisbon. What delight did it
afford the king to give a pleasant summer holiday to his old tutor,
" the German Fénelon," in the neighbouring country seat of Barbing.
Occasionally Louis put in an appearance in the clerical circle which
assembled here, and refreshed himself with the serious conversation
of old canon Wittmann and of Diepenbrock, the young Westphalian.
But almost as gladly as with these gentle priests of Ratisbon did
he associate with Geissel and Weis, canons of Spires, the pugnacious
collaborators upon the staff of the clericalist *Katholik*. Among his
personal intimates were to be found, on the one hand, Baron Heinrich
von der Tann, the moderate liberal, a Franconian of Protestant
family, and, on the other hand, his " beloved little Muckel," the
talented physician Nepomuk Ringseis, a strict Catholic of Old
Bavaria, a mystic alike in matters of faith and of natural
science.

From the beginning of the new reign, the clericalists raised
their voices ever more loudly. It was their custom, in *Eos* and
other journals, to extol Catholic Old Bavaria with much zeal as the
land of Wittelsbach loyalty, and this aroused acrimonious
rejoinders from Franconia. Before long in the new provinces, and

even in diplomatic circles, it became usual to speak of an ultra-montane " Congregation," which was said to carry on secret activities in Munich after the Bourbon model.[1] These rumours were for the most part false or exaggerated, but so incalculable was the king's character that a clericalist triumph seemed by no means unlikely sooner or later. Eduard von Schenk, the new minister for home affairs, a young Rhinelander who had won the king's favour by his romanticist dramas, was suspect to the Protestants, if only for the reason that he was a convert to Catholicism, and he was certainly not strong enough to withstand a sudden onslaught.· Even during the first years of the new reign, the joy of the liberals was already dashed by these anxieties.

On the other hand, the removal of the Old Bavarian university to Munich secured the approval of far-sighted persons. The happy thought occurred in the first instance to Ringseis, and was carried out by the king, with his customary promptitude, in the year 1826. In Landshut the university had evolved somewhat more freely than previously in the Jesuit stronghold of Ingolstadt. But even here it had been far from vigorous. In this paradise of the Lower Bavarian wheat-barons, the danger that the professors would become rustical was all too obvious ; and moreover, the ancient semi-clerical compulsory curriculum continued to exercise its restrictive influence. The king now permitted the university the entire freedom of teaching and study characteristic of North Germany, a freedom he had learned to prize when a student in Göttingen. By combining this university with the Munich academy, he hoped to favour the culture of youth by a stimulating environ-ment, and simultaneously to enrich the capital with an abundance of spiritual energies. For the scientific life of Catholic Germany his Munich was to become such a focus as was Berlin for the Protestant north.

Among the numerous new appointments that were offered, Tieck, Thibaud, Raumer and several others refused, most of them because they dreaded the renowned inhospitableness of the Bavar-ians. Schelling, however, accepted, and for a long time to come his valuable activities as a teacher gave the transformed university its characteristic stamp. He now lived in the mystic circle of ideas of his long-heralded theosophy and gave the watchword for

[1] Küster's Report, February 17, 1830.

the campaign against Hegel. This opposition to the Berlin school of philosophy was likewise manifest in the lectures of Baader the mystic, of Schubert the pious natural philosopher, Stahl the young demonstrator, Puchta, and Döllinger. Most conspicuously, however, was it displayed in the fantastical addresses of Görres, whose appointment threw a glaring light upon the strange mingling of Catholic and liberal sentiments in the mind of King Louis. Thus did the unctuous exhortation to Maximilian receive its due reward, and the grateful Wittelsbach ruler was not to be diverted from his purpose when the Prussian government, upon the express command of Frederick William, inquired whether this appointment, made without prior reference to the Prussian authorities, was in accordance with the federal law.[1] Görres had no gifts as a teacher. The mystically imaginative ornateness of his rhetoric drew a large audience, but the members of this audience carried nothing away from the lecture room beyond the intoxication of a vague enthusiasm. How, indeed, were they to learn anything when an entire term was required for the description of the course of universal history down to the days of the deluge ? All the greater was his influence as party chief, as champion of the church militant. Through religious and personal embitterment, his hatred for Prussia rose gradually to the pitch of fanaticism. The halo of political martyrdom came to his assistance ; the clericalists spoke of Görres with veneration, as the liberals spoke of Arndt and Jahn. Oken received a professional appointment, and following his usual practice was soon engaged in quarrels. The stout-hearted Massmann, too, the book burner of the Wartburg, was enabled not only to give lectures upon " Old German literature " but also to school his young Teutonisers on the gymnastic ground.

Munich university possessed in Thiersch an admirable trainer of teachers, and in Schmeller a highly gifted authority on the German tongue, a man unduly modest and far too little known, whose *Bavarian Dictionary* was a pioneer work in the study of German dialects. Next to Berlin, Munich soon became the most frequented of the German universities outside Austria, contributing much to raise the tone of the capital and to approximate Old Bavarian life to the national civilisation, for although the new

[1] Cabinet Order to Altenstein, December 25, 1827.

streets inhabited by the North German professors were for a long time to come spoken of in the town as " the Protestant quarter," people gradually began to tolerate and to understand one another. During these first terms, moreover, when young men were still gratefully enjoying the newly acquired freedom of study, student life was sound and lively. In the common room, where the young philosopher Beckers and his friends set the tone, a cheerful scientific idealism prevailed. Nevertheless the success of the venture was far from equalling the king's exaggerated expectations. The university of the Bavarian capital could not be compared, even remotely, with the leading university of Prussia. The soil, which had here only just been brought under cultivation, was not as yet fertile enough for such a comparison to be possible. In Berlin Hegel was but one among many. Beside the rich variety of scientific life in the Prussian capital, the learning of Munich, whose dominant characteristics were those of a Catholic natural philosophy, seemed poor, limited, and biased, and at times the royal enthusiast may well have thought of the epigram he had once penned in an hour of depression :

> Like to a swimmer, unskilful, Bavaria, wast thou and art thou,
> Upstriving with forcible strokes, quickly to sink then adown !

Among the non-academic men of learning summoned by the king to Munich, the historian of Tyrol, Hormayr, proved of especial merit. Many years before, he had written *The Austrian Plutarch, Life and Characteristics of all the Rulers of the Austrian Imperial State ;* he had participated in Andreas Hofer's uprising ; and he had roundly abused the Bavarians as " Rhenish Confederate slaves." Having been treated ill by Metternich, he now placed his caustic pen at the disposal of the liberal minded king of Bavaria, and at once proceeded to write, concerning the historical frescoes of the Munich arcades, a booklet which for Bavarian self-adulation and courtly servility would be difficult to parallel ; again and again he reminded the Bavarians how in earlier days, when their state was barely a third of its present size, their influence had often been decisive in European politics. This sudden change of sentiments was hardly likely to awaken confidence, but since Hormayr was familiar with all Metternich's weaknesses he was not to be despised as Wittelsbach court publicist. The indefatigable Cotta, too, who had just established a steamship service upon the lake of Constance, was induced by King Louis to found in Munich a branch of his book-selling business. Here was to be published a great liberal newspaper, *Neue Politische Annalen*, a continuation of Murhard's undertaking ; Lindner, the confidant of the court of Stuttgart, and the youthful Heinrich Heine, were entrusted with the editorship. The newspaper, however, succumbed within a few months, and Lindner subsequently made a quiet living on the staff of the *Bayrische Staatszeitung*, where he continued for years to sing his old song of " pure Germany," but did so with muffled voice, securing little attention.

The king zealously promoted the reform of the gymnasia. He wished to reconstruct them after the fashion of the Saxon and Würtemberg classical schools, and to do away altogether with the lycées, which still occupied an untenable intermediate position between the university and the gymnasium. With Schelling's support, Thiersch brought forward a profoundly considered scheme of education whose aim it was, by the simplicity of a thorough humanistic culture, to teach young men, first of all practice, and subsequently theory. The overburdening of the scholar with divers items of instruction, which was already increasing to a serious extent at the Prussian gymnasia under the guidance of Johannes Schulze, was to be avoided ; the soul-destroying curse of examinations was to be restricted ; the number of school hours was to be sufficiently reduced to enable the teachers to give equable instruction in all branches and to exercise a spiritual influence upon their pupils by the vigour of their personalities.

But when this admirable schools' ordinance appeared (1829) resistance was offered to it on all hands, so that it became only too plain with what difficulty the new century, influenced by such manifold interests, was able to adapt itself to the essential conditions of culture. Schrank, the ecclesiastical councillor, and his associates wished to return to the educational methods of the Jesuits, whereas the *Sophronizon* of Paulus scented hierarchical leanings in the new schools' ordinance. Franconia, a land of industrial progress, demanded the favouring of instruction in natural science (which beyond question was unduly neglected in Thiersch's scheme) ; and Oken, the spokesman of these realists, bluntly demanded that the pupils should be introduced to " the entire culture of the world," and that they should be instructed in advance concerning everything which they might possibly require to know during life. To the older officials, on the other hand, it seemed that the demands of the new plan of education were excessive. Zentner, in especial, an ex-professor, spoke with the utmost contempt of science (resembling in this many professors who have abandoned the professorial chair for a life of affairs); it was his opinion that all the state ought to demand of the schools was that they should train future officials for the practical needs of state service. These opponents were joined by Grandauer, the influential cabinet secretary, a man of second-rate intelligence, but one who knew well enough how to make himself indispensable to the monarch. Thus assailed from all sides, the king, after a year's delay, determined in a new schools' ordinance to reduce classical instruction to some extent. The lycées, unhappy hybrid structures, continued to exist ; and, worst of all, the proposal made by Thiersch that the teachers' miserable salaries should be increased was never carried into effect, the result being that the majority of the teaching posts were soon filled by priests and even by monks. Thus, while the well-intentioned reform of the Bavarian gymnasia certainly effected a few improvements, these schools were very far from resembling the Saxon classical schools.

The king was much more fortunate in his efforts on behalf of art. Less than science, is art affected by the vicissitudes of public life, and in Munich it found a soil far from ungrateful. These Old Bavarians, with their keen love of sensuous delights and their natural joy in colour, unperturbed by the over-refinements of criticism, only needed some one who could arouse their dormant energies in order to make them capable of learning to build and to create once again as vigorously and well as in the days when the conspicuous steeple of the church of St. Martin at Landshut and the ponderous masses of the Frauenkirche at Munich were designed by Bavarian masters. In most cases, too, artists made themselves at home here more rapidly than professors. The mistrust felt at first by the born Bavarians soon waned, and the newcomers enjoyed the freedom characteristic of this pleasure-loving city. The painters wandered on foot through the adjoining mountains, or spent their days merrily in summer time on the island of Frauenwörth in the

Chiemsee ; at their festivals there prevailed a rough humour which
had been almost unknown to the Germans since the carnival sports
of Hans Sachs.

Leaving out of account the expenditure of state, public
corporations, and municipalities, King Louis disbursed from his
private treasury upon buildings and works of art no less a sum than
18,000,000 gulden ; nor would even this amount have sufficed had
he not attended to details with meticulous exactitude. Paying
no attention to the unjust reproach of stinginess, he openly
declared his opinion that artists had no reason to be ashamed
of working for monetary reward ; but he knew how to pay
them due honour, and secured for them a worthy position in
the state and in society. When quite a young man he had entertained the idea of providing a comfortable home for Schiller in a
villa upon the Palatine. After he had become king he paid a visit
to Weimar on Goethe's birthday in order to render homage to the
poet. With his support was erected the first monument to be
devoted in Germany to the commemoration of artistic services, the
statue of Dürer in Nüremberg. Taking a lofty view of the civilising
power of art, he considered that works of art were not solely for
critics and connoisseurs, but for the people at large. He would
never allow a charge to be made for visiting the collections, or
guardians to be appointed for the protection of costly monuments ;
his Bavarians were to become accustomed to endure, and ultimately
to love, the beautiful.

That which art must discover for itself could not be bestowed
by its royal protector. Unity of style was impossible in a disturbed
epoch which overlooked all the literary creations of an earlier age,
which almost succumbed beneath the burden of new and contradictory ideas, and which had to learn for itself once again to pass
beyond prosaic tastelessness by acquiring the alphabet of the form
sense. To Munich painting, its " Peter the Great," Cornelius, gave
from the first a tendency towards the sublime and the monumental.
But the king could not find among his architects a single one competent by the overwhelming force of a great personality to dominate
the architecture of Munich as completely as Schinkel dominated
that of Berlin ; and although he himself preferred the classical, he
was practically compelled to direct his architects to undertake the
free imitation of various other styles. He was tasteful in his

selections, and the chosen style almost invariably corresponded with the function of the building. But when compared with the picturesque narrow alleys of the old town, wherein the quiet Catholic life of the two previous centuries was so faithfully reflected, the wide streets and squares of new Munich had a strange, motley, and characterless aspect, above all during these early years, when the commercial life of the city was as yet unable to keep pace with the king's bold designs. Greek temples, Roman triumphal arches, and Florentine palaces, towered quaintly above mean lines of houses, or stood quite alone upon some desolate building site; and such a man as Heinrich Heine, who would see nothing but the defects of Munich architecture, found ample opportunity for mocking at the artificial glories of the German " Beer-Athens." Moreover, the burning impatience of the master builder was disastrous to his work. Ever busied with new plans, he could seldom devote the requisite affection to the half completed, and pressed on ever to get the work finished, although the untrained hands of German craftsmen still needed consideration and patience on the part of their employer. He abounded in proposals, until at length it seemed as if there was hardly a great Bavarian left to whom a monument could still be erected ; and since he considered himself to be the real creator, he would occasionally mar the artist's handiwork by some capricious order. Among the numerous artists who flocked to the Isar, many men of distinguished powers were unjustly treated, one of whom was the magnificent draughtsman Bonaventura Genellis. The rivalries inevitable in this turmoil speedily led to odious quarrels, for the king was completely lacking in the easy assurance of Charles Augustus. With a jealous eye to his own prestige, he at once furnished a rival for anyone who seemed inclined to play the part of " grand vizier." But despite all its human weaknesses, this was a rich epoch, full of bold creation and sanguine hope, which now dawned for German art, when Cornelius, surrounded by respectful pupils, erected his painter's scaffolding in the Glyptothek ; and in later years the master continued to look back with yearning to this ecstatic springtime.

Hardly had Louis ascended the throne when he resumed the design for a Walhalla which he had first conceived in the days of the foreign dominion. At Ratisbon, high above the Danube, was to rise the German temple of fame, a sober Doric building standing upon mighty terraces. Whilst this scheme was still under discussion, the foundation stones were laid almost simultaneously for the Königsbau, the Allerheiligenkirche, and the Pinakothek. The architect of all these was Leo Klenze, a Lower Saxon from the Harz region, an admirer of Hellenic ideals, less rich in original ideas than Schinkel, but endowed with a fertile imagination, and sufficiently pliable to adapt himself to the monarch's moods ; an abundance of building material dear to the architect's heart was provided from the marble quarry which the king had purchased at Untersberg. The Königsbau, copied from the Pitti palace, bore all too plainly the stamp of deliberate imitation, and failed to attain the overwhelming sublimity of Brunellesco's stone masses, placed as if by the hands of Titans. More successful was the interior of the Byzantine Hofkapelle, an imaginative and harmonious structure in which the king had incorporated his favourite dreams, shining with gold and marble, almost as beautiful as its glorious prototype, the Cappella Palatina of the Norman kings in Palermo ; when contemplating in the half light that played around the arches the sombre frescoes of Heinrich Hess, the observer was overcome with a feeling of hallowed devotion such as the cold religious edifices of our worldly century are seldom able to arouse. In the Florentine palace of the Pinakothek, Dillis, the director, installed, in addition to the collection of the brothers Boisserée, the newly acquired Wallerstein gallery, so that both the Rhenish and the High German art of old days were magnificently represented. Here were also to be found the great Rubens pictures from Düsseldorf, splendid Murillos, and works by Italian masters, the whole constituting a collection which was excelled in Germany by that of Dresden alone. Nüremberg had had to sacrifice many of its treasures to enrich the Pinakothek. But Louis was by no means inclined to rob his provincial towns, issuing an ordinance for the protection of ancient monuments, and seeing that it was strictly observed. The vandalism of Rhenish Confederate days had come to an end. The Bavarians were once again able to rejoice in their beautiful towns, now that Heideloff, the Swabian, and a whole school of architects with Old German sentiments, had in Nüremberg, Bamberg, and Ratisbon, restored the crumbling churches and other edifices in conformity with the original design, acting, in most cases, upon the king's orders.

In Munich, sculpture did not thrive satisfactorily at the outset, and the king frequently recalled Thorwaldsen's saying, that Protestantism was favourable to sculpture, Catholicism to painting. Louis, therefore, looked abroad for aid, and had his father's monument designed by Rauch, and the equestrian statue of Elector Maximilian I by Thorwaldsen. At length, however, in Ludwig Schwanthaler there appeared a native artist who was exactly what the impatient Mæcenas needed, a man whose imagination worked with marvellous ease, who was always graceful, and whose touch was ever sure, but who had little competence for executing sketchy designs charmingly in respect of individual detail. Statuary which was to exercise its own independent influence was work in which he was seldom entirely successful; but no one understood better than he the art of providing in reliefs and statues brilliant and thoughtful adornment for the pediments of temples of art and for the halls of palaces. The art of bronze-founding likewise exhibited new life. Although the first cast of the monument to Max Joseph was a failure, the king did not rest until his new foundry, under the management of Stiglmayr, was equal to the best in Europe.

But the crown of Munich art was painting. Hardly had Cornelius finished the frescoes in the Glyptothek, when he began another great cycle of paintings, the History of Painting in the loggias of the Pinakothek. Even those artists who, like Schnorr, the painter of the mighty Nibelung pictures, went their own way, could not escape the heroic influence of this epic genius. Landscape painting actually became inspired by the wealth of ideas of the historic style. The Italian landscapes with which the Palatiner Rottmann adorned the arcades adjoining the palace did not merely awaken an indefinite lyrical mood, but told of the human greatness which had made its way athwart these scenes, and did this with such eloquence that the onlooker could condone the abominable royal distichs inscribed beneath. A considerable period had to elapse before the Munichers became accustomed to the presence of the busy community of artists. They grumbled at the mad expenditure ; they mocked at the king's philhellenic adviser Thiersch, who had given not only the library (Bibliothek) but also the Glyptothek and the Pinakothek ; and they were delighted when one morning there was found on Thiersch's door the word *Nepiotheke* (the storehouse of fools). Gradually, however, they began to notice that their royal town was by these strange artistic activities being raised to the rank of a great city ; and ultimately (though late, for the restless experiments in one style after another were by no means favourable to the growth of sound taste) the day arrived when art reacted upon craftsmanship and Munich handicraft flourished abundantly.

King Louis's most characteristic energies were displayed in this field. " Now I can lay aside my chains and live," he was accustomed to say when, almost every year, throwing off the cares of government, he took refuge in Rome. Here he could enjoy himself, in the Villa di Malta on the Pincio hill, just opposite the dome of St. Peter's. In Rome he could devoutly follow the tracks of Goethe, whose favourite spot, the quiet fountain of the Acqua Acetosa, he had some years before had adorned with trees and benches. Here he visited Thorwaldsen's studio, and here he forged new plans for Bavarian art, by the thought of which he was at times so greatly excited that he would positively leap for joy. Anyone who saw him in this poetic ecstasy necessarily gathered the impression that in the mind of this prince there was no place for statecraft. Never would he have admitted this himself. He considered that he was predestined to greatness in the realm of action as well as in that of thought, and, like the Medicis of old, his artistic creations were simultaneously inspired by dynastic aims. It was his hope that an aesthetic reputation would gain for the house of Wittelsbach a brilliant position in Europe. He loved Germany ardently, cherishing the memories of the War of Liberation, and naming his new streets after the battles of Arcis, Bar, and Brienne, to the annoyance of the French envoy, who was still unable to understand that the Rhenish Confederate days of Bavaria were at an end. But he considered also that the German fatherland must permit the crown of Bavaria free scope for its European policy. Consequently the loose constitution of the Germanic Federation was congenial to the king, and he expressly declared that he had no desire to see a federal state, but only a harmonious federation of states. Quite in conflict with his usual thrifty habits, he immediately recalled several diplomatists. He then sent Lerchenfeld to Frankfort, Cetto to London ; he worked much with the ambitious Count Bray ; and the foreign envoys had marvels to relate concerning the great European designs of the court of Munich.

Outside Germany, this Bavarian impulse to activity had but

one primary aim, to support the beloved land of Greece, now becoming re-established. Shortly after the opening of the new reign, a philhellenist appeal was circulated in the Bavarian newspapers, containing the words, " However divergent opinions may be in other matters, in respect of effective participation here, we are all agreed ! " This phrase could have issued from one pen alone. In Vienna the personality of the illustrious author was immediately detected, and with growing anger Metternich learned that Colonel Heideck and several other Bavarian officers had gone to help the insurgents, and that large sums of money had been sent to Greece from the court of Munich.[1] Thiersch, in the intoxication of philhellenist enthusiasm, now conceived the idea of having the Greeks trained for civilisation by Bavaria, and of having the king's son, the youthful Prince Otho, established at the head of the growing Hellenic state. Never, assuredly, could a stranger whimsy have originated in the brain of an excellent professor, for in the whole of Europe there could hardly have been found two races more remote in nature than were the crafty and temperate Greeks and the straightforward and pleasure-loving Bavarians. King Louis, however, embraced the idea with enthusiasm, opening in Munich a Panhellenion where the sons of the Greek heroes, Bozzaris, Miaulis, and Kanaris were to be educated ; and he assailed the great powers with proposals which were to secure for the house of Wittelsbach the undying glory of being the restorer of Hellenic freedom.

In German politics it was his aim that Bavaria should take her place proudly beside the two great powers as the mightiest of the " purely German states," and as the born leader of the minor courts. He hated Austria in accordance with the ancient tradition of his race, and his hatred had been increased by recent wrong-doing ; never could he forgive the court of Vienna for having simultaneously cheated his house of Salzburg and the Palatinate. He looked up with cordial admiration towards Prussia's warlike greatness. Thankfully did he remember the protection which his ancestors had once secured in Berlin, and would often say, " Had it not been for Frederick the Great, perhaps I should not stand here." Nevertheless he could not free himself from that old family superstition which accounts for so many of the transformations of neo-Bavarian policy. It was only by the blind caprice of chance

[1] Blittersdorff's Report, September 4 ; Küster's Report, May 19, 1826 ; etc.

that " the historical parvenus " of the north had been raised to an elevation which accrued by right to the more distinguished house of Wittelsbach ! He desired to live upon terms of loyal understanding with Prussia, but the " semi-Slav state " must not interfere in purely German matters. For support in his German plans he counted chiefly upon the king of Würtemberg, who did actually overcome his personal antagonism, and entered into confidential relationships with his new neighbour.

Bernstorff, who was under no illusions about the character of Louis, regarded this sudden friendship with indifference. He instructed the Prussian envoy to assure the court of Munich that Prussia's sentiments were friendly, but this was not to be done in unduly cordial terms lest the king should presume upon it.[1] Metternich, who was at first extremely suspicious, soon became easy in his mind, and allayed the anxieties of the Badenese government in his usual ponderous and didactic manner. " If we enter more deeply into the matter, if we raise ourselves to a high standpoint, and contemplate the questionthere from in its essence and in its probable and possible consequences, we soon perceive that the artificial structure undergoes dissolution into a tenuous and airy tissue which utterly lacks internal fixity and any sort of potentiality for vigorous persistence. It can find no fulcrum in the character of either of the two princes, for in so far as they can be said to possess characters at all, these exhibit the most glaring contrasts. There is but one point wherein, perhaps, these two temperaments may be said to present a certain similarity, and this is the fondness of both for strutting upon the stage. The independence of which the king of Bavaria dreams is so extensive in its scope that the independence of his less powerful neighbour will necessarily be driven from the field. Both these princes have likewise an itch for popularity, and two men who court the same bride are not disposed towards harmonious personal relations "—a malicious play upon words involving a reminder of the long-forgotten days when Louis, then crown prince, had aspired to the hand of the princess who subsequently became Queen Catharine of Würtemberg. " They are rejoicing in false imaginings," concluded the Austrian, " they are building castles in the air, when they are really unable to give any clear account of what they desire, and when they certainly desire a great

---

[1] Bernstorff, Instruction to Küster, November 19, 1825.

deal more than they are competent to perform. In this case also time will not fail to exercise its rights."[1]

The ill-humour unmistakably displayed in these lines was not occasioned solely by the constitutionalist utterances of the Bavarian autocrat, nor yet by the hosannas of his liberal admirers. King Louis hardly troubled to conceal his sentiments towards the hereditary enemy of Bavaria ; commanding, for instance, that Ingolstadt should be fortified, although he knew that Emperor Francis regarded this as a direct manifestation of hostility ;[2] and profoundly mortifying the Hofburg by promptly reviving the unhappy dispute about the Badenese Palatinate, which had seemed finally buried since the decisions of the congress of Aix-la-Chapelle. Having been brought up in Rohrbach and Mannheim, the monarch regarded himself as a Palatiner, and just as when crown prince he had with the utmost obstinacy defended the alleged claims of his house, so now did he consider it a point of honour to bring his former home under Wittelsbach rule at any cost. An abundance of blessings was to flow over the fortunate land ; the Otto-Heinrichsbau in Heidelberg was to re-arise upon its ruins ; Mannheim was to become the brilliant meeting-place of the Bundestag ; and when the chain of fortresses of Philippsburg, Germersheim, and Landau had been completed, Bavaria would be the Prussia of the Upper Rhine.

There was naturally no reason to anticipate that the great powers would without just cause repudiate the pledges they had given the court of Baden. But Louis believed that Russia, which had in Aix-la-Chapelle championed the rights of Baden, would suddenly come over to Bavaria's side. After the accession of Nicholas I, he sent Wrede to St. Petersburg with congratulations, and wrote a holograph letter to the czar declaring that it seemed to him a good augury that they should have received their crowns almost simultaneously. He went on to beg for Russia's assistance, and in his eagerness he actually forgot his renowned German pride. " In Russia," he declared, " I recognise Bavaria's chief pillar of support ; this, I repeat, is my political credo ! " Nicholas, as was to be expected, returned a civil but evasive answer, and it was fruitless to shower marks of consideration upon his envoy in Munich.

[1] Hatzfeldt's Report, November 23, 1825. Metternich, Instruction to the envoy von Hruby in Carlsruhe, March 31, 1826.

[2] Blittersdorff's Report, December 12, 1826.

Next Count Bray wrote a great monograph *Sur la Réversibilité du Palatinat,* which made the round of the European courts. Then the king brought up the extinct Sponheim claims to the succession, and put forward the extraordinary demand that upon the acccession to the throne of the count of Hochberg (whose right to succeed had long ere this been recognised by all the great powers) Baden should cede the Main-Tauber circle in compensation for Sponheim.

How bluntly, too, were these preposterous claims defended ; how tactlessly did the king expose his personal dignity ! Vainly did invidious pamphlets and offensive newspaper articles endeavour to arouse public enthusiasm on behalf of the rightful counts palatine. Winter, the Badenese councillor, routed the adversary in a well-informed memorial. Threats were not lacking, and more than once the good town of Heidelberg had occasion to dread a coup de main on the part of its neighbour, although the Bavarian army was by this time in a state little fitted for bold deeds-at-arms. In August, 1826, the king journeyed from Würzburg to Aschaffenburg, and stayed for a time close to the frontier of the main territory of Baden, which he had marked down as his prey. Concerning this move, the political journals of Munich reported as follows : " Hills and valleys vied one with another to manifest in the most brilliant manner possible the overwhelming delight felt by all the inhabitants at so inspiriting an occurrence. Heaven and earth, delirious with joy, exulted in unison. From the Badenese town of Wertheim came mothers with nurslings in their arms ; artisans closed their workshops ; even journeymen forgot their work and their wages. The enthusiasm of the dwellers in the neighbouring land rivalled in all respects that of the native Bavarians, so that the former gave plain indication of their desire that they also might become subjects of a prince whose pride it is to be loved by his people." When the Badenese envoy made a remonstrance about the use of these remarkable expressions, Count Thürheim, the Bavarian minister, responded with a shrug of the shoulders that the editor had printed the article in the exact form in which he had received it from a certain quarter ! [1]

For several years in succession these childish manœuvres were repeated. In the spring of 1829 the king visited the Bavarian Palatinate, suddenly diverged from the direct route, and, on a

[1] Küster's Report, August 25 ; Blittersdorff's Report, August 30. 1826.

public holiday, appeared at Rheinschanze, opposite Mannheim. Upon this spot, where subsequently under Louis's vigorous care the industrious town of Ludwigshafen flourished, there existed at that epoch no more than a few smugglers' houses, places of ill repute, an inn, and a Bavarian lottery office, designed to effect a neighbourly lightening of Mannheim purses. Precautions had been taken to ensure that the king's advent should be widely known. Crowds of people streamed into the disreputable haunt ; the monarch secured a good reception, showing himself several times at the window of the inn, and glancing tenderly across towards Mannheim.[1] More than once, also, the royal muse gave expression in halting verses to the yearning of the Wittelsbachs ; and when the monarch's hopes began to wane, he gave utterance to the touching complaint :

> In his homeland so fine
> The palsgrave of Rhine
> Now wanders alone.
> Though love fills his mind,
> To silence resigned,
> He by none would be known.

The acquisition of the Palatinate became an obsession by which Louis was affected throughout life. The unsolicited benefits which in old age he continued to shower upon the Palatine towns, the statue of Dalberg in Mannheim, the Wrede monument in Heidelberg, were the issue of the haunting elegiac strains which still became audible to his mind when he recalled the sirens' songs heard in the twenties. The king felt absolutely certain that the Palatiners shared his feelings, although in reality it was in Mannheim alone that isolated traces might still be discerned of Bavario-Palatine sentiment.

The king of Prussia had formally recognised the Hochberg right to the succession, and it was not his way to yield to suggestion where questions of right were involved. He considered the Bavarian claims the outcome of frivolous arrogance ; never would he allow violence to be offered to a German princely house, or Baden and Würtemberg to be cut off from the German north. With just as much right, said General Witzleben to Frankenberg, the Badenese envoy, Prussia might demand the return of

[1] Berstett, Ministerial Despatch to Frankenberg, June 13, 1829.

Ansbach-Baireuth. The crown prince exclaimed in his stormy fashion : " My brother-in-law is mad, absolutely mad ; he wants to become a thoroughgoing Palatiner, and employs to this end ways and means which are unsavoury and altogether unprecedented ! " [1] The court of Vienna also was extremely perturbed about the Munich claims, and advocated at the Bundestag a proposal, plainly directed against Bavaria, that Mannheim should become a federal fortress ; but Austria felt bound by her unfulfilled promises, and gave smooth words to both parties.

At the courts of the great powers, however, the Bavarian grievances, continually reiterated in the confident tone of those who honestly feel that their legal rights have been infringed, began ultimately to make an impression. Russia held back, although Anstett, Russian envoy in Frankfort, an old well-wisher of Baden, was secretly busied on behalf of his protégé. Prussia alone stood definitely upon Baden's side. The king urged the grand duke to make no concessions to Bavaria upon any account. Berstett expressed his thanks in the most gushing terms, saying, " This noble monarch is our best protector " ; while Frankenberg wrote, " The policy of the last years of Frederick the Great has been revived, and Prussia stands alone as the true protector of the lesser German states." A definite declaration was made to Munich that Prussia would not tolerate the resort to force, and at the same time Frederick William had an elaborate memorial prepared to expound to the great powers the rights of Baden in the matter (January, 1828). In this way the integrity of Baden was safeguarded. The sole result of the obstinate repetition of Bavarian grievances was that King Louis kept his own passion alive, and that the eternal Sponheim affair acquired in the diplomatic world a reputation similar to that which had been secured by the Coethen customs dispute.

---

[1] Frankenberg's Report, May 15, 1828.

III

Before the Revolution

Treitschke died before he could extend the History *to the revolution of 1848, but he lived long enough to express his views concerning the forces that made that upheaval inevitable (French radicalism, the influence of the Jews, and the degeneration of German literature) and the factors that enabled Prussia to survive as the hope of the future (faith in the state, as articulated by Hegel, and economic power, mobilized in the Customs Union). His passages on these subjects and his assessment of the Prussian monarch who was to preside over the turbulent events of 1848 show the peculiar mixture of stylistic brilliance and intractable prejudice that marked all of his mature writing, fascinating even those readers who reprobated his opinions.*

THE PRUSSIAN CUSTOMS UNION (IV, 250–60, 286–88;
V, 461, 491–95)

The men who laid the foundations for Prussia's economic dominance of Germany were F. C. A. Motz, who became minister of finance in 1825, and his chief aide, Maassen, who drafted the Prussian Tariff Law of 1818, from which, thanks to his direction and the skillful commercial diplomacy of J. A. F. Eichhorn, grew the Customs Union of 1834. Unorthodox in their views, they had to make their way against the opposition of conservative advisers like Lottum and Ladenburg of the Board of Control and the Lord Lieutenant of East Prussia, Schön, a gifted administrator who was nevertheless more interested in the immediate problems of the landed gentry than in long-range economic planning. Like most of Treitschke's heroes, Motz was a combative nature who gloried in a fight. He was more than a match for his critics and, in the end, won the complete confidence of the king.

Motz was in his fiftieth year when he assumed his new office on July 1, 1825, the solitary statesman in a cabinet of men of short views. Like Eichhorn, this Electoral Hessian had been attracted into the Prussian service by the refulgence of Frederician times. Far more brilliant than Maassen, the quiet man of learning, his nature was no less solid. Vigorous and adventurous, inspired with bold self-confidence which frequently found expression in incisive sarcasms, this efficient and practical man had in a variegated career learned to despise mere book-learning and yet understood how to adapt himself to the living ideas of the time. After he became a minister, he would envy his younger friends for their " fine, bronzed, Landrat tint." Those had been his happiest days when, as a young Landrat he had gone up and down his circle in Eichsfeld, sometimes on horseback and sometimes with a sporting flintlock on his shoulder, visiting the peasants in their farms, rarely giving any orders, but ever ready to show the man of the people the way to self-help, saying, " Spontaneous activity accords best with the energetic character of the Prussians." It was in Eichsfeld that he became accustomed to prize the estate of peasants as the kernel of the nation. " Better," he said, " the most oppressive taxes upon articles of luxury, better to tax everything like Pitt, than to burden the sweat of the countryman." Through the peace of Tilsit he was constrained to enter the service of the detested kingdom of Westphalia. He was in charge of the finances of the department of Harz, twice put in an appearance as deputy at the farce of the Cassel diet, observing meanwhile with delighted anticipation how Prussia was realising the ideas of genuine German freedom. Immediately on receipt of the intelligence of the battle of Leipzig, he summoned his Eichsfelders beneath the old colours, and in Halle and Fulda played an active part in the organisation of the reconquered province. Subsequently becoming president in Erfurt, he helped to conclude with Sondershausen the customs treaty which was to serve as prototype of so many others. Here, in Thuringia, the utter impotence of German particularism was conspicuously displayed. Measureless was his contempt for the petty courts. He had sufficient knowledge of their inclinations from the fate of his own family, which had suffered much from the avarice of the electors of Hesse, and he became even more intimately acquainted with them when the king sent him to Cassel, commissioned to settle the conjugal disputes in the Hessian house—a task in which he was naturally unsuccessful. Proud to be a Prussian, invariably candid and independent, he would never listen to the praises of Austria which were voiced in official circles, expressing his frank detestation of the lazy, ignorant, dishonest Austrian administration. Besides Canning, Motz was the only statesman of this epoch who had fully recognised the essential shallowness of Metternich. Whilst almost all Prussian men of affairs were unable to overcome secret trepidations, in this fresh mind the cheerful confidence of the year 1813 remained unimpaired. " A fine, big war will do us good," he often declared. " But it must be a national uprising, and then we shall develop energies which will surprise everyone."

Motz desired to see the reforms of Stein and Hardenberg pursued to their logical end. A new rural communes' ordinance should supplement the towns' ordinance ; the burdens upon the soil should be completely abolished ; the land tax should be perfectly equalised (as a matter of justice, even if the state were to lose thereby). Just as all the best officials of these days devoted themselves wholeheartedly to political work, so Motz lived entirely for the state, and even in his most intimate personal affairs he kept political ends in view. When his private fortune increased, he purchased a large estate in Posen, feeling himself here to be a pioneer of German civilisation. Without losing a moment, he attacked the neglected property in his energetic and far-sighted manner, attracted German settlers upon the land, and set an example to the province by efficient and well-ordered management. He said to his relatives, with a laugh : " Follow my example, all of you ; I thoroughly understand what I am about."

During his strenuous administrative work in Erfurt and his subsequent tenure of office as lord-lieutenant in Magdeburg, he composed memorials regarding the rounding off of the

Prussian state domain, the incorporation of the minor con-
tingents into the Prussian army, and the reform of the administration. Though rapidly produced, these served to display
his whole method : his keen insight ; his unprejudiced and
magnanimous patriotism ; but also a certain brilliant levity,
which must not be omitted from the picture. Without such
a delight in bold ventures and in the construction of far-
reaching plans, he would hardly, in an epoch of exhaustion
and renunciation, have found energy to pave the way for
the reconstruction of the German state. Those in close
contact with him received the impression that here was a
man with grand natural endowments, one whose intelligence
was full of ideas, restless, productive to excess, but threatening to work itself to pieces within an unduly restricted sphere
of activity. He needed an extensive field of operations if
the ideas which were fermenting in his brain were to become
clarified, if his powerful ambition and his cheerful energy of
will were to find free scope for development.

The king had appointed the new minister to make an
end of the deficit. The fortunate performance of this immediate task was also the indispensable prerequisite to the
success of those commercio-political designs which Motz had
never ceased to cherish since the conclusion of the Sondershausen treaty. Only when the equilibrium of the national
finances had been secured, could the crown venture upon
customs treaties the prospect of whose financial success was
dubious. In high official circles the general opinion regarding the state of the finances was extremely unfavourable.
Six years earlier it had been found simply impossible to believe
that a deficit could exist in Prussia ; and now the position
was regarded as absolutely desperate because the yield
of the new taxes could not be precisely foreseen. Motz
did not share these gloomy views. He was convinced that
the much lamented deficit would long ere this have been
done away with, if only unity, foresight, and order had
been introduced into the financial administration. " But I
was careful," he said later to his daughter, " to guard myself
against promising that surpluses should be forthcoming ; had
I done so, they would have thought me mad." [1]

[1] From the Memoirs of Frau von Brinken.

A man of less courage might well have been alarmed by the condition of the market. At the very time when Motz entered upon his new duties, England became affected by a terrible commercial crisis, one of the worst convulsions known to mercantile history. The opening up of South American trade had given rise to feverish speculation, which was now followed by a natural reaction. During a period of fifteen months, seventy banks and three thousand six hundred business houses failed. Modest as was still Germany's share in world commerce, our country was not exempt from the disaster ; the great firm of Reichenbach in Leipzig and some of the leading houses of Berlin collapsed. But the significance of these troubles was trifling in our case in comparison with the incredible misery of German agriculture ; and the agricultural crisis, as always happens, was more enduring in its effects. The years of famine had hardly come to an end, when there occurred a rapid and permanent fall in the price of all agricultural products. Foreign customs laws and the wretched state of the German roads hindered the transport of the exuberant harvests. Even the technical advances which German agriculture owed to its teachers Thaer and Schwerz, now exercised a disadvantageous influence, for consumption could not keep pace with the increased supply. In many regions, land values fell even lower than during the war. It was only the sheep farms which continued to prosper, Germany exporting to England more than twice as much wool as all other countries combined. But even this advantage threatened to disappear when foreigners began to learn from us, and when German shepherds and German stock were sent to Russia, Sweden, France, and Australia. Old Prussia suffered most severely of all. During the war more than half of the live stock had been lost ; now in certain regions the daily wage was only three to four silbergroschen, while in others the *Scheffel* of rye was offered at five silbergroschen. Colonel Brünneck, Schön's brother-in-law, endeavoured to help his neighbours by the introduction of sheep-breeding and by other technical improvements, but very few of them were in a position to venture new undertakings.

In response to the urgent petition of the estates, the king once more granted extraordinary assistance " to this nuclear old province." Roads were built, great purchases of grain were ordered for the army, and public granaries were established with the intention of maintaining the price of the *Scheffel* of rye at one thaler.[1]

Then Schön secured an additional allocation of three million thalers to save indebted landlords from ruin. As a good patriot, it was his chief desire that the old families, those whose names were intimately associated with the history of the region, should be maintained in their hereditary possessions. The same view was advocated in the royal cabinet by Schön's friend, Stägemann. Although an adherent of the new political economy, Stägemann had always considered that the ruin of the old landowners would involve the destruction of the state, saying, " This seems to me quite obvious, for a new state would take its place." But the sum provided was utterly inadequate, although it amounted to almost the sixteenth part of the entire state revenue, and in addition it was necessary at any cost to safeguard from bankruptcy the " Landschaft," the great credit institute of the province, to which the indebted landlords all owed money ; had this not been done, the whole province would have been ruined. Upon Schön's suggestion, the king therefore recommended in 1824 that while the allocation should be primarily employed to save the old landed families, when it proved quite impossible to retain a family in possession of its property, a modest pension should be allotted, and the land should be sold at auction by the Landschaft.[2]

With these almost unrestricted powers, Schön set to work. The fate of the Old Prussian nobility was in his hands. Once again, and even more fiercely than some years earlier at the time of the distribution of the first instalments of

---

[1] Petition to the king from the committee of the East Prussian estates, February 18 ; Cabinet Order to the ministry of state, April 11, 1822.

[2] Schön's Reports : to Schuckmann, August 23 ; to the king, December 6, 1824. Lottum, Cabinet Despatch to Schön, July 2, 1825. Stägemann to Schultz, October 13 ; Stägemann's Memorandum concerning the East Prussian Landlords, June, 1825.

the war indemnity, did all now compete for the favour of
the provincial ruler. He did his best, and many excellent
members of the class of landed gentry owed the preservation
of their property solely to his care, but when he regarded
the position as hopeless, he inexorably authorised the Landschaft to sell the estate by auction. Thus it was that, with
the cooperation of this benevolent government, the counts
Schlieben, the counts Goltz, and many other highly respected
noble families, were expelled from hearth and home, most
of them perfectly innocent, for the ultimate cause of their
poverty had been the patriotic sacrifices made by them during
the war. Hundreds of estates were sold, on one occasion two
hundred and eighteen were disposed of simultaneously, and
the excessive supply depressed the price of land to so low a
figure that the Landschaft could maintain its own solvency
only by securing supplementary grants from the state. In
many parts of the province quite half of the larger properties
changed hands. Side by side with the Käswurms, the
Biehlers, the Reichenbachs, and the other Salzburg exiles who
had already made their way into the ranks of the landowners,
there now of a sudden appeared a crowd of bourgeois landowners,
derived from Mecklenburg, Bremen, Brunswick, and Saxony
Among these were many men of substance who could
invest their capital at 15%, and who soon mingled on equal
terms with the old aristocracy ; but there were also many
rough adventurers who never made a success of their new
position.

Amid this social transformation, no one suffered more
than the severe lord-lieutenant. At times he witnessed tears
of thankfulness, but he was also overwhelmed with abuse.
In the neighbouring provinces the story was current that the
fanatical liberal had made up his mind to replace the slothful
race of Prussian nobles by a new and more vigorous stock.
It is quite possible that, in his haste, Schön may have
jestingly made some such declaration ; but his aims were
just ; he desired to save all that was possible of the old
landed gentry, and it was only the scantiness of the financial

resources which forced him to adopt harsh measures conflicting with his desires. How much more successfully had King Frederick, after the Seven Years' War, cared for the " conservation " of the landed gentry. But such thoroughgoing help would now have been possible in no other way than by pledging the national credit; but since the national debt account was closed, further increase was inadmissible without the assent of a . national assembly. Thus obviously did it once more appear that the monarchy without a national assembly was a mere temporary expedient, sufficing in quiet times, but hopelessly embarrassed whenever extraordinary expenditure became necessary.

The minister for finance had no direct concern with these troubles, but the yield of the taxes made him intimately acquainted with the needs of agriculture, although the king, in furnishing assistance, strictly maintained the principle that even in cases of the utmost need no remission of taxation could be granted. In order to gain a thorough understanding of the difficulties, Motz wished, first of all, to grasp the precise state of the national finances, and he consequently renewed his former demand that the minister for finance should have seal and vote upon the board of general control. The king, following his usual practice, endeavoured to adopt a middle course, for he was unwilling to mortify his tried servant Ladenberg. He commanded that when any difference of opinion occurred the minister of finance should, through the instrumentality of one of his councillors, negotiate verbally with the president of the board of general control.[1] Motz could not be content with any such half measure, for between the two coordinated authorities there had long been in progress a tragicomical contest of official zeal such as is possible nowhere else than in the Prussian bureaucracy. The board of general control endeavoured to prove its vitality by appending to the financial statement innumerable ridiculous comments, ninety-one to the estimates for the domains, a hundred and forty-six to the estimates of the depart-

----

[1] Cabinet Order to Lottum and Motz, November 22 1825.

ment of forestry ; while the accountants of the ministry of finance naturally responded in kind. The dispute became so intolerable that Motz determined to tender his resignation unless his reasonable demands were granted. " I cannot agree," he wrote to Lottum, " to accept the role with which, for many years, to the disadvantage of the national finances, Herr von Klewitz had to put up." By the principles of the old absolutism, such a threat of resignation was a criminal act of defiance, and even Motz thought it necessary to add the assurance : " I 'should regard myself unworthy of the king's favour if, a prey to vanity and folly, I were to consent to retain office on any other terms.

Since, in the spring of 1807, in similar circumstances, Stein had been ungraciously dismissed, no other minister had ventured to assume such a tone. Even Hardenberg had on one occasion only, when he was really sure of the king's approval, uttered a gentle threat of resignation. Now four months were to elapse before Frederick William fully forgave the new minister for his act of self-assertion. But by this time he had through Lottum's proposals been thoroughly convinced that the existing dualism was impracticable, and since he was familiar with the stubbornness of his bureaucrats he at length made up his mind to a measure far in excess of what was demanded by the minister of finance. On April 8, 1826, he astonished Motz by the welcome information that he proposed to abolish the board of general control, and to hand over its powers to the ministry for finance. On May 29th, this command was carried into effect, and Ladenberg, in a doleful frame of mind, had to content himself with the presidency of the audit office.[1] Motz was at length master of the situation, and the other ministers speedily learned that he considered himself justified in exercising strict supervision over all branches of the administration. The slow-moving Altenstein might have good reason for complaining of the finance minister's encroachments, for Motz was a hot tempered man, easily irritated

---

[1] Motz's Report to the king, November 28 ; Motz to Lottum, November 28 and 30, December 5 and 10, 1825 ; March 2, 1826 ; Cabinet Order to Lottum April 8 ; Ladenberg's Petition to the king, May 3, 1826.

by excess of formalities; [1] but no one could complain that he was parsimonious. Considering the resources available, he was free-handed in meeting the demands of art and science ; and when Kamptz consulted him regarding the great expense involved in the revision of the code, he answered that Prussia must always find means for such work.

The vigorous hand of the new leader could be felt in every branch of the financial administration. By a thorough reform of the treasury department, he was able to secure the power of precisely supervising all that went on. He left the control of taxation in the hands of Maassen, the originator of the new customs legislation. In the official world, Maassen and Motz were regarded as rivals, but they were in fact friends. Maassen gladly allowed himself to be swayed by the quick resolution of his more youthful chief, while Motz recognised clearly enough all that he owed to the perspicacity and detailed knowledge of the general director of taxation. " I will always listen to Maassen," he said with a smile, when his cautious friend advised him against an ill-considered venture. Ludwig Kühne, Motz's friend of Erfurt days, worked under Maassen. He was the terror of idlers and mediocrities, and his subordinates hardly dared to breathe when he exclaimed to them, " Stupidity is God's gift, but to abuse it is a scandal ! "

In the provinces, taxation had hitherto been in the hands of the local governments, but the king had of late come to recognise how little the tedious collegial system was suited to this branch of the administration, and in 1822, in the two western provinces, he had therefore placed the entire fiscal administration in the hands of a provincial director of taxation. This arrangement proved thoroughly satisfactory, and was extended by Motz to the other provinces. In accordance with old established custom, the new authorities had frequently to contend with the jealousy of the local governments ; and Schön, in especial, was able to make the tax director's life a burden. Among the populace, too, the officials were regarded with suspicion, for the name of tax-

---

[1] Altenstein to Lottum, February 20, 1828, and subsequent dates.

gatherer was in ill repute, and in the old provinces the
monopoly directors of the great king were still remembered
with terror. But people soon learned to esteem the punctuality
and despatch with which the tax authorities worked, and on
the Rhine Tax Director von Schütz was universally loved.
Every far-reaching fiscal reform needs time to prove its
worth. The business world had by now become accustomed
to the new taxes, and the officials had acquired experience
in the use of the unusual formalities. Even the smuggling
traffic began to subside. By the year 1827 it was possible
to regard the reform as completed, and as firmly rooted in
the national habits.

As a supplement to this reform, Motz undertook to
reorganise the administration of the domains, which had become
chaotic during the great agricultural crisis. Accompanied by
Kessler, the new director of the crown lands, Motz paid a
personal visit to all the domains and forests of the monarchy,
hailed everywhere with rejoicing by the forest rangers and
the tenant farmers, who were hardly able to realise that
the great men in Berlin were at length looking into their
grievances. Motz, in order to make a clean sweep of these
troubles, appointed a special authority to deal with the
question of arrears, and drew up new and more equitable
leases, the terms of which had to be strictly observed, but
which saved hundreds of tenants from ruin. He went to
work cautiously in the matter of the alienation of the
domains. It was only in West Prussia and Posen that he
permitted the sale of a number of outlying areas to German
settlers, "in order to create an independent class of peasantry
devoted to the government."

The best of all was that order was now restored ˙to the
finances. In little more than three years, on May 30, 1828,
Motz was able to report to the king that instead of the
dreaded deficit, there was a net surplus of 4,400,000 thalers,
which the collection of arrears would increase to 7,800,000
thalers ; 3,245,000 thalers had already been paid over to
the state treasury, and 1,172,000 thalers had been devoted
to extraordinary expenses. He gladly admitted that but for
the extensive reforms effected by his predecessor he would

not have been able to give the king this gratifying intelligence ; but he had the satisfaction of feeling that he alone
had been competent to reap the harvest of that seedtime ;
and he already felt so sure of the financial position that he
ventured to recommend a moderate reduction in the graduated
poll tax, suggesting that henceforward the liability to taxation
should begin two years later, at the age of fifteen. In other
respects, declared the concluding words of the report drafted
by L. Kühne, the principles of financial administration
would remain : " Thrift and order in respect of regular
expenditure ; storage of the energies of peace for the needs
of the next war ; the maintenance of credit by punctual
payments ; the utilisation of part of the surplus to provide
for future industrial development."

Henceforward Motz was sure of the king's respect. At
court he was regarded as an upstart, for his ancient Hessian
noble family was new in the Prussian service. Wittgenstein's
party soon scented out the minister's liberalism, while Lottum
and the other advocates of unconditional thrift censured him
for levity because he availed himself of the enhanced revenue
to effect a gradual increase of the restricted expenditure,
to the extent of about 900,000 thalers. Whenever such
criticisms ventured out of obscurity, he always justified himself to the king in a frank personal explanation, for the
finance minister, as supervisor of the whole administration,
could not possibly dispense with the monarch's confidence.

In the year 1824, the ministers for foreign affairs, commerce, and finance reconsidered the question " what line
ought to be taken by Prussia in the negotiations to secure
a customs union." Privy Councillor Sotzmann, son of the
well known geographer and one of the ablest men in the
financial administration, callaborated with H. von Bülow to
expound the outcome of the discussion in a great memorial
which gave expression to several of the main principles of
the subsequent draft of the customs union.[1] They declared
that the accession to Prussia might be effected in either of
two ways : by complete subordination, as had happened in
the case of Bernburg ; or by free association. Where a

[1] H. von Bülow and Sotzmann, Memorandum of December 28, 1824.

larger state was concerned, the latter only could be anticipated, but such a state must in any case make its customs
dues and its taxes upon articles of consumption harmonise
with those of Prussia. Thus the difference between " accession to the customs " (*Zollanschluss*) and " customs union "
(*Zollverein*) was already obvious to the minds of the Prussian
statesmen of that day, although they had not then begun
to employ the modern formal terminology. Since the accession of such a state as Electoral Hesse would involve an
addition to the system of an area " comparable only to one
of our governmental districts," the court of Berlin could not
contemplate making the development of its customs system
unconditionally dependent upon the approval of such an ally.
Hence Prussia must bind herself for a certain number of years
only, so that when the specified term had expired a fresh
agreement might be secured about changes and additions.
Consequently all privileges were to be renounced, the full
equality of the lesser ally was to be recognised ; the only
right reserved, as an indispensable counterpoise, being that
of giving notice that the agreement was to terminate. Each
of the two states was to appoint its own customs officials,
but these were to be pledged to the service of both governments. Thus the plan of securing the supervision of the
frontiers for Prussia exclusively, was abandoned. A very
short step further was required to enable the Prussians to
recognise that the swearing in of the customs officials to both
the allies would be intolerable to the pride of the lesser
courts, and that nothing more could be secured than a
reciprocal control of customs administration. Prussia had
not yet spoken her last word. The memorial did not conceal
that the court of Berlin must be prepared for still greater
concessions. " If only the primary aim be attained, the
genuine introduction of the Prussian customs system and the
Prussian taxes upon articles of consumption, with the prosecution of breaches of the law, then formalities which might prove
offensive to the sense of sovereignty of our respective allies,
may well be disregarded." In conclusion, an important idea
was developed, to which henceforward the Prussian cabinet
remained faithful, and which it carried a stage further.
Should Electoral Hesse desire nothing more than mutual pre-

ferences on imports, this would not merely be more costly
but more dangerous for Prussia on account of the higher
Prussian duties. For every reason, therefore, the complete amalgamation of the two customs systems seemed
greatly preferable. (In actual fact, it was not the height of
the internal tolls which paralysed German trade, but the
very existence of such tolls, and any reform which failed to
attack this evil at the root would inevitably miscarry.)

For the moment, unfortunately, these reasonable principles
could not be carried into effect, for the compilers of the
memorial still adhered literally to the programme of 1819.
They wished to secure a direct advance "from frontier to
frontier," from the nearest neighbour to the most remote.
What could seem simpler than the plan to win over first
of all the most adjacent states, those which lay within the
immediate sphere of Prussian influence, and not till then to
see if the whole of united Germany could perhaps come to
an understanding with the south? Yet this direct route
was impassable. The memorial itself admitted that the
court of Dresden, in any case hostile to all innovations,
would have nothing to do with the Prussian customs system,
were it only on account of the Leipzig fair. No mention at
all was made of Hanover, an English bridgehead; and Danish
Holstein was likewise ignored. Thuringia was "inclined
towards Prussia," but, as explained in a separate memorandum, must first combine to form a customs unit, which was to
serve as "an outwork and cover for the Prussian customs
system." Darmstadt "has no coterminous frontier with us,
and even its Upper Hessian region does not come into the
question unless Electoral Hesse also accedes." The upshot
of all this was that the immediate aim could be no more
than the accession of Electoral Hesse with Waldeck. Even
this aim was unattainable, for the elector of Hesse, after
making a brief trial of a reasonable customs system, resumed
the former hostile attitude towards his great neighbour. As
long as such views, which were plainly associated with the
old and unhappy idea of the Main customs line, continued
to prevail in Berlin, there was no prospect of any enlargement
of the customs system beyond the little enclaves.

It was by Motz that the charmed circle of these North German ideas was first broken. In this matter and in his putting an end to the deficit (whereby a grandly conceived commercial policy was first rendered possible), are to be found his permanent title to gratitude. Before any other Prussian statesman, he asked himself the question whether amid the marvellous confusions of German particularism the roundabout course might not after all lead sooner to the goal than the direct, whether it might not be better to circumvent or to climb over neighbours who were not to be convinced. Since the bold chessplayer could not advance on the board with his pawns, he brought his knights into action. He plucked up courage, directly the favourable hour arrived, to reach out his hand, across Electoral Hesse and the other immediate neighbours, to the South German states. At a time when the official German world regarded the perpetual league between Austria and Prussia as an inviolable law, he marched unhesitatingly towards the attainment of another end, the permanent union, under Prussia's leadership, of all Germany, Austria excluded, by the indestructible bond of economic interests, thus paving the way for enfranchisement from the dominion of the house of Lorraine. As soon as this resolution had been made, the ice was broken. The ascending path had been entered by which Prussia's commercial policy was to advance rapidly from achievement to achievement.

The hardest part of the great work had now been accomplished. The loyal labours of the officialdom were crowned by the blessing of unprecedented order. The published annals of German legislation were swollen to tomes of colossal bulk through all the new treaties and laws. Then came the momentous new year's eve of 1834, which announced even to the masses the dawning of a better day. On all the high roads of Central Germany, long strings of heavily laden freight wagons were waiting in front of the custom houses, surrounded by jubilating crowds. With the last stroke of twelve and the close of the old year, the toll gates were thrown wide. The traces tightened, and amid shouts of exultation and the cracking of many whips the trains of goods moved forward across the

enfranchised land.   A new link, strong though inconspicuous,
had been welded into the long chain of events leading the
margravate of the Hohenzollerns onward towards the imperial
crown.   The eagle eye of the great king looked down from
the clouds, and from a remote distance could already be heard
the thunder of the guns of Königgrätz.   Happier than his
impassioned friend, Maassen lived long enough to enjoy the
hour of fulfilment, but died on November 4, 1834.   No worthy
successor could be found, and the great traditions of 1818
survived only in Eichhorn and the privy councillors of the
ministry for finance.

The enlarged commercial union now took the name of
the German customs union.   Amid the thick vapours of the
Germanic Federation there could already be discerned the
contours of that lesser Germany which was one day to outshine
the glory and the power of the Holy Roman Empire.

The customs union now comprised a territory of 8,253 square
miles [German], with more than twenty-five million inhabitants ;
the frontier of this area was 1,064 miles in length, nine miles
less than that which Prussia had had to supervise singlehanded
in the year 1819.   The work was continued with the same
caution that had been displayed in its foundation, with the
same respect for all economic interests, and some years now
elapsed before the accession of any new members.

Formal equality between the allies was carefully maintained.
Of the four first general conferences of the customs union,
one only was held in Berlin (1839).   The loose federal structure
of the union soon exhibited its deleterious influence, imposing
obstacles in the way of the development of the tariff.   Financial
results lagged far behind expectations ; the costs of administration remained high, being from 10 to 12% of the revenue.   But
no defects could outweigh the enormous advantages of the great
union.   The economic development of Germany had hitherto
been much in arrear of that of her western neighbours, but
it now made such rapid progress as to enable the Germans
to take their places as equal competitors in the world market.
By the close of the first decade of the history of the customs
union, the sins of centuries had been atoned for.   The

prosperity our fatherland had known before the Thirty Years' War had at length been regained.

Owing to the incomparable cumbrousness of the German state system, the political consequences of the customs union were less speedily and less directly secured than many bold intelligences had anticipated. At the beginning of the thirties Hansemann had hoped for a parliament of the customs union, out of which a German Reichstag might perhaps originate; and doubtless many other well-meaning patriots based similar aspirations upon the German "customs state." But the commercial league was not a state, it offered no compensation for defective political unity, and existed for decades without destroying the lie of the federal constitution. In the year 1827, when du Thil had advised the grand duke to take the decisive step in Berlin, the minister had frankly declared: "Let us be under no illusions. By joining the commercial league we renounce an independent foreign policy. Should war break out between Austria and Prussia, Hesse is committed to the Prussian colours." Similarly Dahlmann, who in his grand and profound manner promptly acclaimed the customs union as the one German success since the wars of liberation, confidently declared that the commercial league would safeguard us against the recurrence of civil war. These prophesies were not literally fulfilled. The customs union did not prevent the High German states from taking up arms against Prussia. Nevertheless the year 1866 was destined to display the enormous vitality of this commercial league. The rapid victory of Prussian arms saved our state the trouble of brandishing its mightiest weapon, of promptly converting the High German courts by annulling the customs community.

The consciousness of mutual dependence, the recognition that there could no longer be any separation from the great fatherland, were impressed upon all the life habits of the nation by the petty experiences of everyday life; and in this indirect political influence lies the historical significance of the customs union. The schools of the Albertines and the Guelphs might continue to inculcate upon the mind of youth the fables of intertribal hatred and of particularist self-conceit, but nevertheless there had come an end to the philistinism of old days, to the childish belief in the glories of the system of petty states. The man of business followed with his mind's eye the bales of goods which he had despatched upon their free passage across German territories. He became accustomed, as the man of learning had long been accustomed, to look beyond the frontiers of his little native state. His vision, now adapted to wider relationships, glanced back with ironic indifference upon the pettiness of the narrower fatherland. The very idea that the old barriers of separation could ever be reestablished became strange to our people, and whoever entered the commercial league belonged to it for all time. After every crisis, inexorable necessity refashioned the old limits of the customs union. Men endowed with cool political intelligence could with mathematical certainty foresee the course of the dispute.

The foreign world speedily abandoned the hopeless struggle against our commercial unity. French statesmen, shrugging their shoulders, regretfully admitted that France had nothing to offer the German states which could counterbalance the advantages of the Prussian customs union. It was through Bowring's reports (1839) that the British public first acquired a definite conception of the nature of the customs union, and was wont henceforward to regard Prussia as the representative of German commerce. Austria, after her repeated and futile attempts to disturb the course of events, was invariably forced in the end to leave her rival a free hand in German commercial affairs, and nothing but a tacit agreement to this effect between the two great powers served to secure the maintenance of the Germanic Federation. For Prussia the paths of her commercial policy were now so clearly indicated that even faint-heartedness could not have induced her to forsake them. Her task was to extend the commercial union until it embraced all the German states, but to extend it no further. As early as 1834 the idea was mooted in Brussels (where French lust of conquest was arousing anxiety) whether Belgium should not join the German customs union. Prussia rejected the idea ; and at a later date, when the immaturity which then characterised the national sentiments of German publicists again and again induced them to advocate a commercial league with Switzerland or Holland, Prussia unerringly preserved the national character of the customs union. Thus there had come into existence two organisations within the Germanic Federation : a fictitious Germany centred in Frankfort, and a Germany of honest work centred in Berlin. The Prussian state, by its guidance of Germany's commercial policy, fulfilled part of the duties which properly devolved upon the Germanic Federation, just as Prussia alone, by her army, safeguarded the frontiers of the fatherland. Thus it came to pass that by straightforward industry Prussia grew by degrees to become the leading power of the fatherland ; and only because the European world did not think it worth while to acquire a serious knowledge of Prussia's military system and of Prussia's commercial policy, did Europe fail to note the quiet strengthening of the centre of the continent.

There is a remarkable kinship between the history of the economic unification of Germany and the history of her political unification. Both movements resemble a great dialectical process. Prussian hegemony did not prove victorious until repeated and futile attempts had indisputably proved the impracticability of any other form of unity. A rich heritage of monarchical traditions and of traditions that were federalistic in the best sense of the term was transmitted from the experiences of the customs union to the North German union and to the German empire. In the customs union Prussia became practised in the monarchical leadership of a many-headed and almost amorphous league which would not fit into any known category of constitutional law, this leadership being acquired rather by insight and goodwill and by natural preponderance of power than by any formal privilege. From the thirties onwards there existed two fundamentally diverse schools of German statesmanship. On the one hand were the politicians of the Bundestag, lamentable creatures, in whom the original sin of diplomacy, the interchange of business and chatter, had become second nature ; these men were political children, laboriously kept alive upon the condensed milk of the *Allgemeine Zeitung* of Augsburg and the *Frankfurter Ober-postamtszeitung*, men who knew how to make a solemn and serious use of the forms and the formulas of the vain federal

law.   On the other hand were the sober minded and practical
men   of   the   customs   union,   accustomed   to   the   cautious
consideration of grave interests, accustomed to make just and
benevolent   allowance   for   the   wishes   and   needs   of   their
neighbours.   At the high school of the customs conferences
and   in   the   manifold   deliberations   concerning   commercial
questions, Prussian statesmen became familiar with the methods
of modern German policy ;   acquired the art of guiding irritable
minor allies without arousing ill feeling and without the display
of force ;   and learned how to maintain the essence of monarchy
under federal forms.

The idea of the customs union was not the property of
any single man.   It originated simultaneously in many minds
under the pressure of German needs.   But the clothing of
the idea in flesh and blood was due to Prussia alone, was
due to Eichhorn, Motz, and Maassen ;   and last not least
was due to the king.   It is no mere respect for monarchical
institutions as such, but the obligation of historical justice,
which compels us to maintain that nothing but a firm confidence
in Frederick William's inviolable loyalty could have induced
the German princes to agree voluntarily to the restriction of
their sovereignty.   The unpretentious simplicity of his nature,
which during the wild Napoleonic days had often made this
Hohenzollern appear pusillanimous, enabled him in a more
tranquil epoch to sow the seed of a great future.

The Rise of the Hegelian Philosophy (IV, 568–77)

The beautiful sunset glow of philosophy continued to
illuminate this world of struggles and contrasts.   For one and a
half decades, from the close of the twenties to the opening of the
forties, the school of Hegel exercised in German life an influence
comparable only to that of the sophists in Athens.   Abundantly
was fulfilled the prophecy made years before by Stein when he
declared that as a necessary consequence of the lack of political
freedom the speculative sciences would acquire a usurped value.
But no less astonishing than Hegel's early prestige was the subsequent
ingratitude of the nation which, quaffing the fiery draughts of this
idealism, intoxicated at first, on the morrow of sobriety had conceived
and was long to retain a profound loathing for all speculation,

imagining that with the fall of the Hegelian system philosophy itself had been judged and annihilated. The once idolised master was despised, and even to-day of all our great philosophers he is least read and most grossly misunderstood.

Hegel had opened his career with a heroic confidence resembling that which had formerly animated the youthful Kant. The great Swabian felt secure in the possession of all the powers which constitute the speculative equipment of his branch of the German stock, a talent for profound investigation, an ardent imagination, and a many-sided sensitiveness to which nothing human seemed foreign. While still a young man, in 1802, he bluntly declared that the philosophy of reflexion voiced by Kant, Fichte, and Jacobi had risen only to the concept, and had never attained the realm of the ideal. He was emboldened to attempt the conquest of this highest realm, and as his system unfolded itself he did in truth speak what was long to remain the last word. Along the path in which Kant had been the pioneer, German philosophy could not aspire towards a loftier goal. The riddle of existence seemed solved, the unity of being and thinking proved, as soon as Hegel had represented the world as the unending dialectical process of the self-conceiving absolute spirit. In this system were comprised all spirit and all becoming. It was the most consistent monism ever formulated. The idea first traverses the series of necessary forms of thought, then expresses itself in nature, opposes itself to itself as another and objective life, to return finally, after this lapse from the infinite, freely into itself, into the realm of spirit. Thus everything that has been, is, and will be from eternity to eternity, is nothing but the divine reason as manifested in its self-development. Into the mighty framework of this system, Hegel, vaunted by his disciples as a second Aristotle, with colossal energy now fitted the acquirements of all the scientific experience of his day, so that everything in the world of nature and history was assigned its proper place in the unending developmental process of the absolute spirit.

At this epoch a new philosophical doctrine could still take possession of German minds with all the magic of religious revelation. The faithful were undisturbed by crass contrasts between the system and experience, for they knew that it would be impossible for philosophy to wait until that day which will never dawn when the structure of the empirical sciences should be completed. The Hegelian system excelled all others in its power to make its disciples happy in the consciousness of infallible certainty, for if the life of the world was a great process of thought there no longer remained anything unfathomable to the thinker. Consequently, as an inspired pupil of Hegel's declared, thought was thinking of thinking. The method and the substance of the system appeared identical. The law of tripartition which governed the philosophy in its dialectical method likewise controlled the development of the divine reason, for this in eternal recapitulation traversed the three stages of being-by-itself, being-in-relation-to-the-not-self, and being-by-and-for-itself. One who lost himself in this wonder-world felt uplifted as by an elemental force above the common human understanding ; he felt as if the creation of the universe out of nothing was being renewed in his own spirit, as if his thought, self-moved, was by a creative act producing out of itself an objective world and then returning into itself again.

Armed at all points and immeasurably superior in strength was this proud idealism in its conflict with the crude rationalism and utilitarianism of the enlightenment, but it turned no less decisively to attack the desultory fancies of romanticism. This philosophy, seeing spirit and nothing but spirit everywhere, appeared as if it were a last echo from that epoch of pure literature in which the energies of our nation had been almost completely devoted to intellectual pursuits ; yet it was at the same time strictly realist. Only in the real world would it recognise the revelation of God ; inexorably did it condemn those facile thinkers who imaginatively create for themselves that which neither does nor can exist, and those who deplore what is and cannot possibly be otherwise. Self-evident and almost tautological was the great proposition enunciated to overwhelm the doubter : the real is rational and the rational is real.

Nevertheless this grandiose system, however brilliant, was nothing more than an arbitrary invention. Just as all our other philosophers, with the solitary exception of Kant, had been distinguished rather by the boldness and profundity than by the acuteness or definiteness of their thought, so also was Hegel obscure, and especially obscure in the exposition of his fundamental concepts. The main principle upon which the entire system was founded was merely an unproved assumption ; for the high-sounding assertion that spirit expresses itself in nature, opposing itself to itself, really tells us nothing at all. The great enigma, the question how the real world proceeded from the ideal, was and remained a secret, for it is an ultimate secret of the creator. Schelling had already proved that to deduce nature from thought was a task utterly beyond the scope of the human intellect. But at this time no one listened to Schelling. As soon, however, as the fundamental fallacy of Hegel's system was recognised, the imposing edifice collapsed. The bold attempt to demonstrate the unity of being and thinking had miscarried, and if philosophy were to regain solid ground it must return to Kant and to the modest enquiry how the experience of nature is at all possible.

The system proclaimed itself invulnerable, its propositions were to furnish one another adequate mutual support. But the configuration of the world as represented by Hegel could not really be deduced with logical necessity from the philosopher's first principles ; it was a fanciful and arbitrary product of the subjective imagination. The result was that in the carrying out of the system marked inequalities were displayed. Parts were utterly ineffective, while other parts contained the germ of a fruitful outlook upon the universe, one destined to exercise great influence in the future. Hegel's philosophy of nature was an utter failure, for the manifest reality of nature imposed, almost as if in mockery, an insuperable obstacle to any attempt to construct nature out of the idea—besides, in this field the philosopher had no knowledge of his subject. The young masters of exact research who in Berlin were flocking round Alexander Humboldt had good reason for making fun of these dreams, for the real knowledge of nature which Humboldt had just brought home from his Siberian journey was alone sufficient to outweigh the entirety of Hegel's constructions in the realm of the philosophy of nature.

No less unfortunate was Hegel in his philosophy of religion, for in this domain Schleiermacher's religious temperament, working in a congenial medium, enabled him to attain infinitely better results. Hegel started with the assumption, flatly contradicted by experience, that philosophy and religion have the same content, philosophy representing the absolute in the form of thought, and religion representing it in the form of perception. Thus to him religious belief was not a primitive mental energy by which the entire man, his thought and his will, are determined, but an immature form of knowledge. The irrefutable consequence of this, however adroit the attempt to conceal it by dialectic arts, is the necessity of erastianism, for a church which moves only in the realm of imagination must be unconditionally subordinated to the thinking state. If Altenstein, Hegel's docile disciple, continually endeavoured to regulate the inner life of the churches, his master's teaching unquestionably bore part of the responsibility for this disastrous ecclesiastical policy. The idea of redemption, the central feature of Schleiermacher's religious teaching, passed in Hegel's system quite into the background. He was more concerned with the scientific proof of dogmas, not excepting the most difficult of these, the dogmas which will always be too hard for human reason, not excepting the dogma of the trinity ; and the artifices he employed to this end were all the more barren because the pantheistic basis of the system was in manifest contradiction with Christian dogma.

More striking by contrast with these failures was the success attained by Hegel's genius in the sphere of aesthetics. His utterances concerning the unity of idea and form in works of art were great, profound, novel, and so vital that to this day all the aesthetic judgments of the Germans repose consciously on Hegel. His criticism of contemporary poets had the assured justice of a great spirit. Not merely did he understand Goethe ; but he appreciated also the pathos of Schiller, which was less accordant with his own nature ; while, undisturbed by the current opinion of his day, he would not admit that Jean Paul's established reputation was merited.

Yet more fruitful was his philosophy of law. Among all our philosophers, Hegel had the keenest intelligence in political matters. Before him, indeed, Kant had declared that the perfectionment of the bourgeois order was the ultimate aim of civilisation, and Fichte had towards the close of his life extolled the state as the educator of the human race ; while Schelling's writings contained many brilliant expressions concerning the harmony of necessity and freedom in the state considered as a work of art. But none of these men had advanced further than the outer court of politics, and Hegel was the first to enter the very sanctuary. He regarded the state as the actualisation of the moral ideal, as the realisation of the ethical will, and at one blow he shattered the doctrine of natural rights, and overthrew that political romanticism which was fain to derive the state from a primitive contract entered into by individual human beings or else to regard it as a work of divine ordinance.

Thus was resurrected the somewhat hyperbolical conception held by classical antiquity, and an omnipotence accorded to the state which it had never possessed since the Christian world had recognised the right of the individual conscience.   But to this people of ours, which had so long sought its ideal in an anarchic freedom, the idolisation of the state could do little harm.   Only through the overvaluation of the state could the Germans attain to a vigorous sense of the state.   Before all others, Hegel furnished a theoretical justification for the abundant civilising activity which the Prussian state had long been accustomed to display in practice ; he scientifically accounted for the energy of the German idea of the state ; he routed the arid legalist doctrine of the state ; and he provided the historian with an implement wherewith to effect, without philistine pettiness, an ethico-political valuation of the heroes of history. Recent historians and the pupils of Savigny had, indeed, long been aware that the state is a primal and necessary institution, through which alone national morality can attain perfection ; but Hegel was the first to provide the philosophical foundation for this great doctrine, and to make it intelligible to the cultured classes in general.   The philosopher's acute political insight was displayed even in the details of his doctrine of the state.   Before any other German writer he recognised, although by way of suggestion merely, that between the individual and the state there lies a peculiar world of economic interests and relationships of dependence, and to this world he gave the name of bourgeois society. How great a service was it, too, that a Swabian, a professor, who had practically stood aloof from the national movement of the wars of liberation, should expressly indicate to the Germans what they possessed in Prussia, should show them why this state was not simply the most powerful but also the noblest and most rational of the German states, and that its strict order stood on a morally higher level than the celebrated German freedom of old days which fought for its own hand alone. Despite much exaggeration, all his writings on the subject breathed a serious understanding of the state which had been unknown to earlier German philosophers.

This understanding of the nature of the state was the necessary outcome of Hegel's well-developed historical sense.   A thinker to whom all the life of the world was a process of becoming, must necessarily be affected even more powerfully than Schelling by the impulse towards historical comprehension which dominated the

entire epoch.   He saw that mortals can grasp the divine reason only
when it is broken up into a thousand rays, and that the idea of
humanity finds completion in nothing short of the totality of
history.   For this reason he did not pass his time in pondering, as
had so many philosophers before him, over the obscure riddle of the
genesis and the purport of history.   He would neither look back
longingly towards the lost innocence of a golden age, nor attempt to
console the world with thoughts of a happier future, but, standing
firmly upon the soil of historic reality, he found here, in the endless
multiformity of civilisation, the unfolding of the divine thought.
Hegel's philosophy of history was his greatest scientific achievement,
and was hardly less fruitful than had been Kant's doctrine of duty.
Like all fertile ideas, it was not absolutely new, for the way had been
prepared for its formulation by Kant and Herder.   From Kant's
essay concerning the beginnings of the human race, Hegel derived
the idea of the progress of mankind, but he made it more profound
and vital in that he did not conceive of progress as represented by
simple ascent in a straight line, but, like Herder, discovered in every
nation its own peculiar emanation of the divine thought, and conceded to every epoch its own modicum of morality.   In each age of
the world he recognised that there had existed one leading nation,
which had held the torch of life for a time, and had then yielded it
into the hands of another.   In this conception, the historic human
being appeared at once immeasurably great, as bearer of the idea,
and infinitesimally small, in contrast with the creative laws of the
divine reason.

It is true that the arbitrariness of the philosopher's constructions
is repeatedly manifested in this field also.   Although he spoke of the
rationality of the real, he had but little respect for facts, and would
forcibly amend the historical record, doing this in many cases merely
for the sake of the holy triad.   A philosophy of history directed only
towards the future was of necessity too remote from the human
struggle ; in such a philosophy the victor was always right ; it had
no appreciation for the heroism of the vanquished, for the sacred
sense of duty which impelled a Hannibal or a Demosthenes to
attempt the rescue of a declining nationality ; it had no comprehension of the lofty tragedy of historical struggles.   Enmeshed in
contented optimism, it could find no answer for the heart-searching
problem, why, despite the unending progress of the race, the

individual human being remains as weakly and sinful as ever. Nevertheless, amid a plenitude of errors, there was left an imperishable gain. Hegel was a pioneer in grasping with admirable scientific penetration the idea of historical evolution, of the progress from lower forms of civilisation to higher forms, the germs of the latter being contained within the former ; and he showed at the same time how this new thought was to be manipulated, giving in masterly outline a sketch of the hidden connection between the epoch of unconscious creation and the epoch of conscious reflection.

For this reason his ideas exercised a direct or indirect influence even upon historians who detested the philosopher's interpretation of history. What was imperishable in Hegel's philosophy of history lived on in the works of Ranke ; Droysen, too, and many others among the younger historians, acquired a wider horizon in the school of Hegel. The dominion of the Hegelians in the educational institutions of Prussia and Würtemberg lasted for years, favouring many-sided culture and promoting discipline of thought. Even those who would not accept the formulas of the system, learned nevertheless from its teachings that amorphous knowledge is not knowledge at all.

No less conspicuous, however, were the dangerous consequences of the new doctrine, as displayed in the unbounded sophistical arrogance with which it infected its adherents. The orthodox Hegelian was competent to deal with everything that had happened, everything that had been thought or done, by showing it to be a settled detail, a surpassed standpoint, which had already been treated in some paragraph of the all-embracing system. For him there was but one question remaining insoluble, and this was the one which a pert desciple did actually moot, namely : What remains for the world-spirit to do now it has arrived at perfection in the philosophy of the absolute ? The philosophers were encouraged to such excesses by the use of a scholastic jargon intelligible only to initiates. The master, when he let his pen run free in annotations and excursuses, displayed the linguistic powers natural to genius, restoring to modern usage a number of excellent words and phrases that had become obsolete, for instance, the expressive " von Haus aus." At times, however, he made use of monstrous artifices of speech, darkening that which was clear and confusing that which was simple, and his disciples did not hesitate in this respect to outdo the follies of the master. Since the foundations of the system were established in the air, with the aid of the universally effective dialectical method its adherents arrived at conclusions which pointed to all quarters of the compass at once, and this philosophy which prided itself on its objectivity ended by letting loose an unending succession of confused and fluctuating subjective opinions.

The proposition " the rational is real " contains a profound truth, but not the whole truth   It does not tell us that in this real and rational world there exist also the irrational and the speciously rational ; still less does it tell us that the vocation of the creative spirit is to discern the completed work in that which is in process of becoming, and in the germs of new life to recognise in advance the reality of the future. Baldly stated, therefore, the proposition may readily be misinterpreted to support an unthinking quietism. Hegel, it is true, nowise merited the reproach of servile sentiments which the envious were not slow to make ; in his writings on political science he went far beyond the actualities of Prussian conditions, demanding parliamentary government and trial by jury, conceding to the monarch no more than the right to put dots on the i's.   But by temperament he was conservative.   In the later years of his life he adhered closely to the side of the government, and did not hesitate to avail himself of the favour of Altenstein and Johannes Schulze for the discomfiture of his scientific opponents ; and he would have been glad to see his *Berliner Jahrbücher* transformed into a state undertaking like the *Journal des savants*.   When he termed the real " rational," it was certainly with no intention to advocate an arrest of progress, but he desired the establishment of a definite system of statecraft which should base its reforms upon contemporary and extant realities.

There had already appeared, however, a number of intemperate and ultra-conservative disciples, led by Göschel the jurist, and these declared in the name of Hegel that everything was rational which then actually existed in state and church.   Simultaneously it became evident that the same ambiguous saying could be twisted also to the uses of the most destructive radicalism.   If nothing but the rational was real, a man of crude intelligence might well consider himself justified in remodelling the world in accordance with his own reason, unceremoniously replacing the speciously real by the truth of philosophy.   This arrogant conclusion, unquestionably the very opposite of what Hegel intended, was in fact drawn at this early date by isolated hotspurs, young fellows who believed that they understood the master better than he understood himself.

The first inception of young Hegelian radicalism was manifest when Eduard Gans entered the lists against the historical school of law. Gans was a versatile Jew, acute rather than brilliant, and an adept in that art of reproducing others' ideas which secures such facile successes in the professorial chair. Gans detected the weaknesses of Savigny's disciples, who often lost themselves amid a maze of unmeaning details, and he revived, far more adroitly than Rotteck, the old and senseless struggle on behalf of the law of reason against the historical law—although the essential ideas of Hegel's philosophy of history were in truth far more closely akin to those of the historical school of law. The unedifying dispute strongly recalled the unfortunate misunderstanding between Kant and Herder, but it had one good result in that it led Gans to set seriously to work and to produce in his *Erbrecht* a study in the comparative history of law which furnished a happy complement to Savigny's doctrine. But the enthusiasts of the Hegelian school had now discovered that which is indispensable to every growing party, a common enemy. War against historical doctrinaires became the watchword. Under this device there assembled a troop of radicals who, going far beyond the liberal views of Gans, contested everything which was sacred to the master, above all his prussophil tenets and his lofty sense of order, while continuing to declare that they were fighting in his name. The Hegelian school began to split into a right and a left.

Hegel's great works enshrined a tragical contradiction. He aroused in German science a definite sense of the state, but through the sophistical arts of his dialectical method he likewise fostered that undisciplined spirit of presumption which was beginning to derange and undermine the established order of state and church.

HARBINGERS OF A NEW AGE

Radicalism and the Jews (IV, 531–32, 553–68)

THE treaty between the two customs unions of the south and the north opened for the Germans the prospect of a national market such as had not existed for centuries, and therefore paved the way for an unprecedented development of economic forces. Years, however, were still to elapse before preliminary understanding was to be succeeded by permanent union, and there was to be yet another interval before, under the protection of the new customs barriers, a great manufacturing industry was to rise and flourish. Not until 1840, with the growth of factories and stock exchanges, of railways and newspapers, did there begin to appear in German society also the class struggles, the restless hurry, and the adventurous self-assertiveness of modern economic life. Up to this time most people had persisted in the parochial customs of the first years of peace. They had remained upon paternal acres or quietly engaged in traditional handicrafts, satisfied with the modest joys of their simple homes. But towards the end of the twenties there were already numerous indications that a great transformation in national customs was in course of preparation. Just as had happened after the golden era of poesy in the middle ages, so now were the days of Jena and Weimar to be succeeded by a prosaic epoch, an epoch in which energy was for the most part to be directed outwards, into political, ecclesiastical, and economic struggles.

Our literature has long been the faithful mirror of all the secrets of the German heart, and thus it was that the harbingers of this revolution were earlier perceptible in literature than in practical life. Poetry no longer maintained its dominance in the realm of the spirit. Just as in former days the decline in Italian architecture had disclosed itself in the extensive and yet sterile building activities of the eighteenth century, so now the vast numbers of light and trivial novels and poetical pocket-companions which flooded the book market showed that our imaginative literature was growing rank and could yield but little good fruit. An evil sign of the times was the increasing desire of women to write. As is the case with all great artistic epochs, the blossoming of German poesy would not have been possible without the invigorating participation of women. But as long as the ambition of the leading men of the nation led them to compete for the poet's crown, the natural rule continued to hold good that artistic creation, like all creation, is the work of men. There were few authoresses among the splendid women who, in a sympathetic and receptive spirit, beautified the lives of our classic and earlier romantic poets. But now, when verse-writing had become an elegant method of killing time, and when every impressionable amateur could readily acquire the artifices of literature, there occurred an alarming increase in the number of bluestockings, to use the English word. Caroline Pichler,

Johanna Schopenhauer, Helmine von Chezy, and Caroline von Fouqué, took up the pen in place of the needle, and many of the fashionable pocket-companions were written solely for women and chiefly by women. Goethe noted with concern this new social disease. He did not wish to see the sacred limits of nature infringed, and the profundities of art replaced by futile elegancies, and he vented his opinion regarding this sterile feminine verse-writing, now with good-natured mockery and now with such divine roughness as was permissible to none but the singer of woman's love.

Meanwhile radical ideas, which had once more permeated the western world since the revolutions in southern Europe, began to make their influence felt in German literature. After the disappointment of so many hopes it was impossible that the boastful self-complacency of the Teutonist movement should persist ; reaction was inevitable ; and in Germany, since our people take life seriously, such reversals are apt to be sudden and violent, to be effected with elemental energy. Nevertheless, it was a sign of political immaturity and of perverse conditions that the change of mood should occur so abruptly on this occasion. The new radicalism, which was now becoming predominant among our youth and among the middle classes without affecting the highest strata of our culture, was ungerman to the core. It regarded with contempt all that the heroes of Leipzig and Belle Alliance had held sacred, our art and science, our Christian faith, and even the deeds of the War of Liberation ; while it sought its ideals in the very land which to those of the previous generation had been an object of detestation. To both the neighbour peoples it was disastrous, a necessary outcome of the many unsolved problems of power which still remained open for debate between them, that they could never attain to a peaceful relationship of mutual respect. German judgments of the French oscillated between hatred and over-esteem. In France, the members of a new generation were growing to maturity, the sanguinary horrors of the Revolution had been forgotten, talk of the glories of the storming of the Bastille was again widely current ; and a crowd of Germans, whose numbers increased year by year, enthusiastically joined in the French chorus of self-praise. From the middle of the twenties onwards, French political ideas made their way irresistibly across the Rhine.

Never before in history had the victor bent his neck thus willingly beneath the yoke of the vanquished. In the age of

Louis XIV, when France dominated our culture, for Germany, depopulated and mutilated, little else was possible but passive acceptance of the Gallic conqueror. But now it was only in the exact sciences that the French occupied the premier position ; in all other fields of literature and art they were equalled or excelled by the Germans. While the German might well envy his neighbour for the earlier acquirement of national unity, Prussia at least, in her national crown, her compulsory military service, her educational system, her local self-government, and her upright officialdom, possessed all those foundations of an ordered and free political life which were lacking to the French state. But by the radical youth of Germany, the party struggles so brilliantly conducted by the parliamentary orators and journalists of Paris were not regarded as a proof of hopeless internal restlessness, but as a sign of highly developed liberty ; for among wide circles of the half-cultured there still prevailed, as Niebuhr noted with profound regret, a view dating from the early days of the Revolution, a sentiment of hostility to the state, the opinion of those who held " that freedom finds expression in conflict alone—in the struggle of the parliamentary deputies with the government, and in the struggle of the individual with the sovereign." In reality the Germans had little to learn from the unnatural cross between English parliamentary practice and Napoleonic administrative despotism which was extolled by the French as constitutional monarchy. That which now made its way over from France as the last word in political wisdom, should have been recognised as nothing but an anachronism, a new concretion of that formalist doctrine of the state according to which the essence of freedom is to be found in a constitution alone— a doctrine whose scientific foundations had long ere this been overthrown by Niebuhr and Savigny. Admiration for French methods could not now fail to confuse and to lead astray. Thereby our young men were estranged from the fatherland ; they were robbed of respect for the heroes of the nation ; they were deprived of an understanding of the actual beginnings of a sound national political system ; while their mood, already sufficiently unwholesome, was in addition artificially corrupted by the revolutionary catchwords and the unmeasured violence of faction which they adopted from their French neighbours. The young Germans who grew to manhood under the spell of these French ideas hardly realised that Gneisenau was still living among us in the full vigour of his prime, and Motz was not even a name to them, whilst they all knew and admired General Foy, who in the Paris chamber had demanded that France should once again adopt the tricolour, the banner of the Marseillais.

The new radicalism found a powerful ally in the youthful energy of literary Judaism. Modern Jewry had long ceased to possess sufficient intellectual energy to generate a sound culture of its own, as had been possible centuries before to the Jews who lived amid the oriental civilisation of the Moorish empire in Spain. The old civilisations of western Europe possessed so definitely national a stamp that in politics and literature the Jews could not venture to display themselves as an independent force. Thus the first German Jew to attain a notable position in our literature, Moses Mendelssohn, followed the current of German national life, helping to the best of his ability in the intellectual tasks of the German philosophy of enlightenment. When he defended the faith of his fathers against Lavater, as he was well entitled to do, it was by no means his intention to permeate the German world with Jewish ideas, and he was far more concerned to diffuse German culture among his co-religionists. Since then, the seed he had sown had ripened, a number of the Jews had become more or less Germanised, and several Jewish writers were already regular contributors to the newspaper press ; but in these circles there soon began to prevail a dangerous spirit of aloofness and arrogance. In Germany the Jewish population was far more numerous than in other countries of western Europe, and since the Polish stock of Jewry to which our German Jews belong had always been less ready to adapt itself to western civilisation than had the Spanish Jews (from which stem the majority of Jews then resident in England and France had sprung), it resulted that in Germany, and in Germany alone, a peculiar semi-Jewish literature came into existence, concealing under accidental forms its orientalist outlook and its hereditary hatred of Christianity. A well-established national pride which would have nipped all such attempts in the bud was non-existent. The patient soil of Germany had served as an arena for all the nations of Europe, and there was no reason why the Jews should not try fortune in their turn.

The finer spirits among the German Jews had long recognised that members of their race could not claim civic equality unless they were prepared to abandon a separatist position and to participate unreservedly in German life. A few decades after Moses Mendelssohn

had issued his appeal, talented men of Jewish descent, baptised
and unbaptised, men who felt themselves to be Germans and whose
work displayed thoroughly German lineaments, had acquired
distinguished positions in art and science : in music, Felix
Mendelssohn-Bartholdy ; in painting, Veit ; and in theology, the
simple-minded and pious Neander. But in contrast with these, the
crude Jewish geniuses whose pens found a market in the columns of
the daily press boldly insisted on the display of Jewish peculiarities,
while simultaneously demanding respect as spokesmen of German
public opinion. These Jews without a country, vaunting themselves as a nation within the nation, exercised upon the still inchoate
national self-esteem of the Germans an influence no less disturbing
and disintegrating than similar Jews had exercised of old upon the
declining nations of the Roman empire.

   In so far as the Jewish cosmopolitan was competent to understand western nations, he was chiefly attracted towards the French,
not merely from reasonable gratitude, but also from a sense of inner
kinship. To a nation which for centuries had ceased to possess a
political history, nothing seemed so alien as the historic sense. To
the Jews, German veneration for the past appeared ludicrous ;
but modern France had broken with her history, here they felt
more at home, in this raw new state, created, as it were, by pure
reason. Thus it came to pass that the Jewish litterateurs encouraged
German radicalism in its uncritical preference for France. Moreover, the cries of haro with which, in accordance with their national
custom, the Jewish publicists loved to make the welkin ring, did not
serve to ennoble our political manners, more especially since the
Germans are themselves prone to become tasteless in polemic.
When Jewish hatred of Christianity came to fan the flames of
controversy, the well-grounded political discontent of the day
found degenerate expression in boundless exaggeration.

   Above all corrupting in its influence upon German radicalism
was the strange Jewish perversity of self-mockery. This people
without a state, widely scattered throughout the world, adopting
the tongues and the customs of other nations while still clinging
to its own isolation, lived in perpetual contradiction, which
might appear either tragical or comical according to the observer's
standpoint. To the nimble Jewish wit, the ludicrous contrast
between oriental nature and occidental form was necessarily
apparent. The Jews of Europe had long been accustomed to make

mock of themselves with utter ruthlessness, and the severest things
ever said about Jews proceeded from Jewish lips. The racial pride
of the chosen people vis-à-vis the Gentiles was, indeed, so deeply
rooted that the Jew remained undisturbed by the bitterest
expressions of self-mockery. But now this evil Jewish custom made
its way into German literature, where the soil was already prepared
by the playful irony of the romanticists and the political bitterness
of the liberals. It came to be regarded as a mark of genius to speak
dispassionately, with shameless disrespect, of the fatherland, as if
the speaker had neither part nor lot therein, as if the mockery
of Germany need not inevitably cut every individual German
to the heart. But the German jokes with difficulty. Least of all
could he understand this orientalist wit, and he consequently took
at its face value many a vituperative onslaught which was not really
meant in bad part. Our radical youth soon began to look upon
impudent abuse of the fatherland as the true index of intellectual
ability, simply because the German state, hemmed in by a thousand
difficulties, could not instantaneously grant all the wishes of its
impatient children. They continued to rail against the cringing
humility and the sheeplike patience of the Germans until they
believed in their own grotesque caricature of Germany, honestly
imagining that the most passionate nation in Europe, the nation of
the *furia tedesca*, was phlegmatic.

During the years when everything German was being decried,
the national caricature of the German Michael acquired a new and
repulsive configuration. The German Michael of old days, as
befitted his warrior name, had been a great hulking fellow, clumsy
and uncouth, but valiant, downright, and cheerful, like John Bull
or Robert Macaire, not unworthy of a great nation, a nation that
believed in itself and could therefore venture to laugh at itself from
time to time. But now, under the old name, he was portrayed and
described as a cowardly and sluggish dolt who, maltreated by everyone
he met, pulled down his nightcap over his ears. This caricature had
come into vogue during the romanticist campaign against the
philistines, making its first appearance on the title page of the
Heidelberger Einsiedlerzeitung, but Achim von Arnim had solemnly
declared that this good-for-nothing was intended to typify the well-
to-do reading public, "not my people, whom I honour, and about
whom I shall never lightly jest." The new generation of radicals
knew nothing of such discretions, and was not ashamed to make a

mock of the nation whose victorious sword had just overthrown the Napoleonic world empire, depicting it in the repulsive lineaments of a cowardly lazybones.

The stimulating and destructive efficiency of radical Jewry was all the more dangerous because the Germans were subject to a long-standing illusion as to the nature of this new literary force. They ingenuously accepted as German enlightenment and German freedom of thought that which was in reality Jewish hatred of Christianity and Jewish cosmopolitanism. It was only Wolfgang Menzel and a few other publicists whose eyes were open to the danger, but since they all belonged to the high church school their warnings were disregarded. Not until much later did the nation recognise that from the end of the twenties a foreign drop had been mingled with its blood. The Germans had justly prided themselves on their freedom from irreverence, for the liberal spirits among them had spoken boldly, but had always approached sacred things with respect. This could not be said henceforward, for in Germany, too, were to appear writings characterised by all the impudence of Voltaire, though lacking the Frenchman's genius.

The intellectual father of this hybrid Judaico-German literature was Ludwig Börne of Frankfort, a man essentially upright, gentle and warm-hearted, but destined never to rise above a tasteless amalgam of German sentimentalism and Jewish facetiousness, vacillating hopelessly between patriotism and cosmopolitanism, equally incompetent to discover a definite creed and to attain to a genuine national feeling, and ultimately giving himself up to the uncouthness of an arid and stormy radicalism. In a simpler and more vigorous epoch, a character so inharmonious would merely have aroused the interest of the mental pathologist, but amid the confusion and bitterness of German party struggles he was able for a time to play the part of tribune of the people. The great figures of our classical literature were too lofty for his understanding. He gave his admiration to Jean Paul, and in youth was so devoted to lachrymose self-portraiture that when he was in love with pretty Henriette Herz he was careful to describe in his diary all the hours and minutes of his " spiritual hypochondria " and the sublime sentiments by which this state was characterised. Subsequently pulling himself together, as dramatic critic he acquired a reputation which was not altogether undeserved, though unduly exaggerated by the zealous trumpetings of his co-religionists. Lacking a cultured sense of beauty, he was nevertheless endowed with the healthy naturalism of the human understanding. Not merely did he aptly satirise the absurdities of the fate-tragedy and other gross aberrations of taste, but had in addition an eye for unrecognised talent, as in the cases of Kleist and Immermann.

He now began to write on politics and social questions in the *Wage*, the *Zeitschwingen*, and other newspapers, and these activities soon monopolised his energies, for it was as a political writer that he displayed all the arts of his scorn. But scorn is justified only when it arises from the noble wrath of genius, and this man lacked all the qualities requisite to the publicist—a feeling for realities, a sense of proportion, foresight, and even a common knowledge of affairs. Industry, by which the Jews are usually characterised, he considered superfluous in politics. His political articles are frothy and ephemeral journalism, for not one of them bears witness to a serious study of the matter with which it deals. Börne was the first to establish the dominion of " the sovereign feuilleton " which worked such unspeakable harm to the unripe political culture of the Germans, and emboldened crude smatterers, helping themselves out with a few jests, puns, figures of speech, and cries of indignation, to discuss all the serious problems of statecraft.

Wherever wit could carry him, Börne was in his element. He satirised the Gothamites of the German petty towns amusingly enough, though raising a clamour thereanent which hardly conformed to the triviality of the topic. Wit is a child of the hour which ages prematurely, and to which posterity can rarely do full justice. Börne, however, had the gift of being genuinely amusing about serene highnesses, aulic and commercial councillors, privy councillors' wards, the Taxis postal service, and the epicures at the ordinary ; these witty sallies are the immortal elements of his writings, in which there is nothing else to attract even passing attention to-day. Directly he endeavoured to rise above such trivialities into the sphere of politics, he displayed the poverty of a dull understanding, whose only resource when faced by complicated political problems is a barren statement of alternatives. " Is the state our end, or the individual within the state ? " seemed to him the great problem of the future, for he could not recognise the futility of such a question, although Kant had demonstrated its absurdity. Thus without ever indicating a definite and comprehensible goal, he abandoned himself to empty praises of anarchy, the mother of freedom, and to equally vain tirades about the hopeless miseries of Germany, saying, "We are dumb driven cattle, handed down from the past to the present, which the present will bequeath unchanged to the future."

He had but one clear political aim, the emancipation of the Jews. His conversion to Christianity was not dictated by religious conviction, nor yet by the desire to become a thorough German, being merely the outcome of a wish to do away with obstacles to easy social progress. But shame was unknown to him, and though a renegade he had no sense of impropriety in playing the advocate on behalf of the coreligionists he had abandoned. After his conversion he still retained the racial pride of the chosen people, and scarce troubled to conceal that he regarded the Jews as the salt of the German earth—and yet, when the fancy took him, he would roughly attack Jews and Germans in one breath, and would satirise German Jews as eight-footed hares. " I well know how to prize," he wrote on one occasion, " the unmerited good fortune through which I was born both German and Jew, so that I am able to aspire to all the virtues of the Germans without sharing any of their faults ! " But he could not endure that Christians should even speak of " Jews," and raised clamorous complaints of intolerance when the newspapers reported as a simple statement of fact that Levi, a Jewish merchant, had gone bankrupt. Among the grievances he was never weary of airing, there were many of which he could justly complain, but there were many others that were simply the outcome of the sensibilities of a morbidly inflated self-esteem. On the occasion of the centenary of a great conflagration, the town of Frankfort proposed a commemorative festival, and the council issued the following decree : " At the close of the festival, on Sunday 27th, a solemn religious service will be held in all Christian churches, and it is likewise ordered that prayers be said in the Jewish synagogues." Both in form and content this proclamation was perfectly innocent, but since the wording in the case of the Jews differed slightly from that used about the Christians, Börne wrote a furious article, and despairingly exclaimed: "Oh, unhappy fatherland in which these things can happen ! " Notwithstanding such exaggerations, the persistent iteration of complaints made an impression, and the Jews, so recently regarded with hatred, were now by young men of radical views esteemed as noble fighters for freedom.

In the year 1822 Börne journeyed to Paris, and as soon as he reached Strasburg delightedly exclaimed, " Now I can breathe freely ! " How remote were the days when Rückert had prophesied to the Germans that here in the ancient imperial city a German princely castle must and should one day arise. Our new champion of German freedom wrote from Paris : " I was no longer shivering among fishes, I was no longer in Germany ! " He was not utterly devoid of appreciation for the greatness of his fatherland, and in his better hours he unquestionably felt the futility of " coquettish glory," recognised the superiority of the German tongue, and even valued German freedom of thought. But after such bursts of German sentiment he invariably relapsed into Judaico-French phrases, bombastic to a degree which none but Victor Hugo has ever excelled, saying, for instance, " Paris is the telegraph of the past, the microscope of the present, and the telescope of the future ! " He was never weary of holding up before the " fragmentary men " of Germany the brilliant example of the " complete men " of France. Without noticing the ludicrous contradiction, he went on to commend to us, in especial, the rigid one-sidedness of French party sentiment. " The Frenchman," he said, " praises and favours everyone belonging to his own side, and censures and injures everyone attached to the opposite party ; this is why the French can do anything, while we can do nothing." Looking over Paris from the Vendôme column, he declared : " This view would do a German good if the reed could grow larger and stronger because the storm has overthrown the oak." Thus within seven years of the second entry of the German army into Paris he had forgotten that we were the storm which overthrew the oak. French vanity had long ere this begun to cherish the illusion that the power of the *grande nation* had been broken solely by the mysterious caprice of destiny, without any cooperation on the part of the Germans ; now the victors were beginning credulously to repeat the fables of the vanquished.

Börne's books served to direct the glances of our German youth towards Paris once again. Before, the splendours of court life had allured to the Seine ; now, the attraction was the parliamentary struggle. It speedily became the rule that every young radical author must prove the soundness of his political faith by a pilgrimage to the Mecca of liberty. Börne was followed by Eduard Gans, a man of much keener political insight, and able to perceive the defects of French political life. Yet he also was bewitched by the theatrical tumult of party struggles. When, in a journalistic prosecution, the loud applause of the liberal-minded public thundered through the court, he imagined himself to be listening to " France's heart-beat " ; and in comparison with the politically awakened young men of Paris, those of Germany seemed to him superficial triflers. Thus matters went on, German men of letters crossing the Rhine in unending succession, their spirits rising directly they.reached Kehl bridge. All of them set out with the fixed determination to admire everything French. Since they learned nothing of France but Paris, and while in Paris associated only with a small circle of radical journalists, they furnished utterly false reports to the German papers. The Prussian officers quartered in France during the war had not failed to observe that most of the inhabitants of the country were thrifty, hard-working, rather timid people, and that the military spirit was incomparably weaker than in Prussia. These sound opinions were now abandoned by the Germans, for Börne and his disciples unceasingly declared that the chivalrous French nation concerned itself little about base economic cares, and was glowing with ardour to win liberty for itself in order to share the acquirement with other peoples. The cult of the so-called ideas of '89, which in Germany during the actual years of the Revolution had been restricted to a group of men of learning, was first diffused throughout the broad masses of our middle classes by this German-French journalistic campaign. It was the worst conceivable of political schools for a nation already prone to doctrinaire excesses.

After his return from Paris, Börne was in a state of feverish excitement, longing for the revolution. He himself did not know how the revolution was to be brought about or what its coming was to effect. Since the Germans remained calm, be abused them as coarsely as had Saul Ascher. In the years following the War of Liberation, the nation had exercised its domestic rights, and had shown Ascher's Jewish impudence the door. But now had come a change of sentiment. Advanced radicals looked at one another with meaning smiles when Börne, in ever-new invective, reiterated Ascher's idea, saying: "The Germans are a nation of servants, and at the word ' fetch ' would wag their tails and bring lost crowns back to their masters." They thought it witty when he recommended the burning of the Göttingen library, and announced his intention to abuse the Germans until he had spurred them on to an awakening of national pride. They greeted him with applause when, with a spitefulness which nowise fell short of the zeal exhibited by the persecutors of the demagogues, he examined the political sentiments of the more notable among his contemporaries, bluntly accusing of servility all who held moderate views, and aspersing with his mean suspicions the leading spirits of the nation, men too great for his understanding. His nickname for Goethe was " the rhyming knave," and for Hegel " the prosy knave." Who could take it amiss of the younger generation that it should use the living man's right in the case of the correspondence between Schiller and Goethe, and should declare, even if crudely and unjustly, that this world of beauty was out-of-date. But Börne did more. He declaimed against the anti-popular sentiments of Goethe and even of Schiller, regarding the latter as a yet more pernicious aristocrat. He dragged the poets' friendship in the mud, sullying their greatness, although in these very letters it spoke so convincingly to all German hearts. " It is tragical," he exclaimed, " that our two greatest geniuses should be so null when we see them at home, so petty that, were it possible, they would be even less than null ! " Summarising his judgment of Goethe, he said that for sixty years, favoured by unexampled good fortune, this man had imitated the handwriting of genius and never been found out. He extolled Voltaire, in order to emphasise a contrast with the offensive repose of Goethe's style. " How different is Voltaire ! His vanity takes us captive. We are delighted that so great a man should tremble before our criticism, should fawn upon us, should seek to win our approval ! "

The hubbub was so senseless that it was hardly possible to say how much of it was seriously meant, and yet herein lay the danger. Börne, though he reviled Germany's greatness, remained a patriot after his own fashion. But our German youths who lent an unnatural ear to this Jewish self-mockery lost all veneration for the fatherland, and thus Börne's influence, though it was in a sense inevitable in the circumstances, was disastrous to the coming genera-tion. Dipping youth in gall, he was unable to offer youth a single new idea. Moreover, he sinned deeply against our language. At the opening of the century Germans for the most part wrote well, though at times somewhat cumbrously (for many of them carried the lengthy periods of the classical tongues from school into every-day life). But Börne formed himself upon Jean Paul's over-elaborate style, and subsequently on French models; not his that refined understanding for the genius of language which is akin to the historic sense. His abstract, journalistic, and cultured writing was brilliant, piquant, elegant, anything you like—except German. It could wrangle, but could not express a noble wrath ; could inflict painful pinpricks, but could not overwhelm ; played with fanciful images, and yet never acquired expressive warmth ; lacked the soul, the energy of nature. " History numbers great men ; they are the index to the book of the past ; such are Goethe and Schiller : and history numbers other great men ; they are the table of contents to the book of the future ; such are Voltaire and Lessing." In sentences of this character everything was ungerman, thoughts, structure, and words ; but they shone and dazzled. Soon they found busy imitators. Journalists vied one with another in the use of transcendental images, dislocated words, over-refined allusions ; they fell in love with their own unnaturalness ; they took as cordial a delight in their own artifices as had of yore Lohenstein and Hoffmannswaldau. Even in Goethe's lifetime the German tongue began to run wild, and only men of science and a few poetic souls were able to withstand the temptations of hyperculture.

In German poesy a loud echo was promptly awakened by the Greek lyrics of the great radical poet of the age ; but Lord Byron's weltschmerz, the defiant self-assertion of the revolutionary ego, rebelling now menacingly, now despairingly, against the order of the world, while it secured in the twenties many admirers among the Germans, found but few imitators. Romanticist irony still sufficed discontented spirits as a medium for expression, and doubtless to many young poets the Byronic weltschmerz seemed quite inimitable. The individual appears so small when contrasted with the great moral forces constituting the nexus of historic life that an attempt to stem these forces, when made by any other than a divinely gifted poet who carries the whole world in his heart, seems ridiculous vanity. Byron, as his friend Shelley phrased it, "had gazed on Nature's naked loveliness, Actæon-like," and had then, like Actæon, been torn to pieces by raging hounds. In his finest and most audacious work, *Don Juan*, we find side by side with an abundance of frivolous mockery so wonderful a knowledge of the sweet mysteries of the heart, and side by side with a radicalism which challenges all titles to sanctity so serene an inspiration for true human greatness, that the poem, while it might well lead immature minds astray, could not but fascinate all profound and liberal spirits. All his works breathe that charm of personal experience to which poetry owes its power. He was what he wrote ; he, a bold exile, was entitled to declare war against all traditional order. Banned by the hypocritical morality of his own land, he stood alone and self-sufficient, until he found a glorious death in the struggle for the freedom of the nations.

Despite his many failings a great and genuine man, he towers above the German writer who first endeavoured to inspire our poetry with a flavour of Byronic weltschmerz. Heinrich Heine grew up in Düsseldorf amid the glories of the Rhenish sagas. Like all the younger romaticists he was an enthusiast for the lays of the *Wunderhorn*, but it was impossible for him to accept this world of miracle with ᐧ the same naivety as did Eichendorff the visionary. His keener Jewish intelligence, trained in the school of Hegel, and the precocious cynicism of a mood influenced by experiences gained among the licentious millionaires of Hamburg, led him to revolt unceasingly against romanticist dreams. He never rose superior to these contradictions. He was altogether devoid of the human greatness of our classical poets. He had talent without profundity ; he had wit without conviction ; he was egotistical, lascivious, untruthful, and withal at times irresistibly charming ; as a poet, too, he lacked character, and was therefore extraordinarily unequal in his creative work. He had moments of real inspiration, when he received the benison of the muse, when he struck the keynote of strong sensibility, and could limn vivid pictures with admirable plastic power. In many cases, however, he prostituted his virtuoso's talent for form to the work of soulless imitation. Still more frequently was he overpowered by an impulse towards self-mockery, so that from the heights of ideal sentiment he would suddenly leap down into the abyss of obscenity or of cheap witticism, and, with faunish grimace, would convey to the reader the insincerity of the assumed mood of lofty emotion.

His verses, which seem so spontaneous, were elaborated with unremitting industry until they satisfied his keen and sure sense of style ; but the supreme artistic diligence which leads a man to devote himself year after year with single-minded energy to a mighty task, was to him unattainable. He lacked the architectonic talent which marks the master ; of all the great works he planned, not one was ever completed, not even the *Der Rabbi von Bacharach* which opened with so much promise. Aware of his own weakness, he positively vaunted his desultoriness. He spoke of himself as a devoted enthusiast, contrasting his own characteristics with Goethe's concentred egoism ; but he was too shrewd and too fine an artist to decry the old man of genius publicly, as did Börne. His zealous journalistic comrades extolled him as the poet with laughing tears in his blazon, who had discovered the secret of being simultaneously drenched and ardent, and his hopeless vacillation between derision and tender yearning was by them termed Heine's sublime weltschmerz. But this weltschmerz did not spring from the despair of a strong and defiant spirit ; it arose from the man's incapacity for the enduring maintenance of the poetic mood.

Heine began by writing insipid love songs to entrancing maidens and all kinds of pretty-pretty humorous newspaper articles. His first notable work was the *Harzreise* (1824), greeted with a storm of applause, in which court society participated. In the dull and oppressive life of those days a sense of liberation was induced by the author's jovial and unrestrained humour, which led him to look at everything from the ludicrous side and to administer his drubbings to high and low alike. Next, in *Die Nordsee*, he utilised his talent for the description of nature in a hitherto untilled field. As yet all our poets had been men of the inlands, and Heine was the first to portray for the Germans the majesty of the ocean. But the continuation of the *Reisebilder* did not fulfil the splendid promise of the opening volume. The author's descriptive faculty was manifestly weakening. Echoes of Sterne's *Sentimental Journey*, fragments of story, political and philosophical observations, were strung loosely together ; and this tasteless amalgam of fact and fiction, being easy to write and easy to read, was congenial to the indolence both of the author and of his admirers. It resulted that the German poesy of the next decade volatilised almost exclusively in piquant journalistic trifles. The sole distinctive feature of the concluding volumes of the *Reisebilder* was the impudence of their uncleanness ; never before had the temple of the German muse been defiled with sodomitic scurrilities as Heine defiled it in his base polemic against Platen. His worship of the shade of Napoleon was idolatrous to a degree which outrivalled the unctuous flatteries of the Napoleonic senate, and this servility appeared all the more nauseating since it was manifestly due in great part to a wish to ingratiate ; in glorifying genius, the vain poet desired incidentally to illuminate his own greatness.

In the *Buch der Lieder* are to be found many futile imitations, but also a few poems which vie with the best productions of the German romantic school. For Heine was not merely a man of incomparably richer endowments than Börne, who poured all the wine of life into the goatskins of politics, but was also far more of a German than his Frankfort fellow-tribesman. In the hours in which he was a poet he was German to the core. German emotion spoke from those few of his love poems which genuinely represented personal experience. It spoke from his spring songs. It radiated from his stanzas on the pine tree and the palm, which gave vivid expression to the nomadic impulse of the Teutons—stanzas that have lost their witchery solely through perpetual repetition. When, as a skilled technician, he took the lay of the Lorelei, Clemens Brentano's treasure-trove, and reminted it, he could plume himself on giving to a piece of fine material a form accordant with national sentiment, and he asserted the artist's right to seize his inspiration wherever he could find it.

Heine never awoke that spontaneous and joyful understanding which the great poet knows how to induce in his fellow countrymen. The Germans always took him too seriously, and were consequently unable to grasp his drift. The idle fellow desired to amuse his readers, to move them, to astound them, and above all to please them ; he cared not a rap whether his words had any real meaning. He early assumed the role of political martyr, although no one had touched a hair of his head, and although the placing of a few of his writings on the index had had the customary effect of increasing their sale. In truth, exercising the humourist's right, he regarded politics merely as a field for the display of his literary talents. Whereas Börne pursued political aims in good faith, and failed only because of his incompetence to discover a single political idea, it was simply in order to dazzle and to titillate that Heine interspersed his writings with empty political chatter. No fault of his that readers sought a profound meaning in his jests. The solitary political idea to which he clung faithfully throughout life was his deadly enmity to Prussia, nor was this enmity utterly frivolous or devoid of elemental energy, for it betrayed in him the instinctive feeling of the Rhinelander. When Heine made fun of the Prussian soldiers, writing " the queue that hung behind of yore now hangs beneath the nose," one seemed to be listening to a Düsseldorf guttersnipe or to a clown in the carnival of Cologne, and was gratified to recognise that this German Jew did after all possess a home. For the rest, his political views were wholly dictated by the caprice of the moment and by æsthetic inclination. Following Byron's example, he sought the finest blossoms of humanity in the heights or the depths of society ; the middle classes, the strata in whom the newer German literature was rooted, were to him tedious and ridiculous, and to him middle-class virtue denoted that financial solvency which was the ethical touchstone of the Hamburg bourse. After his manner he loved Germany no less sincerely than did Börne, and he loved with greater penetration ; but like Börne he unceasingly showered upon the land of his affection the invectives of his elfin Jewish wit. It seemed funny to radical youths when Heine flung in their faces the saucy sophism : " The Englishman loves liberty as his legal wife ; the Frenchman, as his betrothed ; the German, as his aged grandmother."

Like Börne, Heine submitted to baptism on contemptible grounds and without profit ; yet the tolerance of public opinion found it nowise amiss that these two regenade Hebrews should make a parade of their " Jewish woes." Heine's hatred of Christianity glowed far more fiercely than Börne's. " Certain species of ideas are dirty," he once wrote. " If you crush one of these bug-ideas it emits a stench which is perceptible for thousands of years. Of such is Christianity, which was trodden under foot eighteen centuries ago, and which has continued ever since to poison the air for us unfortunate Jews." Yet at times he would commend the power of Christian love and would feel the aesthetic attraction of Catholic ritual ; the heavenly smile of a Madonna would enthral him no less completely than the mysterious light of the Sabbath lamp. Whereas the great artist gains fresh illumination with the passing of the years, this man, without firm standing-ground and devoid of spiritual peace, declined ever lower towards the level of a vulgar buffoon. His evangel of the joy of life, which in his youth was still ennobled by the cult of beauty, became blunted and coarsened to an unclean and prosaic religion of the flesh, and before long he set the crown upon his self-mockery in the frank confession to his readers :

'Tis rare that you and I foregather
In the abstract realm of mind.

> Roll' we in the dung together,
> Quick we understanding find !

With Börne and Heine, with the inroad of Judaism, there was heralded a new literary epoch, destined happily to be of brief duration, but the most odious and sterile period of our recent literature. Since the days of Lessing, no school of German imaginative thought sowed so many dragon's teeth, and none created so little of permanent value, as that of the radical journalists of the thirties.

The Dominion of the Feuilleton (V, 511-24)

The noisy activities of the new generation that gathered round the banner of Heine were pursued in fields remote from there luminous hilltops of poesy. Since Heine had taken up his residence in Paris his lyrical talent had undergone a speedy decay ; and in a dissolute life, one devoid of concentration, his mind became empty, his feelings blunted. In any case he could not venture the creation of comprehensive works, for as a rule the massive energy of the Aryan is alone competent to produce artistic composition in the grand style. Even the marvellous products of oriental art, even the forest of pillars in the Mezquita at Cordova, or the scintillating arches of the Alhambra, fail, for all their magnificence, to produce the impression of a coherent whole. Apart from a few songs and the fragment of an unsavoury tale entitled *Schnabelewopski*, in this decade Heine wrote no notable imaginative work. His energies were monopolised by the day's gifts and the day's demands. He elaborated his fugitive impressions into all kinds of literary capriccios, the fragments being then assembled under such titles at *Zustände*, *Zeitbilder*, and *Reisebilder*—new names for which he secured the freedom of the city among the German feuilleton writers. To excuse these dispersed activities, he boastfully announced to the world that he felt it to be his vocation to mediate between the civilisations of the two neighbour nations, and the German liberals loyally accepted his assurance.

The French took his measure more accurately. They

speedily perceived that he knew nothing whatever about French politics, whilst for their part they could learn nothing about German literature from Heine's jocular comments. The most perspicacious of his Parisian friends considered that he was forsaking his poetic calling when he imagined himself predestined to play the part of teacher to the nations. They were, however, adroit enough to encourage by their flatteries " France's new ally," for never before had any foreigner so servilely licked the dust from their boots. Englishmen and Frenchmen, visiting Germany, were accustomed to express their astonishment that the Germans did not talk English or French ; but the goodnatured German was filled with shy veneration when he discovered that in France every dull-witted peasant could actually talk French. Even this talented Jew was awestruck like the simple German philistine. Everything in France seemed to him more refined,· more beautiful, more distinguished, than what he had seen at home ; and he expressed his astonishment (writing as his manner was half in jest and half in earnest) that a " Dame de la Halle speaks better French than a German canoness with sixty-four ancestors. In his *Französische Zustände* he could find no words adequate for the expression of his antipatriotic enthusiasm. " The French are the chosen people of the new religion, Paris is the new Jerusalem, and the Rhine is the Jordan separating the sacred land of freedom from the land of the philistines." Indefatigably did he sing the praises of the new " bourgeois king without court etiquette, without pages, without courtesans, without pimps, without diamond trinkets and similar splendours." He sang the praises likewise of the men of the mountain who from the highest benches of the national convention in Paris had preached their tricolored gospel, in harmony with the gospel of him who of old delivered the sermon on the mount. He sang the praises likewise of the great Napoleon, overthrown in the War of Liberation solely by the might of stupidity, after all a matter of small importance seeing that " through their very defeats the French are able to put their opponents in the shade." When the Paris mob was shouting beneath his windows " Warsaw has fallen, death to the Russians, war against Prussia ! " he impudently declared that none but the foes of democracy would stimulate national prejudice, that French patriotism embraced with its love the entire territory of civilisation, whereas German patriotism constricted the heart as with leathern thongs.

At the same time he posed as a political refugee, speaking tearfully of his exile when in reality nothing kept him in Paris but love of pleasure and his French leanings. Declining soon to lower depths, he sold himself to the French court, begging for and accepting for many years in succession a state pension. He displayed his gratitude by continuing to slander his native land, whilst ceasing to pen the mocking sallies against Louis Philippe which hitherto he had from time to time permitted himself. Then, desiring to found a periodical intended to circulate in Prussia, through the mediation of Varnhagen he applied to the Prussian government, giving solemn assurance of his thankfulness to Prussia for her services to the bastard population of his Rhenish home. The Rhinelanders, he said, these Belgians endowed with all the faults of the Germans and possessing none of the virtues of the French, had through Prussia's instrumentality been made German once more. In the ministry at Berlin his asseverations were taken for what they were worth, and directly Heine learned that his application had been fruitless, he hastened to resume his invectives, speaking of the "ukasuists and knoutologists of Berlin," and appealing to the Rhenish bowmen to shoot the detestable black eagle from its perch. Yet the admiration felt by the German liberals was unaffected when in the year 1848 the secret dealings between Guizot and Heine at length came to light. In their eyes the unmasked mercenary of France was still an apostle of German freedom, and anyone who timidly ventured to maintain that even for Heine the principles of honour and uprightness ought to be valid was dismissed as a man without understanding by the protagonists of the dominant literary school.

A trifle more solid was the small talk with which Heine attempted to enlighten the Parisians upon the history of German religion, philosophy, and literature, for in this department the pupil of Hegel was not quite so rudderless as upon the high seas of politics. Even here, it is true, the core of things eluded him, for what could a man hostile to all deep religious sentiment find to say about religion ? Following the usual method of the dilettantist, he helped himself out with a rigid formula, reducing the entire multifarious struggle of ideas in history to the simple opposition between sensualism and spiritualism, between acceptance and renunciation of the world, and dividing the entire human race into well-fed Greeks and hungry Nazarenes. Everything now turned to uncleanness in his hands. In the rare moments in which he was still poet he endeavoured to justify " religious transfiguration, the rehabilitation of matter " as a cult of beauty ; but as soon as he was launched in this direction, he prayed no longer to the Olympian gods of the Hellenes, but to Astarte and to the golden calf of the Semites. Too able and too widely experienced to venture upon the open display of his fierce hatred of Christianity, he passed from contradiction to contradiction, in one breath comparing Christianity to a contagious disease, and in the next referring to it as a benefit to suffering humanity. In Luther he could only see the champion of rigid spiritualism—Luther, the very man who revived acceptance of the world upon the soil of Christendom, the very man who reestablished the moral justification of the state, of the household, of all honest mundane labour. With equal superficiality did he regard German philosophy solely as a force of destruction and decomposition, and in this way he had no difficulty in attaining to the desired conclusion that pantheism is the esoteric religion of our nation, and that the Germans, as soon as their philosophy was complete, would be the first to follow the French example and " to elaborate their revolution." He had just as little understanding for the moral severity of the Kantian doctrine of duty as he had for the conservative and constructive ideas of the Schelling-Hegel philosophy of history, and utterly beyond his grasp was the quiet growth of religious piety which arises as a necessary reaction against the arrogance of philosophic radicalism. How empty, how arid, how tedious, seemed this new form of unbelief. The old enlightenment retained faith in the eternal progress of mankind, and continued to hope for a day of light ; the modern doctrine of fleshly transfiguration scorned everything which binds men together in human bonds, and ultimately nothing was left for the disciples of that transfiguration beyond the sovereign individual, able to devote himself at will to the enjoyment of countless grisettes and unnumbered truffle pasties. In his artistic criticism Heine described the Paris Salons with fine understanding, being the first to direct the Germans' attention to the richly coloured canvases of the French school, and many of his appreciations of the newer paintings were inspired with splendid poetical enthusiasm. Yet his pretentious ego, continually craving for admiration, never failed to manifest itself. His best works were spoiled by obscenities or personal invectives, by political tirades, or coarse attacks upon his literary antagonists, whom, with all the insatiability of Judaic hatred, he continued to assail even when they had entered the shelter of the tomb. At this particular epoch, French literature was in a state of distressing ferment, for the brief and beautiful blossoming of the restoration had been succeeded by a lamentable decay. All the best intelligences of the day were drawn within the whirlpool of this struggle. In the universal haste, hardly anyone found it impossible to collect his energies for purely artistic creation, and amid numberless noisy mediocrities the new time produced but one figure endowed with a vigorous imaginative gift, the figure of George Sand. The classical beauty of form characteristic of the age of Louis XIV was deeply rooted in the sentiments and traditions of the nation. Hence the struggle against academic rules did not lead here, as it had led formerly in Germany, to a new and freer idealism, but resulted in the dissolution of all artistic forms, in the decomposition of all ideals. French romanticism perished amid a desolate social radicalism. The obscene and the horrible—sensual, obscure, and futile—replaced passion; attacking the state, society, and marriage; revelling in blood and filth; luxuriating now in avaricious dreams, and now in the weltschmerz of satiety; but ever incapable of any new creative effort. The arbitrariness of this unbridled subjectivism found its only definite standing ground in an attack upon the existing order; now that Béranger and Chateaubriand had struck up a new friendship, the men of literary talent belonged without exception to the opposition.

Heine, whose mind was eminently receptive and utterly lacking in independence, surrendered himself unresistingly to all the confused ideas issuing from this peculiar literature which, for all its febrile excitement, was decadent and affected with the palsy of old age. He greedily swallowed the foam of every fiery drink offered him in Paris. For a time he was even inspired with enthusiasm for the socialistic cobwebs spun from the brain of Père Enfantin, until the æsthetic repugnance of the poet and man of the world made him draw away from "crude and naked communism." All this desultory scribbling left nothing of permanent value beyond a few fine poems and a mass of witticisms, good, bad, and indifferent ; but its momentary influence was enormous. Heine, outsoaring even the French themselves, became master of the European feuilleton style, the banner bearer of that journalistic impudence which disposed of the heights and depths of human life wth a few fugitive comments. His internationalist fellows, who were now everywhere, though cautiously at first, engaged in newspaper enterprises, overwhelmed him with admiration. They spoke of him as a second Aristophanes, the naughty darling of the Graces, forgetting the obvious difference that the unrestraint of Aristophanes resulted from the excessive energy of creative genius, whereas Heine's naughtiness was due to the artistic incapacity of a pygmy spirit, incapable of great things, and forced to console itself by mocking exuberance.

Heine befooled his forsaken fellow countrymen by that charm of the exotic which the broadminded German nature is so rarely able to withstand. Ever since the Germans had first poetised, beauty of form had for them invariably been a sequel to richness of content, and of how many of our great poets could it be said that they had never succeeded in discovering the true artistic form for the clothing of their lofty thoughts. In Heine there appeared among us for the first time a virtuoso of form who was utterly indifferent to the content of his words. He boasted of his "divine prose," a prose which, indeed, ever striving after effect, became with the progress of the years more and more a prey to mannerism, yet never lacked careful polish. By this affected, careless, iridescent, and pretentious style, he endeavoured to make everything, no matter what, palatable to his readers. He possessed what the Jews have in common with the French, the gracefulness of vice which makes even the base and the odious seem alluring for a moment; he had the trick of turning out a fine-sounding sentence about a pretty trifle; and above all he was endowed with what Goethe had so often condemned as sterile, wit which can play over the surface of things without mastering them. All this was utterly ungerman. The language of Martin Luther, born in the struggles of conscience, had at all times remained the language of candour and truth; in this tongue sin was termed sin, nothing, nothing, and once again did Goethe speak from the very heart of the nation when he declared: " When we speak German, we lie when we are polite." But for the very reason that the Germans felt unable to vie with this clever Jew in the artifices of piquancy and charm, they allowed themselves to be dazzled by him, mistaking for the magic of art what was in reality no more than the stimulus of novelty.

Slowly, very slowly, did the understanding gain ground that Heine's witticisms could never be truly congenial to German minds. Of all our lyric poets he was the only one who never wrote a drinking song; to him heaven seemed full of almond cakes, purses of gold, and street wenches, for the oriental was incompetent to carouse after the German manner. It was long before people realised that Heine's " esprit " was far from being " Geist " in the German sense. Whenever he had spoken in earnest, he proved a false prophet; what he regarded as dead lived on, and what he spoke of as living was dead. Heine could not read the true signs of the times, which had already been clearly recognised by Thomas Carlyle in his profound work on the French revolution; Heine could not recognise the decay of France and the quiet strengthening of Prussian Germany. Years were to elapse before ephemeral journalistic literature was appraised at its true value; but Heine's reputation collapsed as soon as the world became accustomed merely to skim the feuilleton, and to forget in a day the thoughts conceived in a day.

Upon contemporary imaginative writers, however, the example of the widely acclaimed Parisian feuilletonist exercised a disastrous influence. Lord Byron, by the brilliant arbitrariness of his digressions and incidental descriptions, had often endangered the purity of artistic forms; but he wrote in verse, and in verse of marvellous beauty, so that the nobility of poesy was never utterly lacking. Heine, with his feuilleton style, was the first to throw down the barriers which must ever separate poetry from prose. His judgments on art, his notes on opinion, his literary and political disquisitions, meagre in content, were decked out with tinsel and with flowers of rhetoric which were not genuinely poetic but were intended to exercise a poetic influence. Hence his admirer Arnold Ruge honoured him with the ridiculous name of " critical poet." His prose did not march straight forward towards its goal, but sauntered along, continually straying from the path in search of flowers. In earlier days, when academic rules were dominant, poetry was in bondage to prose, and was termed by the French " the finest species of prose." But in Germany poetry had long ere this learned to stand on its own feet; and even prose had now acquired such constructive energy that, on occasions, it could allow itself unheard of liberties. Heine's writing, however, was not the permissible poetic prose of the romance or the novel, but a morbid mongrel style that was neither fish nor flesh. Prosaic matter appeared in prosaic form, and yet entered a claim to be enjoyed as a free work of art. It is not surprising that the critical poet, who in his own vein was after all incomparable, should be succeeded by a long series of poetic critics, who imagined themselves artists because they interwove into their judgments a few fragments of plunder from the imaginative treasure-house of German poesy. Many writers of real talent misapplied their powers to the production of this iridescent prose, wandering far aloof from poetic euphony.

Whilst Heine utilised the changing impressions of Parisian life for the production of these elegant trifles, Börne, in his *Parisian Letters*, lapsed into sheer fanaticism. He could not mention a new opera or one of Paul de Kock's frivolous romances without a discharge of stage thunder. If Heine represented social radicalism, Börne was the advocate of political radicalism. He, too, had no definite aim, being concerned merely to rail at everything that existed in Germany, and to manifest his enthusiasm for " the rights of man " which were to be above every law. Should he occasionally go so far as to offer his readers any morsel of fact, he showed a childlike lack of critical faculty; and several of the apocryphal documents from the archives of the Bundestag upon which the liberal legend was nourished for many subsequent years, were first published in his *Paris Letters*. Since he was incapable of development, and could never find anything new to say, he was reduced to screaming. " Turks, Spaniards, and Jews," he exclaimed, " are much nearer freedom than the Germans. They are slaves, but one day they will break their chains and will then become free. The German, however, is a born servant ; he could be free but will not." His old hatred for Goethe became a positive fury, and he wrote : " Kotzebue's tepid tear-soup is a thousand times better than Goethe's frozen wine." To such an extreme did he go with these invectives that Carl Simrock, though a liberal, felt impelled to ask Börne whether he hoped to annihilate the German nation by this abuse of its leading mind.

Börne accepted the new doctrine regarded by the radicals as essential to salvation, that in this enlightened century history had suddenly changed its character, and no longer fulfilled its ends through the instrumentality of great men, but through the reason of the masses. He consequently spoke of modern France, a country whose culture was produced by rule of thumb, as " the school of the world, the great railway of freedom and morality"; whilst Germany, with its wealth of individual energies, its manifold and yet unified civilisation, became ever more unintelligible to him. Since all true culture is aristocratic, he was opposed to German science as an enemy to liberty, contending : " Every university makes the whole country stupid for fifty miles round ; a few are to know everything in order that all may know nothing." Refined sophistical images, which in truth had always been the outcome of mere wit, never of reflection, gradually became rarer in his writings. They were replaced by unmeaning demagogic catchwords, by references to " the horny hand of the honest man, the sugary leaden hearts and lecherous lavender souls " of the servants of princes. His revolutionary spleen could find pleasure in roughness alone. When his watch was stolen amid the press at the Hambach festival he wrote maliciously: "At length the Germans are awakening to action; tremble, tyrants, for we also have learned how to steal!" At times his rage overmastered him so completely that he lost all sense of the respectable, and would lapse into the modes of expression which in his Frankfort home were denoted by the term "mauscheln." "I have no freedom to look back upon and have consequently no freedom to look forward to. I drive others because I am myself driven, I exasperate because I am exasperated. The wind is violent and shakes me. Is the violence mine? Did I make the wind? Can I say 'Peace, be still." In the clubs of the German handicraftsmen and refugees he was ever busily engaged, and although these heroes manifested their lust of battle mainly in threatening phrases and in the display of black-red-and-gold flags, it was not without bearing on the future that in every German town of moderate size there were before long to be found a few individuals who had graduated at the high school of demagogy on the Seine.

Through this continuous railing and mocking, his German national sentiment, which had never been characterized by vigorous and spontaneous development, underwent utter decay, and he sank into a radical cosmopolitanism akin to treason. He founded a French journal, *La Balance*, openly declaring in its columns: "I am as much Frenchman as German. God be thanked, I was never a devotee of patriotism." In the French tongue he poured forth scorn upon the Germans for their "national vanity," asking: "Is egoism less a vice in a country than in a private individual?" He assured the French that in three days they had done the work of a century, whereas in three centuries the Germans had done nothing at all. In Voltaire and Rousseau they possessed men of genius whose like was unknown in Germany. As if he wished to incite his hosts to engage in a war of revenge against the land of his birth, he solemnly assured them that the German courts had not only brought about the execution of Louis XVI by the coalition war, but had also, through their secret advice, been responsible for the July ordinances of Charles

X—an impudent calumny, recognized as such even in France. He continued to revile his political opponents as servile souls with no more spirit than dogs. Since the liberal press docilely followed the example of this terrorism in the field of ideas, public opinion soon came to regard the holding of conservative principles as the sign of a weak character, and a German writer needed to be a man of considerable courage to give frank expression to monarchical sentiments.

Just as in France all the opposition parties made common cause, so did Börne extend the hand of fellowship to everyone who attacked monarchy. Lamennais had just been doing penance in Rome for the democratic sins of his journal *L'Avenir*, and had humbly accepted the fierce papal encyclical of August 15, 1832, which first announced with perfect clearness to an unsuspecting world that the pugnacious spirit of the counter-reformation had reawakened in the Vatican. In the encyclical we read : " From this stinking source of indifference flows the equally erroneous opinion, or rather the delusion, that to every man must be assured freedom of conscience." A year after his submission, the hotblooded Breton was no longer able to control himself, and (to the horror of his milder tempered friend Montalembert) he wrote *Paroles d'un croyant*, a book full of apocalyptic images, which in words of flame attacked kings as children of Satan : " They blaspheme the Saviour, who brought freedom to earth, who will tolerate no rulership in the city of God, but desires only the mutual obligations of all." The writing never departed from the Catholic outlook, for it was merely a restatement, in fantastic and exaggerated terms, of Augustine's doctrine of the city of God, and had no more in common with the ideas of unbelieving German radicalism than the works of Mariana and the Jesuit monarchomachists had in common with the political doctrines of the Huguenots. Börne, however, translated the book and recommended it to the Germans, for his political culture was too slight to enable him to penetrate the essentially religious ideas of the French radical.

Sinister was the patience with which many of the German liberals endured Börne's invectives against their fatherland, and since he said the same thing over and over again in varying forms, he won the approval of all those simple souls who ask no more of the politician than that he should hold immutably to his confession of faith. Even Rotteck magnanimously forgave him for his personal attacks, and never ceased to admire the Paris tribune's fidelity to conviction. But the liberal camp contained a few men whose national pride was of tougher fibre, and who found the Jewish self-mockery as contemptible as the perpetual rain of abuse. C. F. Wurm of Hamburg, Wilibald Alexis, the young poet of Berlin, and subsequently Gervinus and other serious publicists, entered the lists against Börne, and showed that he was a man utterly without original ideas, "rioting in commonplaces." In witty poems Carl Simrock made fun of the cheap heroism of the apostle of freedom who shot his poisoned arrows from a safe distance, and had not even to suffer pecuniarily in the cause, seeing that the Germans, "good natured fools," bought his books just the same. To the allurements of revolutionary propaganda, the Rhenish poet proudly rejoined that the Germans would build no altars to idols, and that they would merely expose themselves to the foreigner were they to strive for freedom without a fatherland.

Less vociferously than Heine and Börne, but with almost equal success, did the circle of Rahel Varnhagen strive to diffuse neofrench ideas. In his books the language used by Varnhagen was invariably cautious. With great industry, but quite uncritically, he collected from Prussian history materials for his *Biographical Monuments*, giving in well-rounded and monotonous periods a solemn narration of mingled truth and fiction, of fact and anecdote. If he had to describe an elegant courtier, a Besser or a Canitz, he could produce a neat picture, almost as graceful as the black paper figures he was wont to cut with scissors in his drawing-room. But his hand lacked the strength requisite to carve the oak of which heroic characters are made. The figures of Blucher and of the Old Dessauer, which are quite unmeaning without an atmosphere of passion and rough humour, appear lifeless and even silly in Varnhagen's smooth, spruce presentation. To high society this cool mannerism was agreeable, and Metternich extolled the shipwrecked diplomatist as a master of historical style, doubtless tacitly intending to frighten the inconvenient man away from political activities. Varnhagen's liberal views found somewhat more definite expression in the Hegelian *Jahrbücher für wissenschaftliche Kritik*, to which he contributed almost as indefatigably as the editor, Eduard Gans.

But he was entirely himself only at his Rahel's tea table. Here, amid authors, men of the world, and diplomatists not in active service, he gave free rein to his malicious tongue, and, knowing everybody, always ready to do a service, he played the patron to young men of talent. It was here that Gans, among a number of new political ideas, discovered also the great æsthetic truth : " The Taglioni dances Goethe." Here everyone was called upon to contribute brilliant impressions, and everyone was expected to know better than other people (the crown of life to the true Berliner). Then Rahel, " thyrsus-swinger to the thought of the time," would send the lightnings of her spirit across the wide world, inspiring initiates to smiles of intimate comprehension. Everything about her breathed the restless weltschmerz of a noble but profoundly unsatisfied feminine nature. To quote her own words, she was affected with " a peculiar melancholy, an impulse to advance, a claim, a desire for something to happen." Something new and unprecedented was to take place. With dialectical audacity she disregarded all the limits which nature and history have imposed upon humanity ; fatherland and church, marriage and property, everything was subjected to her disintegrating criticism. Why should not water burn ; why should not fire flow ; why should not a man bear children ? " Had Fichte's wife written Fichte's works, would they have been any less worthy of attention ? " In such a phrase she would victoriously proclaim the mental equality of the sexes. In the moral world the only thing that seemed to her of account was the arbitrary choice of personal feeling. She considered it " dreadful " that in wedlock many children should be procreated whose parents were not inspired by genuine mutual love. Her blunt conclusion was : " Jesus had only a mother. All children should have an ideal father, and all mothers should be held as blameless and honourable as was

Mary." Such expressions of opinion could be tolerated when the kindly and brilliant woman used them to enliven casual conversation ; but they acquired undeserved importance in the minds of youthful listeners, who had already learned from Hegel to discard all moral laws as obsolete, and who now turned to account in their writings the oracular utterances of the " mother of young literature."

Wilhelm Humboldt, who succumbed for a time to the charm of these conversations, soon came to recognize that the only note here was that of an arrogant egotism incapable of any sacrifice for the common weal, and he wrote to his friend :

> Entwined thy heart with every earthly feeling,
> With every mundane action and enjoyment—
> This know'st thou not, the links that bind in heaven.

In 1834, after Rahel's death, Varnhagen published her letters and conversations in a volume of *Souvenirs*. Here we find a strange medley of profound thoughts and cordial admiration for true human greatness, intermingled with sparkling nonsense, hysterical lamentations, and empty witticisms, which can only impose upon the reader for a time owing to the grace with which they are expressed. For many years the unhappy work remained a storehouse of aphoristic half-thoughts for the feuilleton writers.

Young Germany (V, 524–41)

From these sources in Paris and Berlin there was nourished a new school of literature, to which Wienbarg, one of its members, gave the name of Young Germany, although it was neither young nor German. All its associates belonged to North Germany, the cultured but unimaginative section of the fatherland, as Goethe used to term it ; and in all of them the reason was enormously stronger than the imagination. Every previous revolution in our literature had, like the present one, proceeded from the more active north, and invariably the new ideals had first been perfected by the superior imaginative energy of the High Germans, the classical ideal by Schiller and Goethe, the romantic by Uhland and Rückert. On this occasion, however, at the outset, South and Central Germany were indifferent, and were subsequently hostile; for in the warm and lovable nest of German fancy, in the original home of the German tongue, it was speedily recognized that the new literary movement was of Judaic and French origin, and was consequently predestined to infertility.

Since these younger writers were all lacking in lyrical faculty, making a virtue of necessity they maintained that prose alone contains " literary germs." The creation of figures instinct with life, the expression of the enduring sentiments of the human heart, they left to those soulless handicraftsmen who before their day had been known as artists. Desiring to expound the tendencies of the zeitgeist, they cared little whether they incorporated their topical reflections in the form of a novel, a description of travel, or a feuilleton causerie—the last being the most suitable form of all. No longer was poesy to illumine life by its ideals; but life, with its finite aims and ephemeral caprices, was to dominate poesy. Consequently the writings of Young Germany passed into utter oblivion as soon as history outgrew the tendencies of the thirties. The men of the new Sturm und Drang loved to compare themselves with Lenz, Heinse, and the other brilliant spirits of the days of *Werther*. They never noticed that they were merely breaking down doors already opened, that the regime of philistinism had been destroyed by Goethe long before their day, and that the society of the new age, although not invariably free from accesses of demure sanctimoniousness, exhibited on the whole tolerant consideration for the hot blood of youth. They imagined that their " young criticism " would exercise an influence no less creative than had been exercised by the critical writings of Lessing, whereas the German imagination, now proudly independent, had long ceased to need a liberator. Their radicalism was artificial, devoid of seriousness, and uninspired by lasting passion. Many of their catchwords were merely a background for the better display of the greatness of their own detached egos.

Theodor Mundt, the Berlin journalist, acted as herald of their renown. In Rahel's salon he garnered the new ideas; in the *Dioskuren* and other short-lived journals he described the labours of the youthful titans; in *Madonna* he acclaimed the right of free love; in *Moderne Lebenswirren* he revived

Börne's old witticisms about the " highly well born," about
the " polypi of the age," and so on ; and in a tedious work
upon the unity of Germany he showed that henceforward great
monarchs would be neither possible nor necessary, for constitutional monarchy merely made kingship " devoid of physiognomy," and could consequently be no more than a transitional
stage on the way to republicanism.   More noteworthy were the
Æsthetischen Feldzüge and other minor critical essays by Ludolf
Wienbarg, the Holsteiner.   Sensation and reason were, in his
opinion, the forces of the new age ; Luther had freed the
understanding, and now the senses must come into their rights.
It was therefore reserved for the modern " writers of destiny "
to fulfil poetry with reality.   " Poesy and life are inseparables ;
the female frets to death when severed from the male."   Add
to this an overplus of enlightenment and cosmopolitanism, for
" pantheism and pancivism spring from the same root."
Neither Mundt nor Wienbarg was capable of continued growth,
for the former lacked talent, the latter industry.

Heinrich Laube was endowed with a larger share of vital
energy, and brought with him a breath of Silesian cheerfulness
into the blasé world of Berlin authorship.   Unfortunately
he carried his wares too early to the literary market, and
having at this time nothing original to say, he was compelled
to claim notice for himself by whip-crackings and bombast.
In *Das neue Jahrhundert* he endeavoured (to quote what he
himself said in maturer years) " to judge everything possible
and impossible by the standard of liberalism."   He extolled
Rotteck as the German Lafayette ; declared reason to be the
foundation of liberalism and the supreme source of all rights ;
and admired Polish freedom with a naivety truly remarkable
in a Silesian.   *Das junge Europa*, too, contained nothing
profounder than feuilleton comments, but to these comments,
as he himself phrased it, he gave " the physiognomy of a
novel," and· youthful readers of his descriptions of free love,
characterised rather by truth than by charm, might well think
that they had to do with a work of imagination.   It was
devoid of artistic beauty, but from the occasional gleams of
a sound human understanding it might be inferred that the
young poet would soon weary of these unripe boastings.   Laube

spoke of Goethe in admiring terms, but he was not free from
a sense of superiority, for Young Germany was firmly convinced
that the newer literature was advancing with giant strides far
beyond anything that had been attainable by the old pleasure-
seeking prince's servant. "As long as Goethe lived in a petty
time, Goethe was great ; but when the time became great,
Goethe was small. It may be that freedom will rise from
his tomb. With other maidens has he dallied, but never
with the most beautiful of them all."

Even earlier than Laube, when no more than twenty-one
years of age, Carl Gutzkow made his first essays in authorship.
A typical Berliner, quite estranged from nature, he was all
understanding, all culture, so that even his passions had a
doctrinaire flavour. However earnestly in later years he might
endeavour to contemplate, to experience, to feel, throughout
life there clung to him the influences resulting from his having
grown up in this metropolis, where even the mob knew no
stronger term of abuse than "uncultured man," where the
children in their earliest years became acquainted at menageries
with their own resemblance to monkeys, but seldom or never
caught sight of a herd of German cattle. Gutzkow invariably
aspired towards intellectualism, and it was impossible for him
to express a simple thought in simple words. Ardently desirous
of fame, the successes of others preyed upon his mind, and
distant observers could readily regard this man who, though
irritable, was essentially good-natured, as a person of malicious
and envious disposition. In rapid succession he published
a number of short stories, all defective in point of character
drawing, and overloaded with weltchmerz   Next came *Briefe
eines Narren an eine Närrin*, a sentimental sketch in the inflated
style of Jean Paul, but devoid of the latter's geniality. This
was followed by *Nero*, a shapeless drama, ostensibly intended
to represent "the struggle of the beautiful with the good, a
struggle still undecided " ; but the work achieved nothing more
than confused freethinking utterances and tepid witticisms,
failing even to arouse a sentiment of awe by its delineation
of the mania of Caesarism.

It was through a great literary scandal that Gutzkow's
name first became known to wider circles. The sultry vintage

years of 1834 and 1835 were to involve our literature in severe storms. In the autumn of 1834 occurred the death of Schleiermacher. The church mourned for its great teacher, and whoever was competent to understand the hidden tragedy of the life of the thinker was profoundly moved in contemplating the career of this man who had only attained his splendid power of bringing consolation to heavy laden hearts because he had himself suffered so greatly, because he himself had come into such intimate contact with the great forces of destiny. How marvellously had God guided him! How many were the struggles through which this shy spirit had at length fought down the repugnance towards all public activities, to wield in the end a mighty influence over the nation. How many aberrations of sentiment, how many disillusionments elaborately concealed by a keen wit, had to be endured, before this richly endowed heart, stretching all its roots and leaves towards love, could come to terms with the weakly and misshapen body, and could at length find peace in work of pure inclination. How many doubts must be surmounted before the feeling of dependence upon God became elevated into a joyful consciousness of appurtenancy, of sonship to the Father, until the bold investigator felt himself in perfect harmony with his church, and on his deathbed, as was his Protestant right, administered the sacrament to himself and his family.

Yet this tomb, contemplated with veneration even by Varnhagen, was one which Gutzkow, with youthful impudence, ventured to desecrate. To make fun of the unctuous laments of the theologians, suddenly, quite without authorisation, he republished the dead man's long forgotten and weakest work, the only one unworthy of its author, *Vertraute Briefe über Friedrich Schlegels Lucinde*, published in the year 1800. These letters had been penned by Schleiermacher in the desire to assist his friend Schlegel against the attacks of the conventional moralists, and whilst actually engaged in writing them he had been uneasy about his own work. The mysticism of love, which doubtless unriddled many a fine secret, but likewise coarsely desecrated many another, did not arise from the natural force of a strong passion, but from the half unconscious sophistry of a hypercultured sentiment influenced by external suggestions. At a later date, when Schleiermacher outgrew romanticism, he recognised how impossible it is to deduce the moral laws of society solely from the idea of individuality. But this subjectivism of the youthful romanticist was the very thing which pleased the Young Germans, whose principal talent it was to trot out old errors in a new dress. His cordial defence of sensual delights was a dainty morsel for their lustful palates, and in Gutzkow's hands it was accentuated to become the " soulless and unworthy libertinage " which the young Schleiermacher had expressly repudiated. Gutzkow took the theologian's name in vain, writing a lengthy introduction in which he bluntly preached unchastity and godlessness. " Is it not true, Rosalie ? Only since you have worn spurs on your little silken boots have you known the meaning of the words, ' I love you ' . . . Come here, Franz ! Who is God ? You don't know ? Innocent atheist, philosophical child ! Had the world never known of God, it would have been much happier ! " The writer really imagined that with this foolish chatter he was performing a great act of spiritual enfranchisement. " I believe," he wrote, " in the reformation of love, as I believe in every social problem of the century "—and his associates acclaimed this remarkable reformer, who believed in all problems. Wienbarg wrote with delight : " The most beautiful and the most talented of Schleiermacher's children has hitherto been disowned and calumniated because it was a love child and did not bear its father's name."

The Young German writings were but little read, but they were much talked of, and this was already success, for modern society believes it to be its duty to discuss everything, whether this be understood or not, and thus is apt credulously to accept any established reputation. With the ideas of the newer Parisian literature, the industrious business habits characteristic of that literature and all the evil arts of log-rolling had crossed the Rhine. It was fruitless for Scribe to make mock of these abuses in his clever comedy *La Camaraderie* ; they had become indispensable to the French, especially since the newspapers, following the example of

Girardin's daily, *La Presse*, had assumed purely democratic forms, and had learned how to secure extensive circulation by low prices and numerous business advertisements. As far as was possible in our modest conditions, Young Germany, too, knew how to promote the ephemeral reputation of its adherents. Gutzkow was presented to the nation by Wienbarg with drums and trumpets. He was "the talented author of *Maha Guru*, the writer of the epoch-making literary supplement of *Phœnix*, the youthful templar, the boldest soldier of liberty and the most charming priest of love on German soil." Hardly less ludicrous did it sound when Heine sang the praises of blusterous young Laube on account of his "notable tranquillity and self-realised greatness." In this fertilising rain of mutual admiration, many of the mere camp-followers of Young Germany suddenly found themselves on the way to become literary giants. In Leipzig lived Gustav Kühne, editor of *Europa*, a man of no account, and so dull a writer that a Leipzig student suffering from boredom was wont to say: "Es kühnelt mich." But in his well-ordered house the younger literati were sure of a hospitable welcome, so they praised him as a German man of letters, and his name is still copied from one history of literature to another although no one ever reads him.

What a gulf between the Teutonist followers of Jahn and the new literary apostles. The former displayed energy pushed to the point of roughness, the latter's work was artificialised and over-adorned; the Teutonists displayed faith, the Young Germans mockery; whilst instead of the overstrained patriotic zeal of the purifiers of German speech, we find in the Young Germans an unceasing parade of foreign locutions, in which they outdo even the South German parliamentarians. The notable adaptability of our tongue has ever been a sign of strength, for the Teuton, a born conqueror, takes his property where he finds it; but, like every great talent, it is liable to misuse, and never was it more grossly misused than in these days. Simply from vanity, because they considered everything French especially distinguished, and because they wished to suggest that they themselves were quite at home in Paris, the writers of the Young German school loaded their style, even without this unduly artificial, with a mass of foolish French words and phrases. When Wienbarg published a new volume, he sublimely announced that he was placing " his critical effort under the reverbère of the book trade."

The evil example was all the more disastrous to German journalistic style because the younger writers on the daily press were many of them Jews, almost invariably devoid of a feeling for the niceties of language. How great had become the power of Jewry during these few years ! Börne and Heine, Eduard Gans and Rahel, set the tone for Young Germany, whilst a fifth in the company was Zacharias Löwenthal, the busy publisher of Mannheim. Cosmopolitanism and hatred of Christianity, bitter mockery and corruption of speech, utter indifference towards the greatness of national history—everything in the movement was Jewish, although the Young Germans never constituted a definitely circumscribed school, although Börne did not even correspond with most of his German imitators, whilst Gutzkow at least was no lover of the Jews. It is true that the Hebraic choir-masters were few in number, but the Jew's mysterious faculty for multiplying himself is familiar to all, and any one who in a narrow alley sees twenty Jews standing at their thresholds is prepared to take his oath that there must have been hundreds there. Moreover, since the five leaders were really of much greater intellectual force than the members of their Germanic following, the Judaic spirit exercised for a brief period an influence upon German literature such as has never since been paralleled. It is true that the number of Jewish authors is now much larger than in those days, but they do not gain the respect of the nation unless they are fully Germanised. Such a reputation as Heine's was possible only in a generation whose cosmopolitan dreams had expunged for a time the memory of the primeval contrast between Aryan and Semitic sensibilities. This semi-Jewish radicalism had no creative faculty whatever, but it assisted in undermining the foundations of state, church, and society, thus contributing to the revolution of 1848. For this reason alone does the movement find a place in history.

The hopeless confusion of all moral ideas in Young German

circles was manifested with cynical impudence in Georg Büchner's drama *Danton's Death*. When the police were already on his heels owing to his intrigues in Upper Hesse, with feverish zeal the young poet was studying the newspapers of the revolutionary epoch. In a number of loosely threaded dramatic scenes, a faithful chronicler, he described to the life the doings of the men of blood who sat in the national convention—described this unadulterated revival of the Celtism of druid days, with its blood drinking, its voluptuousness, its gloomy misconceptions, and its nauseating superaddition of modern boredom. No contemporary writer except Carlyle reproduced the horrors of the revolution with such terrible truth, but whereas the Scottish author gave passionate expression to his moral reprobation, the German seriously undertook to glorify the revolution in a work that can only arouse our loathing. Who can tell whether this most gifted of all the Young German poets might not one day have outgrown his deplorable materialism? Büchner aspired towards artistic truth; he detested phrase-making, even going so far as to dislike the emotional note of Schiller's writing; and would give his full approval only to the profound simplicity, the repressed passion, of the folk-song. In his long story *Lenz*, dealing with the favourite epoch of the Young Germans, the age of Sturm und Drang, he eschewed all bias, relating with pitiless veracity and a sinister sympathetic comprehension how illusion gradually mastered the friend of Goethe's youth. Ere the work was completed, Büchner died suddenly, in February, 1837, a few days after Börne's death, and German radicalism, so poor in men of talent, did not hesitate to glory in this name. Young Herwegh sang Büchner and Börne as the German Dioscuri.

Prince Pückler-Muskau, like Büchner, had no more than an indirect connection with Young Germany, the association being not so much personal as due to kinship of views. But in Rahel's salon he had developed his gift for amiable small-talk into a fine art, and upon Varnhagen's advice he published *Letters from a Deceased Person*, an able description of travel, far superior to the youthful writings of Gutzkow or Laube.

The distinguished man of the world had had real experience, whereas the others drew upon specious imaginings. He said many an apt word upon the hypocrisy of English morals ; the quiet humour of his narrative was in correspondence with his personal character ; and the infusion of foreign idioms, which he carried to an extreme, did not in his case sound so unnatural as it did in that of the Young German plebeians, seeing that aristocratic society was still in the habit of talking such semifrench gibberish. As an unprejudiced cosmopolitan, and as one who despised the smug middle classes and above all the Prussian officialdom, the prince was at first given a kindly reception by the critics of Young Germany. In the long run, however, he could not escape the curse of amateurishness. His attitude towards penmanship was merely one of indulgent contempt, and he soon wrote himself out. For a brief period his marvellous adventures, some true and some fictitious, in every country under the sun, procured for him a world-wide reputation. In the end, however, readers began to weary of Semilasso's peregrinations and his increasing pose of nil admirari. Such creative artistic faculty as he possessed was displayed in his remarkable work as landscape gardener on his estates of Muskau and Branitz.

The dissensions over the tomb of Schleiermacher had not yet ceased when another death incited the champions of Young Germany to fresh deeds of glory. In December, 1834, Charlotte, the beautiful and high-minded wife of the young poet Heinrich Stieglitz, stabbed herself. In a few lines written just before the suicide, she expressed the wish that her husband might " become happier in genuine unhappiness," her hope apparently being that the intensity of his sufferings would heighten his poetic faculty and would increase his power of tragic passion. To one who knew the female heart, there could hardly be anything enigmatic about this act of self-destruction. Heinrich Stieglitz was one of those pitiable mediocrities in whom unjustifiable ambition has been induced by brilliant success in examinations, and his artistic aims were quite beyond his power. His proud young wife shared these sterile torments for a few years, but when it became clear to her that the man of her choice could not fulfil her ideals, she was unable to survive the disillusionment.

To spare her beloved, and it may be also because her mind
was deranged, she endeavoured to wrap her woman's motives
in freethinking phraseology. Like most suicides, this also
was the outcome of weakness, of pusillanimity. But it was
impossible that so simple an explanation should content an
epoch avid of sensation. All Berlin looked upon Charlotte
Stieglitz as a heroine, regarding an act which deserved nothing
more than humane sympathy as the manifestation of an
unprecedented spirit of self-sacrifice, as a literary matryrdom
comparable with the martyrdom of the saints of the church.
Even Rauch and other serious-minded men were carried away
by the wave of universal admiration. Böckh, in Greek distichs,
extolled the new Alcestis, "who had voluntarily gone down
to Hades for the good of her spouse." Theodor Mundt, a
family friend, did not hesitate to turn the horrible incident
to business account ; he promptly erected a biographical
"monument" to the deceased, roughly withdrawing the veil
from the hidden sorrows of this profoundly unhappy marriage.
Then the widower made a journey through Germany, carrying
with him his wife's dagger, and boasting of his own shame.
In his *Memories of Charlotte*, which was not published until
some years after his death, he says : "Her last lines are
henceforward my diploma, my promotion to a higher rank."
It was impossible that sorrow should awaken profound thoughts
in this weakling. In 1849 he died of cholera in Italy, a
commonplace writer of travels. Not the desperate deed itself,
but the echoes it awakened, was a tragical sign of the times.
a sign of sensibilities perverted by hyperculture.

By the death of Charlotte, Gutzkow was stimulated to
write his romance *Wally*. With this work (such was the
announcement promptly made by the chorus of Young German
criticism) the men of the new Sturm und Drang ventured their
boldest cast, as those of the earlier movement had ventured
it with Heinze's *Ardinghello*. But how shameful was the
decline. In Heinze's work are displayed naked and unfalsified
nature, blazing sensuality, vigorous portraiture, and a charming
art of narration, by which the reader is readily induced to
overlook the infamous character of the contents. Moreover,
in the interwoven observations on art are to be found many

excellent ideas, worthy of a time which still possessed enthusiastic faith in beauty. But in Gutzkow we find nothing but a desert of reflections, of immature and precocious utterances concerning the rights of the flesh, the unnaturalness of marriage, the folly of Christianity. We are shown a bored and impotent hero, and an equally stupid and world-weary heroine, who is ashamed of her feminine modesty as a prejudice, who exhibits herself nude to her lover in order to wed him symbolically, whilst contracting marriage with a man whom she does not love. Naturally the work closes with a suicide. This detestable piece of obscenity does not contain a trace of vigorous passion or a single natural word.

It was impossible that in a moral nation such an overplus of uncleanly impudence should be allowed to pass unchallenged. In September, 1835, Wolfgang Menzel opened a campaign against Young Germany in the columns of the Stuttgart *Literaturblatt*, of which he was editor. One of the most zealous members of the Würtemberg opposition, on intimate terms with Welcker and many others among the South German parliamentarians, he had been an eager participant in the petition issued from Boll by the Swabian liberals, and had on many occasions warmly espoused the cause of the ill-treated Jews ; but he remained a firm adherent of the Protestant faith, and would not allow the wisdom of the newspapers to shake his conviction that France was on the decline, Germany in the ascendant. When the ungerman and unchristian tendencies of Young Germany had been plainly demonstrated in Gutzkow's *Wally*, he gave vent to his feelings in his rough, arrogant, and blustering manner, but with honest courage. He must have known that the majority of his liberal associates were half estranged from the church, and that they would be likely to look askance at his defence of Christianity. In the course of the prolonged dispute, in which retort was perpetually followed by counter retort, he at length openly declared that *sanspatrie* Judaism was disintegrating all our ideas of shame and morality, and that whilst the mob frenzy of the middle ages had falsely accused the Jews of poisoning springs, the old accusation might now be justly revived in reference to the domain of literature.

The aberrations of art cannot be fought with moral indignation alone. More dangerous to Young Germany than Menzel's essentially prosaic moral sermons was the aesthetic opposition voiced by the circle of Swabian singers. With well-grounded pride Justinus Kerner had written:

> Among the hills and o'er the lea, where songs of harvesters are heard,
> The school of Swabia's bards is held, where Nature speaks the master-word.

As the Swabians had in former days stoutly upheld the clarity of Protestant reason against the fantastic extravagances of Schlegelian romanticism, so now with no less stoutness did they reject the artificialities of the new feuilleton style, preserving rhymed euphony, the nobility of lyrical form, and the natural innocence of the uncorrupted pleasures of the senses. Their muse

> Sang a song not free from error,
> But yet untouched by earthly stain—

as Gustav Schwab expressed it with amiable modesty. Among the young men who now sat at the feet of the two patriarchs Uhland and Kerner, one only, Eduard Mörike, was endowed with a wonderful gift of illuminating everything with poetic light. But in fortunate hours the two Pfizers, Schwab, and Carl Mayer, would sometimes produce a vigorous ballad, a well-turned epigram, or a pretty nature poem; and whereas the Young Germans, luxuriating in weltschmerz, looked upon poesy as a ruthless fate, to the Swabians it seemed a splendid gift from heaven which was to fill the poet with joy, thus rendering him capable of lifting others to heights of happiness above the confusion of daily life. Merry were the hours when the Swabian poets sat over their tankards, and when Lenau and Auersperg, the two young Austrian poets, paid them a visit, or the brothers Adolf and August Stöber came over from Strasburg, where, in the Frenchified western march, they were the trusty champions of the German tongue and German poetry.

This was German life, German art and fancy. How prosaic in comparison seemed the activities of the thought-choppers round Rahel's tea table, or the foolish chatter of the grisettes at Heine's little dinner-parties.

Gustav Pfizer therefore considered himself justified, in the name of German art, in taking the field against Heine and his followers. Pfizer's poetical creations were extremely unequal. The prim forms he employed were not always well adapted to the rich content of his verses, most of which were contemplative; a few only of his characters, like that of Hermes Psychopompos, stand out clearly before the reader's eyes, "always beautiful and always serene"; but he possessed a sure and highly cultured understanding of the beautiful. His brother, again, Paul Pfizer, a declared liberal, could not possibly be accused of partisan fanaticism when in the year 1838, in Cotta's recently founded *Deutsche Vierteljahrsschrift*, he pointed out the æsthetic errors of Young Germany in unsparing but worthy and measured language. Was the widely trumpeted and stimulating confusion of the feuilleton style anything more, he asked, than a foolish attempt to break down the lines of demarcation long since established by Lessing between poetry and prose? What could result but the destruction of all beauty if the younger poets were to vie with one another in brushing back their hair in order to display their faun's ears and satyr's horns? All Swabia agreed with him. Even Vischer, the young writer on æsthetics, a strong radical in politics and religion, under the spell of the sound sense of beauty characteristic of the Swabian stock, straightforwardly declared that such works of reflection as the novels of Gutzkow or Laube could not properly be classed as works of imagination. We owe it to the Swabians that the Young German movement never made its way into the highlands, the rank growth being confined to the great towns of the north. The victorious resistance of national sentiment to the Judaico-French hybrid literature originated in the liberal south, which in the political field had proved so willing to accept the doctrines of salvation made in France. The consoling conclusion might be drawn that even the process of political Frenchification had merely touched the surface of things among these people who were

German to the core, and that the German spirit would one
day remodel its constitutionalist ideas. But who at that time
would have ventured to express such hopes ? All the world still
sought the strength of the South Germans where their weakness
lay, in the Gallic verbal displays of the chambers.

Since Menzel's *Literaturblatt* was much read in conservative
circles on account of its high church tendencies, his attack
attracted attention at the courts, and accelerated the long
pending intervention of the Bundestag. Wienbarg, when he
introduced the name of Young Germany, had unfortunately
been unaware or had ignored that there already existed another
Young Germany, the revolutionary secret society of refugees
and handicraftsmen which had been founded in Switzerland
under Mazzini's leadership. This Young Germany was but
too well known to the demagogue hunters in Frankfort, and
obvious, though quite unfounded, was the suspicion that there
must be some sort of connection between the two associations.
The most savage of the numerous attempts to assassinate
Louis Philippe had just miscarried. Fieschi's infernal machine
struck terror throughout Europe, and demagogic intrigues
were supervised more closely than ever. At this juncture
Wienbarg and Gutzkow issued a bombastic manifesto inviting
all German freethinkers to cooperate in founding a German
review which was to outdo Schiller's *Horen* and the *Revue
des deux mondes*. It was impossible that the Germanic
Federation, in view of all it had said against the political
press, should tolerate the undertaking. General von Schöler,
the new Prussian federal envoy, an acknowledged connoisseur,
gave the Bundestag an unflattering but just description of the
character of this new literature. In essentials it was, he said,
no more than a revival of the doctrines of the Encyclopædists ;
but it was able " to make up for deficiency in genuine wit
and novelty of ideas by smartness of expression and by
impudent mockery of sacred things." On December 11, 1835,
upon the proposal of Austria, all the governments undertook
to check the diffusion of Young German writings by every
legal means.[1] In accordance with federal custom, the resolution

---

[1] Schöler's Reports, November 3, 1835, and subsequent dates.

was so indefinitely worded that after the lapse of seveıal months Hanover enquired whether all the writings of the Young Germans, even the earlier ones, were really to be suppressed. Schöler rejoined that the resolution had not intended anything so drastic as this, but no further resolution was adopted to throw light upon the precise meaning of the one previously carried.[1]

Everything was therefore left to the individual states, and these took action as pleased them best, for the most part with notable lenity. Here and there proceedings were taken against particular books written by the Young Germans. In Prussia, the import of all publications of the Hamburg firm Hoffmann and Campe, which issued Heine's writings, was actually prohibited for several years. Speaking generally, however, the prohibition was very ineffectually enforced, and in the end lapsed entirely. The only writings of the Young German school for which there was a real demand among the reading public, the works of Heine and Börne, were obtainable almost without hindrance. There could be no talk of any serious persecution ; the Young German literati got off far more easily than the editors of the suppressed political journals. Nevertheless, Heine continued to assume the role of the unhappy exile, comparing himself with Dante, who had likewise had to eat the bitter bread of the stranger. Gutzkow was the only one who had to pay a somewhat higher penalty. His *Wally* indisputably contained a " despiteful description of the Christian religion," and on this account he was condemned by the Mannheim law court to a brief term of imp·isonment.

Trivial as were these troubles, they sufficed to adorn with the halo of martyrdom the heads of the Young German leaders. In the public eye everyone was right who had a quarrel with the Bundestag. Besides, was it not shameful that belletristic literature, which in Germany had always enjoyed unrestricted liberty, should now be subjected to the arbitrary control of the police ? Influenced by these considerations, Paulus of Heidelberg, advocate for the defence in all such cases, entered the lists on behalf of Gutzkow's *Wally*. His involved sentences showed, indeed, how much self-constraint the old rationalist

---

[1] Schöler's Report, April 18, 1836.

had been forced to exercise before he could undertake to champion this thoroughly atheistical book. Other defenders of Gutzkow contented themselves with the flattering opinion that this novel could not possibly lead anyone from the paths of virtue. Most of those who were attacked displayed very little heroism vis-à-vis the government. Not long ago they had boastfully undertaken to shake bourgeois society to its foundations ;. now they humbly protested that their sentiments were harmless, and that their influence had been extremely restricted. Heine despatched a missive to the Federation which among friends he himself described as a " childlike, syrupy, and submissive letter." Referring " to the example of the Master, that inestimable man Martin Luther," he declared " with the profoundest respect " that he would never cease to obey the laws of his fatherland. But the Bundestag knew its man, and shelved the address as irrelevant.[1] Heine wrote also to Metternich, with no better success, humbly begging that victorious Austria would be magnanimous enough to rescue him from his afflictions.[2]

Fainthearted before the authorities, the Young Germans reserved all their anger for Menzel. He alone, they held, was responsible for the prosecution, although he had merely done his duty as critic, and had employed the honest weapon of literary polemic. He was far from approving the measures taken by the Bundestag, and his rough language was more reputable than were the malicious suspicions wherewith the Young German writers aspersed their opponents. But for five years thenceforward he remained the target of the radical writers. Börne twisted the sense of his words and wrote a booklet entitled *Menzel the Devourer of Frenchmen*, although Menzel had made no attack on the French, having merely visited upon the German Jews, men without a country, the well-deserved reproof that no Frenchman would ever sink so low as to attack his own people before strangers and in a foreign tongue. This writing was Börne's swan song. For several years it was extolled even in the schools as a masterpiece. Yet it merely proved that his radicalism had no better foundation than arid negation and rage against

[1] Schöler's Report, May 24, 1836.   [2] Maltzan's Report, July 1, 1836.

all those who held different opinions. "What," he asks,
"are we to think of the man who sells his opinions for an
Austrian smile, a Prussian flattery, a Bavarian shrug, or a
Jesuitical commendation?" Again: "For these reasons, the
man who hates France or reviles that country for sordid
lust for gain, is a foe to God, humanity, right, freedom, and
love." This fanatic was unable to see that a German might
have other reasons for resenting the avaricious war clamour
of the Parisians. Nor was there lacking a lament for free
Frankfort, now enslaved by federal troops; the Frankforters
were Jews who had to do with Christian Austria and Prussia,
and must be made to mind their manners!

Heine's conduct was yet more equivocal. In earlier days
he had been a fellow member of the Bonn Burschenschaft
with Menzel and Jarcke, and he was familiar with their strict
religious views. It could not escape his perspicacity that the
present struggle was inevitable, and that the romanticist and
radical elements which had comprised the old Burschenschaft
must now part company. He could not fail to know that
Menzel's conduct had been perfectly straightforward. Yet he
gave his rejoinder the lying title *Against the Informer*. Being
himself far out of range, he indulged quite without restraint
all the gross inclinations of his Falstaffian nature, referring to
his opponent as a mouchard, a blackguard, a recreant, a
scoundrel, a ruffian, and a poltroon. He attained his purpose,
for in those days, when everyone dreaded the heavy hand
of the police, nothing could be more terrible than to be accused
of being an informer. Heine's fierce calumny was promptly
adopted by the whole liberal press, and despite its obvious
untruth was so obstinately reiterated that it finds a place even
to-day in most histories of literature.

In the *Schwabenspiegel* which he launched against Pfizer,
Heine made use of a trick no less effective. Since Uhland
and Rückert, the two greatest poets of the south, were not
personally participating in these struggles, he endeavoured
to represent the dispute as if it had been merely due to minor
poets, envious in their mediocrity, setting themselves up against
his own superior talent, as if the prim bourgeois respectability
of the highlands were arraying itself against the free thought

of the north. The real truth was that South German poesy
was arrayed against Jewish witticism. The Swabians' pens
were set in motion, not by sanctimonious censoriousness,
which has ever been alien from the temperament of the
cheerful German south, but by æsthetic repugnance. One
weakness of the Swabians could not, indeed, be overlooked.
Whilst the Young German writers were wholly a prey to their
prepossessions, the southern poets on the other hand were
too remote from the passions of the day, and their refinedly
sensuous and peaceable verse was incompetent to give full
expression to the ideas of a fermenting and struggling time.
Heine knew how to turn this defect to good account, for the
art of making a diabolically clever use of half truths was the
one quality which he shared with his idol Napoleon. He
described the Swabians as a clumsy rout of children at play,
and thus brought some of the laughers over to his side.
Finally, the younger radicals had had their taste quite corrupted
by the mockeries of the new literature ; they could laugh
when Heine spoke of the diarrhœal flux of the Swabian poets,
or when he accused his opponent Pfizer of unnatural vice.
Nevertheless the tide of the radical feuilletons was already on
the ebb. The lesser men of the Young German movement
were quickly forgotten ; and the stronger personalities, Gutzkow
and Laube, were beginning to collect their forces, and to atone
by maturer works for the follies of youth. Whilst still in
prison, Gutzkow wrote a brief work on the philosophy of history
which, though full of empty phrases, showed that he was
beginning to come to his senses.

But the Parisian colony of the Young Germans first showed
its true colours to the world when its members began to fall
out. Börne and Heine had never got on well together, for
no understanding was possible between doctrinaire obstinacy
and unmeaning frivolity. Börne gave frank expression to his
views, but Heine evaded a chivalrous combat, and did not
discharge his long-retained spleen until Börne died, and Raspail,
the French republican, extolled the hero of international
democracy in a stirring funeral oration. For the third time,
as after the death of Schleiermacher and after that of Charlotte
Stieglitz, did Young Germany manifest its humane delicacy

beside a freshly made grave. Heine's work on Börne gave utterance, as usual, to a number of brilliant half truths, but the tone was so spiteful and so vulgar that even the liberal press was angered. The liberal Aristophanes might revile conservatives and poets as much as he pleased, but it was unpardonable of him to attack a tribune of the people. The dispute was utterly nauseating, and the notorious feud between Voss and Stolberg seemed in comparison to have been an amiable interchange of ideas. When Börne's friend Frau Wohl now opened her packets of letters and sedulously extracted all Börne's private opinions about Heine, the vapours of the ghetto were wafted across Germany, and many an honest German began at length to recognise the nature of the idols before which he had once bowed the knee.

The Fine Arts (V, 555–58, 562–68)

Even the opera felt the growing influence of France. The leading dramatist among the composers, Giacomo Meyerbeer of Berlin, had removed to Paris, and thence pursued his internationalist artistic activities, remaining always in sympathy with French moods. His *Robert the Devil*, which opened the long series of his European triumphs, was closely akin to Victor Hugo's neoromanticism, and when religious differences became more accentuated, this turned his thoughts to the effective subject of *The Huguenots*. By brilliant dramatic incident and charming melody, he exercised an irresistible influence over the masses, mingling all possible forms and styles as long as they could stimulate the nerves. He had no trace of the simple greatness of German art.

Since his style expressed all the bad tendencies of the day and a few of the good ones, it would probably have become supreme in Germany as well had not a greater genius taken possession of the field. Felix Mendelssohn, like Meyerbeer, grew up in the luxurious circles of Berlin wealth, but his pure and amiable nature adopted none but the good and vigorous traits of the metropolitan environment, its many-sided culture, its free insight, its skill in the arts of social life, and its gift of sympathy. A thorough German, even the charm of the south could not permanently attract him, and,

among all foreigners, the Teuton English have alone fully
understood him, the French never. By his *St. Paul* he
awakened the Protestant oratorio to new life, and he gave to
German song a deep and ecstatic musical expression.   Hardly
less important than these compositions, which raised him to
a rank far above that of all composers then living, was his
activity as conductor.   In 1829, when no more than twenty
years of age,. he made his debut in this field by the production
in Berlin of Sebastian Bach's forgotten *Passion*, and from
that time forward he never remitted from his endeavours to
revive among the cultured the taste for the noble and genuinely
German artistic forms of the symphony, the oratorio, and the
sonata.   He made comprehensible to the nation the works
of Bach and Handel, and also Beethoven's last symphonies,
which had long been considered impossible of production.
From the days when Mendelssohn, universally known and
loved throughout Germany, began to wield his baton in Berlin,
Düsseldorf, Frankfort, and Leipzig music, which had sunk
almost to the level of a pastime, regained honour as a lofty
art.   It was to him that the Germans owed it that when
anarchy came to prevail also in the world of opera, audiences
continued to preserve a kernel of sound taste.   Thus did a
German of Jewish descent lead back our cultured society
to the old traditions of national art, in the very days when
the German Jews of Paris were sinning so grossly against
German nationality.   Mendelssohn's noble and grand activity
showed for all time that the German Jew can attain true
fame only when he gives himself up wholly and without reserve
to German life.

Painting, too, was affected by the realistic impulse of the
day.   A long time must always elapse before the world can
recognise the limits imposed upon the talent of creative spirits.
Happy is the artist who, like Schiller, after the production
of raw and immature works, can strive steadily upwards,
attaining to an ever freer development of his genius, to depart
as soon as the nation begins to understand him fully.   Different
and tragical was the destiny of Cornelius.   Impetus, nobility,
greatness, a world of new ideas, were infused by him into

the petrified graphic arts. The Germans looked upon him as a second Goethe ; King Louis was almost inclined to regard him as a greater painter than those of the cinquecento ; in 1831, when he returned from Italy, the artists of Munich received him as if he had been a prince, detaching the horses from his carriage, and drawing it themselves in triumph through the town. But to this excess of esteem a reversal was to succeed. Cornelius was no more than the Klopstock of our new painting, more richly endowed, doubtless, and more forcible than the writer of the *Messiah*, but like Klopstock rather a pioneer than one of those who complete their work, and, unfortunately there was no Goethe to follow in his footsteps, no one to gather in the focus of a single burning glass all the rays of the newly discovered light. He lacked the true imagination of the painter, unrestrained delight in the play of form and colour. The first thing to enter his mind was always a great poetic thought, and not till then did he seek to discover the forms in which he might incorporate this freely created ideal. For this reason he lacked humour, and for the same reason feminine beauty had comparatively little charm for him, since this beauty rarely gives expression to ideas. He could teach little, for he despised the rules of technique that can be conveyed by teaching, and it was impossible for him to communicate to lesser spirits the essential charm of his works, the power of his great personality. Thus did he pursue his career, a serious little man with the vigorous head of a thinker, idolised by his pupils, but fully understood by few. It was a saying of his, "Nature is the wife, the genius is the man," but he was a masterful husband, and it did not suit him to immerse himself lovingly in the life of his wife. Those who painted simply and truly, but were unable to accept his grandiose conception of the cooperation of all the arts, were despised by the proud master as "men of one groove." Since he continued to look upon the Bavarians as savages, what did it matter to him that he never felt truly at home in Munich? What cared he for the censure of the French, who reproached him with being a poet merely, and not a genuine painter? The French were foreigners, and therefore incapable of understanding German art.

Such was his mood when he received the commission to decorate the new church of St. Louis with frescoes, and the artist at once conceived the design for a third great picture cycle which was to outdo the two first, which was to be a Christian epic, a painted Divine Comedy. Much of his draft was vetoed by the master-builder. What remained was still magnificent enough, and it was above all in the picture of the last judgment, the largest fresco in the world, that Cornelius hoped to display the spirit of enlightened Christianity. A quarter of a century earlier, when, in Rome, he had still been an enthusiast among the young Nazarenes, he might perhaps have attained success with such a production, might have achieved a work as strong in its simplicity, as profound in its faith, as Memling's last judgment in the church of St. Mary at Danzig. Since then, however, he had experienced an extensive cultural development, traversing the world of Faust, of the Niebelungen, of Homer, passing through the entire domain of the history of art. How could he now throw himself wholeheartedly into a conception which, of all the Christian myths, is the most alien to the modern mind—for however notably the sense of responsibility before God may become accentuated with the ripening of civilisation, it is no less certain that the separation of the goats from the sheep and the graphic depiction of the punishments of hell must appear childish to an experienced and cultured century. Cornelius' genius was wrecked upon this anachronism. His work was more pious, was richer in religious sentiment, than the kindred paintings by Michelangelo and Rubens, neither of which represented anything more than a struggle of titans; and for this very reason it failed to attain the elemental sublimity of the one, or the material strength of the other. On this occasion even his well-tried talent for composition, his wonderful gift for representing a great event exhaustively in a few figures, failed; the picture fell into groups, and though some of the angelic and saintly personalities still displayed the old greatness, the arch-fiend and his servitors could awaken no horror.

The whole undertaking was ill-omened. The cheerful artistic activity which had once filled with bustle the painters' scaffolds of the Glyptothek, was not renewed in the church of St. Louis. The royal master-builder could not conceal his disappointment when he looked upon the unsuccessful and ill-painted picture, and he said sharply, "A painter ought to be able to paint." Remote were now the days when Crown Prince Louis had modestly said to Ludwig Tieck: "You too are called 'Louis.' It is a great honour to me to bear the same name as a distinguished poet." Since he had worn the crown his feeling of self-complacency had greatly increased ; even as artist he imagined himself the equal of his painters and sculptors, since his poor works had found so many flattering admirers. Cornelius was not the man to accept contumelious treatment. Shortly after this manifestation of royal displeasure he left Munich for ever, and his school disappeared with him. His lofty idealism was no longer in harmony with the new time.

More in tune with the times, and more congenial to Treitschke, were the realists of the Berlin school, like Eduard Meyerheim.

He lived in Berlin, entirely devoted to his easel and to music ; during the summer faring on foot through the mountains of Thuringia or the Harz region, collecting there his materials among the petty bourgeois and the peasants. A man of tenderer feelings than are usual to-day, but free from false sentimentality, he loved to depict the grace and the kindliness which animate the simple folk-life, and those who visited exhibitions soon found his homelike pictures almost as indispensable as readers of that day found stories of village life. Franz Krüger, on the other hand, moved in the upper levels of society. The artist of the world of fashion, he painted princes and courtiers as admirably as he painted their fine horses, but truly and faithfully, with that joy in the real which Chodowiecki had first aroused among the painters of Berlin. In the great pictures of military reviews which the court commissioned him to do, he had to deal with the most refractory of conceivable material, the straight lines of grenadiers with their hideous tunics and stiff stocks, the tall plumed hats of the generals and the docked tails of their horses. Yet how rich, significant, and pithy did his paintings seem. What an abundance of

life was there in the history of Prussia if you only knew how
to get hold of it.   No one was better aware of this than young
Adolf Menzel, who was still comparatively unnoted.   His
genius was to complete what the Berlin realists, Chodowiecki
and Krüger, had begun.   Pictures of manners and review
pictures were to be succeeded by pictures of heroic incidents
in Prussian history.

The same Prussian pride glowed in the heart of Rauch.
Long ago the days of disaster and the subsequent marvellous
resurgence had moved him to the depths of the soul.   It was
always like a breath of fresh life to him when in brass or
in marble he could commemorate the men who had participated
in these struggles.   He spoke of his noble handicraft as the
true historical art, and was fond of recalling Goethe's saying,
" Man's best monument is man himself."   Even in Schleiermacher's ugly head he was able to see and reproduce the
living, the immortal element.   He had made himself intimately
familiar with the lineaments of the king, who became ever
dearer to him as a man ;   one bust of Frederick William
followed another, while the sculptor, simply for his own
gratification, reproduced his memorial of Queen Louise.   No
labour seemed to him too trifling if done for the sake of
Prussia.   Again and again he shaped the eagle for the gates
of fortresses and for the pillars of bridges, until at length
the   beloved   heraldic   bird   secured   perfect   monumental
representation.   It was he who designed the embellished death's
head for the busby of the   black hussars   He was delighted
to accept a commission from the town of Gumbinnen to carve
the statue of Frederick William I, for it gave him immense
pleasure that in the grateful eastern march he could reproduce
the strict soldier-king in his human worth as " the restorer
of Lithuania."   But he was too much the classicist to feel
entirely at home in this shapeless northern world.   His favourite
memories were of Italy, of those happy days of youth when
the new Teutonic migration had been attracted to the eternal
city for the rescue of a degenerating art, just as of old for
the rescue of a degenerating church.   What an expansion of
mind he had experienced roaming among the statues of the

Vatican, or when admiring in Carrara the snow-white peaks thrusting upwards like sugar loaves into the blue sky and when, in the company of his friend Tieck, clambering through the rifts in search of the finest marble.

Herein lies the rarely understood but splendid beauty of modern German history, that all the little streamlets of tribal history, as if impelled by a mysterious force of nature, gradually coalesced to form a single stream, until ultimately every part of the nation came to share in the greatness of the fatherland. Certainly as the south excelled the north in imaginative and poetic energy, no less certainly were the North Germans in advance of the highlanders in intellectual power and in the art of sculpture. The Low Germans, Winckelmann and Carstens, Schinkel and Rauch, were the first to awaken in Germany a sense for the formal beauties of the classical antique, their nearest collaborators in this field being Thorwaldsen, the kindred Dane, and Zoega the archæologist, a Holsteiner. In Berlin, Rauch was never happier than when with Wilhelm Humboldt, his loyal patron since Roman days, or when with Schinkel—for all three were firm believers in the affinity of the Hellenic with the Teutonic genius. It was his pride that Prussia did more than any other state for the study of the antique. He eagerly promoted the establishing of the new collections of casts at the universities of Bonn, Königsberg, and Breslau ; and he had an extensive supply of marble blocks brought to Berlin.

As he grew older his pleasure in classical forms increased. With ecstatic delight, therefore, did he accept a commission from King Louis to adorn the Ratisbon Walhalla with six colossal Victories. At last he could throw into the corner "the everlasting trousers" of the statues of Prussian commanders, and feast his eyes upon "the noble nude." These magnificent female forms remained the joy of his life for years. But he still had time to spare for the realistically conceived Dürer monument at Nüremberg ; whilst with touching simplicity he incorporated Christ's saying, "Suffer little children to come unto me," in the Halle statue of the pious Francke. On one occasion he was somewhat influenced by echoes of romanticism, when he produced the charming statuette of the

Virgin of Tangermünde riding on the stag. His powers ripened slowly, and did not attain full development until he was sixty years of age. Each new work was meticulously prepared, as if it had been the first. When travelling he noted every shapely tree, every graceful hill, and grew unhappy only when darkness fell. When visiting his daughter in Halle, he never failed to model reliefs to adorn the walls of the hall, making a plastic album which was to remind her of her father's life and thought. For him art was all in all. He felt like a king in his own kingdom. He was the cynosure of every eye when in winter, wrapped in his light-coloured voluminous cloak, he stalked majestically down the lime-tree avenue. Under his firm guidance the Berlin school of sculpture led the world for a generation. Many able artists, almost all born in northern and central Germany, issued from its portals. Among these may be mentioned Drake from "the little home of genius" in Waldeck which had been Rauch's own birthplace and that of Kaulbach and Bunsen; Kiss, Bläser, Wolff; and, excelling all the others, Ernst Rietschel of Electoral Saxony, a man of gentle and romantic disposition who was first introduced by Rauch to the antique world, and who soon became the master's favourite pupil.

How poor, when contrasted with this classic realism of the Berlin school, seems the crudity of Schwanthaler. He was and remained a romanticist. No one could fail to recognise this who saw him in his eyrie at Schwaneck, overhanging the Isar, where he lived like a mediæval knight. To him the self-denying industry which the severities of classical sculpture imposed upon its pupils was unknown. In the plastic arts of Munich, the sole truly living department was that of foundry. When Miller became director of the foundry it acquired world-wide fame, even the bronze doors for the capital at Washington being ordered from this distant spot.

It was fortunate for Rauch that the Bavarians gave him so much to do. Prussia had now to be sparing in her commissions, for the war preparations had swallowed all available means, and the little that still remained for artistic ends had to be mainly devoted to the completion of the museum.

This building provided Schinkel with another task worthy of his genius. In most of his previous achievements he had reluctantly had recourse to the vanity of ornamentation. He knew that the architectural works of his beloved ancients owed their majesty, not solely to nobility of form, but also to the chaste elegance of the raw material. Since the state finances were not equal to the purchase of freestone, he returned to the popular and natural architecture of the plains, and in the Berlin academy of architecture produced a fine example of unadorned brickwork, which since then has flourished once more in its old North German home. It was perhaps the most distinctive of his works, a mighty block, defiant as the mediæval palaces of Florence, and yet full of grace. The walls were dull red, relieved with stripes of blue brickwork, an entirely new scheme in these days when a colour sense had been lost; while terra-cotta decorations in the classical style harmoniously surmounted the wide windows.

Apart from these two buildings, lesser works only were entrusted to Schinkel, and it was a great distress to him that the difficulties of the time should thus have clipped his pinions. The victory of Hellenic civilisation over the darkness of the primeval age, which he depicted in his designs for the atrium of the museum, was for him the essential content of history. But even in less ambitious works he remained ever true to his saying: "Art is nothing unless it be new; those who aspire will never fail to create something truly living." If commissioned to build a church for the Berlin suburb of Moabit, or for Darkehmen, a remote Lithuanian town, he invariably endeavoured to solve the problem in a new manner, asking himself how the practical needs of the Protestant ritual might be harmonised with the laws of beauty, and it is manifest that his answers were most successful when he had recourse to southern styles. Gothic was alien to this Protestant Hellene. In the sober Werdersche church in Berlin there was little trace of the heaven-storming and rapturous mysticism of Gothic. When planning a château in the centre of a green park, Schinkel's imagination was indefatigable in its inventiveness, for, now a thorough Teuton, he felt that supreme beauty was attained only when the works of man fitted perfectly into natural surroundings. Some of these buildings, like the charming Villa Charlottenhof, were finished by his own hand; others, such as the châteaux of Babelsberg and Camenz, were completed by other architects; but the majority of his essays in this field, like the marvellously beautiful design for the castle of Orianda, were never carried out. He wished to demolish the library in the Opernplatz in Berlin, and to replace it by a fine palace for Prince William, but the prince's means were restricted, and Schinkel had to allow his friend Langhanns to build in the corner of the square a palace which, though finely conceived, was of extremely modest proportions. No more than a fraction of his colossal energies bore fruit in German life. Down to the days of 1848 the after effects of his genius could still be traced in new churches and museums, and also in many of the pleasant country houses which, as general prosperity came, sprang up in the neighbourhood of large towns. But the quiet and peaceful generation to which he had devoted his labours passed away, and the new epoch of clamorous commerce, of railway stations, exhibitions, and banks, imposed upon architecture tasks of an entirely new character.

For all the restrictions by which it was hampered, Schinkel's work had a far profounder influence upon national life than had the febrile architectural activity of the court of Munich. In Gärtner, from Rhineland, King Louis had at length found an architect after his own heart, a nimble and hasty artist, ever ready to produce all that the impatient employer demanded. In rapid succession were now erected the romanticist structures of the Ludwigsträsse, cold and uninspiring for the most part, although the great staircase of the library is not without artistic charm. Fortunately at one end of the desert street was the gate of victory modelled upon the arch of Constantine, whilst at the other end was a somewhat unsuccessful imitation of the Florentine Loggia dei Lanzi, which, however, from a distance had a stately appearance. The street was spoken of as "the Gallery of Bavarian Generals," statues of Tilly and Wrede being erected there—but the name gave much amusement to neighbours, for Tilly was no Bavarian, and Wrede was no general. Nowhere was the artificiality of this monumental art upon a soil without a history more painfully displayed than in the bronze obelisk commemorative of the thirty thousand Bavarian soldiers who had perished in Russia. This was a masterpiece of the founder's art. On each face of the pedestal was a ram's head, while the inscription read : " They too died for the liberation of the fatherland." But the citizens of Munich who knew nothing about the Roman battering ram, enquired with pardonable astonishment why their ruler had thought of doing honour to his valiant warriors by depicting four large sheeps' heads ; whilst when Czar Nicholas viewed the obelisk, King Louis had need of all his eloquence to persuade the Russian that the inscription really had some meaning. Nevertheless, Ziebland's basilica of St. Bonifacius and Ohlmüller's Gothic church in the Au suburb showed that the architectural academy of Munich was likewise competent to train sound talent. Many of the art-loving king's undertakings which seemed strange to his contemporaries were justified in after days, when commerce grew and when stately mansions clustered round these fine buildings.

Historians and Natural Philosophers (V, 568–90)

Literature and the fine arts were unable to escape the morbid moods of the epoch, but science continued to preserve the pith of German genius almost unimpaired. It now simultaneously took up the heritage of the great traditions of the classical and of the romantic epoch, and the distorted evolution of our people, descending from the clouds to reality, is witnessed by the fact that in the domain of political history Germans studied the achievements of other nations at a time when the simple efficiency of Prussian statecraft (poor indeed, as yet, in striking successes) had not been sufficiently recognised either at home or abroad. Leopold Ranke, meanwhile, had set out on his travels. In Vienna he made the acquaintance of Gentz, and was confirmed in the view that the state is in the first instance power, and that dominion over Europe is exercised by a concert of the great powers. While at Vienna, freshly influenced by the memoranda and conversations of Wuk, the Serbian patriot, he wrote the *History of the Serbian*

Revolution, a model of vivid narration, giving actuality to the remote and the distant, perfectly free from the cumbrousness of German professorial learning, and yet soundly critical. He next removed to Rome, and in that city, where the art and the archæology of the Germans had created new life, research into modern history was also to find its fountain of youth. In the sixteenth and seventeenth centuries, which long remained Ranke's chosen field of work, papal policy had still been world-embracing. From Rome and Venice he could survey the changes in international relationships, if not completely, at least with an approximation to completeness, and the treasures collected in Italian archives formed the basis of his incomparable diplomatic learning. Thus equipped, he produced the finest of his works, the *History of the Popes*, a book that only a German could have written, and among the Germans Ranke alone. The many-sidedness of his knowledge and his insight was dependent upon a brilliant power of concentration which in most cases is found only in men of unsociable and adamantine disposition. But Ranke from the first combined with a lively and receptive spirit an unruffled calm which enabled him to face what was happening with the same equanimity as if it had already happened. When a lad at Schulpforte he had had a close view of the battles of Grossgörschen and Leipzig, not regarding them unfeelingly, and yet unaffected by the ardent patriotic enthusiasm which at that day led so many young Electoral Saxons to fight in the allied ranks. Through the partition of Saxony he became a Prussian subject, and gratefully recognised the order, justice, and culture of the state in which he was newly enrolled ; but the blunt Prussian manner, the characteristic mentality of the Brandenburgers, was as foreign to him as the Prussian sense of the state ; and in so far as in his thoroughly independent outlook on German history traces of old traditions can be recognised, they lead back to Electoral Saxony, not to Prussia. Thus his choice of profession was determined, not by direct experience of life as in the case of notable men in general, but by a direct process of ratiocination. Having read numberless historical works, in the fulness of knowledge he resolved to show the world the reality of historical life, purely, authoritatively, and definitely, so that his own personality should completely disappear behind the picture.

When he began the *History of the Popes* he took a very low estimate of the power of the Vatican at that particular time. "The relationships of papal authority to ourselves," he writes laconically, "no longer exercises any important influence. The days when we had occasion to feel alarm have passed away, and we are convinced that we are absolutely secure." This was an error which Ranke shared with all his contemporaries. In later years he retracted it, and admitted that a new epoch of the papacy had begun. But it was precisely to this happy feeling of security that his book owed its artistic charm. With a freedom from prejudice incomparable in the ever-contentious field of religious history, he described the great tragedy of the counter-reformation, for the first time applying Niebuhr's critical method to the study of modern history. Whether he was freely surveying the widely ramified plans of the papacy, or with fine, clear-cut strokes was depicting the good and the evil done by individual men, with everything in the historical world, great and small alike, he was equally at home. For the first time since the publication of Schiller's vigorous historical portraits did a German historian again produce pictures of living men, but these were not now merely the work of artistic imagination, but were based upon detailed knowledge. Behind the graceful narrative lay a profundity akin to the spirit of Goethe. We are reminded of that master, not only by a delight in the world, a conviction that nothing human is alien, but also by the fundamentally scientific outlook from which all historical activities are regarded as due to the interplay between general conditions and free individual energies. This book actually demonstrates what Goethe had once undertaken to show when returning from Rome, "how from the conjunction of necessity and freewill, of impulse and desire, of action and reaction, a tertium quid energies which is neither art nor nature, and yet is both at once; simultaneously necessary and accidental, purposive and blind."

It was not by chance that this first classic work on history to emanate from new Germany should deal with universal

history. The time had not yet come for a national history
on the grand scale. Generally recognised political ideals were
still lacking, nor did there as yet exist any secure instinct
of unassailable national pride, permeating flesh and blood.
The free cosmopolitan sentiments of the German imagination,
in accordance with which everything great in other ages and
nations was considered as the property of the modern German,
now manifested its power in the field also of political
historiography. Since other talented historians followed Ranke's
example, foreigners speedily came to assume that every vigorous
learned man of German birth who wrote about another nation
was likewise familiar with this foreign nationality, whereas
throughout the foreign world there was but one man, Thomas
Carlyle, who understood German history. Germany, wrote
Emerson, thinks for Europe ; these semi-Greeks grasp the
science of all other peoples. Ranke's work was the first to
secure world-wide renown for German historians. Niebuhr's
Roman History had aroused enthusiasm in none but philologians
who live in a cosmopolitan atmosphere ; but now a thorough
modern, Macaulay, one who neither knew nor loved Germany,
expressed his admiration.

At home approval was by no means unqualified. People
of high culture and men with much knowledge of the world
were able to appreciate the historian's distinguished calm. But
not merely did common radicals, to whom nothing but crude
bias was welcome, rail against him for his detachment ; even
unprejudiced young men like Gustav Freytag felt wounded in
their Teutonic sensibilities, and rightly so. They perceived
obscurely that this book, perfect as a work of art, nevertheless
lacked perfection in the matter of historic truth ; they recognised
that the moral world would go down hopelessly to destruction
were all men to think after the fashion of this distinguished
observer. The historian and the philosopher, unlike the learned
in any other sphere, are enabled by their science to comprehend
man as a whole. Ranke seldom availed himself of this splendid
privilege. Not only did he, with few exceptions, reserve his
own moral judgment; but so thoroughly did he immerse himself
in the mental atmosphere of the time he was describing, that
many of his characterisations produced the impression that

two cunning seventeenth century monsignori were mutually introducing one another. It was with reluctance that he looked down into the lower levels of society from the courts where he had acquired his knowledge of diplomacy. Yet it is beyond question that the reextinction in so many noble nations of the light of gospel truth was effected, not by the diplomatic arts of clever cardinals, but by the rude forces of stupidity, superstition, custom, and hatred, working among the blind masses, forces which proved ready instruments in the hands of the statesmen of the Vatican. Ranke was inclined to overlook these instinctive and elemental forces of history. Neither the raging outbursts of the murderous bands of St. Bartholomew's night, nor the fanatical " ni olvido ni perdon " of the Spanish soldiery, was introduced by him directly beneath the eyes of his readers. He failed to show why Martin Luther was compelled to regard the crowned priest as antichrist. Even the essential irrationality of the Jesuit order, which in the end brought inevitable destruction upon all the states in which it became dominant, was not exhibited with sufficient clearness. Thus the serious question why brute force had been able to secure a partial victory over the ideal was not completely answered.

While at work upon his history of the popes, Ranke himself became aware that the book failed to give due weight to the moral superiority of Teutonic Protestantism, and he was already entertaining the design of writing a new history, the counterpart of the first, which was to deal with the great epoch of the opening of the German reformation. He knew how much more difficult would be this task. Referring on one occasion to a book by Augustin Thierry, Ranke said that the Germans were not competent to produce such a work, for it was obviously easier for Frenchmen to grasp the full significance of their country's past. But he believed that he would be able to make up for the lack of patriotic passion by the warmth of his religious sentiments. Meanwhile he resumed his lectures at Berlin, founding there the first of those historic seminaries which since then, further developed by his pupils, have encouraged at all our universities the methodical study of original documents. His school became the nursery of a new generation of historians. Waitz, Sybel, and many other aspiring men of talent, followed in his train ; and even the smaller fry soon proved unable to elude the influence of his creative spirit. Since Stein's enterprise, the great collection of the *Monumenta Germaniæ*, had made rapid progress under the guidance of Pertz, Ranke urged the younger historians to work up the raw material, and with the *Annals of the German Realm under the Saxon House* there began a long series of exhaustive treatises which placed the facts of our mediæval history upon a far more stable footing than had been possible to Raumer.

The free spirit now prevailing among historians at length began also to permeate political science. It was time, for the pupils of Niebuhr, Savigny, and Eichhorn had almost without exception devoted themselves to philology or to the history of law, and for this reason the pioneer conceptions of the historical jurists long remained entirely unknown to the professionals of political science. Liberal sociologists were content to graze upon the communal pastures of natural law, and boasted of progress when they were in the toils of reaction. What a wealth of commonplaces was brought to market by Pölitz in his book upon constitutionalist life. All earthly existence was subsumed by him in " the two ideas of religion and civism "; and the freedom of the citizen could be guaranteed in no other way than by " written charters "— for it was impossible to get on without a scrap of paper. Even more hopeless seemed the scientific errancy of German liberalism in the *Staatslexikon* which Rotteck and Welcker had been editing since the year 1834. The well-planned and ably edited undertaking numbered among its contributors almost all the notabilities of South German liberalism, and many North Germans as well. Its vogue in middle-class circles was even more extensive than that which had previously been secured by Rotteck's *Universal History*. How much easier to read than a detailed historical disquisition were these brief articles arranged in the convenient alphabetical order which the Brockhaus encyclopædia had already made palatable to the great reading public. The bourgeois of sound views had merely to look up the key-word in order to learn without further trouble what he ought to think about every political or religious question. No objection could possibly be raised to the infallible accuracy of this oracle. In the preface Rotteck succinctly undertook "to elucidate those doctrines alone whose rejection must be regarded as a manifestation of illwill."

In the library of every diet, in every editorial office, and in every private study, the long series of volumes of the *Staatslexikon* graced the shelves; but the crown prince of Prussia and his romanticists' friends henceforward used the term "Rotteck-Welcker" as an abusive denomination for all aberrations of the zeitgeist. There were a few excellent articles in the compilation, and above all two good essays on economics by List and Mathy; but the fundamental conception was untenable and obsolete; the impassioned and verbose introductions by the two editors sang in all cases the old song of the only true law of reason, revealed by the French Revolution, and to which positive and historical law were now at length to give place. Even in the historical articles the spirit of liberal philistinism paraded with as much self-complacency as if Niebuhr had never lived. Like a parsimonious paterfamilias lecturing a prodigal son, Kobb, the Palatine radical, lectured Frederick the Great for having wasted so much blood and treasure in the conquest of Silesia. While such a work might well gain new adherents for the liberal party, it could do little to further the political culture of the nation, and least of all in Austria, where the counterpoise of living historical science was still almost completely lacking. The average reader, always a lazy thinker, was merely confirmed in his inclination to voice in sounding catchwords his judgment upon things beyond his understanding, and was encouraged to cherish that belief in authority, a belief at once blind and opinionated, which makes the centuries of polymathy seem so much more detestable than those epochs of youthful civilisation wherein naive credulity was still well-nigh universal.

By his *Politics* (1835) Dahlmann now dragged political science from the charmed circle of the formulas of natural law. "Restoring politics to the basis and the standards of existing conditions," he at once raised the lifeless constitutionalist doctrine to the free heights which historical research had long before attained, and for the first time gave German liberalism a firm scientific foundation. Like his friend Niebuhr he rejected the fancies of natural conditions and the social contract, conceiving the state as "an original order, a necessary datum, an asset of mankind"; but whilst the historical jurists had hitherto attacked the constitutionalist state as the spawn of the illusions of natural law, Dahlmann's historical method led him to the conclusion that constitutionalist forms arose by inner necessity from the evolution of German political life. Thus was strict scientific proof at length provided for that which had been merely suggested in the political writings of the Stein period of reform. This completely new demonstration was so convincing that even Heinrich Leo, a fierce enemy of liberalism, was for a time (not, unfortunately, for always) converted, and admiringly declared, "Dahlmann was the first from whom I learned that these constitutionalist forms can embody a vigorous political life."

The bold endeavour to arrive at a historic view of the entire nature of the state was not fully successful at the outset, for political doctrine must try to discover general ideas and imperatives, whereas throughout history the incalculable freedoms of struggles for power and of the individual will are at work. Dahlmann was not always able to surmount this contradiction. Involuntarily, at times, he relapsed into the method of natural law, which regarded the living state as no more than the issue of a thought process; and although he expressly insisted that "the idealist solves riddles which he has propounded to himself," he went on to speak of constitutionalist monarchy as "the good state," thus suggesting that he himself was subject to the illusion of an absolute political ideal. In those years no thinker could as yet completely escape the persistent influences of the old philosophy of abstract right. Even of the British state, which now, as twenty years earlier, he maintained to be the model of freedom, he gave no more than an incomplete picture, for the ultra-aristocratic character of the old English methods of self-government and party rule were not as yet fully understood by any German. In the matter of the threatening social contrasts of the age, too, his judgments remained those of the self-complacent liberal bourgeoisie, for he wrote : " Almost everywhere the nucleus of the population consists of a diffused middle class, which grows continually more widely homogeneous."

These defects, however, were of trifling import when compared with the new and vivid ideas of the book. The doctrine of popular sovereignty and the fierce struggles of the day had long ere this led Rotteck's school to regard monarchical authority as nothing better than a necessary evil. But Dahlmann termed the monarchy the sole bond of custom in the world of German states, contending that for all other political elements a centre of gravity was still in process of formation. To those who sang the praises of the barricades, he said sternly : " A revolution is not merely the sign of terrible misfortunes, but is at the same time a self-imposed misfortune." He thought very little of the boasted freedom " of, if the term is to be used, constitutionalist Germany " ; and for the future estates of Prussia he demanded only such rights as would be compatible with the living monarchy. All this was written in fine, thoughtful, and impressive language, strongly reminiscent of Jacob Grimm's monumental style. Throughout there was displayed a clear recognition of the freedom of historical greatness, of the nobility of our classical culture, of those pious emotional energies which combine to maintain the state—an elevated outlook which had nothing in common with the arrogance of the enlightenment. This confession of faith of cultured liberalism first found acceptance, therefore, in the north, where monarchical sentiment remained a natural growth, and where Stein's legislation had not been forgotten. Dahlmann believed that in externals also there would be a completion of human affairs at the close of history, and this belief, which in our experienced days is cherished only by youthful enthusiasts, gave his words a proud confidence which made them irresistible to his contemporaries. Though it was more difficult for the South Germans to abandon their law of reason, in the south, too, there gradually arose a moderate liberal party which would at least hear no more of the old radical catchwords, which had outgrown talk of popular sovereignty, the social contract, and revolutionary right. Unfortunately Dahlmann's book was never finished. A taciturn man, he found writing almost more difficult than speaking, and he had no successor in his chosen field of science, for the road along which he led the way could be traversed only by men of quite unusual gifts. Down to the present day we still lack a work explaining on realist lines the whole life of the state as an issue of actual conditions, a book which deals only with demonstrable historical truths instead of with subjective political opinions.

Shortly afterwards he wrote the *History of Denmark* for the series of many volumes on the " History of European States," edited by Heeren and Ukert. Its extensive sale showed how accurately Perthes, the farseeing publisher, had gauged the newly awakened historical appetite of the day. Dahlmann's book was the pearl of the collection. Even his old enemies the Danes could not deny that the civilisations of Norway and Iceland, Denmark and Lower Saxony, had never before been subjected to so exhaustive a study, that the legal institutions which had been the outcome of the reciprocal interplay of these civilisations had never before been so thoroughly examined and so vividly described. He believed that he himself was of Swedish blood, and he had passed the greater part of his life in the frontier domain between the German and the Scandinavian worlds, so that this northern region was one in which he felt quite at home. Moreover, he was able to interweave into his narrative something of the poetic beauty of northern saga, for although with the freedom of prejudice that had been characteristic of Niebuhr he made a vigorous clearance of old traditions, he was not inclined to reject them in their entirety. Of the disputants he spoke sternly, but with a benevolent humanism, and with that genial humour which remains indispensable to the understanding of Teutonic natures. At the right moment he always took the field in person, to survey with his serious and profound gaze the upshot of the developmental process, for the historian cannot, like the epic poet, allow Nemesis free play in an imaginative fable. **The historian must candidly explain the moral significance of the confused facts with which he is dealing, and this is why** the compelling force of a historical work subsists ever in the strong personality of the narrator. This book likewise remained incomplete, and the remote topic was unattractive to the mass of the reading public.

Schlosser, in the most popular historical work of the day, the new edition of the *History of the Eighteenth Century*, exercised far greater influence upon public opinion than either Ranke or Dahlmann. In Schlosser the middle classes found what they had failed to find in the other two historians: material that was universally comprehensible; unsparing moral judgments; and the defiant Frisian spirit which, with manifest delight, "democratically utters the truth" to all the mighty ones of the earth. The terrible accusations against the sovereigns and against those miserable beings who as ministers had "displayed all the vices of ministers," pleased embittered readers, although a false picture was obviously given of a great century which had furthered civilisation precisely owing to the exercise of absolute sovereign authority, introducing reforms for which as yet there was no popular demand. Even at the courts feeling was not wholly adverse towards "the friend of mankind, the contemplative philosopher," as he loved to name himself, and the grand duchess Stephanie of Baden bestowed her favour upon him, for his continuous moral indignation was the outcome of a profound and cordial disposition, and amid the petty partisan hatreds of the day, the old blusterer continued to preserve much of the broad-minded humanity of the previous century.

Nor was any objection raised to the rough-hewn character of his presentation. On the contrary, people rather admired him for his staunch courage in declaring that he "deliberately despised" all elegance and gentleness, failing to notice how closely this rude shapelessness approximated to the frivolous disregard of form characteristic of Heinrich Heine. Schlosser, like Heine, regarded style as a cloak with which content might be invested or not at will. Neither of these writers knew what Goethe had long ago shown, that an idea which has been quietly ripening evolves the right form of expression with a certainty akin to that with which the flower evolves the fruit and that fine prose arises quite spontaneously from perfect command of the subject under discussion. Schlosser's work was formless because he scorned the self-denying industry of Ranke, and because with the aid of moral catchwords he passed facile judgments upon matters that were only half understood. The severest of his many unjust judgments were the outcome of ignorance. When he bluntly opined that the system of levying troops introduced by Frederick William I might readily have been made better and juster, he did not know what he was talking about, for he had no idea how insuperable a resistance the rude masses of the population had offered merely to the limited cantonal system. The literary sections of the book were the best, and were best liked ; and since they were the outcome of fuller knowledge, they gave expression to sounder views. It is true that in this first attempt he was not yet able to demonstrate the inward connection, the continuous interaction, of literary life and political struggles. In his treatment they are still presented as altogether independent entities. Moreover, the decisive years of his own education had been before the blossoming time of our poetry, and for this reason he placed Lessing, " the originator and perfecter of German culture," high above Schiller and Goethe, whilst he was manifestly more familiar with the writings of the Anglo-French enlightenment than with later and greater works.

Wonderful was the way in which this antediluvian book floated down the midstream of modern life. For the very reason that Schlosser always held aloof from the liberal party, his cruel and often monstrously unjust severity was regarded by his contemporaries as the impartiality of an incorruptible judge. They looked upon him as a revivalist preacher of the middle ages ; his sonorous voice had the note of a passing bell heralding the oncoming of the revolution for which so many were longing ; and although at times he would rail against " this lax and servile generation," his readers continued to derive the welcome impression that all the evils of which the writer complained were an outflow from the higher levels of society. Although he knew how to maintain the distinction between public and private morality, he pitilessly subjected all the heroes of history to the measuring rod of his Kantian private morality. The freedom of genius remained no less incomprehensible to him than the right of the saving deed ; and only to the ignoble greatness of Napoleon would he concede privileges which he denied to a Frederick. He lacked the historic insight which leads the modest thinker to recognise the mutability of human moral ideals, so that, instead of prematurely usurping the function of the eternal judge, he appraises each epoch in accordance with its own finite aims. An aristocrat in life and inclinations, Schlosser unintentionally stimulated middle-class dissatisfaction with the existing order ; despising academic professionalism, he no less unintentionally ministered to the self-conceit of the men of learning—for above the slime of princely worthlessness which he depicted for his readers, none but a few great writers rose as solitary pinnacles. Here alone did he find " truth, simplicity, tranquil life, self-control, a modest demeanour, and that virtue without which freedom remains a dream, right a shadow." Here alone did he consider himself able to breathe pure air, failing to recognise that this life of tranquil contemplation also has its arrogance, its sins and temptations, though these may seem a trifle less glaring than the sins of men of action. It was pardonable, therefore, that young Gervinus and others among Schlosser's pupils should also consider themselves enormously superior to statesmen in the field of action, so that university professors soon came to play in Germany a part similar to that played by lawyers in France, for not everyone is able as was Schlosser to master the politicians and yet with all modesty to keep out of public life. His intense moral emotion, which it was impossible to ignore, preserved German historiography from an anæmic frigidity ; but his works speedily became antiquated as soon as the agitations of the time subsided.

Now that the writing of history had regained a political complexion, it was inevitable that some historians should become shrewd political partisans. Heinrich Leo, when he had outgrown the wild radicalism of his student days, had devoted himself for a time to the Hegelian philosophy, and had then returned to the romanticist outlook which was in conformity with his temperament. His activities in Halle both as teacher and author were extremely fruitful, for he was an ardent spirit overflowing with energy, straightforward and amiable even in his insatiable pugnacity but unmeasured in all things, and so dominated by passion that despite his abundant learning whole epochs of history necessarily remained incomprehensible to him. Only in the world of the middle ages, and especially with the richly coloured life of mediæval towns, was he thoroughly well versed ; this is shown by his best work, *The History of the Italian States*, and still more plainly by his *History of the Netherlands* and by his *Universal History*. The formal purity of the antique world seemed to him soulless, whilst the centuries of modern history were in his view a period of " progressive decay," characterised by the prosaic dominance of material interests—as if it could be ignored that town life in the middle ages was likewise regulated by material interests.   Thoughtful was his description of the stormy wedded life of Germany and Italy in Hohenstaufen days : " The man, full of energy, courage, and claims ; the wife full of cunning and skill, mistress of every wile ; the two continually getting on one another's nerves, and yet inseparable." But the way in which, in modern history, the old community of destiny between the two great nations had been renewed ; the way in which the patriots on both sides of the Alps were displaying enthusiasm for like ideals ; the way in which Piedmont was becoming the Prussia of Italy—this wonderful drama was hidden from his eyes, although the curtain was already rising upon it.   In the new century he could see nothing but a manifestation of the " atomistic and mechanical tendency " ; and since he was unable to do justice to its poietic energies, all that he justly alleged against its aberrations was fruitless.   When in pithy phrases he countered over-refined sentimentalism by insisting upon the splendour of war and the indispensability of strict penal legislation, and when he did not hesitate to declare that " the spectre of vain liberty " would punish the French for the crimes of their revolution, the liberal world was of opinion that no one need pay any attention to the roaring of the Halle lion.   His challenging manner secured for him well-deserved recognition, and since he never failed to defend authority, and therefore as far as the middle ages were concerned to defend the Roman church, this loyal supporter of the Prussian monarchy was actually suspected of Catholic leanings. But, as he himself put it, he was far too untrammelled in his thoughts "to adhere to a community so encompassed with arrogance."

The ultramontanes had at length found in Friedrich Hurter the historian to represent their side of the case. His *History of Innocent III and his Contemporaries* gave such plain expression to clericalist fanaticism that Hurter's old friend Haller declared with great satisfaction that the book did not contain a single Protestant word. The church comprises everything, outside the church there is no salvation, such was his reiterated assurance. The gloomy religious frenzy of the centuries of the mendicant orders and of the inquisition was in his eyes the springtime of Christian love, and the more fiercely he attacked free culture, the more confidently did he say of his own recriminations: "This is not dogmatism or polemics; it is the judgment of history." He spent years in the preparation of this book. It furnished abundant material, but offered no penetrating criticism; notwithstanding the enormous assemblage of picturesque incidents, the treatment was clumsy and lifeless, whilst the fundamental outlook was false. Only a dull critic, one whose vision could not pierce beyond externals, could hold that the pope under whose regime the church attained the acme of its power was, for that very reason, the greatest of all the princes of the church. Innocent's crude lust of dominion was as greatly inferior to the sublime religious ideas of Gregory I or Gregory VII as it was inferior to the bold national policy of Alexander III. Moreover, when the panegyrist of Innocent lamented "the secular possessions" of the church, he was merely showing his own incapacity as a historian, for Innocent was the founder of the papal states !

This glorification of the arch-enemy of our Hohenstaufen emperors was all the more welcome to the clericals because it was the work of a highly placed Protestant divine. A chorus of approval and of mischievous delight resounded from the ultramontane camp. Möhler, of Tübingen, promptly brought the book to his lecture theatre to show his priestly auditors a sample of true historiography. The Protestants, on the other hand, at first exhibited towards their renegade co-religionist that weakly consideration which has always been the characteristic defect of Protestant religious freedom. Hurter had vainly knocked at the doors of several Catholic publishers, who had all been afraid to offend a reading public proud of its enlightenment. Perthes, on the other hand, a loyal Protestant, gave the book to the world as inconsiderately as he had in earlier days issued Stolberg's *History of Religion*, for he continued innocently to hope for an understanding between the two sister churches. In the *Berliner Jahrbücher*, Leo paid honour to the opponent of the Ghibellines. In 1834, after the first volume of the history of Innocent III had been published, Hurter's strictly Protestant fellow countrymen in Schaffhausen elected him antistes, chief pastor of the canton, whilst the Protestant faculty of the university of Basle, containing among its members such men as de Wette and Hagenbach, actually conferred upon him an honorary doctor's degree " on account of the abundant knowledge he has displayed of religious history." If Hurter had had the least understanding of the spirit of the Protestant congregational church, as an honest man it would have been impossible for him to continue for an hour to preach a faith whose fundamental truths he absolutely denied. Even Haller implored his friend to break openly with heresy, seeing that his position had become untenable; and it may well be that the old man now looked back with shame upon the days when he had himself been cowardly enough to keep his conversion a secret. But the antistes was entirely under the sway of old family traditions, the traditions of those who as bailiffs had in former days wrought havoc in the confederacy, and he had simply transferred these ideas of rulership to the church. Looking on himself as a priest, he held himself competent to exercise hierarchical authority at will, regardless of the opinions of errant members of his flock. Clumsy, unteachable, and mulish, like most of the Swiss reactionaries, he clung to his Protestant office, and continued the writing of his history, which became more fanatical with every volume. He entered into an alliance with the pope, with nuncios and bishops, with all the leaders of the clericalist party in South Germany, engaging unashamedly in ultramontane intrigues, until, after years had passed, the Protestant population displayed its hostility to behaviour which was tantamount to an impudent falsehood.

Whilst the notable political historians first approached German affairs by devious paths, through the domain of universal history, Jacob Grimm's attention was wholly devoted to the homeland, for he guarded the treasures of our primal age as a pious priest guards a sacred relic. He desired "to encourage more elevated ideas of the fatherland, whose tongue, laws, and antiquities are far from being adequately esteemed," foreseeing that "the future will take revenge upon the present for any contempt of primitive times." He had therefore demonstrated to his countrymen that "our forefathers spoke a well-constructed speech and had excellent legal institutions." Now, in *German Mythology* (1835), the third of his pioneer works, he showed that they had also been "filled with the happy belief in God and gods," and that they had "not abased themselves before idols and wooden images." Never before had he written so movingly. It gave pleasure to his amiable mind to rebuild where ignorant rationalist criticism had demolished. He knew that belief in the gods was the basis of all saga, and that saga is perpetually reborn, whereas history is invariably new, and never repeats itself. He was the first to recognise that, after the conversion of the Teutons, Christianity, wishing to dispel pagan ideas, had endeavoured to conceal paganism under Christian forms, and that for this reason many of the old pagan beliefs persisted in distorted guise throughout the middle ages, as a belief in witchcraft and in the devil, and further that the sacred figures of Christian belief were likewise indued with many of the attributes of the ancient gods, so that Freya lived on in Mary, Thor in Peter, the Æsir in the apostles. Thus by his comprehensive study of pagan and Christian traditions was he enabled to reconstruct an accurate picture of the Teutonic pantheon, and to demonstrate that whilst the gods of our ancestors are obscurer figures, less shapely and more fantastical than the gods of Olympus, yet our mythology was superior to classical mythology through the persistence of a living belief in a continued existence after death and in the moral responsibility of mortals. He showed, likewise, that it was superior through its kinship with Christianity, and superior through its frank naturalness, for how much more homely and congenial are the dwarfs, elves, and giants of the Germans than the respectable and artistically decked nymphs, cabiri, and cyclops. He objected to any learned attempts at systematisation in this world of live figures, which had filled a daring race of heroes with joy in victory and contempt for death. He would not permit the imputation of pantheism to our fathers, for they had venerated many gods of varying strength and dignity ; nor would he admit the charge of dualism, for in this hopeful creed the gentle and kindly gods were enormously preponderant.

No other nation now possesses so vivid and so solidly grounded a conception of the mental life of its primitive forefathers. Equally incomparable in world literature was the essay, *The Diversity in the Structure of Languages*, the last work of Wilhelm Humboldt, wherein the brilliant forces of two epochs, the philosophic universality characteristic of the eighteenth century and the strict study of detail characteristic of the nineteenth, are united even more happily than they had been in the *Essay concerning the Task of the Historian*. In this work, which touches upon the profoundest riddles of existence, Humboldt sketched in bold antitheses a philosophic and historical picture of the nature of man, the subject which had occupied his mind throughout life. He showed that man is man solely through language, but is certainly not the creator of language, for he must be man before he could become competent to discover language. He showed that the enigma of language does not lie in speaking but in understanding, and that the enigma can only be grasped when we recognise that " I " and " thou " are in truth identical concepts. He showed that language is simultaneously foreign to the soul and subject to the soul, dependent upon the laws of thought and nevertheless free, seeing that the contradictory, though it cannot be thought, may be uttered. He showed how the organism of language is fashioned by the entire nation, whereas civilisation is fashioned by individuals, so that language is simultaneously national and individual, dominated by the remote past and yet renewed from moment to moment, not a work but an activity, progressing as a rule by gradations, but advancing suddenly on occasions owing to the direct creative energy of genius which is no less powerful in nations as a whole than it is in individuals. He showed how language may be scientifically treated as composed of mere signs of ideas, but that it may also be treated as a living entity, as an expression of all the experiences which demand the undivided application of human energy, and that all the true culture of our generation therefore is founded upon poetry, philosophy, and history.

Years before, old Blumenbach had given the materialists a knock-down blow by the simple observation, "Why can't the monkey speak? Because it has nothing to say." What is enunciated here as a mere witty hint, was definitely proved by Humboldt, namely, that language is directly given to consciousness in association with reason, that the concept cannot be detached from the word, and that differences of language inevitably imply differing outlooks on the world. With his incomparable wealth of linguistic knowledge, he then proceeded to show in detail how through the verb thought becomes reality, and how a relative clause merely expresses the quality of a substantive, and so on—enunciating creative ideas which for a long time to come were to be guiding principles in comparative philology. This was the last heritage of that magnificent German idealism which had illumined the days of Weimar and Jena. Humboldt died on April 8, 1835, before he had completed his work upon the Kavi language to which the before-mentioned essay was to serve as introduction. The sufferings of his last illness were borne with serene composure. Close to his château, he had years before prepared a beautiful resting place for his wife and his old teacher Kunth on the hill overlooking the blue waters of Lake Tegel. The quiet place is surrounded by pines, and from a slender column a marble statue of Hope (the work of Thorwaldsen) gazes down upon the ivy-clad tombs. Here, too, the great Hellene of German descent was buried.

A generation had passed since the sap had again begun to rise in the tree of historical research, and yet this tree was still continuing with inexhaustible energy to throw out fresh shoots. There had just originated two additional and independent sciences, for Schnaase had undertaken to represent the history of art in its entirety, considered as a complete and necessary development, whilst Gervinus was performing the same task for the history of German literature. In the interim, classical philology had also entered a new domain with the *Corpus Inscriptionum Graecarum* which had been in course of issue since 1824 under the editorship of Böckh. Even during the Napoleonic wars, when Prussian finances were at such a low ebb, Frederick William had approved the expenditure upon this undertaking, for the study of the antique world was ever dear to his heart. For the first time, now, did the life of ancient Greece become personally, directly, and vividly comprehensible to moderns, comprehensible in its everyday activities, and in the multiplicity of its dialects, whose existence can be inferred merely, not directly recognised, in the study of standard classical literature. Yet more vivid became the picture of ancient life when Böckh, in his metrological investigations, discovered the oriental origin of the Hellenic systems of measurement and coinage, thus furnishing a precise demonstration of the connection between western and eastern civilisation, which had been merely a dream vision on the minds of Creuzer and the symbolists. In Böckh's intelligence, a sober mathematical sense was associated with a liberal sentiment for beauty, which even enabled him to appreciate the dithyrambic impetus of Pindar.

These bold voyages of discovery made by " practical philologists " were regarded with increasing concern by the old Greek scholar Gottfried Hermann. It seemed to him as if a raging stream were breaking into the peaceful world of criticism and grammar. He was willing to admit that many areas had been fruitfully irrigated, but the country as a whole was made uninhabitable! The members of his school felt that their ancient possessions were being threatened, and they attacked the historians of philology with unjustified venom, for the two tendencies, far from being mutually exclusive, were mutually explanatory.   Gradually, however, quite contrary to the master's intention, they succumbed to an uninspired micrology.   Classical teaching at the gymnasia began to suffer. Many pedagogues of the Leipzig school came to regard the Homeric poems as merely a means of instruction, to be used in illustrating the grammatical rules of elision, crasis, and the iota subscriptum.   By the end of the thirties it was already plain that pupils were ceasing to take delight in the classical world.   Thus the old and strong foundations of German education began to totter at the very time when the natural sciences were blossoming, and when the interests of an expanding economic system were imperiously demanding new cultural materials.

When Lejeune-Dirichlet, the Rhinelander, went to the university in 1822, he was forced to go to Paris, for in all Germany there was but one mathematician competent to meet his extensive claims, and this one, Gauss, scorned to teach. How different was it now ; how many brilliant men had devoted themselves to the study of all branches of exact science since Alexander Humboldt's return to Germany.   The reign of the abstract natural philosophers was over.   In 1827, in a final outburst, they visited their spleen upon the physicist Ohm.   He had aroused the anger of the *Jahrbücher für wissenschaftliche Kritik*, because the well-assured data of his theory of galvanism were incompatible with the cobwebs of the Hegelian system, and for this reason he was so contumeliously treated by the Hegelians of the ministry of education that, taking offence, he relinquished his teaching post in Cologne. Since then the pride of the young natural philosophers who had assembled under Humboldt's banner had notably increased. They rejoiced to feel themselves the bearers of assured knowledge, demonstrable in its entirety, and, whilst they mocked at the arbitrary constructions of the abstract philosophers, these latter, for the most part, were afraid to retaliate by open attack.   Hendrik Steffens, who taught natural philosophy after the manner of Schelling, was, indeed, summoned to Berlin because the crown prince wished to withdraw him from the odious disputes of the old Lutherans in Breslau.   His princely patron believed that "such a man as Steffens needs for his own advantage to live in the capital, whilst in him the capital will acquire one who ought to be numbered among the distinguished teachers at the university." [1] But the influence of this enthusiast upon Berlinese science remained trifling, although his eloquence drew large audiences. It sounded like a mournful farewell from the old to the new time when in the year 1837, at the examination for the doctorate, Steffens said of the young geologist Beyrich : " The answers indicate that the candidate has paid more attention to objects than he has to the absolute." The other examiners did not join in this censure, for every one of them had by this time come over to the heretical view that for the student of nature the formulation of ideas concerning the absolute must be deferred until objects have been studied.

How radically this new science was destined to transform all national customs could already be recognised in the youthful manufacturing industry of Germany. In the year 1785 the first steam engine entirely constructed by Germans was erected at the Hettstedt copper mines in County Mansfeld. Now, in most branches of industry, steam power was indispensable to large-scale manufacture, and even agriculture had long ere this begun to realise the vivifying energy of the new discovery. During the lifetime of Frederick the Great, Marggraf, the Berlin chemist, had produced sugar from beetroot, but the new discovery was first turned to practical account at the opening of the nineteenth century. By the year 1840, within the area of the customs union there were 145 beet sugar refineries, whose annual yield from 4,800,000 cwt. of beetroot was more than 248,000 cwt of sugar. Professional economists, all of whom were still in the trammels of English theory and were unwittingly defending the interests of British commercial policy, made loud complaints concerning this artificially fostered industry. But the Magdeburg beet growers were delighted at the increasing return from their lands, whilst consumers were pleased at the fall in the price of sugar, and soon, too, people were to realise that in times of activity

---

[1] Crown Prince Frederick William to Altenstein, October 23 and December 30, 1831 ; January 15, 1832.

one discovery invariably leads to another. Since the sugar beet sends its roots to a depth almost four times as great as wheat, the cultivators had to plough their land much deeper, and the inference was soon obvious that if grain growers were to follow the good example they would be able, without exhausting the soil, to exploit its energies more thoroughly.

The great age of natural research now dawning was hailed by Alexander Humboldt with almost youthful optimism. It was during these years that he wrote his volumes upon Central Asia, which happily supplemented Ritter's Asiatic researches. Now, too, he was preparing his *Cosmos*. In Paris and in Berlin this old man of world-wide renown sat among the students to learn from Hase, Champollion, and Boeckh what he still needed to know in the domain of historical philology. Throughout he remained an ever-ready patron of aspiring talent. It was through his advocacy that Justus Liebig gained entry to Gay-Lussac's laboratory. Here the ardent and impassioned young Hessian learned to revere the real. Shaking off the arrogance of abstract natural philosophy, on his return to Giessen in 1826 he furnished chemistry, which in Germany hardly ranked as a science and was left to the apothecaries, with a new method. His pupils were to learn, not in the lecture theatre, but by experiment, at the furnace, and with their retorts. Restricted at the outset almost exclusively to his own scanty means, but subsequently assisted by the Hessian government, he established the first generally accessible chemical laboratory, which soon procured a European reputation for the little university of Giessen. At a considerably later date Liebig's intimate friend, Wöhler, found in Göttingen a fairly adequate centre for his investigations. Prussia, on the other hand, lagged behind in the study of chemistry, for the thrifty system which had rendered it possible to maintain no more than six universities was ill adapted to meet the extensive claims of the new science. At times Liebig's aspiring and many-sided spirit was affected by those gloomy moods which are apt to trouble the chemist in the bad air of the laboratory where he conducts monotonous and laborious experiments. On these occasions he would despairingly exclaim : " At bottom, chemistry is nothing but an arithmetical sum ; its ultimate aim is merely to discover some good boot-blacking or to learn how to boil meat." But Wöhler's tranquillising counsel never failed to restore his equanimity, and the two friends were already in a position to congratulate themselves on numerous splendid successes. Liebig was the discoverer of chloroform, although the uses of this substance were not ascertained till many years later. Wöhler rendered possible an astonishing glimpse into the ultimate secrets of nature by the synthetic production of urea without the intermediation of the energies of living animals. Thereby was refuted an error hoary with antiquity, and the proof afforded that there is no impassable boundary between the organic and the inorganic world.

Nay more, in his researches into vision (1825), the famous physiologist Johannes Müller ascended to those lofty heights where physics and metaphysics touch. By direct scientific observation, he showed what Kant had discovered through abstract speculation, that we see things, not as they are, but as they must appear to us owing to the peculiarities of our sense-organs. Like Liebig, Müller had first to discard the arrogant assumptions of abstract natural philosophy. Standing now upon the platform of exact research, he trained in Berlin a brilliant circle of pupils, and established the physiological foundations of comparative anatomy. When new ideas make their way into German life, the sensibilities too invariably demand their rights. Most of the younger men of science in Berlin associated upon terms of intimate friendship. Among them may be mentioned Dove, Mitscherlich, Magnus, and the brothers Rose. When these men met Poggendorff, the physicist, in the tower of the old observatory in Dorotheenstrasse, the minds of all were filled with the prophetic vision of a great future. The present indeed seemed modest enough ; the developing sciences had first to struggle for their footing. Astronomy alone, whose position had long been established, was reckoned a distinguished pursuit, and could always rely upon financial support from the state. The Königsberg laboratory had actually been founded during the miserable days of the Napoleonic wars, and here Bessel had calculated the position of the clock-stars, thus securing unity for astronomical determinations. Now Schinkel built the new

Berlin observatory, which under Encke's direction became a model institution. Humboldt's advocacy was helpful in this field also, for he was the sun radiating warmth in the centre of the planetary circle. Not until the forties, however, did the blossoming time of German natural science come; but when it came, the French were soon overhauled, and then outstripped.

KING FREDERICK WILLIAM IV AND HIS COURT (VI, 293–336, 339, 342–48, 349–53, 354–62, 364–65)

ON June 9, 1840, Prince Metternich entertained the German federal envoys at a banquet in Vienna, and alluded in moving terms to the glorious league which for a quarter of a century had now secured peace and happiness for the Germans. Princess Melanie, profoundly affected, could not restrain her tears, for tidings of the king's death were hourly expected from Berlin, and who could foresee the events of the new time? Münch-Bellinghausen, the presidential envoy, sat at the festive board. Following his usual practice he had spent the last eight months on the Danube, intending during the hot season to bring the recess of the Bundestag to a close. Many of the guests could not refrain from asking themselves in some dudgeon whether the Federation could really be worth a commemorative feast, seeing the contemptuous way in which it was treated by the Hofburg.[1] By the nation at large no attention was paid to the silver jubilee of the Germanic Federation, except that perhaps here and there some newspaper was found to publish one of the customary sour witticisms concerning the red " incompetence building " in Frankfort.

Who, indeed, could take delight in all the discords that had become apparent during these five-and-twenty years of peace. The old oppositions of our history were confronting one another more crudely, more irreconcilably, than ever before. At the very time when the German federal constitution could be sustained solely by the favour of the two great powers, and when Count Maltzan, the Prussian envoy in Vienna, to Frederick William's lively satisfaction, had summed up the

---

[1] Maltzan's Reports, June 9, 1840, and subsequent dates.

fundamental thought of correct Prussian statecraft in the phrase
"not under but always with Austria,"[1] this same monarch
had already entered a path which must inevitably lead to
severance from Austria. The stately work of this revived
Frederician policy, the customs union, was already so firmly
established, the community of labour between the nonaustrian
Germans seemed so indissoluble, that Michel Chevalier, returning
from a German tour, admiringly declared : " In European
politics I know of nothing more remarkable than the reestablish-
ment of German unity. What a glorious spectacle that a
great nation which seemed about to break up into fragments
should return to nationality, in a word, to life ! "

The crass contradiction between this young and vigorous
economic life and the forms of the rigid federal law, utterly
insusceptible of improvement, could not fail to exercise a confusing influence upon public opinion. Some were still immersed
in the quiet dreams of an unthinking particularism, which
had in truth already been transcended by the far-reaching
relationships of the new national market ; others continued to
repeat the shibboleths of ten years back, the catchwords of
radical cosmopolitanism ; among the best classes of the nation
there was gradually awakening a passionate and sensitive
national pride. Those of the last category realised that colossal
popular energies were being artificially constrained by a
thousand paralysing and perverse political considerations. Bold
suggestions, such as none but isolated enthusiasts had hitherto
ventured to utter, were now being discussed in the newspapers.
People were beginning to ask why this young customs union
should not take example by the Hanseatic league, unfurl its
flag in distant seas, protect that flag with its own warships, play its
part in the conquest of the transatlantic world. The eager glances
of patriotic writers were now directed towards the detached daughter
lands of our race, towards Flensburg, towards Riga and Reval ;
and when during this momentous summer it seemed that the Rhine
frontier was again threatened, there arose with elemental energy a
storm of national wrath which plainly betokened that the spirit
of the wars of liberation was not dead, and that the days of fulfil-

---

[1] Maltzan's Reports, May, 1840. The king's marginal note : C'est bien cela.
Rien de plus correct.

ment were at length approaching for our struggling peoples. Hopes of freedom grew concomitantly with the growth of national pride. After so many struggles and disillusionments, the liberals were beginning to formulate the theoretical ideal of the parliamentary state, to which they continued to cling until in 1866 monarchical conceptions again became predominant. One of the liberal leaders, Carl Steinacker of Brunswick, declared at this time : " The government in the representative state always represents the majority in the state." The thoughtful and well-meaning man could not recognise that with this doctrine he was depriving kingship of all independent power, and was merely smoothing the way for the advance of those republican ideas which were rapidly gaining currency among the refugees and in the impressionable younger generation.

How remote from these continually augmenting doctrinaire claims of liberalism was the reality of German conditions, the extremely modest power of the south German diets, and the arbitrary behaviour of the Guelph king, who could without punishment trample his country's rights under foot. Moreover, liberalism had to encounter influential adversaries in the theoretical field. Hazy reminiscences of Haller and the writings of the historical school of law were the materials whereof young Prince Ludwig zu Solms-Lich compiled his booklet *Germany and Representative Constitutions* (1838), which aroused the lively admiration of the world of good society and was especially prized at the court of Berlin. But old Hans Gagern dismissed the work with the apt comment : " All kinds of sophistical and mystical opinions come our way, deriving especially from the north, to be dispersed by the light of natural reason as mists flee before the sun." From its involved phraseology no more than a single clear idea could be gleaned, and this was that the princely author regarded the entire recent history of the German south as a gigantic aberration, for he held up the Prussian provincial diets as a luminous antithesis. Economic conditions were equally disturbed. Hardly had manufacturing industry begun to flourish under the ægis of the customs union, when the seamy side of the new conditions began to become apparent. Far and wide through the long chain of the " Hunger Mountains " of Central Germany resounded the workers' cry of distress, and bitter poverty made the masses turn a favourable ear to the visionary suggestions of communism.

Grave social disturbances seemed impending, and were likely to prove all the more disastrous owing to the profound disruption of religious life. Whilst from the time of the Cologne episcopal dispute the power of the Roman priesthood increased day by day, and whilst the religious zeal of renascent Protestantism was being displayed in fruitful works of benevolence, the critics of the young Hegelian school despised every form of Christianity. The lees of the old enlightenment had been shaken up once more, and widespread in cultured circles was inability to realise that religion had again become a serious matter. A sign of the times was the publication on the centenary of the great king's accession of a work by young C. F. Köppen, *Frederick the Great and his Opponents*, a brilliant book which victoriously defended against critics the sublime morality of the creative and intellectual hero, and simultaneously overwhelmed with scornful invectives "the Catholic wolves in sheeps' clothing, the Protestant sheep in wolves' clothing, and the zealot frogs croaking in chorus from every marsh." For the young radicals of the day the thought of three generations, the thought which had broken the dominion of Voltaire's ideas in Germany, seemed non-existent. How extraordinary, too, were the contrasts in the domain of literature. Side by side with arduous studies in historical and natural science, there became current an ephemeral literature that was at once impudent and dull, that was hopelessly biased, that mocked in verse and prose at all established order, and that never looked beyond the fleeting successes of the moment.

Germany was in a state of ominous ferment, and Saint-René Taillandier, one of the few Frenchmen who had a clear understanding of contemporary German happenings, wrote with concern that the prevalent mental anarchy was reminiscent of the state of France before the revolution. But the German troubles were not, as had been those of France, revelations of the corruption of a morally degenerate society ; they were obscure intimations of the youthful energy of a noble and aspiring people which was beginning to become aware of its own strength. How readily a great idea could constrain all these brawlers to assemble beneath a single banner, how readily such an idea could completely overshadow the medley of fugitive thoughts not one of which completely dominated the nation, was shown by the marvellous unanimity of warlike enthusiasm which took possession of the Germans when their western frontier was menaced. Had the successor of Frederick William III, by his free royal resolve (such as had hitherto been determinative in all the great transformations of our history), made provision for the wise adjustment of the constitutionalist difficulties in Prussia ; had he thus simultaneously enhanced the prestige of his crown and bridged over the chasm which separated his state from the lesser German territories ; had he, without interfering with freedom of thought and research, loyally fostered that strengthening of religious life which was the noble heritage of the wars of liberation—he could then have ventured to revive Frederician ideas in a new and liberal spirit, to complete the work of the customs union, and, sword in hand, to demand for the state that was leading the working life of the nation, leadership also in the field of German politics.

Rarely has the old truth that men control the course of events been so plainly confirmed. For eight years Frederick William IV remained the man of destiny for Germany. The forces he awakened, and still more the counterforces which sprang to life against him, impelled our people towards the revolution. And yet seldom had it likewise been so conspicuous that men are the product of events. The enigmatic character of the new king was no more than a last fine blossoming of that prolonged epoch of sentimental extravagance which had even now barely drawn to its close, and it was to be left for the vigorous sons of another and hardier generation, for those who had seen the horror of the revolution stalking abroad through the streets, to achieve success where these weaker hands inevitably failed. The peculiar view of monarchical absolutism that this prince cherished in his enthusiast's soul had nothing in common with the frivolous self-deification of the Bourbons or the unthinking hebetude of the Viennese Hofburg, and it had but little in common with the priestly kingcraft of the Stuarts. Like the elaborated despotism of King Louis of Bavaria it could flourish solely upon German soil, upon the soil of that romanticist outlook on the world which found its ideal in the boundless development of all the talents, in the self-confidence and self-gratification of the proud ego. In this harassed and restricted age, all were clamouring for liberty, and none clamoured more loudly than the new king. But before everything the freedom he desired was one that would enable him to live out his own life upon the heights, and to make an active use of his royal wisdom and formative powers. He believed in the existence of a mysterious illumination which God's grace bestowed upon kings as distinct from other mortals ; he had a cordial belief in mankind, and imagined that he understood his era because he had a connoisseur's receptivity for all it had to offer in the way of the grand and the beautiful. Hence he considered it possible for him, in virtue of his unrestricted royal authority, to endow his beloved people with more true freedom than any written constitution could bring.

Frederick William was now nearly forty-five, and his portly figure and the intellectual but placid lineaments of his beardless countenance already suggested the advance of years, despite the youthful restlessness of his movements. Manifold had been his experiences during these long years of waiting. Much homage had been paid him since those distant days when the old Albertina university had chosen the thirteen year old boy to be its rector, and when on his mother's last birthday " the flourishing hope of the fatherland " was honoured by the striking of a medal. At a considerably later date Goethe had prophesied that this great talent must awaken new talents, and everyone had admired the crown prince's intellectual supremacy. He had long sat as president of the council of state and of the ministry, believing himself to be thus supervising all the affairs of state. His father, however, simple-minded but with a good knowledge of men, had been careful to see that this brilliant position, not altogether suitable for the heir to a throne, should not degenerate into a co-regency

The old king had been far more master in his own house than in the state. His children looked up to him with that timid veneration which serious-minded and taciturn fathers know how to inspire even in sons more talented than themselves. The crown prince's political influence was not extensive. His advocacy was doubtless helpful to a few persons, especially orthodox pastors. Such important negotiations as had taken place with the provincial diets had been entrusted almost exclusively to his guidance. But the king had kept all momentous decisions so completely within his own competence that the heir to the throne had soon a painful feeling of powerlessness, and conceived a tacit but continually increasing enmity towards the old regime.

Not merely did he detest bureaucratic formalism, quite failing to recognise its great advantages, and loving to dismiss it contemptuously as " servile bumptiousness " ; but yet more did he detest the whole spirit of this government, which seemed to him closely akin to that of the eighteenth century enlightenment. When as crown prince he stayed at Charlottenhof beneath the hill of Sans Souci, in the rose-garlanded villa which his father had given him and which Schinkel had adorned with Italian grace, the guests would at times in animated conversation institute comparisons between past and future. The aspiring younger generation considered itself enormously superior to the old in its élan, the sincerity of its faith, the profundity of its emotions, its romanticism. Frederick William's bosom friend Prince John of Saxony, writing in formal trochaic verse, referred to the cold marble splendours of the royal halls on the plateau above, and asked of them :

> Seems it not as if re-echoed
> Still the mordant wit of yore ?

whilst in lame dactyls he described the bower beneath, with its youthful merriment :

> Pulses below here what there's ever lacking ;
> Conjoined with mind is a warm glowing heart.

Soon after his ascent to the throne the new king took

a step which neither of his two predecessors had ventured, and established his court in the palace of the great Frederick. He had no fear of the inevitable comparisons, for it was his hope that for the second time from this " historic hill " a new spirit would breathe over the land, though a different spirit from the Frederician, being that of the Christian state. By hard work and through severe mental struggles he had long ere this got the better of the rationalistic teaching of his early tutor, and had come to conceive faith as the highest power of reason. Indelibly graven upon his heart was the saying of St. Augustine : " The immutable light of God was over me, for it gave me existence, and I was beneath it, because it created me." From this he derived his sense of " *the inexpressible difference* between the creator and the creature," and from this likewise he derived the delusion that he could " create divinity " out of his own nature " as an analogy of *the godhead* ! ! ! " [1] Nothing therefore seemed more abominable to him than " the dragon's teeth of Hegelian pantheism." More far-sighted than Hegel, he recognised that every epoch has its own independent value, its own peculiar relationship to God, and that no epoch can be significant merely as a developmental stage on the way to the future. The new age that was now dawning was destined, he considered, to make a clean sweep of the heritage of the old enlightenment, was to overcome the revolution by liberty, carnal freedom by Christian freedom, the mechanical state by the Christian state.

With an artist's imagination he had already conceived a whole world of splendid plans, and, being now master, his amiable disposition, which made him desire to universalise happiness without delay, which made him long to see cheerful faces wherever he looked, impelled him towards realisation. His idea was to supplement the provincial diets by summoning a Reichstag based upon representation by estates, but he had no idea of inaugurating a written constitution, for although he loved to express his contempt for all political theories, his own mind was permeated by an unchangeable political doctrine. The artificial contrast between the revolutionary

[1] Annotations of the crown prince on Bunsen's treatise, Concerning Marriage Law, State, and Church.

representative system and the legitimate representation by estates which Gentz had described in his Carlsbad memorial of the year 1819, seemed to the king an irrefutable truth. Just as the adherents of the old doctrine of natural law had believed in an abstract law of reason far superior to all positive laws, so did he believe in the existence of a historic right of the estates which had arisen independently of the state authority, and could not be suspended by the latter, but merely recognised. The truth that the law-constructing spirit of modern nations displays its strongest activity in the inauguration of state laws was despised by him as an error cherished by the Hegelian idolisers of the state, and his Christian monarchy was ever to remain free from this " all-power of the state." Haller's doctrine of the state now celebrated its greatest triumph at a time when its originator had already passed his seventieth year, but in the mind of Frederick William this crude and prosaic theory of power was transfigured by rich adornments of artistic imagery. For him the unity of the state was as nothing. It sufficed him that all the estates and all the territories of his wide realm should unfold a free and multiform life in their several historical peculiarities. Even the Wends, the Lithuanians, the Kashubes, and the Masurians were to have undisturbed enjoyment of their national speech and customs.

He proposed to mitigate all the severities of the old system. There was to be an amnesty for the demagogues, and also for the Poles, with whom he sympathised as the victims of illegal oppression ; there was to be freedom for the press, and above all for the church. The bitterness of the Catholics on account of the Cologne episcopal dispute would, he hoped, be overcome by magnanimous concessions. The Evangelical church of Prussia and the supra-episcopal authority of the monarchy seemed to him almost devoid of justification. When Protestantism had purged itself of unbelieving elements, the congregations of the faithful were to rebuild their church with their own independent energies, untrammelled by state authority, thus rendering visible the church invisible. Further, he had long regarded with dislike the penuriousness of the old regime. His court was to be brilliant, tasteful, worthy of the Hohenzollern name, and with this end in view he hoped to assemble round his person all that was great in German art and science. Before his accession he had furthered the rebuilding of the Marienburg and the completion of the cathedral of Cologne ; at Castel, he had restored the mortuary chapel of his Lützelburg forefathers, which stands on a precipitous rock high above the Saar ; at Stolzenfels he had magnificently reconstructed the Rhenish palace of the prince bishops of Treves ; and he had thrown open to the public the ruins of Stahleck, at one time a stronghold of his wife's ancestors, the Counts Palatine. Everywhere, now, the ruinous edifices that had belonged to his German forebears were to be splendidly reinstated, the work providing an abundance of new opportunities for the creative talent of the younger generation of artists. The Christian monarch desired to be scrupulously just to all the fresh energies of his country's life—to commerce, to industry, to communications, and not least to the working masses, whose growing power had become apparent to him while he was still crown prince, and earlier than to most of his contemporaries.

It was not his intention to make any radical change in the traditional foreign policy of Prussia. He regarded the league of the eastern powers as a protective barrier against the revolution. His long-standing veneration for Metternich's wisdom had but increased with the passage of the years ; and towards his Russian brother-in-law he was weaker than his predecessor had been. The late king had loved " darling Niks " like a son, but in his quiet way had ever kept the Russian within bounds. To the new ruler the czar's harshnesses were profoundly repugnant, and in the intimacy of private life he would often use bitter expressions concerning " his autocratic majesty " ; but Nicholas impressed him with that secret dread which a man of strong will is often able to inspire in a man of strong intelligence. Yet he felt very keenly that his domestic policy could have nothing in common either with the easy-going slumbrousness of Old Austria or with the slavish tranquillity of the tsarist realm, and he longed for the coming of the time when England should reenter the old quadruple alliance, and when Prussia, fortified by an intimate league between the two Protestant great powers, should secure a

somewhat freer hand in Europe. For years he had felt great
admiration for this kindred island stock, and the ardency of
the sentiment was continually increased by Bunsen's enthusiastic letters. It was a delight to him to see how at the
close of the thirties anglomania spread among the nobility all
over Central Europe and even as far as Hungary, the dress
and customs of English sportsmen being sedulously copied by
good society. The British constitution seemed to him the
model of that organic development which, though in other
forms, he desired to achieve for his own state; and he shared
the opinion widely diffused among the more liberal nobles and
among the bourgeoisie, that England is our natural ally.
Nevertheless his political experience was already more extensive
than that of the liberals; he recognised that the alliances of
states are not solely determined by the ties of inner kinship;
and he considered that a peculiarly close bond between the
two Protestant powers would not be possible unless the old
eastern league remained inviolable.

Yet more lively was his interest in Prussia's German
policy. He had no expectation of a long life, and soon after his
accession said that he did not know whether this short reign
would be glorious; at least he was determined that it should
have a German stamp. Since he despised " the prejudices "
of the Frederician era, and ungrudgingly acknowledged the
precedence of the old imperial house, he regarded the Germanic
Federation under peaceful dualist rule as an institution of the
utmost value, and his only ambition was that Prussia should
invigorate it, should secure for the Federation effective leadership in military affairs, trade and communications, and
commercial policy. He hardly troubled himself to ask the
question how it was possible to harmonise the enlarged federal
authority with the customs union, which had arisen independently of the Federation and in opposition thereto. His
Prussian sense of the state ever remained weaker than his
vague enthusiasm for German unity, and the idea of demanding
the leadership of the nation for Prussia (a leadership that could
be secured only through a struggle with Austria) lay quite
without his circle of vision. Among all the Hohenzollern
kings he was the most pacifically minded, excelling even his

father in this respect, and was therefore the only one who
was never engaged in a serious war. Upon the wall of one
of his museums he had inscribed the well-known utterance of
the Cæsar : " Melius bene imperare quam imperia ampliare "
—a saying that well became the ruler of a world empire,
but was unsuitable in the mouth of the king of a young and
inchoate state, a land with derisory frontiers. He was no
man of the sword. Being extremely short-sighted, he disliked
mounting a horse ; and although at manœuvres he frequently
surprised his officers with keen, critical observations, it was
plain to them that for the king the fulfilment of his military
duties was a matter of conscience, not a pleasure. He was
devoted to the joys of peace. But all the peaceful blessings
which his subjects were to expect under the class-stratified
Christian monarchy were to issue from the wisdom of the
crown. Resembling that of an Old Testament patriarch
was his view of his dignified office, for he really looked upon
kingship as a paternal authority specially instituted by God
for the education of the peoples. Everything that happened
in the state was related, as he thought, to the person of the
monarch. The highest aim of the free press was " the
discovery of errors and abuses concerning which I have no
other sources of information." [1] When he chid his people,
he would say menacingly, " Both Solomon and Sirach
recommend that naughty children shall be chastised in due
season."[2]

If only among all the promising plans cherished by the
crown prince there had been but a single proposal fully matured,
and thought out with statesmanlike intelligence ! But that
passion for results, even inadequate results, which is characteristic of the man of action, was unknown to him. Like
a spectator at the play, he luxuriated in contemplating the
abundant flow of his ideas, and during the long years of
waiting he had almost forgotten how to ask himself in what
way his splendid fantasies were to be realised. Even his
design for the liberation of the Protestant church, the design
dear to him beyond all others, was merely to be promoted
with all his powers for seven years. Should the obstacles

---

[1] Marginal note, June 7, 1843.   [2] Marginal note, June 10, 1847.

prove insuperable, the book was to be closed. Such was not the language of a man born to rule. It was that of a richly imaginative mind ; of one who gave himself up to, rather than determined, the impressions of his life ; a man of soft nature, confiding in God and his fellows, and never ceasing to hope that things would turn out as he wished. Failures were ascribable, not to his own weakness, but to the inscrutable decrees of Providence. Side by side on his writing table at Sans Souci stood statuettes of the Venus of Milo, the pious Gellert, and Czar Nicholas, eloquent testimonies to the marvellously versatile sensibility of one who endeavoured to understand all that was significant in art and science, in state and church, but who never became fully at home in anything.

In converse with the heroes of the German spirit he displayed so dazzling a superiority that Leopold Ranke exclaimed with astonishment : " He is master of us all ! " Yet he was no master, but merely the greatest of those brilliant dilettantes who abound in our complex modern civilisation. In none of the countless provinces of intellectual life with which his restless mind was concerned did he display true strength, genuine creative faculty, and least of all in the field of politics. In later years a peasant with a grievance, being referred by the monarch to the state for redress, mouthed invectives against this " ruffian of a state," and the king would often recall the winged word half in jest. Yet in his mouth, unfortunately, it was something more than a jest. He had an equal loathing for the inexorable regularity of state business and for the asperities of the political struggle, although he conscientiously discharged the duties of his royal office, often working for this purpose far into the night. But he never failed to draw a breath of relief when he could retire from the commonplace world into the recesses of his own rich individuality, and his happiest moments were those wherein, intoxicating and intoxicated, he could in inspired language give free issue to the flow of his thoughts and his feelings. " I could not keep it in, I had to speak," he would say frankly to his friends.[1] Those only who did not know him accused him of an actor's calculation which was altogether foreign to his

---

[1] Frederick William to Thile, June 13, 1846, etc.

disposition. For him it was an essential need to pour from a full heart, to rejoice in the splendour of lofty metaphors, in the euphonies of that mother tongue he loved so fondly and used with such magistral skill. The ultimate effect of these spoken confessions was left by him in the hands of a merciful providence. In this he differed greatly from his predecessor Frederick, who, likewise a born orator, had always spoken with a purpose, weighing every sentence in its effect upon the will of his hearer, and never forgetting that only when they are deeds as well do king's words live on into the days of posterity. It is true that he frequently practised the unconscious dramatic arts to which gifted talkers are prone, and when at the festive board he saw in all eyes a reflection of the radiance from his own victorious personality, he was apt to say a good deal more than he had intended.

Natures of such many-sided sensitiveness are as a rule much dependent upon the caressive support of others, but Frederick William, strangely enough, stood squarely on his own feet. Herein lay the enigma of his character, herein the explanation of the manner in which he was so often over-valued even by men of outstanding intelligence. With careless serenity, with perfect unconcern, he made his way through life. He believed himself endowed, thanks to the sacredness of his royal office, and thanks to his personal gifts, with the power of taking the most comprehensive views, and it amused him at times to veil his intentions in a mysterious but pregnant obscurity, to throw petty mortals into confusion by the use of nebulous and half-unmeaning words. Though he lacked far-reaching energy of will and practical understanding, he remained an autocrat in the fullest significance of the term No one else ruled him; all the glory and all the shame of his regime were chargeable to his personal account. When opposed by his councillors he would sometimes abruptly forego some cherished design, and it would seem for a time as if the thoughts in his uneasy brain had undergone a kaleidoscopic change, but in the end it would suddenly become apparent that with a singular and taciturn obduracy he had clung to his original plan, and had recurred to it, despite all that had happened. He never relinquished anything, and he effected very little. His resolves were determined by emotional leanings and ready-made doctrines, and these could not be overcome by considerations of political expediency.

This independence of others' judgment was fortunate, for, since he had little knowledge of men, he was extremely unlucky in the choice of his advisers, and showed an extraordinary faculty for putting excellent persons into the wrong positions, or for wearying them out by making impossible claims. The consequence was that, apart from his two intimate confidants, Thile and Stolberg, one only of his ministers, Eichhorn, remained in office during the eight years that passed between the accession and the March revolution. Utterly free from the shy inaccessibility of his father, he loved to ask everyone's opinion. In private conversation he would willingly listen to candid contradiction, and almost seemed to invite it by the challenging manner in which he stated his own views. To friends he showed his fondness with an extravagance which often aroused suspicions of insincerity, although it was nothing but the involuntary expression of his temperament. He readily divined all the wishes of his intimates, and fulfilled them with royal munificence, allowing for a friend's human weaknesses with delicacy and consideration. When he desired to charm, he exhibited a fascinating amiability ; and he was not above having recourse on occasions to the petty feminine wile of a fit of the sulks. Nevertheless, he was so greatly uplifted by his sense of royal dignity, that in essentials other individualities were of trifling consequence to him. Astonishing was the callousness with which he could cast off old and tried intimates should they give public utterance to opinions divergent from his own, or should they derange his plans. To him every declared political opponent was a personal enemy ; and like all men of feeling he would treat an estranged friend with harshness and injustice which were the apt counter-parts of the affection and deference previously displayed—and this though he often declared that his greatest wish in life was to be universally just.

His splendidly but unhappily endowed mind, just as much as his physique, recalled the poet's imaginary figure of Hamlet. He was full of beautiful and lofty ideas, and yet was so unstable in his resolves, that at the close of a council his ministers could never feel assured that his opinion remained what it had been at the opening. His piety sprang from the depths of a god-inspired heart, his gentle hand delighted in works of Christian charity about which there was no touch of pretence ; but this man of kindly nature, when overpowered by wrath, would show himself to be vindictive to the point of cruelty. Himself a man of strictly moral behaviour, he was harsh and almost prudish in his condemnation of a loose liver, but this did not hinder his enjoyment of coarse buffoonery and the lewd jests of the Berlin streets. Despite the extent of his knowledge and despite his eagerness for further acquisitions, the finest blossom of culture, simplicity of thought and feeling, was incomprehensible to him and was ever beyond his reach. He was always in search of the peculiar, of that which lay remote from the main road ; and the itch to be witty and brilliant would dominate him even when to yield to the impulse towards paradox was to endanger the success of some political coup. Denied to him was virile force of body and soul, the force which alone could have harmonised these multiform and conflicting endowments, and at times there could already be discerned in him the traces of a positively morbid disposition.

The late king had never failed to attempt, too sedulously at times, to soften contrasts, to allay oppositions ; he had invariably acted in accordance with the old principle that the first duty of every government is to hold firmly to definite political traditions. At length, when his mind had been stiffened by age, it had become possible for Minister Alvensleben to say complacently : " We know our sovereign's opinions perfectly, and can always draft our report so as to be sure of his approval." [1] How different was the new ruler. He, too, aimed at paying due honour to the old traditions of the monarchy, but the many promises made in his speeches, the abundance of his plans, his unstable and capricious conduct, his incessant displays of personal feeling, had so stimulating, so irritant an effect, that a storm of awakened passions soon raged across the quiet land, and the king had to encounter

---

[1] Kühne's Memoirs.

the fate of the magician's apprentice. The weakness of every new government, namely, the incalculability of all relationships, persisted nearly eight years under the fourth Frederick William, until the situation was completely altered by a terrible defeat of kingship. If only the time and its royal awakener had been in the least able to understand one another! But in his marvellously complex course of development he had formed such peculiar ideals, that whilst sometimes as far as words went he was in agreement with average newspaper opinion, the agreement never extended to the substance which those words represented, for the monarch spoke a different language from his people. He was hailed with acclamations because, in accordance with the universal wish, he was preparing to put an end to the coercion and the immobility of the old system, and the form of his speeches seemed to prove that no one can wholly escape the influence of his age, for, just like the poets of Young Germany whom he so profoundly abhorred, he loved to dazzle by the unusual and to give homely utterance to the homely things he despised. But when he spoke of freedom he was thinking of his traditional feudalist system of representation, which was to bridle the power of the officialdom but was never to hamper the monarchical authority, whereas his hearers had in mind the parliamentary representative system, which people were gradually coming to regard as the only political structure worthy of a civilised nation. When the king sang the praises of German unity he was thinking of the Germanic Federation and the continuance of its peaceful development, whereas the cultured classes had long ere this passed sentence upon all the doings in the Eschenheimer Gasse as a spectral puppet show. When he spoke of the independence of the church, everyone agreed with him, for who could withstand the magic word of freedom; but the Christian sentiment he demanded for the free congregations of the faithful was utterly alien from that conceived as essential by the spokesmen of the zeitgeist, and all the noble foundations which were the work of his splendid benevolence, foundations which to-day continue to earn the thanks and blessings of their beneficiaries, were in the eyes of the men of his own time mere ebullitions of sanctimoniousness. When he promised an open path for art and science, he was thinking of the old nature philosophy and of romanticist poesy, spiritual forces which the self-complacent younger generation imagined itself to have long outgrown.

Thus it came to pass that the first phase of his reign was a long concatenation of misunderstandings, and for this mutual confusion the king was just as much responsible as was the obscurely fomenting spirit of the time, which began by acclaiming him as its hero and ended by opposing him with all the bitterness of disillusionment. Even General Gerlach, his faithful friend and servant, would at times say, " The ways of the Lord are wonderful " ; whilst Bunsen, who was no less devoted, on reading the king's plaint, " No one understands me, no one comprehends me," wrote the despairing marginal note, " Even if one could understand him, how could one comprehend him ? " It was impossible for Frederick William, just as it was impossible for his no less imaginative and fanciful Bavarian brother-in-law, to discover by way of despotic severity and an over-elaborated shrewdness, an escape from the complications he had brought upon himself, and he wearied himself with ineffectual endeavours until history marched over him. He lacked energy alike for resolute enjoyment and for resolute action, and although he never completely lost his natural cheerfulness, he suffered always from a sense of inward dissatisfaction. He soon came to recognise with distress that he could achieve no successes, and his contemporaries, irritated and censorious, were in no mood to show human sympathy for the mute sufferings of a greatly gifted soul. The man who had formed so preposterously an exalted estimate of the vocation of king by God's grace had the bitter experience that in a realm where monarchy was traditional his reign had shaken faith in kingship—though the disaster, happily, was not irretrievable. It seemed as if Providence had wished by a tragical example to show this over-cultured generation, this generation whose estimate of the value of culture was so grossly exaggerated, how (in the struggles of national life) intelligence, knowledge, high-mindedness, and amiability are of little worth, unless they are infused with the simple energy of a virile will. In the great complex of German history, this disastrous reign appears, after all, as a necessary and wholesome dispensation, for under a stronger ruler the inevitable transition of the proud Prussian monarchy to constitutionalist forms of government could hardly have been effected without terrible struggles.

Fate determined that several of the most important offices of state should be simultaneously vacated by death. Altenstein's demise took place a few weeks before that of Frederick William III, and the pious Nicolovius had died a little earlier. Before the close of the year occurred the death of the trusty Stägemann, who had so long acted as the monarch's secretary in all confidential concerns. Schinkel, while still in the vigour of his years, was attacked by a terrible disorder which clouded his mind and was soon to bring his life to a close. Both Count Lottum and General Rauch, the minister for war, felt weakened by age, and their lives seemed unlikely to be prolonged. Prince Wittgenstein, now advanced in years, held sedulously aloof from affairs, bitterly complaining that he had nothing in common with the changed world. There was room everywhere for fresh energies, and Peter Cornelius wrote exultantly : " A time of spring and festivity is at hand for all Germany ! " But during the past quarter of a century Germany's life had run an astonishingly rapid course, and owing to the prolonged reign of the late king the natural succession of the generations had been disordered. The new men who came to the top were no longer young. Most of them, like their royal patron, had grown up among the determinative impressions of the wars of liberation, of the restoration epoch, and of the period of religious revival ; and many of them continued to cherish the ideals of liberty that had animated the first Burschenschaft. But the youngest radical generation smiled on them contemptuously as reactionaries, and to the young Hegelians of the new enlightenment their Christo-Germanic ideas appeared even more detestable than did the dryly reasonable bureaucracy of the old system.

Queen Elizabeth was dearest of all to the king's heart. His affection for her was unbounded, and almost exceeded the limits proper to a ruler. When, with tears streaming down his face, he rose in profound distress from beside his father's death-bed, he said to her : " Now give me your support, Elise, for I shall need all my energies." Whenever he returned home, harassed by the superabundance of his thoughts which made every decision difficult, and disturbed by the cares of public business, she invariably gave him a cheerful, sympathetic, and affectionate welcome ; only when anger completely overmastered him did she glance round the chamber with serious mien and say, " I am looking for the king." He attempted to furnish his happy home as cosily as was permissible to a sovereign prince. At Christmas the royal pair would visit the market in the palace square, and on new year's eve the night-watchman had to enter the palace to herald the new year with his horn. The king delighted to do whatever his wife wished. With a high spirit she concealed her distress that her marriage was childless, she did not hesitate to hold at the font her nephew Frederick William, who would presumably succeed to the throne, and she became a second mother to the lad. She found her greatest happiness in inexhaustible benevolence. She helped her spouse in his countless enterprises of Christian charity, dispensing large sums from her private means, at least 60,000 thalers yearly. In all the remoter quarters of Berlin, where the new hospitals and infant schools were being established, everyone was familiar with the queen's carriage drawn by four dapple greys. Nevertheless she was not popular. The Catholics of the west never forgave her for becoming a Protestant. On the other hand, in the rigidly Protestant old provinces, and especially in Berlin, where the spirit of Biester, the Jesuit-hunter, was not yet dead, the report was current, even among the court servants, that the queen had remained Catholic at heart and desired to convert her husband to the Roman church. This rumour damaged the king's prestige, and yet it was utterly unfounded. Elizabeth's conversion to the Protestant faith had been the outcome of free conviction and had ensued upon serious consideration. In later years, with her customary frankness, she told Pope Pius IX to his face : " One married to such a king, whose life is an embodiment of the gospels, is confirmed in the Evangelical faith." It is true that her religious sentiments had a romantic tinge which was suspect to the free thought of the age ; she cherished the ideal of a Christian church no less highly than did her husband. She never repudiated the strictly legitimist views of the Bavarian sisters ; she maintained unbroken intercourse with the courts of Vienna, Dresden, and Munich ; and when she believed the repute of the kingdom to be endangered, this affable princess might to many seem cold and proud. For these reasons not a few considered her political influence disastrous, although less often at this time than in later years did she concern herself about state affairs.

Somewhat more extensive were the political activities of Count Anton Stolberg, who at first assisted Prince Wittgenstein, and subsequently succeeded the prince as treasurer of the royal household. He had fought bravely at Jena. Afterwards, with the aid of the loyal Harz mountaineers, who well knew how to hide this son of the beloved old race of the Harzgraves, he had successfully eluded the clutches of the royal Westphalian police. Later still, during the War of Liberation, he had, as a trusty companion-at-arms, struck up a firm friendship with Prince William the elder, Gneisenau, and York. These memories of the war were ever sacred to him. When after the coming of peace he returned home to aid his father in the government of the country, he had an iron cross erected on the rocks of Ilsenstein in memory of his fallen friends. At a much later date he entered the public service, and alike at Düsseldorf and Magdeburg he acquired as president universal confidence through the distinction of manner conjoined with simple amiability which had from of old been typical of his noble race. His religious sentiments were more active than his feeling for politics. Early joining the circles of the " awakened," in Düsseldorf he seconded the efforts of the two benefactors of the lower Rhine, Count von der Recke and Pastor Fliedner, in their works of charity, and accepted the chairmanship of the new deaconesses' union. His serene and tolerant piety won the esteem of Frederick William. Soon after the beginning of the new reign, " Count Anton " had to move to Charlottenhof that he might ever be at the king's side playing the part of faithful Eckart in all political questions where points of conscience were involved, and he fulfilled this confidential office with fine candour. But since he was himself a man of feeling and was therefore unjust at times despite the natural benignity of his disposition, he could not provide an effective counterpoise to the monarch's moods, and he himself formed a modest estimate of his business acumen and the keenness of his understanding.[1] The religious life of his house exhibited itself in forms which conflicted with Protestant custom. Every evening he, his pious and affectionate daughters, and his entire household, would kneel down together in family prayer, and in new Berlin few were tolerant enough to respect the perfectly unhypocritical fervour of these devotional exercises.

Strictness in religious matters was yet more marked in General von Thile, now a cabinet minister, who henceforward replaced Count Lottum in the duty of furnishing regular political reports to the king. An earnest religious sentiment, straightforward and simple in point of verbal expression, had long prevailed in the Prussian army. Nearly all the distinguished leaders of that army shared the opinion of the Old Dessauer that a soldier who did not fear God was nothing but a simpleton ; unconcernedly performing their duties, they humbly entrusted to the god of battles the uncertain fate of the warrior. But now, under a king of theological and pacifist inclinations, officers of a new and quite unprussian type secured the favour of the court, men to whom the prayer-book was dearer than the sword, men not without merit as soldiers (for in the last war they had all fought in knightly fashion), but lacking that true military ambition which fills the whole soul. Their unctuous piety recalled that of Cromwell's dragoons, although these soft and romantic believers were not endowed with the harsh and terrible strength of the Puritans. Thile was an officer of the new calibre. He was an inconspicuous little man, and his efficiency was not immediately plain to the onlooker, but he was hard-working, conscientious, a ready writer, and even eloquent on occasions. His character was irreproachable ; he was never weary in well-doing ; for years, from his modest means, he secretly provided for the support of a man who had been his personal enemy and who had fallen upon evil days. A friend of Boyen and of many other officers of a

[1] Stolberg to Cuny, January 12, 1841.

comparatively liberal trend, he shunned political extremes, and never hesitated, when he thought it necessary, frankly to contradict the monarch, for whom he had a strong personal affection. But he had no independent statesmanlike ideas, and his political vision was frequently clouded by the overstrained mystical piety which induced the wits of Berlin to bestow on him the nickname of " Bible-Thile." Not long before the opening of the new reign he had entertained serious thoughts of going out as a missionary to Australia or Africa. No less passionately than Frederick William did he loathe the new philosophers, who, as the saying ran at court, " Hegeled their Bible and Bibled their Hegel "; yet more profoundly than the king was his mind permeated with the conviction that the decisive struggle between faith and unfaith was at hand, and that, in view of this one great contrast, differences of creed were matters of no import. Not merely did he believe in the divine guidance of history with a fatalist confidence which was apt to impair his powers of free activity, but he believed in addition in the immediate influence of divine grace upon worldly resolves, and in moments of religious ecstasy his political conduct became utterly incalculable. On one occasion, having given Count Stolberg his opinion regarding the Neuchâtel matter, he wrote to his friend a few hours later : " To-day I regarded the affair solely with the eyes of the natural man, and considered it merely from the so-called political aspect. But in the evening I became ashamed when the words were borne in upon me that greater than all the might of steeds and riders is the might of a nation united with its king in prayer. Where prayer is in question, only the prayerful count ; and if God's word be true they will be victorious over all the mockers." [1] Such was the reasoning by which he explained a change in his judgment of the political situation. A man of this temperament could be Frederick William's faithful assistant, but could never compensate for the monarch's deficiencies.

Living in somewhat monotonous intercourse with these two everyday confidants, the king was always refreshed when another friend belonging to the former Wilhelmstrasse circle, Colonel Joseph von Radowitz, appeared in the capital. On

[1] Thile to Stolberg, December 8, 1846.

these occasions Frederick William would joyfully exclaim :
" Hurrah, old Bruin is back again ! " Radowitz sprang from
an ancient but little known Hungarian family ; his grandfather
had been brought to Prussia as prisoner of war and had
remained in Germany. A precocious boy, Joseph Radowitz
was destined for the Westphalian service and was educated
in French military schools. When fifteen he was already an
officer ; a year later, at Bautzen, he won the cross of the
legion of honour ; at the age of eighteen, after the dissolution
of the kingdom of Westphalia, he became head teacher of
military sciences at the cadet school in Cassel. Being subsequently expelled from Hesse owing to his chivalrous intervention
on behalf of the ill-used electress, he secured an honourable
reception in the Prussian army, where he ably cooperated in
the management of military training colleges and in the
reorganisation of the artillery. The fiery glance of the short-
sighted eyes, deep-set beneath the lofty brow, the bronzed
and yet sallow complexion, the thin lips surmounted by a
dark moustache, gave his clear-cut features a foreign stamp.
His whole nature breathed a mysterious charm. Tall and
powerfully built, his formal and dignified demeanour was not
one to invite intimacy. In society he preferred to sit apart,
sketching or turning over the leaves of a book, until of a
sudden he would interpolate some brilliant observation which
would show the talkers that he had marked every word.
Physical needs seemed almost unknown to him ; he ate
sparingly, drank nothing but water, and looked as if he had
never been young. From his earliest years he had been
dominated by an insatiable thirst for knowledge. Books were
his only passion, and in his exceptional memory he gradually
stored an astonishing abundance of varied knowledge. His
early work, *The Iconography of the Saints*, showed how thorough
was his acquaintance with the history of customs, of art, and
of the church. In the crown prince's salon he soon became an
indispensable oracle, and the *Berliner Wochenblatt* had to thank
him for some of its best articles.

His marriage with Countess Voss introduced him into the
circle of the landed gentry, but among the rigid Old Prussians

he long remained suspect as a foreigner. Though he was of noble character, and a man who utterly despised intrigue, many spoke of him as a new Cagliostro, and he was generally regarded as a masked Jesuit. Witzleben, minister for war, a zealous Protestant and friendly to constitutionalist ideas, at length thought it expedient to have the Catholic legitimist removed from the crown prince's entourage, this being at the time when General Gröben and Colonel Gerlach were likewise transferred to the provinces. The old king approved the proposal, but inspired with his customary sense of justice he appointed Radowitz, a staff officer barely forty years of age, to succeed General Wolzogen on the military committee of the Bundestag. There, too, through his industry and intellectual superiority, Radowitz soon made himself a burden to his easy-going colleagues. The offspring of a mixed marriage and educated at first as a Protestant, shortly before attaining manhood, but with a full sense of what he was doing, he had entered the Roman church, securing there such perfect peace of mind that he bluntly declared all truth to be Catholic. His self-denying life as a thinker led him to take a strict and almost monastic view of the moral world. He could never recognise that the Protestant moral ideal, the unity of thought and will, imposes far more arduous duties upon weak mortal men than the Catholic idea of salvation by works. To him celibacy did not seem a masterstroke of papal policy, a cleverly devised means for promoting the power of the clergy by detaching them, as a circumscribed priestly caste, from lay society; it seemed a lofty moral ideal. The struggle of the Protestants against this monstrous mutilation of nature was to him explicable only as a manifestation of the lusts of the flesh—though he himself was a happy husband and father. Such being his sentiments, it was inevitable that he should be profoundly distressed by the Cologne episcopal dispute. His delight in his adopted fatherland of Prussia received a sudden and painful check, and he considered it a gracious dispensation of Providence that his office was one which rendered it needless for him to show his colours publicly in the struggle.

Notwithstanding all his learning, his æsthetic judgments were no less one-sided. Goethe's cordial sensuality was incompre-

hensible to him.   No less incomprehensible was the whole art
of statuary, seeing that its highest achievements were secured
in the representation of heathen nudity.   For him the primary
source of all the sins of the modern age was to be found in
the great epoch of the cinquecento, in the revival of classical
paganism.   Quite in the spirit of Haller, therefore, he abhorred
the revolution as a devilish principle, and was utterly opposed
to the new sociology because in it the state was regarded,
not as the protector, but as the creator of law.   He could
not yet realise that the law-constructing spirit of modern nations
finds expression above all in legislation, nor had it become
clear to him that the historical evolution of law cannot be
continued to-day without the cooperation of liberally organised
state authorities.   No less fundamentally opposed than his
royal master to the " pseudo-liberal activities " of the officialdom,
he proudly maintained " the higher standpoint which
towers above the view of the absolute state." [1]   He hoped
for a grand Christo-Germanic monarchy, for it seemed to him
doubtful, to say the least of it, whether a Christo-Germanic
republic was at all possible.   During the thirties his mind
was so wholly imprisoned within the circle of Haller's ideas
that he could actually reiterate the assertion that the power
of the crown was based upon the ruler's personal ownership
of land.   In Prussia, where all the domains had long ago
become state property, this doctrinaire contention was now
utterly unmeaning.

None the less, he never became the slave of a theory,
but with keen vision contemplated the world of reality, always
prepared to revise his opinions.   He recognised at an early
date a fact which after the passage of many and turbulent
years was to secure general recognition, that the heartfelt
longing of the Germans was directed, not strictly speaking
towards constitutionalist forms, but towards political acquisitions
of a more practical character—legal security, nationality, self-
government.   Nor did the social foundation of the political
movement escape him.   He saw how the middle classes were
strong only because they posed as representatives of the people ;
it was therefore essential that the crown should prove by

[1] Radowitz to the king, June 23, 1844.

constructive social legislation that in the crown alone could the masses of the people find a watchful advocate and a genuine protector. Especially perspicacious was Radowitz' judgment in matters of German federal politics, for he saw here far more clearly than the king or any of his friends. Since in his view the Roman church was not a power hostile to culture, but was the climax of all civilisation, he was able to undertake an unprejudiced comparison between Austrian and Prussian conditions, and this strict Catholic came to the conclusion that Prussia, aspiring sunwards, had need of the light, whereas the Austrian fungus could thrive only in the shade. The dull sterility of Viennese policy, with its multifarious European interests and consequent estrangement from Germany, was no less plain to him than was the superficiality of Austrian semi-culture, which had no counterpoise to offer to arid Josephanism or to liberal phrasemongering. With this stagnant life he proudly contrasted the healthy energy of the Prussian people and the Prussian state, German to the core. Even before the opening of the new reign (1839) he declared that Prussia alone was competent to lead the nation, that Germany's princes and peoples must learn to look Berlinwards for the defence of their rights and interests. He therefore demanded the continued development of the customs union, and insisted before all that the rights of every German must be safeguarded by the crown of Prussia—a sacred duty which, alas! was so shamefully repudiated in the affair of the Hanoverian constitution. Thus there was already dawning in his mind the idea of the Prussian empery of the German nation, and he did not hesitate to avow that he regarded himself primarily as a German, and only secondarily as a Prussian. The king asked his old friend for counsel upon all the problems of German federal politics, but could never make up his mind to be guided unreservedly by this adviser, nor could he decide to appoint Radowitz to the position in which the latter's influence would have been decisive.

Radowitz expounded his political ideas in the *Colloquies upon State and Church.* This work was published anonymously in the year 1846, and at the time many believed the king to be its author, although the chaste simplicity of its admirable prose style had nothing in common with the emotionalism of Frederick William. It was unquestionably the most notable contribution to German publicism since the appearance of Paul Pfizer's *Correspondence between Two Germans*. But how much better had the Swabian writer understood the first elements of the publicist's art, how much better had he been able to direct the reader's will towards a definite end. Pfizer had employed the controversial form merely in order to vanquish all objections, and to enable him to expound his own aim with the utmost precision, to exhibit the goal of German unity under Prussian leadership. In Radowitz' *Colloquies*, on the other hand, there is an exchange of views between a devout officer, a manufacturer of liberal views, a rigid bureaucrat, and a young socialist, who all express themselves with equal courtesy, in carefully chosen words. Then Waldheim intervenes, unmistakably an impersonation of the author, and with statesmanlike calm he displays to all the interlocutors the narrowness of their respective partisan views. Seldom does he give utterance to his own opinions, and is then always cool, reserved, and diffident. The general impression produced by the writing is that of a brilliant paucity of ideas, for, despite the multiplicity of the outlooks that are displayed, hardly any simple conclusions are drawn. The work lacked the strength of enthusiasm. Its ideas did not shoot up skyward from their root, but were trained over an espalier ; they were more distinguished by nobility of form than by primitive energy. The *Colloquies* proved how liberal and unprejudiced was the author's mind ; and in fact, being more capable of development than the king, he was soon to become convinced that the constitutionalist form of state was now indispensable. But the work gave evidence that its author, too, was affected by that distinguished dilettantism which spread like a blight over all the king's circle of intimates. Radowitz was a little of everything, neither wholly soldier, nor wholly statesman, nor wholly man of learning. His refined and well-equipped mind, abler than that of any other Prussian statesman of his day, could not offer the epoch that which was its essential need, the dread concentration of an elemental energy of will.

Had plans, suggestions, splendid proposals sufficed, Bunsen might have been a help to his age. Little did he care that the privy councillors of Berlin looked at him askance owing to the pitiful failure of his campaign against Rome, and that in memory of his Ancona note they had nicknamed him " the knight of Ancona." He was assured of the new king's favour, and with youthful daring he crowded all sail on his fortunate vessel. Some years earlier, looking forward to the reign of the present ruler, he had hoped that it would witness the establishment of the holy empire :

> A thousand years sufficed not to build a fane so rare,
> But soon will such an artist complete the structure fair.

But pending greater things Berlin was to become a German court of the muses such as Weimar had been in earlier days, and the enthusiast promptly began an exchange of letters with artists and men of learning hoping to induce them to settle in the capital. For himself, since the Berne embassy seemed unworthy his deserts, he wished for the presidency of a great committee to which religious and educational matters were to be entrusted. In such a position, freed from the vexations and tedium of administrative affairs, he could to the top of his bent stimulate, instruct, awaken ideas and promote their spread.

General von Canitz' relations with the monarch were less intimate. He had acquired distinction both as campaigner and as writer on military topics ; from Diebitsch's camp he had sent reports of the Russo-Polish war which were as unbiased as they were far-sighted ; finally, having been entrusted with the difficult embassy to Cassel and to Hanover, he had taken so independent a line that despite his tact he inevitably incurred the ill will of the electoral prince and of the Guelph king. On terms of close friendship with the romanticists Clemens Brentano and Savigny, he considered that the liberation of the church from the state authority, and the firm establishment of the monarchy upon a system of representation by estates, were the two primary tasks of the new government. His residence in uneasy Cassel had borne fruit. He recognised that if Prussia were to carry the customs union policy a stage further, her internal structure must be made to approximate to that of her little constitutionalist neighbours. Prussia, therefore, must summon a Reichstag as soon as possible, but he considered that this body must be composed of representatives of the separate estates. His mind was free from all tendency to narrow partisanship. Handsome and distinguished in appearance, a good conversationalist, witty and trenchant, in ordinary intercourse he was little inclined to parade the strictness of his religious principles. Though in his romanticist circle the Prussian officialdom was as a rule regarded with profound hostility, he gladly recognised how great had been the services of this body. He was on friendly terms with liberals, not excepting Varnhagen. Among the king's pious friends he was most definitely distinguished by the ease of the man of the world.

Very different in type was General Carl von der Gröben, Dörnberg's son-in-law, a long and lean Old Prussian giant, round whose shoulders the white mantle of the Teutonic knights still seemed to cling. This chevalier sans peur et sans reproche could find no rest until, when advanced in years, he was able to make a pilgrimage to the Holy Land. With what delight had he long ago taken part in the preparations for the War of Liberation and in the struggle when it came. So intimate had been his friendship with Gneisenau and Arndt, with Schenkendorf and Görres, that for a time he even aroused the suspicions of the demagogue hunters. Throughout life he preserved the enthusiastic crusading spirit of those pious days. What he lacked in political insight was made good by inviolable fidelity to his Christian king, and by a general love for humanity, which so benevolently embraced without distinction the just and the unjust that Queen Elizabeth once observed, " The good Gröben will begin to talk to us next about the dear and excellent Nero ! "

Whilst Gröben's feeling for the king was nothing more than the knightly sentiment of unconditional loyalty, the three brothers von Gerlach were declared Hallerians. They were sons of the highly respected President Gerlach who had courageously defended Electoral Mark against Napoleonic extortions, and subsequently, disgusted by administrative reforms, had quitted the state service, to accept immediately thereafter the position of chief burgomaster of Berlin. The father's courage, his patriotism, and his conservative sentiments, had been transmitted to his sons, two of whom wore the iron cross. The second son, Judge Ludwig Gerlach, was a learned and able lawyer, just alike to superiors and to inferiors, and a jealous guardian of the independence of the judiciary. The lengths to which his religious zealotry could lead him had been shown some years earlier by his reckless publication of the statements made ex cathedra by some of the rationalist professors in Halle, a coup which secured the approval of his royal friend the crown prince. The Christian state, the free orthodox church, and above all the condominium of the two great powers over the Germanic Federation, were ideals which seemed to him so inviolably sacred, that before long he even came to regard his friends Radowitz and Canitz as renegades in consequence of their more liberal attitude towards Austria, and accused them of radical "Teutonism." Like his brother Leopold, he condemned his political and religious opponents with fanatical and unchristian harshness, and did not conceal his view that differences of opinion seemed to him even more important than differences of nationality. His mind being essentially critical, he had few statesmanlike ideas of his own. He would scourge the sins of a godless age with pitiless severity, but when the question pressed what was to be done, young Otto von Bismarck and the other practical men of talent among his supporters discovered with amaze that this brilliant man could after all do nothing but play the schoolmaster and find fault with everything. It resulted that he could be no more than a dreaded writer in the service of the ultraconservative party, and could never become its leader. How ill-assorted, too, with the sparkling wit and winning cheerfulness of the amiable social companion, was the pious unction, beyond question seriously meant, of his political essays, overloaded with biblical texts. Some traces of this dualism of romanticist irony were likewise seen in the youngest brother, the preacher Otto von Gerlach. He discharged his difficult office among the Berlin poor with apostolic devotion, being a man firm in the faith, and unwearied in ministering to spiritual and physical needs. Twice he defied threats of dismissal for refusing to remarry divorced persons. Yet at times, to the horror of the sanctimonious, he would declaim in the pulpit fine passages from Shakespeare. Thus strangely mingled were religious and ethical ideals in this brilliant romanticist circle.

The king's favourite among the three brothers was the eldest, General Leopold von Gerlach. Whilst still stationed in a provincial garrison town, he was frequently summoned to court ; but after a while he was transferred to Berlin, where his advice was sought in all matters of importance. He was, however, under no illusions regarding the extent of his influence, and openly declared that none of the king's personal favourites had any real power. His most treasured memories were connected with the Silesian headquarters staff, of which he had been a distinguished member. Thereafter for a considerable period he was adjutant to Prince William the younger, who continued later, when their political paths had diverged, to regard him with genuine respect. Anything but a courtier, he would on occasions return a blunt Prussian answer even to the dreaded czar, and though he regarded the Russians as Prussia's natural allies, their servile nature and their routinist sense of order were profoundly repugnant to him. His peculiar romanticist self-complacency made him fond of expressing himself in bold paradoxes, such as that Napoleon was a good-natured fellow enough, but for the rest rather a duffer. In his political views this shrewd and well educated officer went almost further than his brother Ludwig, for he was filled with unquenchable hatred for the despotism of the " hireling officials," though he was himself properly speaking one of their number. He firmly believed in God's direct influence upon crowned heads, and said severely that pretenders whom the Almighty himself had deprived of their high office ought to be in the camp or the cloister, but were out of place in the whirlpool of court enjoyments. Like his brother he was stronger in criticism than in the origination of political ideas.

The brothers found a powerful supporter in Ludwig von

Gerlach's brother-in-law, Baron Senfft von Pilsach auf Gramenz, who, having been appointed a member of the treasury of the household, instituted extensive plans for the drainage of the domains, which were carried out at great cost though rarely with success. Official documents supply practically no information regarding his political activities. Nevertheless, all well-informed persons knew that the king, in so far as he was ever moved by another's opinion, placed great confidence in Senfft's judgment. As crown prince he had espoused the cause of the baron when the latter, ignoring the prohibitions of the rationalistic Stettin government, had delivered pious sermons to his Further Pomeranian peasants, and Frederick William had written : " The conduct of this [the Stettin] government is in truth so colossally stupid as to arouse one's compassion." [1] Senfft was intimately acquainted with all Frederick William's peculiarities, and knew how to adapt his confidential reports and conversations to the monarch's every mood. Nor did he shrink from letting the king know what people were saying about their ruler, frequently reporting current talk without any adornments of his own. Now straightforward, now calculating, but exhibiting always a quiet tenacity, he made considerable headway, and his advice never failed to favour the conservative cause. Through the instrumentality of von Thadden-Trieglaff, who was brother-in-law both to himself and to Ludwig von Gerlach, he maintained lively intercourse with a circle of ultra-orthodox Further Pomeranian nobles who were no less distinguished for their reactionary trend than for their Christian mode of life and their works of charity.

All the other men who were dear to the king's heart had the same high church stamp. Privy Councillor von Voss-Buch had for years been reporting councillor to the crown prince, and was now entrusted with various important functions, chiefly in connection with the department of justice ; Voss-Buch, too, was renowned for his incomparable bachelor dinners. Von Kleist, president of the court of appeal, had been Frederick William's playmate in boyhood ; an ultra of the ultras, he was nicknamed " bloody Kleist " by the demagogues and resigned office in the end rather than swear fealty to the new

[1] Crown Prince Frederick William to Altenstein, May 2, 1830.

constitution. Of the same stamp were C. W. von Lancizolle, the Hallerian, at one time instructor of the royal princes in German constitutional law ; Götze, the learned jurist ; General Carl von Röder, a man of childlike piety ; and others too numerous to mention who during the first years of the peace had belonged to the conventicles of the awakened or to the " Cockchafer Club " of the young Berlinese romanticists. Never had there existed a court circle more worthy of respect. Intelligence, acquirements, nobility of mind, were all admirably represented ; but there was little energy of will, and little understanding of the needs of the age.

Alexander von Humboldt, a regular visitor of an evening at the royal circle, seemed like a foreigner in this Christian environment. Mind called to mind ; the king and the man of great learning could not do without one another ; and their contemporaries involuntarily thought of Frederick and Voltaire, though the comparison was hardly an apt one. Voltaire had had a decisive influence upon the great king's æsthetic judgments, had contributed to form Frederick's philosophical views, but had ever kept strictly aloof from Prussian politics. Humboldt's royal friend had long ago formed his own outlook on the world, and it was impossible that Humboldt could affect this outlook, standing as he did partly above and partly below it. The disciple of the old enlightenment, the man whom in earlier days the Prussian officials at Baireuth had looked upon as a jacobin, had no understanding of the new religious life which was dawning for the Germans and was so joyfully hailed by the king. On the other hand, Humboldt had a far franker appreciation than had Frederick William for the liberal ideas of the rising middle class. Thus differing in almost all other respects, the two found their only common ground in their passionate delight in research and in the growth of knowledge. Humboldt was not slow to perceive that the king was not a man of action and would never secure the happiness for which he longed. The man of science therefore determined to work for good in the one domain of politics that remained open to him, to foster the king's inclinations for playing the Mæcenas, to favour all the aspiring energies of German art

and science more effectively than had been possible under
the thrifty and comparatively inaccessible old ruler. With
unwonted frankness he expressed himself on one occasion
about Bunsen, saying : " It is a weakness of mine to desire
that those whose talent I have early recognised and honoured
shall do something great. Thus do we mutually support one
another, and thus do we contribute towards nourishing and
sustaining like a sacred fire respect for intellectual endeavours."

He wished to be the recognised prince in the realm of
knowledge, but he used his powers in a grand manner for
the realisation of that ideal of the state of Pericles which was
so dear to him as it was to his brother William. He
considered that even the well-equipped and well-ordered state
was valueless in default of the cultivation of the true and
the beautiful. Humboldt had an important share in all that
Frederick William did on behalf of science. The old family
mansion in the Oranienburger Strasse became a place of
pilgrimage for all youthful men of talent. Hermann Helmholtz
and many another promising beginner found there help and
counsel. The little old man sat among towers of books, cards,
letters, articles of every kind sent to him from all quarters
of the earth. Facing him on the green wall was a great map
of the world. Here he would write far on into the night,
sometimes working at his *Cosmos*, sometimes drafting schemes
for scientific institutes, sometimes penning countless letters of
introduction, so that it seemed as if all the threads from the
boundless realm of research were centred in the old magician's
hand. The king overwhelmed him with honours and gifts,
without being able in the end to prevent this man, who had
no thought for the monetary aspects of life, becoming a debtor
to his own servant. Frederick William, in letters to " dearest
Alexandros," displayed all the tenderness, all the cordiality
of his excellent heart, and when Humboldt fell ill the king
would sit for hours at his bedside reading aloud to him.
Regarded as one who knew everything, Humboldt had to furnish
information upon the most divers matters, being now asked to
throw light upon some serious problem, and now to clear up
an idle difficulty—to explain, for instance, why the figures
representing multiples of the number nine, when added together,

always produce the number nine. When the king visited
his friend after nightfall, the servants with the lanterns were
often kept up to an unearthly hour because their master,
after taking his final leave, would renew the delightful conversation on the doorstep.

Less amiable than in such brilliant duologues did the great
man seem at the court festivals, where, dressed in his chamberlain's uniform and wearing the great ribbon of the order
of the black eagle, he would say an affable word to every
nonentity ; and he was a less amiable figure at the tea-parties
given by the royal family. From Paris days he had become
accustomed to be the central figure in the salon, and here
in Sans Souci or Charlottenburg he could not refrain from
drawing all eyes towards himself. He would stand before the
mutinously silent queen, who always mistrusted him, or before
envious courtiers and political opponents, talking about new
books, about what he had read in the newspapers, about his
own writings upon the height of Popocatepetl, upon isotherms,
or upon prisons, always brilliant, always instructive, but
unintelligible to most of his hearers. The king alone would
listen attentively, but even he was at times distrait and would
turn over the leaves of some illustrated book. Humboldt took
a quiet vengeance for the suppressed irritation and tedium
of these weary evenings, from which he would not absent
himself. He carried to his friend Varnhagen, ever ready to
suck up dirty water like a sponge, all the malicious gossip of
the court, not sparing the affectionate king, and displaying
by this backbiting that in capital cities, or at least in scandal-
mongering Berlin, a man of genius, as well as another, could
become petty through seeing things too close at hand. One
thing, at least, was indubitably proved by his odious tittle-
tattle, and this was that the medley at the animated court
lacked a controlling head.

*   *   *

" Farewell now joys, amusements, social delights ! My
highest god is duty "—thus a hundred years earlier, after his
accession to the throne, had King Frederick written to Voltaire.

The successor showed none of his predecessor's resoluteness. Frederick William was utterly unhinged when Czar Nicholas, who had appeared beside his father-in-law's death-bed just before the end, congratulated him on his accession. It was long before he could master his grief and accommodate himself to the changed situation. " Oh, to be like you," he wrote to Metternich, " to unite a warm heart with a cool head ! This is the most certain means for enabling us to possess our souls and always to steer a straight course. I feel all too clearly that to me this fortunate combination is lacking, for I find myself unable to recover from the blow which has crushed us to the earth, and my position seems to me like a dream from which I earnestly long to awake." The whole country shared the king's mourning. The crowd looked on in solemn silence when during the night of June 11th the king's remains were conveyed along the broad central avenue of the Linden to the Charlottenburg mausoleum where the departed had desired to be laid at rest beside his Louise. The street lamps had been extinguished, and the only light was that of the pale moonbeams, which, when the moon emerged from time to time from behind the clouds, fell upon the hearse as it moved silently onward. In all the pulpits from the Niemen to the Saar sermons were preached upon the text, " For the Lord thy God hath blessed thee in all the works of thy hand." The town of Berlin resolved to erect a monument to the dead monarch, to whom it owed so much ; this was placed upon a wooded hill-top and the site was named the Friedrichshain in honour of the deceased.

For all Prussians, memories of the late ruler were keenly revived when the new monarch published the only testamentary dispositions his father had made, apart from directions concerning the funeral. Frederick William IV added to his father's utterances a few deeply felt words of his own. With a plain reference to the warlike preparations of the French, he confidently declared : " If the treasure of a dearly won peace should ever be endangered, my people will arise at my call like one man, just as his people arose at his call." The two testaments had been written thirteen years earlier, long before the July revolution had shaken the life of Germany, and they were couched in the patriarchal style of those tranquil days. One of them, superscribed " My last Will," consisted of nothing more than pious observations. The other, opening with the words " To thee, my beloved Fritz," warned the successor to the throne against a desire for innovations and against unpractical theories, but warned him likewise against an excessive preference for the old, and exhorted him to regard the league with Austria and Russia as " the keystone of the great European alliance." The Berlin council had these legacies from the late king printed for the use of the citizens, and for many years, framed and glazed, they hung on the walls of countless Prussian homes. But the age to which they belonged had passed away ; with these last dues of gratitude the chapter of the past seemed closed ; all glances were now expectantly turned towards the new ruler.

His first doings came from the heart, for it seemed to him a sacred duty to compensate for the harshness of earlier days. He said friendly and encouraging words to all the deputations which came to pay their respects to him. Even the Jews of Berlin, for whom he had little liking, received an assurance that he was no adherent of the blind prejudices of earlier centuries. General Boyen, who had long been the victim of ill-treatment, was recalled to the council of state by an exceptionally gracious holograph letter, and this first act of the new government was universally regarded as a concession to liberalism. Immediately thereafter **Arndt was reinstated** in his post. With the exception of A. W. Schlegel, an enemy of long standing, all the Bonn professors greeted his return with delight, and they promptly appointed him rector for the ensuing year. Never for a moment had he faltered in his allegiance to his country. Even amid the sorrows of an unjust persecution, apostrophising the fatherland, he had written :

> Æons shall last thy life's long span,
>   With German faith and honour fain ;
> Though short the days of mortal man,
>   Undying love shall ever reign.

There was now secured for him a respected old age, cheered by the love of his fellow countrymen. Jahn, too, was freed

from police supervision, and was subsequently decorated with
the iron cross. On August 10th Frederick William signed
a decree granting amnesty to all political offenders, and
promising pardon even to refugees should they return home.
The decree was not to be published until a month later,
when the coronation was to take place, but the king's
compassionate nature left him no rest. He promptly had
the prison doors opened, and many of those set at liberty
were given positions in the state service. This lenity was
a proof of the excellence of his disposition, for he was no less
convinced of the guilt of most of the prisoners than his father
had been. Thus the gloomy epoch of political persecutions
was closed, though a painful epilogue was not lacking. At
the very time when the demagogues were being liberated,
Privy Councillor Tzschoppe, who had been the most rancorous
of their persecutors, became affected with grave mental disorder;
the unhappy man was under the illusion that all the poor
fellows whose youth he had laid waste were persecuting him
in their turn, and shortly afterwards he died insane.

At this early date, however, it became apparent how
dangerous could be the effects of the monarch's goodness of
heart. In an ebullition of brotherly love he entrusted Prince
William, who received the Frederician title of Prince of Prussia,
with the presidency of the ministry of state and of the council
of state. It was the king's hope that his brother would simply
occupy the position which he had himself occupied as crown
prince. But despite his veneration for the wearer of the
crown, the prince of Prussia found it impossible to assume
in relation to a brother but a few years older than himself
the modest role which the late sovereign had demanded from
his sons. It was inevitable that the contrast in character
and temperament by which the brothers were distinguished
should make itself felt, and the next few weeks were to show
that for the heir to the throne the office of minister president
is at once too low and too powerful.

From the first the king had determined that the representative system was not to remain in its present inchoate
condition. He foresaw that this great question was to be
the chief concern of the opening years of his reign, and
it seemed as if, with the aid of a certain amount of determina-

tion, a solution would be quite possible. The promises made by Frederick William III, ill-considered as they had been, contained nothing to threaten the power of the crown in the then posture of affairs. By the ordinance of May 22, 1815, the monarch had pledged himself to summon a deliberative national assembly elected from the provincial diets ; the decision as to the method of election was left to himself, as sole legislator. He had further pledged himself to issue a written constitutional charter embodying the principles upon which the Prussian government had hitherto been conducted, but the form and content of this document were likewise left entirely to him. Finally, in the national debt law of January 17, 1820, the king had promised that the future Reichstag was to receive yearly statements concerning the national debt, and that new loans would not be raised without the Reichstag's approval. Taking the words in their strict meaning, all this signified nothing more than that the estates of the realm must be summoned at regular intervals ; and by coming to an understanding with the Reichstag it might be possible to arrange that the annual statements of account should be presented only to a committee of that body. Moreover, the monarch possessed the uncontested right of repealing laws made by his predecessor, and of issuing new laws, as long as these did not directly infringe the rights of the creditors of the state.

But it now became apparent that a constitutional monarch is in many cases more powerful than an absolute sovereign. The recall of a hasty promise, which in a constitutionally governed state can be effected readily enough with the approval of the Reichstag, could not but seem to the absolute monarch to be a breach of the respect he owed to his father, to seem little short of a moral impossibility. Frederick William felt bound in conscience by the old pledges, and yet all his inclinations and all his doctrines made him revolt against carrying them literally into effect. It was plain that the core of the matter lay in the summoning of a Reichstag at regular intervals. Should this body become an institution, in however modest a form, it could not fail to undergo further development. The construction of the provincial diets had been a victory rather for particularism than for reaction. All the more necessary was it now, therefore, when a quarter of a century had shown that the provinces could live together in tolerable harmony, to establish a weighty counterpoise to the separatist spirit of the territories, and to provide, at length, for the whole nation a common field of labour, wherein a conscious Prussianism, a living sense of the state, could become active.

This was what Prussia's neighbours chiefly dreaded. It was not Prince Metternich and Czar Nicholas alone who listened with deep concern for every breath of tidings from Berlin. King William of Würtemberg was inspired with the same interest, and he repeatedly assured Rochow, the Prussian envoy, that he had now made up his mind about constitutionalism, and regarded the Prussian provincial diets as the best way of providing for the representation of the various interests in the state.[1] The lesser German princes thought with fear and trembling of the possibility of a Prussian constitution. They were all exceedingly well satisfied with the present posture of affairs, for they could deal with malcontents at home, now appeasingly by dangling before their eyes the bogey of Prussian absolutism, now menacingly by referring to the ill-humour of the two great powers. But what would become of their sovereignty if a Prussian Reichstag were to throw into the shade the constitutionalist splendours of the pygmies ; if Prussia, already so greatly strengthened by the customs union, were now to appear upon the stage of German parliamentary life, giving the Germans a daily demonstration how grand a thing it is to belong to a mighty state ?

Frederick William, however, had no comprehension of this unifying force of a national assembly, for the energy of the Prussian idea of the state had no place in his mind. He considered the beautiful multiplicity of the provincial diets a triumph of the historical principle, and as late as the, thirties he had at times still mooted the question whether the old diets of the princes of Magdeburg, Münster, and Paderborn might not be revived as communal diets. He was determined that the provincial diets were to remain the central feature of the Prussian representative system. In cases of exceptional

---

[1] Rochow's Reports, February 29, 1840, and subsequent dates.

need he proposed to summon them all to Berlin, thus constituting a united diet without any further process of election,
a body which, were it simply owing to its cumbrousness,
could meet only at long intervals.   Whilst still crown prince
he had expounded this idea to Leopold Gerlach, and he held
fast to it with his quiet tenacity until he realised it at length
after many years.   Nor was he able to overcome other
objections to the pledges made by his father, objections of a
purely doctrinaire character.   A written constitutional charter
seemed to him to smack too strongly of Rousseau, Rotteck,
and Welcker, and he had determined that he would never
restrict the free power of his crown by any such document.
No less repugnant to him was the pledge that the national
assembly was to be entirely responsible for the national debt,
for it seemed to him intolerable that his monarchical authority
should in times of war be hampered by any limitation of
the kind.   This was a trouble which could disturb only the
over-refined acuteness of an utterly unpractical intelligence.
The surpluses that had of late years been accumulated, together
with the moneys derivable from the bank and the Oversea
Trading Company, would provide ample funds for the opening
of an unexpected war.   Once the war was actually in progress,
there could be no doubt that Prussian patriotism, which had
so often been gloriously tested, would induce the Reichstag
to approve any loans that might be needed.

Harassed by these doubts, Frederick William had not yet
been able to form any definite resolution, but his true instinct
assured him of one thing, that the great festival of allegiance
must be made the occasion for settling the constitutional
question by a royal decree.   Then, in an unhappy hour, there
was put into his hands the testamentary scheme which, not long
before death, his father had entrusted to Prince Wittgenstein.
It was prescribed in this document that only in the event
of the issue of a new loan was a united diet to be
summoned, composed of thirty-two representatives from the
provincial diets with a like number of members of the council
of state ; in addition, the late king had insisted that the
assent of the agnates must be secured prior to any change

in the representative system. It was indisputable that the views summarised in the testament were, in sum, those of Frederick William III. But the document was legally inefficacious, being unsigned and undated. It could be regarded as no more than paternal wishes and advice, and was not a binding testament, for even though by the terms of the civil code the final dispositions made by members of the royal house were, as privileged testaments, exempted from customary formalities, the question after all remained open whether this particular memorandum precisely represented the deceased monarch's will. The new king was long in doubt as to what he ought to do in the matter ; he conscientiously carried into effect all that the testament prescribed regarding the family property, and he communicated its contents to his brothers. Thereupon the prince of Prussia assured him with much earnestness that their father's expression of his desires, though defective in point of form, must be unconditionally respected. Henceforward, said Prince William, any constitutional change would be inadmissible without the assent of all the royal princes of full age.

In view of this exhortation Frederick William determined that at the festival of allegiance, although at the moment there was no question of a new loan, he would announce the prospective summoning of this remarkable diet of sixty-four members. He would lay before the provincial diets, assembled for the coronation, a survey of the finances, and would inform them that he proposed to grant his loyal subjects a remission of taxes in honour of the occasion. This spontaneous concession would, he imagined, secure the approval of the diets, and would make them quite willing to renounce the regular summoning of the Reichstag. Were his father's commands to be thus carried out with the agnates' approval, at some later date, perhaps, when the crown should think proper, a great united diet, an assembly of all the provincial diets, might be summoned. For the nonce the king kept this latter plan to himself, though in the recesses of his mind he clung to it with the utmost firmness. The steps he actually proposed to take at the time of the coronation were communicated to his ministers in the beginning of July. The king wrote that since he did not as yet possess the authority or inspire the confidence which his father had possessed and inspired in virtue of a long and happy reign, he proposed to leave the representative problem unsettled for the time being. Boyen, Voss, and Leopold Gerlach took part in the deliberations which lasted for weeks, and were of an animated character, this remark applying especially to the prince of Prussia.

Of those whose advice was sought, one only, General Boyen, expressed himself in favour of the king's proposal. The old warrior foresaw that popular expectancy could not be much longer repressed. In a memorial under date of August 8th he said : " In such dubious cases the main question is whether the government will wait until it is forced or whether it will take the initiative." Besides, he definitely anticipated another war with France, and just as in the year 1808 he had recommended the summoning of a representative assembly to strengthen the crown for the struggle against Napoleon, so now did he insist that the armed might of Prussia ought to stand " on a spiritually higher level " than the troops of the propaganda. In his view, therefore, " this idea of a representative committee, which has been brought to the front by a remarkable chain of circumstances," was " the best and simplest means for dealing with the domestic and foreign relationships of the state. . . . In God's name, can anyone suggest a better means ? Something must be done promptly for the legislative guidance of the national spirit." In a covering letter he apostrophised the king as follows : " We stand to-day on the brink of the Rubicon, but our aim in crossing the river is not destructive, as was that of Cæsar. No, our aim is the courageous maintenance and timely development of the country's institutions. Such is the task which divine providence has entrusted to your majesty ! "[1] Clearly as the general recognised the goal, he was profoundly deceived regarding ways and means. An assembly of thirty-two deputies from the provincial diets was not a Reichstag, but, as Boyen himself termed it, a representative committee. So pitiful, so derisory, a fulfilment of the royal pledge of earlier days could neither satisfy the Prussians nor inspire them with

[1] Boyen's Memorial, with covering letter to the king, August 8, 1840.

enthusiasm ; it could serve only to stimulate them to demand their chartered rights. The danger was so obvious that even General Thile, who at first took the side of his friend Boyen, soon began to hesitate, while the other ministers and the prince of Prussia were unanimous in their warnings to the monarch.

Thus early did Frederick William display his fatal tendency to mismanage. With the best intentions in the world, he involved the question in such complications that both parties were at once right and wrong. Most of the ministers considered that as far as representation was concerned the legislation of the monarchy was complete, and they were hostile to any innovation. Rochow, in particular, who fourteen years earlier had taken part in the proceedings of the notables in connection with the establishment of the provincial diets, confidently declared in a memorial that " at that time the general constitutional question was universally regarded as settled." Gerlach expressed himself in similar terms, saying definitely that the estates summoned to attend the coronation could not possibly regard themselves as entitled to decide so important a matter.[1] In view of this general opposition the king lost courage. He did not ask himself whether it would not be advisable to abandon the idea of half measures, to concede the whole point at issue, and to announce at the coronation that a genuine Reichstag equipped with all the promised powers should forthwith be summoned. He would have found in Radowitz and Canitz willing helpers for the promotion of such a design. But since his main desire was to manage affairs for himself, and since to him his advisers were never anything more than indifferent tools, he found little difficulty, at this juncture, in making the best of the ministers who opposed his ideas for a representative system. Already half resolved to postpone the execution of the inconvenient plans, he paid a visit to the Saxon court, and met Prince Metternich at Pillnitz on August 13th. He discussed with the Austrian statesman the question of joint military preparations against France, spoke of the necessary reforms in the federal constitution, and

[1] Rochow's Memorial, July 27 ; an unsigned memorial, manifestly by Gerlach, August 4, 1840.

touched also upon the Prussian constitutional problem. Since the Austrian, as was to be expected, vigorously supported the objections of the Prussian ministers, the king allowed himself to be persuaded to abandon his proposals for a time. This was the first occasion on which he failed to avail himself of a wonderfully propitious hour, and in after years he bitterly complained : " I *deplore* another *lost* opportunity, of which there have been so many ! ! ! and for so many years."[1]   Yet even now he was far from being satisfied with himself and sadly observed : " We shall see how evil will be the consequences of this."

Thus the testamentary draft of the old king was never carried into effect, and by command of his successor was henceforward kept strictly secret.   Frederick William now conceived the design of gradually enlarging the competence of the provincial diets, and thus by the highly prized organic process of development paving the way for the eventual summoning of a national assembly.   Prussia's future Reichstag was to be something very different from the South German chambers ; it was not to be a popular representative assembly, but an assembly of estates, each with its own rights to safeguard, a corporation firmly based upon historic tradition, and therefore unable to be an offence to the friendly eastern powers, and equally unable to drive the Prussian monarchy into the arms of the state of the July revolution.   The king's mind was entirely filled with that old Gentzian doctrine of estates which Prince Solms-Lich had recently expounded once more to the courts in acceptable terms.   Frederick William overlooked the fact that the constitutional Bavarian diet was, after all, likewise constructed in accordance with the principle of subdivision into estates, and he failed to foresee that any Prussian Reichstag, if it were more than a petty committee, would necessarily regard itself as popularly representative, and would reflect public opinion.   Dahlmann, more far-seeing than the king, had years earlier, in the finest chapter of his *Politics,* prophesied this necessary development, explaining that the same historic force which had everywhere substituted money for service, knowledge for tradition, public opinion for caste

---

[1] King Frederick William to Thile, June 10, 1847.

opinion, rendered it also inevitable that the old diets should be compacted into a popular representative body. The king could not but regard such words as revolutionary, for the leader of the seven of Göttingen had issued warnings against a doctrine which proposed "to deck out the state, half as a family mansion and half as a church."

But it was precisely this idea of the Christo-Germanic patrimonial state which was sacred to the monarch. He wished to realise it ("for centuries to come," as Prince Solms confidently opined) in deliberate contrast with the states of popular sovereignty and of written charters. Consequently not one of his subjects had power to dissuade him from his hidden designs. He understood in its literal sense the warning which Leopold Gerlach uttered to him in these days, that a king is no longer able to rule when his people has ceased to regard him as king by God's grace. How fiercely nine years earlier had he railed against "these Westphalian Lafayettes," when the Westphalian estates had ventured to remind the king of the promise of a constitution, and when young Fritz Harkort had distinguished himself by the boldness of his language. The people was patiently to abide what the king in his wisdom should in due time think fit to give. Never would he permit his hand to be forced.

Meanwhile preparations were being made for the act of allegiance in Königsberg. It was to be celebrated with peculiar solemnity, for this was the first time that a king of Prussia had ascended the throne as sovereign lord over all his lands.

On August 29th the royal pair entered the ancient coronation city. The butchers rode in the van, this being their privilege here as in Berlin, a privilege gained of old by glorious deeds in war. The members of the other guilds were drawn up in double lines between the festively adorned high-gabled houses, and the ships on the Pregel were gaily decked with bunting. The king was on horseback beside his consort's carriage and responded to the burgomaster's address with apt and cordial words. Thunderous and interminable were the cheers of the masses. The children would not be withheld, and pressed round their sovereign, who with smiling good nature stroked the curly little heads. It seemed as if nothing could ever again disturb the patriarchal relationship between prince and people. The ensuing days were spent by the king in reviewing the troops, in excursions to the beautiful Samland, and in various festivities. The Prussian provincial diet assembled meanwhile on September 5th. It had been summoned by a cabinet order of July 15th, and commissioned before the day of allegiance to answer the two following questions : whether at the festival of homage there was to be a confirmation of the privileges of the estates ; and whether the estate of nobles was to be specially represented at the ceremony. The first of these enquiries, though it did no more than conform to traditional practice, could not fail in existing circumstances to produce the impression that the king wished the diet to express its opinion upon the constitutional question. Frederick William had overlooked the danger, for when the cabinet order of July 15th had been issued, it had still been his intention to announce to the estates the intended summoning of a general or national diet, in accordance with his father's plans. But in the interim he had changed his mind, and since he now came with empty hands he had only himself to blame for what he would above all have desired to prevent, that pressure was to be put upon the crown by its loyal subjects.

Schön opened the diet as royal commissary. He alluded first of all to the deceased king and to that reform period dear to every East Prussian heart when " the ultimate vestiges of slavery " had been annulled. In his cleverly designed speech (which was reinforced in fuller detail by a memorial) he suggested to the diet the answer which they ought to give to the new ruler's enquiry. He advised the estates, in accordance with their ancient and honourable privilege, to offer the king the traditional allegiance-gift of one hundred thousand gulden ; to renounce special representation for the estate of nobles ; and not to lay any particular stress upon the confirmation of old rights deriving from the gloomy epoch of the monasteries and the guilds. The advice of the powerful lord lieutenant was followed almost word for word by the diet. Since, through the instrumentality of Brünneck, the brothers Auerswald, and other faithful adherents, he completely dominated the assembly, we are justified in assuming that he was a secret participator in all that followed ; but so warily did he maintain an attitude of official reserve that it was possible for him subsequently to disclaim having had anything to do with the matter. A Königsberg merchant named Heinrich, a moderate liberal and a well-meaning man enough, who was on this single occasion to play a part in Prussian history and was forthwith to lapse into oblivion, now proposed that the king should be begged to fulfil the late ruler's pledges for a constitution. A memorial from the diet was elaborated in the sense of this proposal. The actual compiler was the deputy Alfred von Auerswald, a member of the Ritterschaft, son of Lord Lieutenant Auerswald, who in former years, prior to the legislative enfranchisement of the peasantry, had been the first to abolish serfdom on his estates. Alfred Auerswald, like his brother Rudolf, who was now chief burgomaster of the territorial capital and was also a member of the diet, had many years before, in the Ordensburg, the Königsberg palace of the Teutonic knights of old, been daily playmate of the young princes, and had ever since remained on terms of friendship with them.

In these brothers Auerswald, in Saucken-Tarputschen (the second marshal of the diet), in Brünneck, Bardeleben, and the great majority of the other Old Prussian nobles, there now to the general surprise became manifest a new political force which had hitherto been quite overlooked because it had been practically concealed in the quiet life of the provincial diets. In South Germany the members of the old nobility had for the most part either held sullenly aloof from the new political life of the nation, or else had joined the ultramontane party, for with many of them the violences of Rhenish Confederate days still rankled. It was therefore natural enough that the High Germans, a people endowed with a large measure of civic pride, should have come to regard " reactionary " and " aristocratic " as practically synonymous terms. But here there existed a patriotic nobility, firmly united to the state to which it belonged, whole-heartedly loyal, proudly cherishing the warlike memories of the black-and-white banners of the Teutonic Knights and of the kingdom of Prussia, and simultaneously characterised by patriarchical simplicity, thoroughly independent, candid to bluntness, far less radical than were the parliamentarians of the south, and yet extremely receptive for the liberal ideas of the age. No one who looked these men frankly in the face could fail to recognise that Prussia had a sufficiency of sound conservative forces to be able confidently to venture upon the necessary reforms—if only the king would lead the way. The political immaturity of the epoch was frequently displayed in the proceedings of the diet. Heinrich, in his proposal, did not distinguish clearly between the asseveration act of the Great Elector and the more recent royal pledges, although the legal basis of these latter was entirely different. But not a single disrespectful word was uttered; the members of the diet all vied one with another in asseverations of inviolable loyalty; and, amid much vague and empty oratory, one point at least clearly emerged, namely, that the Prussian Reichstag would afford the king the safest and perchance the only available means for uniting the different sections of his people, widely separated as they were by space, by language, and by custom.

After serious and thorough discussion, on September 7th, by a vote of eighty-nine against five (the dissentients being all members of the estate of nobles), the assembly approved the memorial which requested the king to maintain and complete the constitutionalist system of representation founded by his father. The diet expressed the hope that his majesty would before long " be graciously pleased to guarantee the continued existence of the provincial diets, and, walking in the footsteps of his father, would proceed to the formation of an assembly of territorial representatives of his faithful subjects." The estates had not in any way exceeded their competence; they had done no more than give a respectful answer to a royal question; and even if it were true that a public exhortation of this character might readily endanger the prestige of the crown, this was the king's own fault for having failed to do the right thing at the right time. The ice having now been broken, the Prussian constitutional struggle, which seventeen years earlier had with difficulty been stilled, was to be renewed.

The court was not slow to recognise this. The prince of Prussia, who was still entirely dominated by his father's strictly absolutist principles, wrote a stinging letter to Schön on September 7th, as soon as he heard of the decision of the estates : " In my eyes it is a mark of the utmost disloyalty to demand guarantees from a new sovereign at the very opening of his reign. Even though in 1815 the king of blessed memory had it in mind to grant such guarantees, nevertheless he reserved for himself and for his successors the choice of a time for carrying out the decision. Moreover, after the introduction of the provincial diets, the king of blessed memory did nothing in the way of promoting a further development of representative conditions, and we may take this as a clear proof, if proof were needed, of his sound practical discernment, for he recognised that the modernity of such institutions in surrounding countries entailed nothing but disadvantages, unrest, and dissatisfaction. . . . A step of this nature would secure the approval of all who desire the overthrow of the existing order, of all who cultivate a self-seeking disposition and give free rein to their own vanity. Not for me nor for any true patriot the desire to be popular with men of that stamp." Schön answered appeasingly that the prince need not consider the matter of any importance, that there was nothing dangerous in the memorial, and that a Prussian diet could never decide anything contrary to the king's will.[1] Minister Rochow, meanwhile, was setting all possible influences to work to prejudice the king against the diet.

When Schön appeared at the castle next day he found the king greatly incensed, and already half determined to dismiss the diet in disgrace. But upon talking the matter over with his old friend, Frederick William gradually recovered his equanimity. He wished, he declared, exactly what the diet wished, but desired to choose his own time, and to act at his own free discretion. He allowed some hints to transpire concerning the plans he secretly cherished for a great united diet. In conversation subsequently with Alexander Humboldt, in the anteroom, Schön said (perhaps from shrewd calculation, but perhaps in the joy of his first surprise) : " The king is even more liberal than I am myself." It need hardly be said

---

[1] The prince of Prussia to Schön, September 7, 1840 ; Reply. September 8th, early.

that this remark was promptly repeated everywhere, and Schön, who in these days received manifold proofs of royal favour, was granted the order of the black eagle, and was accorded the title of minister of state, seemed to the East Prussians the predestined successor of Minister Rochow. In any case, the result of Schön's mediation was that the prorogation of the diet on September 9th was courteously effected. The king said that his father, influenced by what had taken place in other countries, had maturely reconsidered his pledges, and had consequently determined, " holding quite aloof from the dominant conceptions of so-called popular representation," to fulfil his word by the introduction of provincial and circle representative constitutions. " To safeguard this splendid work and to encourage its ever more fruitful development" would be to the new ruler " one of the most important and most gratifying duties of his royal mission."

The request of the diet was thus rejected. The king did not hold out any definite prospect for the future, considering that he would be dishonoured should he allow himself to be driven by meddlesome subjects. Czar Nicholas, it was plain, was greatly relieved, and expressed his thankfulness to his brother-in-law that this thorny constitutional question had been settled " once for all." But the refusal was so graciously made, and Schön had so much that was encouraging to relate to his fellow provincials concerning the monarch's liberal intentions, that the estates really believed that the royal message proroguing the diet, speaking as it did of the further develop-ment of the existing system, contained at least a partial concession. They hailed the reading of the document with acclamations. Thus was the train laid for a disastrous mutual misunderstanding. But who at this moment, when rejoicings at the opening of the festival of homage were making people deaf to all other considerations, could devote himself to quiet reflection? Moreover, the diet had no definite and well-developed popular conviction to appeal to for support. Since no segregation of parties had as yet been effected, it is probable that many members of the assembly had given but little thought to the matter before registering their votes, and the leaders only of the majority definitely understood what they wanted. On the other hand, the five members who had composed the minority had a strong following in the province. Twenty-seven of the noble landowners summoned to the festival assembled on September 8th under the leadership of Count Dohna-Schlobitten to protest against the memorial of the diet. They assured the king that they were perfectly content with the existing provincial diets, and that they had no desire for any innovation.

Amongst the populace no one was as yet paying any attention to these political oppositions ; the minds of all were filled with thoughts of the royal guest and how best to do him honour. On the evening of September 9th the province gave the monarch magnificent entertainment. The many great figures of territorial history were presented in tableaux vivants ; men of all classes and all shades of opinion worked harmoniously together ; Cäsar von Lengerke, the liberal theologian, had written the descriptive verses, and these were declaimed in a sonorous voice by Eduard Simson, a young lawyer. Next day the deputies of the provinces of Prussia and Posen assembled for the act of allegiance. More than twenty thousand persons stood in the spacious courtyard or were thronged round the windows of the castle. The throne was set up on a platform, approached from the courtyard by a great flight of steps. The chancellor and the marshal of the diet of the kingdom of Prussia delivered their addresses in traditional form, but Count Poninski, marshal of the Posen diet, did not miss the chance of giving a plain reminder of " the sublime and paternal pledge of the great king," who had promised his Polish subjects to safeguard their nationality and their language. When the formal oath of allegiance had been read, in the hush that ensued there suddenly sounded, shrill, piercing, and twice repeated, the warning cry of a mad woman, " Do not swear, do not swear ! " The sinister impression produced by this interruption was, however, instantly forgotten when the king arose from his throne and, with right hand solemnly uplifted, pledged himself before all the people to be a just judge, a trusty, careful, and compassionate ruler, a Christian king. Then in inspired words he acclaimed the land of Prussia as unparalleled in valour, and extolled the harmonious union of its prince and people : " Thus will God preserve our Prussian fatherland for itself, for Germany, and for the world ! Manifold, and yet one. Just as the noble bronze, an alloy of many metals, is subject to no other rust than the verd-antique which beautifies its surface as century follows century." Indescribable was the effect of this rhetorical masterpiece which, like all the sayings of the born orator, sounded much finer to the hearers than it seemed afterwards to those who read it in cold print. There was no one to enquire soberly whether all these passionate asseverations, all these glorious metaphors, had any tangible political content. One of the new political lyricists, Rudolf Gottschall the student, sang :

> The people
> Is standing, filled like Danae with longing, ardent, voluptuous, and glowing,
> Waiting to receive the shower of golden words !

Joy was ecstatic, and the bacchantic frenzy continued for several days.

Less gracious was the reception of the Prussian estates, when on September 11th they waited on him to express their gratitude for his prorogation address. " More firmly than ever, if possible," said the diet, " is now secured the adamantine bond uniting Prussia's royal ruler with his loyal people." But the king made a didactic speech to the deputies, an oration packed with elevated observations, which could not fail unfortunately to increase the general perplexity. He expressed his most vehement dislike to all state fundamental laws that were inscribed on parchment, and declared that England, owing to her peculiar history, afforded the solitary example of a successful constitutionalist regime. Having thus said what he did not desire, he left his real intentions in the dark. It was therefore natural enough that very different reports of his speech should become current, and Rochow had to explain in the *Königsberger Zeitung* that the king's words had been misunderstood. Immediately after Frederick William's departure a deplorable dispute broke out in the newspapers, a controversy in which several of the members of the above-mentioned deputation from the estates participated. It was plain to all that Rochow and Schön stood behind the respective groups of disputants, that the rivals were waging war through the instrumentality of others' pens, and that both were animated with the same personal and political enmity. Finally Rochow induced the king to issue the cabinet order of October 4th announcing what had actually taken place in Königsberg, " in order to put an end to all possible erroneous interpretations and to any suggestion that I agreed to the proposal for the development of the territorial constitution in the sense of the ordinance of May 22, 1815." The order said practically nothing more than had previously been said in the address proroguing the diet, but its phrasing was vigorous and cutting, and at one blow it destroyed all the fine dreams of the East Prussians. It was as if scales had fallen from their eyes ; they believed that they had been mistaken in the king ; and the opposition forces, which during the festival seemed almost to have disappeared, now gathered strength. Schön, however, who would not abandon hope, diligently circulated the report that this cabinet order, which unquestionably expressed Frederick William's deliberate opinion, had been cunningly extorted from the monarch by Rochow.

Outside East Prussia this unedifying epilogue passed quite unnoticed, for, owing to the institution of the provincial diets, there was as yet hardly any political intercourse between the separate territories of the monarchy. The Berliners were unwilling to await the coming of the second festival of allegiance, which was to be attended in the capital by representatives from all the king's German federal territories. They expressed a wish to give a festive greeting to their sovereign immediately on his return, and Frederick William agreed to the suggestion with one of those brilliant phrases, dazzling rather than convincing, of which he was so fond. His father, said the king, who had done so much for the country, had the right to be modest, but he himself had not yet earned such a right. The triumphal entry took place through the Frankfort gate on September 21st, to the sound of pealing bells and thundering cannon, as if the monarch had been returning from a victorious campaign. Impassioned speeches and poems gave assurance of the boundless devotion of " the most loyal city in the land." There were triumphal arches, banners, garlands, everywhere, and the crowd displayed a frenzied delight such as had not been known to Berlin since the days when the fighters came home from the War of Liberation. When the king, quite exhausted by the overplus of joy, at length dismounted at the palace steps, he remarked apprehensively to Chief Burgomaster Krausnick : " What a frenzy, a true fit of intoxication. I hope it won't be followed by crapulence ! "

The great act of allegiance was to take place on October 15th, but long before that day the deputies, filled with joyful excitement, came to the capital. Amid the cheerful social intercourse that now ensued, the representatives of the different provinces were able for the first time to make one another's personal acquaintance, and they discovered with astonishment and delight that notwithstanding their many differences they were one and all good Prussians. But whilst provincial prejudices were thus overcome, the force of the old social contrasts was still undiminished. This was shown by a trifling dispute about etiquette. The Brandenburg Ritterschaft had the traditional right of swearing fealty personally to the sovereign, and had exercised this right at the opening of the last reign. Since the king could not think of depriving his loyal Markers of an ancient privilege, he determined to receive in his private apartments all the representatives of the estate of nobles and of the Ritterschaft, deputed from the six provinces ; the municipal delegates and the representatives of the estate of peasants were subsequently to tender allegiance under the open sky, since there was not room for the ceremony in the palace. The intention underlying this arrangement was perfectly innocent, but much indignation was aroused among the municipal deputies, and the flames of anger were sedulously fanned by the liberal press outside Prussia. Burgher pride was gravely affronted at such a preference being shown to the nobility. Chief Burgomaster Francke of Magdeburg, aided by Count Stolberg, attempted to mediate, and the king gave the towns permission to send a deputation into the castle. But the Brandenburg knights, being well within their prerogative, declared that whilst they would, if needs must, obey the monarch's command, they would never voluntarily surrender any privilege of the

Mark. The municipal deputies now met to take council in the greyfriars' monastery, and Rochow, who assumed a most conciliatory attitude on this occasion, was ultimately able to persuade them to content themselves with the original arrangements. Nevertheless, strong and almost threatening words were used during the deliberations, and the fact was noted, surprising and ominous for the future, that the deputies from the west, who had been generally dreaded on account of their radicalism, were but little troubled about the whole dispute, whereas the representatives of Frankfort, Breslau, Prenzlau, and other cities of the old provinces, gave fierce expression to their long repressed hatred of the nobility.[1]

But all these matters were soon forgotten in the unmeasured rejoicings of the festival of allegiance. In the palace, the king first of all received the oaths of the princes, the clergy, and the Ritterschaft, and assured them that they had not to look forward to a so-called glorious reign, which to posterity would seem filled with the thunder of ordinance and the sound of trumpets, but a reign whose character would be simple, paternal, genuinely German and Christian. Then he betook himself to the dais, flaming in gold and purple, where the throne stood, facing the platforms gaily decked with bunting and occupied by the municipal representatives and the deputies of the estate of peasants. Between, and on a much lower level, were assembled the guilds of the trusty capital, banners unfurled. Around, at all the windows and on the roofs of the houses in the great square, were masses of people, all in exemplary order. Before the oath of allegiance was accepted from the two lower estates, the king arose from his throne to address his people, with fuller detail than in Königsberg, and even more impressively. He promised to rule after his father's example as a just and peaceful king, and went on to demand of all present : " Will you give me your help and support to develop ever more splendidly the qualities through which Prussia, with her fourteen million inhabitants, has become a companion of the great powers of the earth— the qualities of honour, fidelity, aspiration towards the light,

[1] From Kühne's Memoirs, which are here based upon the detailed reports of his intimate friend Francke.

towards the right, and towards the truth, a continued observ-
ance of the wisdom of our forefathers in conjunction with
the heroic energy of youth? Will you be careful not to
forsake me nor to renounce me in this endeavour, will you
sustain me faithfully through good days and through evil?
If so, make answer now in the clear and most beautiful tone
of our mother tongue, make answer with a heartfelt ' Ja ' ! "
Indescribable was the impression produced by these words,
wherein the ˙artist soul of Frederick William discharged itself
with elemental energy. The most beautiful tone of the mother
tongue resounded from thousands of honest throats, nor was
the universal ecstasy seriously damped by the sudden downfall
of a violent shower of rain. The king now exclaimed : " Your
' Ja ' was for me ; it is mine, and I will keep it for my own ;
it binds us indissolubly together in mutual love and troth ;
it gives courage, strength, comfort ; and even on my death-bed
I shall not forget it ! " Thereafter the legally prescribed oath
of allegiance was taken, and the passionate enthusiasm of this
ever-memorable moment endured for several days, until the
end of the splendid festivities, which were tastefully conducted
throughout.

What moved these faithful royalists in Berlin was, after
all, despite the differences in political sentiments, in essence
nothing more than the same impulse towards great words and
great sensations which had years before animated the popular
orators of the Hambach festival. The lyrical mood of the
golden age of our poesy had not yet completely evaporated.
The Berliners, like the Hambach celebrants, desired after a
tranquil and all too sober epoch to give free vent once
again to strong patriotic feelings. Just as the Palatiners, men
without a state, yearned for a fatherland somewhere in the
clouds, so were the Prussians able to rejoice in their glorious
and mightily armed state. And just as in Hambach the
true-hearted enthusiasm of the German disposition had been
clouded by radical lack of discipline, so now had the powerful
uprush of genuine loyalty carried to the surface in its train
the nauseating lees of servility which are never lacking even
in the noblest monarchies, and which are accustomed to display
themselves in their fullest baseness at the opening of a new

reign. Many of the orators and poets who hastened to make the most of the occasion were utterly immoderate in the flatteries they lavished upon a king whose great deeds still lay hidden in the womb of time. Unctuous theologians spouted the praises of the throned Chrysostom, whilst Ludwig Tieck was not ashamed to sing :

> What were the triumphs
> Of the Cæsars, of all the emperors
> Born in the tyrannous ages of Rome,
> What, even, was the career of the young hero
> Who carried his victorious arms to the distant Ganges,
> In comparison with the progress of our sovereign
> Through the streets of his capital,
> Where heartfelt love and trust
> Encountered him everywhere, in field and forest too
> No less than in the city,
> Where tears of joy were shed on his behalf,
> And where, strong and manly, he was gloriously crowned,
> Not with laurel, but with the foliage of his country's oaks ?

The book entitled *The Prussian Festival of Allegiance,* wherein Privy Councillor Streckfuss depicted the celebrations at the two capitals and in the provinces, was necessarily regarded with mingled feelings by men of liberal mind. There was far too much obsequiousness in all these manifestations of Prussian loyalty, and the excellent elderly author lapsed at times into a Byzantine tone which no one would have permitted himself, under the sober-minded Frederick William III, a man impervious to flattery.

But after the excesses of the days of allegiance, in a people inclined to reasonable views speedy reaction was inevitable. Disillusionment showed itself first in the circles of the monarchist extremists. It seemed to them that the immoderate adulation of the son was a manifestation of ingratitude to the father, and people were not slow to note with how much emphasis the prince of Prussia, in his speeches to the officers, alluded to the ever-memorable services of the late king.[1] The very men to whom an oath was a matter of grave import could not but ask themselves the question what was implied

[1] Berger's Report, January 6, 1841.

by the new king's demand for a second pledge in addition
to the oath of allegiance which he was legally entitled to
exact. One who in such a manner asked for a free Yes
from his subjects, surely gave them likewise the dangerous
right to say No. Did this solemn Yes establish any new claim
beyond the universal claim upon subjects to do their duty?
The king firmly believed that this was the case. He considered
that by the questions which he had as it were scattered
over the heads of those who had come to pay him homage
he had instituted a quite peculiar tie between himself and his
people, an extremely intimate personal relationship such as
that which had existed between the mediæval princes and
their *fideles*. He continually returned to this idea. Five
years later, when the Magdeburg municipal authorities entered
a strong but perfectly legal protest against one of his religious
ordinances, the king angrily enquired whether this was " the
fulfilment of the solemn promise given at the festival of
allegiance to sustain me faithfully, to help me loyally, upon
my difficult path? " [1]

This touching pledge, which he had as it were extorted,
had induced people to give by a sudden impulse when carried
away by the greatness of the moment, thus strengthened his
unfortunate inclination to regard all his political opponents
as personal enemies, or even as renegades or perjured caitiffs.
Directly people began to think matters over calmly it became
plain to all that the king's high-sounding speeches did not
contain a single political idea. They merely heralded the
advent of a new time without saying a word about what
the future was to bring. This led Milde, a clever Silesian
manufacturer, to say dryly that the king was a great comedian
—though Frederick William was never this by intention.
Friedrich von Gagern's criticism was juster, for he said that
such sermon-stuff was not the language of the man of action.
The wind of popular favour suddenly veered, and veered most
quickly of all in the capital. The Berliners felt ashamed that
they had shown so much strong feeling, and now that they
had come to their senses once more they began to cherish
a grudge against their sovereign for having led them astray

---

[1] King Frederick William to Thile, May 29, 1846

by the charm of his personality, and for having induced them once in a way to forget their ingrained and uncongenial shrewdness. In proportion to the violence with which enthusiasm had flamed during the days of rejoicing were now displayed all the disagreeable traits characteristic of Berlin life—gossip, backbiting, and censoriousness. With a malice which recalled the shameful times of the peace of Tilsit, everything that came from above was criticised, mocked at, despitefully torn to pieces ; and many of the steps taken by the king were already showing how insecure he felt his seat to be. In Königsberg, in connection with the customary bestowal of titles of nobility, he had recommended that the new titles should pass only with the landed possessions of the family to the eldest son, but, like his brother-in-law Louis of Bavaria, he was to learn that this well-meaning attempt to introduce the English custom into Germany was to encounter the insuperable resistance opposed for good or for ill by national traditions. As early as the days of the Berlin allegiance festival he had found it necessary to modify the new ordinance because the old nobility refused to regard a title of nobility passing only with the estates as fully equivalent to their own. Henceforward the Berliners greeted with loudly expressed and spiteful delight every defeat sustained by their king. They made fun of themselves for the enthusiasm they had displayed during the festival of allegiance, and mocked the words they had so frequently heard reiterated, " this do I pledge myself on oath " by pattering the charming phrase " to this to pledge myself am I loath."

During the ensuing weeks a number of important appointments were made. Privy Councillor Eichhorn was nominated to succeed Altenstein, and this promotion was pleasing to the public, for although the dwellers in the capital, exceptionally ignorant about political matters, had absolutely no idea of this man's importance in connection with the history of the customs union, they knew none the less from town talk that he was in ill favour at Vienna as a demagogue. Moreover, he had one advantage which seemed of supreme importance to this keen-witted township—he was of bourgeois origin. The appointment of the brothers Grimm to the Berlin academy

met with universal approval. Negotiations were opened with
Albrecht, but out of gratitude to his Saxon patrons he refused
the Prussian invitation. It was undeniable that the king's
magnanimous intention was to atone for the ill-treatment of
the seven of Göttingen. But joy was short-lived, for simultaneously the Grimms' brother-in-law Hassenpflug was summoned
to preside over the supreme court of Berlin. After his
misadventures in Hesse, he had been a minister, first in
Sigmaringen and subsequently in Luxemburg, and in the western
march had honestly done his best to maintain the independence
of the German grand duchy vis-à-vis the Netherland kingdom.
No one gave him credit for this. Public opinion continued
to regard him as the reactionary minister of Electoral Hesse.
Although the judicial position now assigned him was no more
than a proper recognition of his great juristic capacity, and
although he never attempted to exercise any kind of influence
in Prussian domestic policy, people feared the worst because
he was a friend of the Gerlachs. Some verses became current
set to the tune of the new Rhine song, *Sie sollen ihn nicht
haben, den freien deutshen Rhein.* They began, *Wir wollen
ihn nicht haben, den Herrn von Hass und Fluch.* " For never
will we have him, this man of hatred and cursing " (a play
upon the name of Hassenpflug)—and went on to speak of him
as the hypocritical associate of the pious gang of courtiers,
as the companion

> Of Stolberg, Gerlach, Thile,
> Of Radowitz and Voss.

Such was the tone in which the Berliners were already
talking of their king's entourage when the foolish exultations
attending the festival of allegiance had hardly ceased to rever-
berate. The verses, too, served to disclose the real cause of
this venomous spirit of opposition. The capital as yet had
little thought of political partisanship, being still far more
interested in ballet dancers, operas, and pianoforte players.
But it was the town of Nicolai, and its self-complacent enlightenment, able to deck itself at will with any mantle, Jewish or
Christian, was now wearing the colours of the young Hegelians.

Everyone who differed from the epigones of Hegel was calumniated. This was the experience of Julius Stahl, the Bavarian, appointed in these days professor of public law at Berlin university, in succession to Gans, prematurely deceased. Stahl, like Gans, was a convert from Judaism, but, unlike his predecessor, was profoundly convinced of the truth of Christianity, and regarded the Burschenschaft, of which he became an enthusiastic member, as nothing other than a Christo-Germanic brotherhood. Having attained intellectual maturity, in the first and critical portion of his *Philosophy of Law* he devoted himself to the refutation, with victorious dialectical skill, of the doctrine of natural rights in all its embodiments, and was now engaged upon a systematic exposition, in accordance with the views of the historical school of law, of the ideal of a feudalist monarchy, which he conceived in no narrow spirit. When he seated himself pencil in hand at his little writing table, with nothing before him but a sheet of blank paper, it seemed as if he were able to spin ideas spontaneously out of his mind. His sagacity was not altogether free from excessive subtlety, and there ran through his nature a vein of fanaticism, which was to be disclosed later, when oppositions became more pronounced. But he was firm and serious-minded ; he was free from personal ambition ; and he lived wholly for the political ideal which seemed to him to be true. For these reasons he ever remained on terms of close friendship with the brothers Grimm, who with the brilliant discernment characteristic of their sublime simplicity were attracted always towards men of sterling fibre. Quite equal to Gans as an orator, he greatly excelled his predecessor in the depth and acuteness of his ideas. But how deplorable was his welcome, for the Hegelians had sworn to rid the lecture theatre of this dreaded adversary of the doctrine of natural rights. But the delicate-looking little man with the glittering eyes and the sharp Jewish physiognomy stood his ground valiantly, lecture after lecture. He compelled his audience to pay heed, and the result was that for many years his discourses were the most thronged of any delivered at the university.

The condition of dissatisfied expectancy was to prove more disastrous than any such unpopular appointment. After all

the big words of the festival of allegiance, confident hopes
had been entertained that something remarkable would take
place, and now, when nothing happened, the general ill-humour
waxed day by day with alarming rapidity. During this period
of disappointment, Schön again tendered the monarch a helping
hand. He was continually at feud with Rochow, but the
king, accustomed as an autocrat to regard with good-humoured
contempt quarrels among his instruments, endeavoured, as he
phrased it, to glue the disputants together once more, for he
believed himself still to have a use for both of them, and his
confidence in Schön had not been at all shaken by what had
happened in Königsberg. Meanwhile a Berlin publishing
house produced a picture of the late king accompanied by a
table recording the memorable deeds of his reign, among which
was enumerated Stein's political testament of the year 1808,
which had been composed by Schön. This was Schön's favourite
child, and it was upon the strength of the document that
he chiefly based his claim to historical renown. In 1817,
when he had recommended the formation of a constitutional
ministry, it had been printed for the first time, some unknown
individual having communicated the long-forgotten document
to a liberal newspaper. Anyone with some knowledge of
human nature might well suspect that in this second resurrection
of the favourite child the young authors and freemasons of
liberal views whose services were always at Schön's disposal
had somehow been concerned. It was natural that the liberal
press should seize the opportunity of reminding an ungrateful
world of the services performed by the East Prussian statesman,
but the police authorities took alarm, and had the dangerous
picture removed from the bookshops. Schön now sent the
king a facsimile of the original document, which certainly
served to show that Schön had been the chief author of Stein's
parting words. In a covering letter he attempted to interpret
the vague doctrinaire utterances of the testament in the most
harmless manner possible.

Thus was everything carefully prepared for the main attack.
A few days later he sent the monarch an anonymous writing
consisting of six pages of print entitled *Whence and Whither?*
Its leading idea was borrowed from an article upon Prussianism

which Arnold Ruge had recently published in the *Deutsche Jahrbücher*, masking its authorship by the signature of " A Würtemberger." Schön believed the essay to be the work of Strauss, and adopted from it the contention that Prussia as a state had hitherto remained Catholic, and had been led by a political priestly caste. In vigorous phrases he went on to show how Frederick the Great had found his people " one hardly competent to think," and had endeavoured through the instrumentality of his " servants " to educate his subjects ; but in the course of time the officialdom had got out of hand, had embittered the landed gentry by an intolerable tutelage, had led the entire nation in leading strings, had hampered the working of the towns' ordinance and of the provincial diets, and had made the Landwehr come rather to resemble " the professional military service." For these reasons the landed gentry of the Königsberg diet had stepped forward, as leaders of the people, to demand " general estates," which might take over a considerable part of the administrative work, reduce the number of officials, check extravagance, approximate the Landwehr to the people once again, speedily put an end to all cabals and police intrigues, and which, thanks to their knowledge of popular conditions, would always have public opinion on their side. " Only through general estates," declared the document in conclusion, " can and will a public life originate and thrive in our land. . . . If we fail to take the time as it is, if we fail to seize the possibilities for good that it offers and to favour the development of these, the time will take its revenge." In this direct exhortation and in the personality of the author were to be found the only importance of the leaflet. It contained no noteworthy ideas, and although the repeated references to the " servants " was obviously intended to play upon Frederick William's personal dislikes, it was inevitable that the presumptuous tone, the arrogant vilification of all Prussia's past, and finally the appeal to the pagan young Hegelians, should affront the king to the soul. Privy Councillor von Voss, therefore, Frederick William's confidant, after he had learned with astonishment the name of the author, wrote as follows to Thile : " I thought the writing extremely silly, and had imagined it to be the work of some eccentric landowner. For a man in Schön's position to compose such a document seems positively insane, and it has produced a very melancholy impression upon my mind." [1]

Yet, however bunglingly composed, the leaflet unquestionably embodied Schön's ministerial programme. He hoped either to win the king over to his views, or else, should he fail in this attempt, to unfurl by his demand for a national representative assembly a banner visible from afar, around which the dispersed and aimless opposition of the country might rally its forces. The scheme was doubtless well-conceived but it was one hardly suitable to a man holding the position of lord lieutenant. At a later date, indeed, Schön contended that his *Whence and Whither?* had been designed merely as a historical document which would enlighten posterity concerning the state of civilisation in the kingdom of Prussia during the year 1840. But it was impossible that the experienced old statesman could have believed that such a writing by such an author should remain permanently secret, after it had been printed at the Königsberg court printing office, distributed to various archives, and sent in confidence to five friends of different shades of political opinion. The king regarded this idea of privacy as inconceivable, and on December 26th, writing in answer to the lord lieutenant, said very frankly that a testing time for their old friendship had now arrived. "*Whence and Whither?* does *not* please me." So shortly after the death of the late king the "whence" should have been otherwise conceived. As for the "whither," "this will bring sorrow to your friends and joy to your enemies." Frederick William went on to recount all the incautious liberal phrases used in the writing, such as the assertion that the Landwehr was as an army of representatives of the people to be contrasted with the army of the crown, or that the general estates ought to take over the work of administration. "This last," wrote the king, "is for me a cheerful prospect!" He reiterated the fundamental ideas of his own policy, which he believed to be sublimely elevated above all the meddlesomeness of his subjects. "I feel that power is vested in me wholly by God's grace, and with God's help I shall continue to feel this to the end. Believe me, upon my royal word, that in my day no prince, no peasant and no peasant boy, no diet and no Jewish school, shall appropriate anything which has hitherto rightly or wrongly appertained to the crown *unless I have myself in the first instance given it away.* . . . . Resplendency and astuteness I leave ungrudgingly to the so-called constitutional rulers whom a scrap of paper has converted into a fiction, an abstract idea, vis-à-vis the people. Paternal rule is in accordance with the manner of German princes, and because dominion is a legacy from my ancestors, is my patrimony, I confront my people boldly ; for this reason I can and I will guide immature children, chastise those that are froward, but permit the worthy and the well-behaved to participate in the administration of my possessions, indicate what is their own patrimony, and safeguard them against the arrogant pretensions of servants." In conclusion, he forbade his friend to communicate the writing to the next East Prussian diet, where it could work nothing but mischief. It might appear subsequently, but must be authenticated by Schön's signature.

The letter did credit to the king's gentle heart, but hardly to his political acumen, for if he disapproved of the ideas in the writing he should not have allowed Schön to remain governor of a province whose mood became daily more difficult. Yet at the bottom of his soul Frederick William really desired to establish the national assembly for which Schön asked, but to establish it in a different form ; and since he did not desire to hurt his friend's feelings, he finally decided on January 1, 1841, though Schön had twice tendered his resignation, that in the next diet the lord lieutenant should hold the post of royal commissary as the king's friend and plenipotentiary. Thus Schön remained in office, with Rochow as his superior. Rochow could not deny himself the malicious pleasure of informing the lord lieutenant that a dangerous writing entitled *Whence and Whither ?* was being circulated, and that it was essential that proceedings should be taken as soon as the identity of the anonymous author could be ascertained. Schön responded by a gruff despatch acknowledging the authorship and declaring that the writing was not intended for publication.   How was it possible that these two mortal enemies should work harmoniously together? The constitutional question seemed ever more enigmatic and confused. The first call to arms from the Prussian diet had been followed by a second summons, the pennon of the national assembly was fluttering in the breeze, and unless the crown took prompt and decisive action no power on earth could hinder a movement from below upwards such as was unprecedented in Prussia.

  ... elsewhere in Germany, where people had at first shaded their eyes before the new glories radiating from the crown of Frederick, the old prussophobia began to gather strength once more.   Onlookers were rubbing their hands delightedly because the great promises seemed likely once again to show but little fruit of performance.   Franz Dingelstedt, author of *The Songs of a Cosmopolitan Nightwatchman*, and the ablest of the newer political lyricists, expressed the heartfelt sentiments of the radical youth of Germany in his mocking ghazals :

A year 'tis now since erst you preached the times so new, so good, so free ;
Is not their coming overdue, the times so new, so good, so free ?
Long time you sat upon the egg, and cackled loud to all the world ;
Your eagle never yet is hatched, the times so new, so good, so free.
Full bold you prophesied the day ; but hasten now, make good your words,
Reveal to us in splendour rare the times so new, so good, so free !

Index